Critical Pedagogies of Consumption

"This book is long overdue. It is time for educators to take consumption and consumer culture seriously. . . . This volume brings a new language to the table, outlining new pedagogies and theories of consumption, new dialogues, and new terms. . . . Utopian in theme and implication, it shows how the practices of critical, interpretive inquiry can help change the world in positive ways. . . . This is the promise, the hope, and the agenda that is offered."

Norman K. Denzin, From the Foreword

"Its focus on learning, education, and pedagogy gives this book a particular relevance and significance in contemporary cultural studies. It will certainly be useful to all those who have an interest in a critical pedagogy that is concerned with the central source of meanings and values in our society. Its impressive authors, thoughtful structuring, wide range of perspectives, attention to matters of educational policy and practice, and suggestions for transformative pedagogy all provide for a compelling and significant volume."

H. Svi Shapiro, University of North Carolina at Greensboro

"A powerful lineup of international scholars . . . This book adds an international perspective to issues that have been taken up more specifically in the U.S. and Canada."

Deron Boyles, Georgia State University

Distinguished international scholars from a wide range of disciplines (including curriculum studies, foundations of education, adult education, higher education, and consumer education) come together in this book to explore consumption and its relation to learning, identity development, and education. Readers will learn about a variety of ways in which learning and education intersect with consumption. This volume is unique within the literature of education in its examination of educational sites—both formal and informal—where learners and teachers are resisting consumerism and enacting *critical pedagogies of consumption.*

Jennifer A. Sandlin is Assistant Professor in the Division of Advanced Studies in Education Policy, Leadership, and Curriculum, Mary Lou Fulton Institute and Graduate School of Education, Arizona State University, Tempe.

Peter McLaren is Professor in the Division of Urban Schooling, the Graduate School of Education and Information Studies, University of California, Los Angeles.

Sociocultural, Political, and Historical Studies in Education

Joel Spring, Editor

For additional information on titles in the Sociocultural, Political, and Historical Studies in Education series visit **www.routledge.com/education**

Critical Pedagogies of Consumption

Living and Learning in the Shadow of the "Shopocalypse"

Edited by

Jennifer A. Sandlin
Arizona State University

Peter McLaren
University of California, Los Angeles

Routledge
Taylor & Francis Group

NEW YORK AND LONDON

First published 2010
by Routledge
270 Madison Ave, New York, NY 10016

Simultaneously published in the UK
by Routledge
2 Park Square, Milton Park, Abingdon, Oxon OX14 4RN

*Routledge is an imprint of the Taylor & Francis Group,
an informa business*

© 2010 Taylor & Francis

Typeset in Minion by
Book Now Ltd, London
Printed and bound in the United States of America on acid-free paper
by Edwards Brothers, Inc.

Library of Congress Cataloging in Publication Data
Critical pedagogies of consumption: living and learning in the shadow of
the shopocalypse/edited by Jennifer A. Sandlin, Peter McLaren.
    p. cm—(Sociocultural, political, and historical studies in education)
Includes bibliographical references and index.
1. Education—Economic aspects—United States. 2. Education
and globalization—United States. 3. Capitalism—United States.
4. Consumption (Economics)—United States. 5. Consumer
behavior—United States. I. Sandlin, Jennifer A. II. McLaren, Peter.
LC66.C74 2010
370—dc22   2009018965

ISBN10: 0–415–99789–5 (hbk)
ISBN10: 0–415–99790–9 (pbk)
ISBN10: 0–203–86626–6 (ebk)

ISBN13: 978–0–415–99789–8 (hbk)
ISBN13: 978–0–415–99790–4 (pbk)
ISBN13: 978–0–203–86626–9 (ebk)

To Joe Kincheloe, Bill Talen, Rudy Espino, and Grant St. Clair

Contents

Foreword

Norman K. Denzin

This book is long overdue. It is time for educators to take consumption and consumer culture seriously. Consumption's pedagogies teach today's children and adults how to fashion identities connected to gendered celebrity culture, advertising, fashion, and the media. Our educational institutions are sites where consumer practices are taught, bought, sold, and exchanged. In classrooms and playgrounds, children are taught how to consume popular culture. Educational institutions produce gendered, classed, and racialized subjects—subjects whose identities are forged out of exchanges in the consumer marketplace. A child consumer is a person who knows how to buy, wear, eat, watch, drink, and exchange cultural signifiers of childhood.

At the beginning of the 21st century, there is a pressing demand to intervene in the neoliberal capitalist economic-consumption system. The contributors to this volume bring a new language to the table, outlining new pedagogies and theories of consumption, new dialogues, and new terms, including: green consumerism, consumer citizen, branding, student entrepreneurship, consumer education as resistance, public pedagogies, signs of the burger, anti-Barbie doll discourses, regimes of skin care, beefscapes, lifestyle food advertisements, ethical parent-consumer subjects, unlearning consumerism, re-imagining consumption, radical cultural workers, culture jamming, and the Shopocalypse.

Utopian in theme and implication, these chapters show how the practices of critical, interpretive inquiry can help change the world in positive ways. Each contributor examines new ways of making the practices of critical qualitative inquiry central to the workings of a free democratic society. Each chapter brings these practices more centrally into the fields of consumer research and education. This is the promise, the hope, and the agenda that is offered by the editors and contributors in this important volume. Together they show how critical pedagogy can be put to strategic advantage by consumer researchers, by educators, by adults, by parents, and by children.

Critical Pedagogies of Consumption

Within a critical pedagogy framework, consumption refers to more than the acquisition, use, and divestment of goods and services. Consumption represents a site where power, ideology, gender, and social class circulate and shape one another. Consumption involves the study of particular moments, negotiations, representational formats, and rituals in the social life of a commodity. The consumption of cultural objects by consumers can empower, demean, disenfranchise, liberate, essentialize, and stereotype. Consumers are trapped within a hegemonic marketplace. Ironically, as Holt (1997) observes, consumers who challenge or resist these hegemonic marketing and consumption practices find themselves located in an ever-expanding postmodern market tailored to fit their individual needs.

The interpretive rituals and practices surrounding consumption are anchored in a larger system, called the "circuit of culture" (du Gay, Hall, Janes, Mackay, & Negus, 1997, p. 3). In this circuit meanings are defined by the mass media—including advertising, cinema, and television. This circuit is based on the *articulation* or interconnection of several distinct and contingent processes, namely the processes of representation, identification, production, consumption, and regulation (du Gay et al., 1997, p. 3). These processes mutually influence one another, continually shaping and creating consumers who conform to postmodern market conditions.

Human beings live in a second-hand world. Existence is not solely determined by interaction or by social acts. Mills (1963) puts this forcefully when he argues, "The consciousness of human beings does not determine their existence; nor does their existence determine their consciousness. Between the human consciousness and material existence stand communications, and designs, patterns, and values which influence decisively such consciousness as they have" (p. 375). After Smythe (1994, p. 285), I understand that the basic task of the mass media is to make this second-hand world natural and invisible to its participants. Barthes (1957/1972) elaborates, noting that the media dress up reality, giving it a sense of naturalness, so that "Nature and History [are] confused at every turn" (p. 11). This is the case because the media's purposes are to "operate itself so profitably as to ensure unrivalled respect for its economic importance in the [larger cultural and social] system" (Smythe, 1994, p. 285).

The prime goals of the mass media complex are four-fold; the first three are to create audiences who: (1) become consumers of the products advertised in the media while (2) engaging in consumption practices that conform to the norms of possessive individualism endorsed by the capitalist political system and (3) adhering to a public opinion that is supportive of the strategic polices of the state (Smythe, 1994, p. 285). At this level the information technologies of late capitalism function to create audiences who use the income from their own labor to buy the products that their labor produces (p. 285). The primary commodity that the media produce "is audiences" (p. 268). The fourth goal of the media is clear—to do everything it can to make consumers as audience members think they are not commodities.

Each process within the circuit of culture becomes a nodal point for critical, interpretive consumer and educational research. Critical researchers seek to untangle and disrupt the apparently unbreakable economic and ritual links between the production, distribution, and consumption of commodities. Critical researchers are constantly intervening in the circuits of culture, exposing the ways in which these processes over-determine the meanings cultural commodities have for human beings. The moral ethnographer becomes visible in the text, disclosing, illuminating, and criticizing the conditions of constraint and commodification that operate at specific points in these circuits (see hooks, 1990).

Complex discursive and ideological processes shape the rituals of cultural production and consumption. Each historical period has its racially preferred gendered self. These selves are announced and validated through these circuits of representation, identification, and consumption. The cultural studies scholar interrogates these formations and the circuits they forge. A single question is always asked, namely "How do these structures undermine and distort the promises of a radically free democratic society?" Phrased differently, "How do these processes contribute to the reproduction of systems of racial and gender domination and repression in the culture?"

An antifoundational, critical social science seeks its external grounding not in science, in any of its revisionist, postpositivist forms, but rather in a commitment to a post-Marxism and communitarian feminism with hope but no guarantees. It seeks to understand how power and ideology operate through and across systems of discourse, cultural commodities, and cultural texts.

In Conclusion

How can we use critical, interpretive consumer and educational research to communicate across racial, gendered, and classed barriers? How can we use this research to criticize the commercial signifiers of neoliberal culture? Can we imagine new forms of consumer culture, forms that do not rely on the images and sounds of sexism, violence, and mindless consumption? Over 50 years ago Ralph Ellison asked whether Americans can "use their social sciences, and their art, cinema and literature to communicate across [the] barriers of race and religion, class, color and region?" (Ellison, 1952, p. xxii). Today Ellison's questions are more poignant then ever: "How can we share in our common humanity, while valuing our differences?" "How can the interests of democracy, post-consumerism, environmentalism, education and art converge?" "How can we use our literature, cinema and critical social science to advance the goals of this democratic society?" (p. 11). Can we overcome the structures of racism and sexism that are so deeply engrained in the marrow of this consumer-based democracy (Feagin, 2000, p. 270)?

I believe that a critical consumer and educational research agenda can advance this project. With John Sherry (2000), I am convinced that critical pedagogy and critical interpretive consumer research has "a vital moral and political role to play in the new millennium" (p. 278). I too am concerned with how our patterns, practices, and philosophies of consumption estrange us from and threaten our place in the "natural" world. And with Sherry, I believe we need to craft new humanistic "interdisciplinary methods of methods of inquiry and inscription" (p. 278). The problem is clear—work must be focused around a clear set of moral and political goals. The editors and contributors to this volume explore several ways in which this could occur. For this we are deeply in their debt.

References

Barthes, R. (1957/1972). *Mythologies*. New York: Hill & Wang.

du Gay, P., Hall, S., Janes, L., Mackay, H., & Negus, K. (1997). *Doing cultural studies: The story of the Sony Walkman*. London: Sage.

Ellison, R. (1952). *Invisible man*. New York: Random House.

Feagin, J. R. (2000). *Racist America*. New York: Routledge.

Holt, D. B. (1997). Poststructuralist lifestyle analysis: Conceptualizing the social patterning of consumption in postmodernity. *Journal of Consumer Research, 23*(4), 326–350.

hooks, b. (1990). *Yearning: Race, gender, and cultural politics*. Boston: South End Press.

Mills, C. W. (1963). The man in the middle. In I. L. Horowitz (Ed.), *Power, politics, and people: The collected essays of C. Wright Mills* (pp. 374–386). New York: Ballantine.

Sherry, J. F., Jr. (2000). Place, technology, and representation. *Journal of Consumer Research, 27*(2), 273–278.

Smythe, D. (1994). Communications: Blindspot of Western Marxism. In T. Guback (Ed.), *Counterclockwise: Perspectives on communication* (pp. 266–291). Boulder, CO: Westview Press.

Preface

Consumption has become a term much more prevalent today than perhaps at any other time in history as the scourge of capitalism continues in its reckless fury to excoriate every vulnerable and hitherto uncommodified space while it takes root, germinates, and inflicts its pestilence on a planetary scale. The term *consumption* permeates not only academic disciplines such as marketing, consumer behavior, anthropology, consumer psychology, and sociology, but it is also the *point d'appui* for much of the work in cultural studies, where scholars have investigated how the brand-names of the corporate capitalist order help to shape identity. What is often missing in this work is a focus on the *learning* and *education* involved in the process of becoming both consumer literate and also a living commodity, the latter of which has affected all of us in this age of the postmodern spectacle and its orgy of consumption. *Critical Pedagogies of Consumption* attempts to redress these lacunae by bringing together researchers from a wide range of subfields within education who represent a range of age levels and types of education.

While in the face of the world's unspeakable suffering and tribulation amidst the downward spiral of the economy caused by capitalist overproduction that has produced the boom-and-bust-cycle for the last several centuries or more—culminating in the Crash of 2008–2009—executives from the recently bailed-out insurance giant AIG continue to receive $165 million in bonuses, and workers continue to be laid off in record numbers. The full-throated chorus of "no government interference" that was sung by the right-wing corporate press for decades is suddenly nowhere to be heard, even in the business community.

Gore Vidal presciently noted in 1963 that the U.S. government prefers that "public money go not to the people but to big business. The result is a unique society in which we have free enterprise for the poor and socialism for the rich" (quoted in Vidal, 2002, p. 129) and the truth of this statement is no more evident than in the recent nationalization of Fannie and Freddie where you can see clearly that the USA is a country where there exists socialism for the rich and privatization for the poor, all basking in what Nouriel Roubini (2008) calls "the glory of unfettered Wild West laissez-faire jungle capitalism" (¶ 6) that has allowed the biggest debt bubble in history to explode out of control, causing the biggest financial crisis since the Great Depression. Indeed, socialism is only condemned when it profits the poor and the powerless and threatens the rich. But capitalists are quick to embrace a socialism for the rich—which really is what neoliberal capitalism is all about. But of course, it's not called what it really is—a system of mass destruction—but rather bears the euphemistically coined phrase, "free market capitalism" and is seen as synonymous with the struggle for democracy. In fact, for the last 60 years the military budget has propped up capitalism, which would have fallen into crisis much sooner had it not been for imperialist wars waged by the United States. And now we are witnessing the most massive transfer of wealth to the rich in human history to the tune of more than eight trillion dollars, which has been funneled to the biggest banks, investors, corporations, and insurance companies. This helps explain why democracy works for the rich, while the poor are cast into quasi-feudal steampunk landscapes of dog-eat-dog despair. Those whose labor is exploited in the production of social wealth—that is, the wage and salaried class—are now bearing most of the burden of the current economic crisis in the United States. Those financiers and institutions that precipitated the crisis that has destroyed the jobs and homes of millions of people are bailed out while the poor are left defenseless in the face of a massive structural collapse of capitalism.

This book is an attempt to heed various calls by educators such as Usher, Bryant, and Johnston (1997), who urge scholars to begin taking consumption seriously within the field of education. It is simultaneously a call for education scholars to explore consumption and investigate the "lines that disrupt and overturn the brand-name corporate order" (Reynolds, 2004, p. 32). This edited volume represents the first attempt to bring together scholars from across a wide range of disciplines within the broader field of education to explore consumption and its relation to learning, identity development, and education. Moreover, this volume brings a variety of education scholars together to focus on resistance to consumerism and to envision what we are calling a "critical pedagogy of consumption."

Structure of the Book

This book is divided into four parts, plus the Introduction. In the Introduction, we (**Jenny and Peter**) set the stage for the rest of the book, as we argue that educators must begin to take consumption seriously as a site of learning and education, and as a potential site of production and resistance. In order to facilitate this engagement with consumption's pedagogy and to work towards envisioning a "critical pedagogy of consumption," we provide an overview of various perspectives on consumption, and of various ways in which education, learning, and consumption intersect.

Part I, *Education, Consumption, and the Social, Economic, and Environmental Crises of Capitalism,* expands upon many of the points we make in the Introduction, as contributors set the context for the study of education and consumption by providing overviews of various theoretical approaches to examining the intersection of education, learning, and consumption; historical overviews of consumption; and overviews of the many crises that are connected with consumer capitalism and the implications these hold for education and learning. **Michael Hoechsmann** tracks the long history of the growth of a pedagogy of consumption that culminates in the Parisian experience of the late 19th century. In doing so, he pays attention to historical moments where consumer goods played an instructive—or pedagogical—role in people's everyday lives. He argues that the emergence of consumer desire, and the cultural production of imaginary wants and needs, involves a re-enchantment of the world for populations undergoing tremendous and ruptural social, cultural, and economic change.

Robin Usher delves into the theoretical terrain of consumption studies, and discusses how consumption is linked to learning. As the focus of modern life has become crafting meaningful lifestyles, Usher posits that the desire to create these lifestyles motivates individuals to *learn* in multiple and varied ways. Usher raises questions about what it means for educators to operate within this new consumer world where individuals are constantly engaged in expressive, aesthetic, and identity-based learning as they enact lifestyle practices.

In their respective chapters, **Richard Kahn** and **Ramin Farahmandpur** each focus on the various crises—including social, cultural, economic, and environmental crises—connected with hyperconsumerism and overconsumption. Kahn focuses on how global capitalism and hyperconsumption are implicated in massive global environmental destruction; he also highlights how a critical ecopedagogy can address these issues. Farahmandpur presents an overview and analysis of the current social, political, and economic crises facing the United States, arguing that these crises are inextricably linked to capitalism and U.S. imperialism. He examines how these crises manifest in the commercialization and corporatization of public education, focuses on how Marxist analysis is needed more today than ever, and describes how activists across the globe are engaged in anti-capitalist struggles.

Authors contributing to **Part II, *Schooling the Consumer Citizen*,** examine how formal institutions of education are implicit in crafting what Spring (2003) calls "consumer-citizens." Molnar (2005) and Spring (2003) argue that formal institutions such as schools help establish consumer culture, and work to craft consumer-citizens through formal curriculum as well as other spaces where commercialism has risen within schools. Spring (2003) states,

> While schools are teaching consumerism through conveying the message that education is a form of consumption, in-school ads, and consumerism-oriented courses, the school's most important contribution is creating a peer group of teens who relate through brand names and consumerism-oriented activities.
>
> (p. 188)

This "consumer education" continues into higher education, which has increasingly become a site where education is branded, marketed, and corporatized. In this part, authors critically examine how schools have operated with the best interests of the *market* in mind, and how educators are beginning to problematize and challenge the ways in which schools socialize learners to be consumers.

In his chapter, **Joel Spring** provides an historical look at how consumerism grew to be the dominant ideology in the United States. Spring examines how children and adults were crafted as consumers throughout the 19th century through the information contained in and disseminated through advertisements, newspapers, textbooks, home economics teachers and courses, and spaces of consumption such as the department store. Spring also examines the particular gendered and racial craftings of "the consumer" that these spaces fostered.

Alex Molnar, Faith Boninger, Gary Wilkinson, and **Joseph Fogerty** examine how K-12 schooling has become a corporatized space, as school commercialism has been steadily on the rise. Drawing upon their recent work, the authors examine the many ways commercialism manifests in schools, and how this commercialism is crafting consumer-citizens.

Matt Mars' chapter is situated in the context of higher education. He discusses what he calls *state-sponsored student entrepreneurship,* that is, the idea that some student entrepreneurs now have the market agency to utilize university capital as a lever for creating independent entrepreneurial ventures. Mars outlines the privatized dimension of collegiate entrepreneurship education through an exploration of privately endowed entrepreneurship faculty positions and collegiate entrepreneurship centers, and argues for a more critical perspective on entrepreneurship, one that is explicitly centered on how entrepreneurship can be used to foster social change.

Gustavo Fischman and **Eric Haas** approach the issue of the corporatization and commodification of education—and in their case, specifically higher education—through examining the prototypes about higher education that are crafted and distributed through the opinion-editorials of three influential U.S. newspapers. Drawing upon Norman Fairclough's notion of "mediatization," they found that there are only three consistent framings of "higher education" in the media, and that two of these—what they call "educational entrepreneurship" and "redemptive consumerism"—are closely connected with consumerist conceptions of higher education.

Sue McGregor traces the history of consumer education since the 1960s, focusing mainly on formal consumer education that is taught in K-12 and higher education settings. She shares how consumer education has moved from a preoccupation with teaching consumers how to function efficiently in the free-trade marketplace, towards encouraging them to strive for citizenship, solidarity, and sustainability.

Part III, *Popular Culture, Everyday Life, Consumption, and the Education of Desire* focuses on public pedagogy and everyday life as sites of education and learning that are possibly even more influential than formal educational institutions. Critical educators view forms of mass media such as soap operas, television, and movies as forms of public education, and consider popular culture and everyday life powerful sites of pedagogical practice. Giroux (1999), for instance, argues that "public pedagogy" is performed through popular culture, a site that produces meanings, social practices, and desires among the public. He explains that media culture

> has become a substantial, if not the primary, educational force in regulating the meanings, values, and tastes that set the norms that offer up and legitimate particular subject positions—what it means to claim an identity as a male, female, white, black, citizen, noncitizen. The media culture defines childhood, the national past, beauty, truth, and social agency.
>
> (Giroux 1999, pp. 2–3)

and, we would add, *it helps define what it means to be a citizen and a consumer.* Authors in this part explore how public pedagogy works to craft consumers with particular relationships with consumer culture.

Many of the authors in this part provide analyses of specific sites of popular culture that help shape who we are as consumers. For instance, **Joe Kincheloe** and **Shirley Steinberg**, in their respective chapters, provide critical analyses of two icons of American consumer culture—McDonald's and Barbie. Kincheloe explores how McDonald's public relations strategies have worked to equate the idea of "McDonald's" with "America," "freedom," and "democracy." While Kincheloe asserts that McDonald's and its advertisers want to transform children into consumers, he also posits that children are not simply passive consumers, but negotiate their own meanings within this corporate climate. Steinberg, on the heels of Barbie's 50th birthday, provides an analysis of Barbie's cultural and consumptive aspects. She discusses how Barbie has influenced generations of children and adults, providing a role model of a particular kind of "true American" who embodies dominant capitalist consumerist hegemonic ideologies.

Jane Kenway and **Elizabeth Bullen** explore how skin functions as a site where female subjection and abjection are both produced and reproduced, and examine what skin teaches us about femininity, feminism, and consumerism. They examine the dermographics of regimes of skin care (such as hair removal) and the mechanisms of consumer-media culture that drive them—and show how the pedagogies of consuming skin rely on processes of subjection and abjection. These processes, they argue, seek to erase the signifiers of girls' and women's life stages and life stories that the skin narrates.

Anne Marie Todd argues that food advertisements commodify food products that are far from their natural states in ways that portray an intimate connection between food and nature, and investigates how this process works in two specific food advertising campaigns: the California Cheese advertisements that portray "happy cows" that make "good cheese," and the American beef industry's advertisements that depict larger-than-life cuts of meat.

Lydia Martens focuses her chapter on "The Baby Show," which is a consumer extravaganza showcasing baby care products for new parents held in various sites across the UK; she explores how the Show constitutes new parents as pedagogical subjects in consumer culture, which she argues is a process that mirrors an analogous development in the medical-health field.

In the last chapter of Part III, **David Greenwood** uses an "ethic of place" framework to explore the political and economic relationships between his own consumption and people and places across the globe. Using case studies from his own teaching, and specifically conversations about the politics of chocolate that emerged in his classes, he connects everyday consumption to social, political, and economic inequalities; he also urges us to unpack the "invisible knapsack" of consumer privilege we all carry, so we can begin the process of transformation in our individual and collective stories of consumption.

In **Part IV,** *Unlearning Consumerism: Sites of Contestation and Resistance,* contributors focus on sites of contestation and resistance to consumerism. In a recent article focusing on the brand-name corporate order currently permeating Western society and American schools, Reynolds (2004) asks, "Where are the confrontations, the protest, and the resistance?" (p. 29). He goes on to argue that there has yet to be a "major political or policy battle on classroom commercialization" (p. 29). However, there *are* some educators across the globe who are taking consumption seriously, and are particularly interested in learning and enacting consumptive resistance. This part explores how children, youth, and adults learn and "unlearn" consumerism, how learners in a variety of settings are participating in learning and education around issues of consumption, how educators are enacting critical consumer education in a variety of settings, and how social movements focused on issues of consumption operate as sites of critical learning.

In their chapter, **Darlene Clover** and **Katie Shaw** discuss consumption and production in Canada—highlighting specifically the gendered nature of consumption and production practices and discourses—and explore how environmental adult education, non-governmental organizations, and the government of Canada are responding to these issues.

Stephen Brookfield provides an analysis of critical adult education occurring within the realm of popular culture. Brookfield discusses how educator-activists have created political forms of consumption that themselves serve to challenge the ideology of consumerism. In particular, Brookfield examines the pedagogy of activist-educator Paul Robeson, and how he used popular culture and media as anti-capitalist forces.

Valerie Scatamburlo-D'Annibale discusses the links between capitalist production, consumption, and revolutionary critical pedagogy. More specifically, she focuses on the forms of resistance captured under the umbrella term of "culture jamming," which seek to confront and contest the hegemonic discourses of consumer society. She argues that culture jamming fails to provide an adequate challenge to the fundamental injustices of capitalism and often perpetuates the very ideological discourses it claims to resist. In contrast, Scatamburlo-D'Annibale discusses how a revolutionary critical pedagogy can operate as a more effective challenge to capitalism.

David Darts and **Kevin Tavin** take a different perspective on culture jamming, exploring its potential to counter the ideology of consumption. They discuss their teaching work with pre-service art education students, through which they encourage critical projects focused on consumption and inspired by culture jamming; and urge other educators to create educational experiences that support critical self-expression, political agency, and careful interrogations of consumer culture.

Henry Giroux, in a reprint from his 1999 book, *The Mouse that Roared*, discusses how the Walt Disney Company wields ideological influence over the global cultural landscape. He also focuses on a variety of ways children, adults, teachers, and policy-makers can counteract the commercial onslaught of Disney and other multinational corporations. He urges educators and citizens to engage in the kinds of pedagogical and political work that move towards enacting a "critical pedagogy of consumption," including critical pedagogy, critical media literacy, public debate, and other actions that link cultural battles with policy battles.

Nicolas Lampert, who created the cover art for the book, provides a description of how he uses collage and other media to create art with political and social content. He urges artists and educators to engage in creative actions, including visual projects, as small parts of a larger struggle to challenge consumer capitalism and to reclaim public space against privatization and corporate control.

Conclusion

We have fashioned our work under the assumption that researchers and practitioners, especially those interested in social contexts of learning and education, cultural studies in education, environmental education, informal and incidental learning, social movements, curriculum studies, and critical pedagogy, will be drawn to the importance—even the urgency—of examining the politics of consumption. We also believe that this book will be of interest to educators who are interested in learning more about contemporary social and cultural theory. There could not be a more precipitous time to engage the issues set forth by the leading scholars of this volume.

References

Giroux, H. A. (1999). *The mouse that roared: Disney and the end of innocence.* Lanham, MD: Rowman and Littlefield.

Molnar, A. (2005). *School commercialism: From democratic ideal to market commodity.* London: Routledge.

Reynolds, W. M. (2004). To touch the clouds standing on top of a Maytag refrigerator: Brand-name postmodernity and a Deleuzian "in-between". In W. M. Reynolds & J. A. Webber (Eds.), *Expanding curriculum theory: Dis/positions and lines of flight* (pp. 19–33). Mahwah, NJ: Lawrence Erlbaum.

Roubini, N. (2008, Sept. 18). Public loses for private gain. *The Guardian.* Available: http://www.guardian.co.uk/commentisfree/2008/sep/18/marketturmoil.creditcrunch

Spring, J. (2003). *Educating the consumer-citizen.* Mahwah, NJ: Lawrence Erlbaum.

Usher, R., Bryant, I., & Johnston, R. (1997). *Adult education and the postmodern challenge.* London: Routledge.

Vidal, G. (2002). *Dreaming war: Blood for oil and the Bush–Cheney junta.* New York: Thunder Mouth's Press.

Acknowledgments

This book, like all edited books, is truly a collective effort. Together, the contributors, Routledge editors, and other friends and colleagues with whom we have had extensive conversations about consumption and education have collaboratively engaged in the production of knowledge—all of this collective work has helped create this book. We would like to thank Naomi Silverman, our editor at Routledge, for her support, patience, and guidance through the entire process of bringing this book to fruition. We could not have done it without her. We also thank Meeta Pendharkar at Routledge for helping us through many of the technical aspects of the process, and Joel Spring for encouraging us to pursue this project and for including it in his book series. Additionally, we would like to thank the external reviewers of this book, Rebecca Martusewicz, Deron Boyles, and H. Svi Shapiro, for their helpful comments, critiques, and suggestions. They particularly pushed us to consider ecological issues we had not yet thoroughly explored, and guided us to include more authors who focus on the environmental consequences of overconsumption. The book is stronger now because of these additions.

We would also like to thank all of the contributors to this book. Through the process of editing this book, we have benefited and learned from the diversity of perspectives authors have brought. The process of working on this book has brought forth new intellectual as well as social relationships, and for that, we are grateful. Additionally, we want to acknowledge and thank Carly Stasko and Trevor Norris for their infectious enthusiasm for this project; and Brian Schultz for his "super sleuth" editing eyes. And special thanks goes to Bill Talen, aka Reverend Billy, who created the concept of the "Shopocalypse," and in many ways was and remains the original inspiration for this book. As the Reverend exclaims, "Change-a-lujah!"

Jenny would also like to thank Jim Scheurich and Yvonna Lincoln. In the early Spring of 2007, when I first had the idea for this book, Jim and Yvonna spent hours listening to my ideas, reading drafts of the proposal, providing me feedback, connecting me with potential contributors, and, most importantly, encouraging me to move forward with the project. I am grateful to Jim for introducing me to Peter McLaren, who was enthusiastic about the project and graciously climbed onboard to help. I am also grateful for Shirley Steinberg, and want to wholeheartedly thank her for all of her help and patience, for embracing this work, and for her mentorship through this process. I would also like to thank Jake Burdick, not only for his help with editing, but also for co-teaching a consumption and education graduate seminar with me at Arizona State University in the spring of 2008. During that semester, and since then, Jake and I have spent countless hours discussing issues related to consumption and education, popular culture, consumerism, the wonders of *One Tree Hill*, the cute yet scary ideology of Hello Kitty, the hilarity of failblog, and the healing powers of tsoynamis. Jake has introduced me to new theoretical perspectives on curriculum, consumption, and popular culture, and I am grateful to have him as a friend and colleague. Finally, I want to thank my husband Rudy Espino and my son Grant St.Clair, who graciously participated in many book-inspired discussions over dinner—about the public pedagogy of Disney, the horrors of fast food, commercialism in schools, the connection between playing online games at lego.com and Grant's growing desire for legos, and why we all can't stop singing "Chocolate Rain." And I want to give extra special thanks to Rudy for the beautiful garden he created during the last few months of the editing process. I was sustained by gorgeous greens as I stayed up late nights editing.

1 Introduction

Exploring Consumption's Pedagogy and Envisioning a Critical Pedagogy of Consumption—Living and Learning in the Shadow of the "Shopocalypse"[1]

Jennifer A. Sandlin and Peter McLaren

In a world where Michael Jordan is paid more for a single Nike advertisement than the combined wages of workers in a Southeast Asia Nike factory, is it any wonder that Mattel has brought out a new 'Cool Shoppin' Barbie,' the first doll with a toy credit card. The offspring of a Mattel and MasterCard initiative to secure a future generation of lifetime credit card addicts (similar to the way that the Joe Camel advertisement was designed to addict a generation of children to cigarettes), Cool Shoppin' Barbie is a shameless exploitation of children in a country in which 1.35 million people filed for bankruptcy in 1997 because of the easy availability of credit. Is this any more ethically repulsive than the media's glorification of wealth, or celebration of violence, or its anointing of high-priced consumer items with a sacerdotal status, and its overall linking of consumption to identity? Is it any wonder that gun-obsessed children are feeling alienated and blowing away their classmates with high-powered rifles and then complaining that they can't order pizzas in their jail cells? Should we blink an eye at the fact that the former president and chairman of the Communist Part of the Soviet Union, Mikhail Gorbachev, was paid one million dollars by Pizza Hut to play his character on a TV commercial, where he is praised by the Russian people for introducing them to the delights of pizza, democracy, and Western-style freedom.

(McLaren, 2005, p. 79)

This opening quote sets the stage for this book, as it describes the current state of consumption in our hypercapitalist world, and its oppressive cultural, social, economic, and ecological consequences. In this book, we take the acts and processes of consumption as our starting place—being ever mindful of consumption's inextricable links to capitalist production—and explore how education and learning are impacted by, grounded in, implicated with, and tied to consumption. This edited volume focuses on the connections between consumption, education, and learning. It explores the present context of consumer capitalism and the various implications our current times hold for lifelong education and learning; it also examines how consumption is tied to learning and identity development. In this book, authors explore the learning and education that are located in the hegemonic aspects of consumption, as well as those that are situated in the more playful, ludic, creative aspects of consumption. Finally, this book explores educational sites of contestation and resistance—both formal and informal—where learners and teachers are enacting critical pedagogies of consumption.

The ideology of consumerism is currently one of the most dominant forces in society; we undoubtedly live in a consumer world, and we enact processes of consumption in almost every aspect of our lives. Scholars of consumption, however, take various perspectives on consumption. Some scholars focus on the destructive economic, social, and cultural impacts of rampant overconsumption, while others, like Twitchell (1999), praise consumption as a creative way of forming identities and materialism as a form of freedom. Our own theoretical perspectives on consumption are more complex, lying somewhere in between these two views (see the section later in this introduction where we briefly discuss our own conceptualizations).

Regardless of one's theoretical perspective on the meanings and consequences of consumption, many argue that consumer behavior, "rather than work or productive activity has become the cognitive and moral focus of life, the integrative bond of society" (Usher, Bryant, & Johnston, 1997, p. 16). Usher et al. (1997) assert that contemporary consumer capitalism—for better or worse—encourages and requires both consumption and "people who develop their identities through consumption" (p. 16).

Given the omnipresence of consumption in our lives, Usher et al. (1997) insist that it is currently impossible to understand education and learning "without a conception of the part played by consumption and consumer culture," (p. 18) and urge educational researchers and practitioners to begin taking consumption seriously as a site of education and learning. We, in turn, call upon educators to not only consider consumption as a space of education and learning, but also to critically analyze what it might mean to *resist* consumerism and overconsumption. This activist work exists both inside of schools and in more informal spaces of learning such as the broad and diverse social movements focused on resisting consumerism and consumption, which include groups working towards labor rights and opposing global sweatshops, fighting against globalization, advocating for fair trade, and fighting against the ecological destruction that accompanies massive overconsumption.

We, in this introductory chapter, and the other contributors in this book, in their chapters, reiterate these calls to educators to begin to take consumption seriously as a site of learning and education, and as a potential site of production and resistance. In order to facilitate this engagement with consumption's pedagogy and to work towards envisioning what a "critical pedagogy of consumption" might look like, we believe it is important for educators to understand various perspectives on consumption, and to get a sense of the many ways in which education, learning, and consumption intersect. In explicating these issues, we hope to convince educators to more vigorously begin discussing, reflecting upon, learning about, teaching, and researching consumption and its intersections with education, learning, and resistance. While there is a small but growing interest among educators in issues of consumption, learning, and education (Haiven, 2007; Hoechsmann, 2007; Jubas, 2007; Kenway & Bullen 2001; Molnar, 2005; Sandlin, 2005; Sandlin & Milam, 2008; Spring, 2003), this work is only just beginning to build an understanding of the kinds of learning and education that are intertwined with the processes of, participation in, negotiation of, and resistance to, consumption.

Historicizing, Defining, and Theorizing Consumption

The practices and processes of learning and education exist within a context of consumer capitalism that is increasingly structuring how social, political, and economic life around the world is organized (Finger & Asún, 2001). Consumption is defined by McCracken (1990, p. xi) as "the processes by which consumer goods and services are created, bought, and used" and has become perhaps the most significant organizer of twenty-first century life. And Paterson (2006) argues that individual *acts* of consumption are embedded in larger *processes* of consumption. That is, a particular *act* of consumption is part of a series of *processes* that extend beyond processes of production. An individual act of consumption, then, has "taken account of branding, images, [and] notions of self-worth," has "responded to themes and signs that trigger elements of the sensory consciousness and the nonconscious states," and has "exercised the temporary satisfaction of a desire or felt need" (Paterson, 2006, p. 3). Others within the field of critical environmental economics position consumption as the "using up" of natural resources, and focus on the "commodity-chain approach," which sees consumption decisions as being "heavily influenced, shaped, and constrained by an entire string of linked choices being made, and power being exercised, as commodities are created, distributed, used, and disposed of" (Princen, Maniates, & Conca, 2002, p. 15). Princen et al. (2002) craft what they call an "ecological political economy" of consumption—which combines an analysis of the effects of consumption on the environment with a look at the social and political dimensions of consumption, especially the ways in which power benefits some and harms others. Thus, they place environmental concerns within the context of issues of "community, work, meaning, freedom, and the overall quality of life" (Princen et al., 2002, p. 3).

It is widely posited that contemporary "consumer society"—and, along with it, a new era of consumer capitalism—has its roots in the post-World War II era, where there was an "explosion of consumption in the industrialized nations," as "many industries, such as automobiles, chemicals, domestic appliances, electrical and electronic goods, took off, fueling as well as feeding off a culture of consumerism" (Gabriel & Lang, 1995, p. 12). This new "consumer capitalism" involves "a shift towards consumption as a central social, economic and cultural process" as well as the globalization of capital and proliferation of multinational corporations (Bocock, 1993, p. 78). As this frenzy of consumption has moved from the modern into the postmodern era, the meanings of consumption have shifted accordingly, and have become tied much more to identity formation. Within current times, lifestyle choices and consumption patterns have come to shape people's senses of identity, rather than their work roles, a change Bocock (1993) sees as ushering in a new phase of capitalism. Indeed, Bocock (1993, p. 77) argues that consumption is "the characteristic socio-cultural activity *par excellence* of late twentieth-century post-modern capitalism . . . Consumption is *a*, even *the*, major characteristic of post-modernity."

Consumption is sometimes described as a *process*—a "set of social, cultural, and economic practices" (Bertelsen, 1996, p. 90), which in capitalism is supported by the *ideology* of consumerism which "serves to legitimate capitalism in the eyes of ordinary people" (p. 90). The promise that the ideology of consumerism makes is that "consumption is the answer to all our problems; consumption will make us whole again; consumption will make us full again; consumption will make us complete again; consumption will return us to the blissful state of the 'imaginary'" (Storey, 1996, p. 115). While some sociologists and cultural studies theorists who study consumption focus on the "negative" ideology of consumerism that they assert underlies all processes of consumption, others seek to remove the tone of "condemnation" (Sassatelli, 2007, p. 2) inherent in many descriptions of consumption, and focus more on the complexity of actual, contextualized, consumer practices.

Within the sociology of consumption, there are various theoretical perspectives on consumption (Martens, Southerton, & Scott, 2004); these various theoretical perspectives are in turn categorized differently by different authors (see, for example, Giles & Middleton, 1999). Drawing upon these various ways of categorizing different approaches to consumption within the sociology of consumption, we briefly discuss four different perspectives on the meaning of consumption. The first perspective is grounded in critical theory and conceptualizes consumption from the vantage point of the sphere of production. This perspective focuses on how consumer culture helps reproduce capitalism (Kenway & Bullen, 2001) and is grounded in Marxist and Frankfurt School approaches to the study of culture and consumption. This approach views "individuals as trapped within a system of exchange over which ultimately they have little control" (Giles & Middleton, 1999, p. 220). Storey (1996) explains that for Marx,

> men and women are denied identity in (uncreative) production, and are therefore forced to seek identity in (creative) consumption. But this is always little more than a hollow substitute (a fetish). Moreover, the process is encouraged by the so-called ideology of consumerism—the suggestion that the meaning of our lives is to be found in what we consume, rather than in what we produce. Thus the ideology legitimates and encourages the profit-making concerns of capitalism (a system demanding an ever increasing consumption of goods).
>
> (pp. 113–114)

This approach is perhaps best exemplified by the work of Adorno and Horkheimer (1944/2000), who focused on the "culture industry" and how it mass-produced homogenized and commodified culture, art, and entertainment to be consumed by a manipulated public. In this view, "late capitalism, through the entertainment and information industry, promotes an ideology of consumption which generates false needs which function as control mechanisms over consumers" (Sassatelli, 2007, p. 76), all for the benefit of furthering consumer capitalism. From this point of view, the system of production drives the system of consumption; the culture industry—which is made up of television, advertising, the entertainment industry, and commercial culture of all kinds—creates false needs in individuals in order to sell products. Individuals then seek to fulfill those manufactured needs through consuming the products they see advertised through these various media. From this perspective, consumers have very little agency to resist the culture industry.

A second perspective on consumption, exemplified early on by the work of Veblen (1899/2000) and more recently by the work of Bourdieu (1984) and others who have pursued Bourdieu's line of research (see, for example, Holt, 1998), as well as those who take more anthropological approaches to consumption (Douglas & Isherwood, 1979, for example) pays more attention to modes of consumption and consumption as a means of communication. This view focuses on why and how individuals consume, and how these patterns of consumption help to distinguish different social groups and "mediate the social relationships between different groups" (Martens et al., 2004, p. 156). These perspectives broadly emphasize the idea that consumers and the objects they consume "communicate positions in the social world, and that this is more fundamental than any idea of simply fulfilling a particular concrete need" (Corrigan, 1997, p. 17). These authors, in various ways, convey the idea that consumption communicates social meaning, and is also where struggles over social distinction take place. One's consumption choices reveal certain social positions and "tastes" that are not natural but are, in fact, conditioned by growing up in a certain environments with particular kinds of social, economic, and cultural capital. Furthermore, one's choices of food or any other kind of commodity, service, or experience communicate such social positions to others.

A third approach takes a more postmodern perspective and focuses on how consumption is used aesthetically (Baudrillard, 1996), or as a part of the "individualizing tendencies of modern society" (Martens et al., 2004, p. 156)—see, for example, Giddens (1991). To these authors, consumption does not necessarily fill existing "needs" that have been "created" by the culture industry; nor does consumption simply express already-fixed identities that are attached to belonging to a particular race, class, or gender (as Bourdieu, 1984, or Veblen, 1899/2000, might argue). Instead, consumption becomes integral to the process of creating identities in a postmodern world; consumption becomes symbolic, as it is centered on signifying ideas and creating meaning. In this perspective, individuals do not simply accommodate themselves to particular styles on offer; rather, they actively produce their own styles and identities through appropriating, changing, and individualizing what is offered in the marketplace (de Certeau, 1984), in order to create their own sense of identity.

More recent conceptualizations of consumption focus on what de Certeau (1984) refers to as everyday life practices (see, also, Paterson, 2006, who draws upon de Certeau and focuses on consumption and everyday life). Martens et al. (2004) argue that these more recent perspectives are in part an attempt to define consumption as more than simply *purchase* (a focus on the economics of consumption) or *display* (a focus on the symbolic functions of consumption); rather these new "everyday practices" conceptualizations focus on the everyday life practices that are embedded in, enacted through, and reproduced by consumption. Paterson (2006) argues that these everyday actions hold more complexity and meaning than typically assumed; in fact, they "reveal very complex dialogues and transactions to do with identity, status, aspirations, cultural capital, and position within a social group" (p. 7). Paterson (2006) also argues that everyday practices of consumption also "potentially show reflexive consideration of ethical, creative, and environmental concerns" as consumers place "their conscious experiences of acts of consumption into larger processes of globalization" (p. 7). These ideas are demonstrated by the practices of "ethical consumers," whose decisions to buy or not buy particular commodities are based on political, religious, spiritual, environmental, and ethical convictions (Sandlin & Walther, 2009). An ethical consumer might choose to spend more money on "sweat-free" clothes that are not made in sweatshops but, rather, are made in factories where workers are earning living wages and working in clean and comfortable conditions. These consumers are thus concerned with the effects consumption purchases have "on the external world around them" (Harrison, Newholm, & Shaw, 2005, p. 2).

Others who adopt this "practice" perspective focus on how goods are used once they are consumed, and focus on the resistant aspects of consumption. McCracken (1986), for instance, explores the appropriation of commodities, or on what happens to goods after they are initially bought, and presents a series of "consumption" rituals consumers use to alter the meanings of goods as they incorporate them into their lives. And authors like de Certeau (1984) and Fiske (2000) focus on how consumers, through what de Certeau calls "production through consumption" actually enact resistance through using goods and spaces of consumption in ways that run counter to what producers expect or envision. Finally, some authors such as Sassatelli (2007, p. 109) view the practices of consumption with more ambivalence, and advocate approaches that seek to explore consumption as it is situated in particular contexts, and to position consumers as agents who enact a sort of "bounded reflexivity." This approach sees consumption as both an expressive and a performative act. That is, consumption helps shape identities; through consumption, individuals

> not only contribute to the fixing of a series of cultural classifications, not only express themselves through symbols or communicate their social positions, but also constitute themselves and their social identities . . . in so doing, social actors reorganize their surrounding world while being shaped by it.
>
> (p. 109)

Consumption, Education, and Learning: Exploring Consumption's Pedagogy

Education and learning intersect with consumption in multiple ways. Martens (2005) argues that although these intersections have a "distinct" presence in the sociology of consumption literature, they remain "somewhat implicit" and not fully explored. We, in turn, argue that the literature in education has also to a large extent failed to fully explore these intersections.

The Market as Educator

It has been stressed that the market has taken over a primary role as educator or pedagogue (Martens, 2005). The market teaches learners—in informal and incidental ways—how to consume, how to behave in the marketplace, and how to interact with consumer capitalism. That is, the market "produces a raft of 'educational' materials (apart from aids to formal teaching), including self-help books, magazines, television, advertising, websites and product manuals and information on packaging, all of which operate as conduits of consumer information and education" (Martens, 2005, p. 345). These teach "consumer knowledge about the rules of the market and the social organisation of the sphere of exchange" (p. 345). Consumers are thus acculturated into "appropriate forms of behavior in the marketplace" (p. 346). The market also teaches learners about culture more generally, an idea echoed in Giroux's (2000) arguments about how the public pedagogy of the culture industries works. In this view of the market as an educator,

> consumption is akin to communication, and goods are better than, for instance, prayers or stories in making visible the categories of culture . . . Routine and ritualised consumption practices train participants in the relevance and cultural content of social categories, inequalities and diversities associated with gender, race, class, and age.
>
> (Martens, 2005, p. 346)

This "market as educator" perspective has had the most attention within the sociology of consumption (Martens, 2005). Within the limited field of educators who write about consumption, this perspective has also been popular. From this general perspective, individuals are viewed as learning from everyday practices of consumption and from participating in various sites of consumption, including shopping, tourism, leisure pursuits, theme parks, movies, and fashion magazines. Educators such as Giroux (1999; see also his chapter in this volume) and Kincheloe (2002; see also his chapter in this volume), for example, focus on sites of consumption such as Disney and McDonald's as spaces of education and learning. Giroux's *The Mouse that Roared* (1999), for instance, analyzes the Disney Company as a large corporation that holds great power in shaping the culture of childhood and the everyday lives of children and their families. Giroux shows how the Disney Company does not simply produce neutral or harmless entertainment, but, rather, how Disney is implicated in a complex web of power, politics, and ideology. And Kincheloe's (2002) *The Sign of the Burger* explores how McDonald's has come to play so many powerful roles in our global society, and focuses specifically on the power McDonald's has exercised to influence or educate the world, as it has "produce[d] and transmit[ed] knowledge, shape[d] values, influence[d] identity, and construct[ed] consciousness" (p. 9). Both authors position these sites of consumption as spaces where identities are shaped, childhood is created, and nostalgia is crafted.

Within the "market as educator" perspective, researchers have also discussed the educational or pedagogical aspects of advertising and branding, particularly how they are related to learning and identity formation (Hoechsmann, 2007;

see also his chapter in this volume). Other researchers focusing on the sociology of childhood have examined how "childhood" is constructed and commodified for consumption, and how children become socialized into becoming consumers through advertising, marketing, and media such as television shows aimed at them (Giroux, 1999; Kenway & Bullen, 2001). Others have focused on the consumption and commodification of food (Molnar, 2005; VanderSchee, 2005). Researchers within education (Giroux, 1999; Spring, 2003) have focused on how consumption shapes identity, "American-ness," and ideas about family, gender, and power. Still others have focused on how identity, race, ethnicity, and power are taught and learned through the realm of consumption (Spring, 2003; Willinsky, 1998).

In these various works, however, as in much of the literature that focuses on the "market as educator," despite many authors providing some evidence of resistance to the public pedagogies of consumption, the overwhelming message is focused on the hegemonic power of these various sites of consumption to shape individual identities in the service of consumer capitalism.

Institutions as "Consumer Educators"

Martens (2005), focusing specifically on children, argues that while the "market as educator" is an important perspective, those interested in the connections between learning, education, and consumption, should also look at other realms of influence that help determine how individuals learn consumption. For instance, she argues that both the school and the family teach children how to be consumers. Thus children (and, we would argue, youth and adults) learn within the realm of the market, as well as within the realms of the family and various educational institutions. Martens (2005) presents two models depicting the intersections between consumption, education, and learning, bringing together multiple factors including

> *social actors* (parent, child, kinship and friendship networks), *institutions* (the market and schooling), *cultural discourses on 'good hoods'* (which includes understandings and constructions of good parenthood, motherhood, fatherhood and childhood), *household contextual issues* (such as whether the household contains one or two parents and whether adults engage in paid work outside the home) and *individual biographies* (of adults and children).
>
> (Martens, 2005, p. 350, emphases ours)

Within the educational literature, some authors have focused on how consumption, consumerism, and commercialism intersect with formal educational institutions, and thus help to shape the learning and education that occur within those institutions. Within the field of education, Molnar (2005) is one of the leading scholars examining the intersection of these issues within K-12 schooling arena; his work specifically explores how schools operate as consumer marketplaces. Other educational researchers working in similar veins include Boyles

(2005) and Breault (2005). Equally compelling work has been conducted by educational researchers focusing on the commodification of higher education, and the ways in which corporate culture has become tightly enmeshed with higher education (see, for example, Johnson, Kavanaugh & Mattson, 2003; Noble, 2001).

Other educators seek to understand how schools and other formal educational institutions are not simply sites where commercialism is invading, but are also spaces of contestation. McGregor (2005) and other consumer educators, for example, have begun to focus on how consumer educators within school contexts can create a more critical practice of consumer education that focuses less on the naturalization of consumption and helping people to better navigate that world, and more on questioning consumer capitalism. These consumer educators advocate a consumer education that embraces sustainability education, critical pedagogy, critical citizenship, critical consumer education, and critical consumer empowerment education (Benn, 2004). Other educators writing from within curriculum studies and art education focus on classrooms where educators are encouraging students to question commercial culture through learning about and enacting critical pedagogies such as culture jamming (Darts, 2004; Tavin, 2003).

Learning (Through) Consumption at the Intersections of the Market and Institutions

Others seek to work at the intersection that combines "market as educator" or "everyday practices" perspectives with the institutional perspectives. Spring's (2003) recent work, for example, provides an historical overview of how the combined actions of educational institutions, advertising, and the media resulted in what Spring (2003) calls the "triumph of consumerism" as a prominent American ideology. And Kenway and Bullen (2001), grounded in the disciplines of childhood and youth studies, examine how "consumer-media culture" constructs children and youth as consumers; how this culture acts as a primary socializer for children and youth; how the lines between education, entertainment, and advertising have blurred; and how educational institutions such as schools have become spaces where corporations are targeting children and youth.

Lifelong Learning Through Consumption-Related Social Practices

Writing more specifically from the perspective of adult education and lifelong learning, Usher et al. (1997) also point out several ways consumption, education, and learning converge. They see consumption as being inextricably tied to learning, as they argue that consumption is connected with a variety of social practices—including lifestyle practices, confessional practices, and critical practices—all of which involve *learning*. *Lifestyle practices* involve expressive modes of learning, are focused on the creation and re-creation of identity, and involve "the self-referential concern with style and image" (p. 18). Usher et al. (1997) explain that this ongoing re-creation of identity, with its concern with aestheticization, creates the need for "a learning stance towards life as a means of self-expression and autonomy" (p. 18). This form of learning is grounded in postmodern conceptions of consumption as a means that people use to differentiate themselves from others, belong to particular groups, and to express individuality (Featherstone, 1991). Therefore, given the emphasis within lifestyle practices on "novelty, fashion, taste, and style," lifestyle practices "are practices of consumption and moreover of a consumption which is potentially unending, since as desire can never be satisfied, there is always the need for new experiences and new learning" (Usher et al., 1997, p. 18). Individuals use *confessional practices* to help them understand themselves; these practices take the self as the object of study and involve self-reflection and introspection. Usher et al. (1997) argue that within confessional practices, what is consumed is the *self*, as individuals engaging in confessional practices assume that "there is deep hidden meaning buried 'inside' which, once discovered, opens the door to happiness, psychic stability and personal empowerment" (p. 19). Like lifestyle practices, confessional practices are never complete—"there is a constant need to change in order to adapt a changing self and a changing environment" (p. 19); thus confessional practices as self-consumption also necessitate engaging in lifelong learning.

Finally, *critical practices* occur both inside and outside of formal educational institutions, and engage with processes of both production and consumption, especially against products of consumer capitalism such as waste and environmental pollution. Usher et al. (1997) argue that in postmodern society, these critical practices consist of techniques of "ludic subversion and the creation and manipulation of seductive images" (p. 20). That is, critical resistance takes place not only by working against material products and processes of oppression tied to consumption, but also in the symbolic realm, through images "and the signification of, and investments made in, particular images" (p. 20). Critical practices necessitate critical learning and a stance of reflexivity about self and society. Within all of these practices, learners embark on both formal (institutionalized) and informal acts of learning, most of which have not been taken seriously by educators.

Echoing the ecologically focused concerns captured under Usher et al.'s (1997) notion of "critical practices," a growing number of educators are exploring the negative environmental consequences of consumption and are increasingly calling for ecologically focused education and learning, both inside and outside of formal educational institutions. Some scholars who focus on the environmental impacts of consumption (Jucker, 2004; Martusewicz & Edmundson, 2005) draw on the frameworks of ecojustice popularized by Bowers (2001). Martusewicz (2004) explains that this work emerges from the "desire to recognize and preserve traditional knowledges and cultural practices as critical to addressing the ecological crisis" (p. 4). Other educators who draw attention to the environmental effects of consumption are grounded in critical pedagogy, and focus on how global capitalism has spurred an enormous environmental crisis that is deleterious to both humans and nonhuman nature. To address this crisis, educators such as McLaren and Houston (2004) call for what they term a "critical revolutionary pedagogy" that is "informed by a dialectics of ecological and environmental justice that highlights the situatedness of environmental conflict and injustice toward nonhuman nature without obscuring its historical production under capitalist value forms" (p. 27).

Positioning Ourselves Within the Complexities of Consumption

I (Jenny) embrace what might be called a "critical postmodern" (Agger, 1992) or "critical practice" perspective on consumption. That is, I acknowledge some of the pleasurable, expressive, performative aspects of consumption but do not embrace them uncritically. I also acknowledge the hegemonic aspects of consumption but do not see them as completely totalizing. Like Sassatelli (2007), I view the everyday practices of consumption with some ambivalence; while I see and denounce the destructive, oppressive forces of multinational corporations and their ideologies of consumerism, I also see consumers as having some amount of agency, and see them enacting "bounded reflexivity" (p. 109). I encourage educators to explore consumption as it is situated in particular, everyday contexts. I long and hope for a world where the ideology of consumerism is no longer the force driving our society. I see moments of hope and resistance in critical pedagogies of consumption, but also believe we are fighting a battle characterized by incredibly unequal power relationships.

I (Peter) locate my work within what I take to be the fundamental condition of late modernity—a brutal and systematic extraction of surplus value from proletarianized regions of the world (usually festering in a climate of bourgeois-comprador nationalism) culminating in a condition of substantive inequality and an egregiously unequal division of labor—a condition that is structurally inescapable under the regime of capital. This regressive situation has spawned alienated lifeworlds festering in the swamp of reification and the commodification of everyday life by means of the generalization of exchange-values mediated by the machinations of capital accumulation on a global scale. Since the mid-1990s, the focus of my work has shifted discernibly, if not dramatically, from a preoccupation with poststructuralist analyses of popular culture (with a focus on the politics of representation and its affiliative liaison with identity production) in which I attempted to deploy contrapuntally critical pedagogy, neo-Marxist critique, and cultural analysis to a revolutionary Marxist humanist perspective with a focus on the role of finance capital and the social relations of production. I came to view the assertion of many poststructuralists—that Marxism constitutes a totalizing pressuring of meaning into semiotic foreclosure, placing an overlay of determinism on the free interplay of cultural discourses with their free-floating auto-intelligibilities, their aleatory and indeterminable play of the sign, and turning the jazz of signification into a military march of pre-ordained procrustean meanings—as an exclusion of causality from the domain of history by replacing it with difference and play. In effect, by situating the social as a contingent totality, the avant-garde politics of representation articulated by the poststructuralists become part of a larger ensemble of textual reading practices that obscure the production practices of capitalism (Ebert & Zavarzadeh, 2008). Against a utopian theory of entrepreneurial individuality and agency backed by a voluntarism unburdened by history, I came to see the necessity of transforming the very structures of white supremacist capitalist patriarchy by means of a pedagogical praxis guided by the revolutionary knowledges of historical materialism. In so doing, questions of patriarchal and sexist ideology are connected to their material origins—of social labor—that emphasize the relations between the sexes and how the distribution of labor in capitalist economies has generated the alienating conditions in which men and women relate to themselves and to one another (Ebert & Zavarzadeh, 2008).

Around the same time, I also had serious problems with what progressive educators were describing as the struggle for democracy in the public sphere because so much of this discourse involved pedagogically fostering a respect for the values of democratic citizenship and appealing to moral sentiments and critical reasoning. Of course, this is bound to fail because it rests on an appeal to the individual's consciousness—a move that does little to parry the most devastating effects of capital and is ineffective in bringing about capital's inanition. As Istvan Meszaros (2008, p. 341) notes, an appeal to individual consciousness ultimately remains insufficient because "it avoids the social causes of the denounced negative symptoms." He adds that "what is absolutely excluded is the possibility of changing the structural determinations of the established social order that produce and reproduce the destructive effects and consequences" (p. 341).

I believe that it is the social relations of labor that determine a person's class location, not the opportunities a person has to go shopping. The market distributes the already available wealth. While, for instance, the stock market may seem to produce wealth, it is really just redistributing the wealth produced by the labor of the workers. Profit does not come from market relations (buying low and selling high) but from human labor power. Those who have to sell their labor power to earn a living (those who produce the profit for the capitalist) are part of one class. Those who purchase human labor and take the profit away from labor are part of another class (Ebert & Zavarzadeh, 2008). I follow Marx's focus on the development of human productive forces—a very complex process that is historically related to the material conditions of production and the class struggle. This profound incompatibility between the forces and relations of production produces tremendous social conflict.

In the field of education, Marxism's protean focus on proletarian self-activity and the self-organization of the popular majorities are anathema to much of the work that falls under the dubious category of social justice education. While well-meaning progressive educators might be willing to criticize the manner in which humans are turned into dead objects that Marxists refer to as fetishized commodities, they are often loath to consider the fact that within capitalist society, all value originates in the sphere of production and that one of the primary roles of schools is to serve as agents or functionaries of capital. Furthermore, they fail to understand that education is more reproductive of an exploitative social order than a constitutive challenge to it precisely because it rests on the foundations of capitalist exchange value. This is because, as Glenn Rikowski (2000) writes, "the inequalities of labor-power quality generated within the capitalist labor process require re-equalisation to the socially average level *in order to attain the equalisation of labor-power values that is the foundation of social justice in capitalism*" (¶ 6, italics in original).

The unmeasured condemnation and broadside assaults on Marx by the academy in general and education in particular treat Marxism as a chthonic adventure, akin to what Valerie Scatamburlo-D'Annibale (2009) refers to as "a form of ideological Neanderthalism, an antediluvian memory invoked by those trapped in the mental furniture of a bygone era" (p. 23). The retrograde, opportunistic, and banal and banalizing politics of the critics situates itself in a culture of liberal compassion and a polyglot cosmopolitanism that effectively masquerades an unwillingness to comprehend neocolonialism and to ignore the contradictions inherent in the system of commodity production and its manifold mediations of our concrete quotidian existence; it further constitutes a refusal to consider uneven and combined development, a structured silence and motivated amnesia surrounding the urgent task of historicizing power relations in concrete material conditions of production and reproduction, a grand refusal to disclaim the limitations of bourgeois ethics in the project of social transformation and a studied reluctance to engage the concrete multilayered totality of everyday life (read as a determinate socio-historical process) in which use value is subordinated to exchange value (see San Juan, 2002).

Human decisions are always conditioned; and human history is not unconditional—praxis is a world-changing activity since human beings are able to change the circumstances in which they find themselves intractably enmeshed. Production relations maintain what has already been achieved, whereas material and intellectual productive forces push society forward. As Marx (1950) writes: "Men make their own history, but they do not make it just as they please; they do not make it under circumstances chosen by themselves but under circumstances directly encountered, given and transmitted from the past" (p. 225).

Local and transnational movements for social justice have been significantly impacted by what has been taking place on a global basis since capital began responding to the crisis of the 1970s of Fordist–Keynesian capitalism—which William I. Robinson (2008) has characterized as capital's ferocious quest to break free of nation state constraints to accumulation and twentieth-century regulated capital-labor relations based on a limited number of reciprocal commitments and rights. Accordingly, we have witnessed the development of a new transnational model of accumulation in which transnational fractions of capital have become dominant in part because of new mechanisms of accumulation which include a cheapening of labor and the growth of flexible, deregulated and de-unionized labor where women always experience super-exploitation in relation to men; the dramatic expansion of finance capital; the creation of a global and regulatory structure to facilitate the emerging global circuits of accumulation; and neo-liberal structural adjustment programs which seek to create the conditions for frictionless operations of emerging transnational capital across borders and between countries. And while there still exists national capital, global capital, and regional capitals, the hegemonic fraction of capital on a world scale is now transnational capital. So we are seeing the profound dismantling of national economies, the reorganization and reconstitution of national economies as component elements or segments of a larger global production and financial system which is organized in a globally fragmented and a decentralized way and that is controlled by the concentrated and centralized power of the transnational capitalist class (Robinson, 2008). The role of the nation state has changed to meet globally uniform laws that produce capital against the interests of the international working class. The nation state still serves local capital but it can no longer fetter the transnational movement of capital with its endless chains of accumulation. But the nation state still serves the interests of capital against labor. As Marx and Engels (1977) put it, the nation state remains "a committee for managing the common affairs of the whole bourgeoisie" (p. 44).

The cultural turn in much of current postmodern and postcolonial criticism is not a passing trend but rather a structural feature of capitalism. Particularly during times of crisis, capitalism turns to culture to solve the contradictions that it cannot resolve in its actual material practices (Ebert & Zavarzadeh, 2008). Class has less to do with status and lifestyle and the politics of consumption than it does with the distribution of labor in the capitalist economy.

Because through the medium of experience, the individual is mistaken as the source of social practices, this process of misidentification becomes a capitalist arche-strategy that marginalizes collectivity and protects the individual as the foundation of entrepreneurial capitalism. As a consequence, the well-being of the collectivity is replaced by the "politics of consumption" that celebrates the singularities of individuals by valorizing the desire to obtain and consume objects of pleasure. Experience in this view becomes nontheoretical and beyond the real of history. This is why we need to locate all human experience in a world-historical frame; that is, within specific social relations of production. Critical revolutionary pedagogy, as I have been trying to develop it, attempts to create the conditions of pedagogical possibility that enables students to see how, through the exercise of power, the dominant structures of class rule protect their practices from being publicly scrutinized as they appropriate resources to serve the interests of the few at the expense of the many (Ebert & Zavarzadeh, 2008).

The overall agenda that I have been trying to develop since the mid-1990s is captured in the description of what Meszaros (2008) calls *socialist education*: "the social *organ* through which the *mutually beneficial reciprocity* between the individuals and their society becomes real" (p. 347). My concern has been with marshaling critical pedagogy as a broad, non-sectarian coalition or social movement into the service of altering historical modes of production and reproduction in specific social formations, including, if not especially, educational formations. The thesis here is that capital as the medium for social interaction is based on the logic of abstraction and in order to control capital its basis of value production must be uprooted. In other words, the destructiveness of capital cannot be solved through the welfare state or government intervention into the economy. The path to socialism can only be made by the abolition of value production itself. Hence, I reject the call for a post-Marxist and post-structuralist pedagogy of consumption.

Towards a (Critical) Pedagogy of Consumption

The theoretical perspectives on consumption discussed at the beginning of this chapter are taken up in various ways by the authors in this edited volume. Contributors' essays draw from a range of theoretical approaches to the study of consumption, while also representing a variety of different aspects connecting education, learning, and consumption. This diversity of approaches and contexts—even among us, the editors—makes it difficult to pigeon-hole or easily categorize the critical work in which contributors are engaged. While the contributors may study different aspects of consumption/education links, and may be grounded in different theoretical perspectives, we posit that all would agree that there are many aspects of consumption and consumerism that are inextricably linked to the learning and enacting of oppression, and to ecological, environmental, natural resource, and cultural destruction across the planet. McLaren and Farahmandpur (2005) argue that we are currently indulging in "millennial consumer orgies celebrating the unending promise of 1,000 years of uninterrupted shopping at Planet Mall" as we "pretend that the social and economic horrors that we have come to associate with Western capitalist democracies have been a temporary spike in global capitalism's blood pressure" (p. 25). And Taylor and Tilford (2000) focus on the negative environmental and cultural impacts of rampant consumption, stating that this consumer "binge" has resulted in "devastating levels of environmental deterioration" (p. 464). Of course, there are some authors in this volume who recognize the destructive aspects of consumption yet also argue that consumption is not only a matter of "passive and alienating consumption of goods, services and images"; they argue that consumption can also be constructed as an "active, generative process" embedded in social practices that involve learning (Usher et al., 1997, p. 21). What draws the contributors in this volume together, however, is that we all agree that we need to take consumption seriously within education, and that we need to move towards not only understanding how consumption operates as pedagogy, but also understanding what a resistant "critical pedagogy of consumption" might look like.

We urge educators to begin making more connections between consumption, education, and learning. We challenge educators to explore the consumptive aspects of the everyday educational and learning sites that we teach in or learn in. We also challenge educators to explore the educational and learning aspects of various sites of consumption. These sites can be formal learning or educational sites (within schools, formal consumer education, curriculum materials, adult literacy programs, community educational programs focused on consumer issues, etc.) or informal, popular culture, or media-based sites of learning (shopping malls, sporting events, leisure sites, fast-food restaurants, television shows, video games, magazines, movies, etc.). We urge educators to investigate sites of hegemony as well as sites of resistance and contestation, or sites that enact both roles.

Researching these sites would help push us to further articulate consumption's pedagogy, that is, to further understand what a "pedagogy of consumption" currently looks like. These questions also help us think through what a *critical* pedagogy of consumption might look like, in both formal and informal spaces of learning and education. While consumption's pedagogy typically frames consumption as the "acquisition, use, and divestment of goods and services" (Denzin, 2001, p. 325), a critical pedagogy of consumption would construct consumption as a "site where power, ideology, gender, and social class circulate and shape one another" (p. 325) and would view consumption as "a social activity that integrates consumers into a specific social system and commits them to a particular social vision" (Ozanne & Murray, 1995, p. 522). A critical pedagogy of consumption would ask, "What kind of consumers are being created?" and "In whose interests do those constructions work?" It would also investigate how consumer resistance works as a space of critically transformative learning and of critical public pedagogy. Through a critical pedagogy of consumption, learners would learn not just technical skills, but would come to investigate the naturalization of the consumer world within which they as consumers operate. A critical pedagogy of consumption would help learners recognize that the "hegemonic cultural logic of consumerism systematically permeates public, discursive, and psychic spaces, dictating that our lived experiences are increasingly shaped and monitored by marketers" (Rumbo, 2002, p. 134); here learners would engage in problematizing the naturalization of consumer culture and would form a "different relationship to the marketplace in which they identify unquestioned assumptions and challenge the status of existing structures as natural" (Ozanne & Murray, 1995, p. 522).

Note

1 The "Shopocalypse"—a combination of "*Shopping*" and "*Apocalypse*"—is a term coined by anti-consumption social activist Bill Talen, who takes on the persona of "Reverend Billy." Reverend Billy, along with the "Stop Shopping Gospel Choir" stage "Retail Interventions" inside big box stores, chain stores, traffic jams and other monuments of our current mono-culture.

References

Adorno, T. W., & Horkheimer, M. (1944/2000). The culture industry: Enlightenment as mass deception. In J. B. Schor & D. B. Holt (Eds.), *The consumer society reader* (pp. 3–19). New York: The New Press.

Agger, B. (1992). *Cultural studies as critical theory*. London: Falmer Press.

Baudrillard, J. (1996). *Selected writings*. Cambridge: Polity.

Benn, J. (2004). Consumer education between 'consumership' and citizenship: Experiences from studies of young people. *International Journal of Consumer Studies, 28*(2), 108–116.

Bertelsen, E. (1996). Post mod-cons: Consumerism and cultural studies. *Critical Arts Journal, 10*(1), 87–107.

Bocock, R. (1993). *Consumption*. London: Routledge.

Bourdieu, P. (1984). *Distinction*. Cambridge, MA: Harvard University Press.

Bowers, C. A. (2001). *Educating for eco-justice and community*. Athens, GA: The University of Georgia Press.

Boyles, D. R. (2005). The exploiting business: School-business partnerships, commercialization, and students as critically transitive citizens. In D. R. Boyles (Ed.), *Schools or markets: Commercialism, privatization, and school-business partnerships* (pp. 217–240). Mahwah, NJ: Lawrence Erlbaum.

Breault, D. A. (2005). Jesus in the temple: What should administrators do when the marketplace comes to school? In D. R. Boyles (Ed.), *Schools or markets?: Commercialism, privatization, and school-business partnerships* (pp. 59–68). Mahwah, NJ: Lawrence Erlbaum.

Corrigan, P. (1997). *The sociology of consumption*. London: Sage.

Darts, D. (2004). Visual culture jam: Art, pedagogy, and creative resistance. *Studies in Art Education, 45*(4), 313–327.

de Certeau, M. (1984). *The practice of everyday life*. Berkeley, CA: University of California Press.

Denzin, N. K. (2001). The seventh moment: Qualitative inquiry and the practices of a more radical consumer research. *Journal of Consumer Research, 28*, 324–330.

Douglas, M., & Isherwood, B. (1979). *The world of goods.* New York: Basic Books.

Ebert, T., & Zavarzadeh, M. (2008). *Class in culture.* Boulder, CO, and London: Paradigm Press.

Featherstone, M. (1991). *Consumer culture and postmodernism.* London: Sage.

Finger, M., & Asún, J. M. (2001). *Adult education at the crossroads: Learning our way out.* London: Zed Books.

Fiske, J. (2000). Shopping for pleasure: Malls, power, and resistance. In J. B. Shor & D. B. Holt (Eds.), *The consumer society reader* (pp. 306–328). New York: The New Press.

Gabriel, Y., & Lang, T. (1995). *The unmanageable consumer.* Thousand Oaks, CA: Sage.

Giddens, A. (1991). *Modernity and self-identity: Self and society in the late modern age.* Berkeley, CA: University of California Press.

Giles, J., & Middleton, T. (1999). *Studying culture.* Oxford, UK: Blackwell.

Giroux, H. A. (1999). *The mouse that roared: Disney and the end of innocence.* Lanham, MD: Rowman and Littlefield.

Giroux, H. A. (2000). Public pedagogy as cultural politics: Stuart Hall and the 'crisis' of culture. *Cultural Studies, 14*(2), 341–360.

Haiven, M. (2007). Privatized resistance: AdBusters and the culture of neoliberalism. *Review of Education, Pedagogy, and Cultural Studies, 29*(10), 85–110.

Harrison, R., Newholm, T., & Shaw, D. (Eds.). (2005). *The ethical consumer.* London: Sage.

Hoechsmann, M. (2007). Advertising pedagogy: Teaching and learning consumption. In D. Macedo & S. R. Steinberg (Eds.), *Media literacy: A reader* (pp. 653–666). New York: Peter Lang.

Holt, D. B. (1998). Does cultural capital structure American consumption? *Journal of Consumer Research, 25,* 1–25.

Johnson, B., Kavanaugh, P., & Mattson, K. (Eds.). (2003). *Steal this university: The rise of the corporate university and the academic labor movement.* New York: Routledge.

Jubas, K. (2007). Conceptual con/fusion in democratic societies. *Journal of Consumer Culture, 7*(2), 231–254.

Jucker, R. (2004). Have the cake and eat it: Ecojustice versus development? Is it possible to reconcile social and economic equity, ecological sustainability, and human development? Some implications for ecojustice education. *Educational Studies, 36*(1), 10–26.

Kenway, J., & Bullen, E. (2001). *Consuming children: Education-entertainment-advertising.* Buckingham, UK: Open University Press.

Kincheloe, J. L. (2002). *The sign of the burger: McDonald's and the culture of power.* Philadelphia: Temple University Press.

Martens, L. (2005). Learning to consume—consuming to learn: Children at the interface between consumption and education. *British Journal of Sociology of Education, 26*(3), 343–357.

Martens, L., Southerton, D., & Scott, S. (2004). Bringing children (and parents) into the sociology of consumption. *Journal of Consumer Culture, 4*(2), 155–182.

Martusewicz, R. A. (2004). Editor's corner. *Educational Studies, 36*(1), 1–5.

Martusewicz, R. A., & Edmundson, J. (2005). Social foundations as pedagogies of responsibility and eco-ethical commitment. In D. W. Butin (Ed.), *Teaching social foundations of education: Contexts, theories, and issues* (pp. 71–90). New York: Routledge.

Marx, K. (1950). *The eighteenth Brumaire of Louis Bonaparte,* in K. Marx & F. Engels, *Selected works. Vol. 1.* Moscow: Foreign Languages Publishing House.

Marx, K., & Engels, F. (1977). *Manifesto of the Communist Party.* Moscow: Progress.

McCracken, G. (1986). Culture and consumption: A theoretical account of the structure and movement of the cultural meaning of consumer goods. *Journal of Consumer Research, 13*(1), 71–84.

McCracken, G. (1990). *Culture and consumption.* Bloomington: Indiana University Press.

McGregor, S. (2005). Sustainable consumer empowerment through critical consumer education: A typology of consumer education approaches. *International Journal of Consumer Studies, 29*(5), 437–447.

McLaren, P. (2005). *Capitalists and conquerors: A critical pedagogy against empire.* Oxford, UK: Rowman & Littlefield.

McLaren, P., & Farahmandpur, R. (2005). Educational policy and the socialist imagination: Revolutionary citizenship as a pedagogy of resistance. In P. McLaren (Ed.), *Red seminars: Radical excursions into educational theory, cultural politics, and pedagogy* (pp. 25–58). Cresskill, NJ: Hampton Press.

McLaren, P., & Houston, D. (2004). Revolutionary ecologies: Ecosocialism and critical pedagogy. *Educational Studies, 36*(1), 27–45.

Meszaros, I. (2008). *The challenge and burden of historical time: Socialism in the twenty-first century.* New York: Monthly Review Press.

Molnar, A. (2005). *School commercialism: From democratic ideal to market commodity.* London: Routledge.

Noble, D. (2001). *Digital diploma mills.* New York: Monthly Review Press.

Ozanne, J. L., & Murray, J. B. (1995). Uniting critical theory and public policy to create the reflexively defiant consumer. *American Behavioral Scientist, 38*(4), 516–525.

Paterson, M. (2006). *Consumption and everyday life.* New York: Routledge.

Princen, T., Maniates, M., & Conca, K. (2002). *Confronting consumption.* Cambridge, MA: MIT Press.

Rikowski, G. (2000). Education and social justice within the social universe of capital. Paper presented at the British Educational Research Association, April 10, 2000. Available: http://www.leeds.ac.uk/educol/documents/00001618.htm

Robinson, W. (2008). *Latin America and global capitalism: A critical globalization perspective.* Baltimore, MD: The Johns Hopkins University Press.

Rumbo, J. D. (2002). Consumer resistance in a world of advertising clutter: The case of Adbusters. *Psychology & Marketing, 19*(2), 127–148.

San Juan, E. (2002). *Racism and cultural studies.* Durham, NC: Duke University Press.

Sandlin, J. A. (2005). Culture, consumption, and adult education: Re-fashioning consumer education for adults as a political site using a cultural studies framework. *Adult Education Quarterly, 55*(3), 1–17.

Sandlin, J. A., & Milam, J. L. (2008). "Mixing pop [culture] and politics": Cultural resistance, culture jamming, and anti-consumption activism as critical public pedagogy. *Curriculum Inquiry, 38*(3), 323–350.

Sandlin, J. A., & Walther, C. S. (2009). Complicated simplicity: Moral identity formation and social movement learning in the voluntary simplicity movement. *Adult Education Quarterly, 59*(4), 298–317.

Sassatelli, R. (2007). *Consumer culture: History, theory and politics.* Thousand Oaks, CA: Sage.

Scatamburlo-D'Annibale, V. (2009). Imagining the impossible: Revolutionary critical pedagogy against the 21st-century American Imperium. In M. Eryaman (Ed.), *Peter McLaren, education, and the struggle for liberation: Revolution as education* (pp. 19–54). Cresskill, NJ: Hampton Press.

Spring, J. (2003). *Educating the consumer citizen.* Mahwah, NJ: Lawrence Erlbaum.

Storey, J. (1996). *Cultural studies and the study of popular culture.* Athens, GA: The University of Georgia Press.

Tavin, K. (2003). Engaging advertisement: Looking for meaning in and through art education. *Visual Arts Research, 28*(2), 38–47.

Taylor, B., & Tilford, D. (2000). Why consumption matters. In J. B. Schor & D. B. Holt (Eds.), *The consumer society reader* (pp. 446–487). New York: The New Press.

Twitchell, J. (1999). *Lead us into temptation: The triumph of American materialism.* New York: Columbia University Press.

Usher, R., Bryant, I., & Johnston, R. (1997). *Adult education and the postmodern challenge.* London: Routledge.

VanderSchee, C. (2005). The privatization of food services in schools: Undermining children's health, social equity, and democratic education. In D. R. Boyles (Ed.), *Schools or markets: Commercialism, privatization, and school-business partnerships* (pp. 1–31). Mahwah, NJ: Lawrence Erlbaum.

Veblen, T. (1899/2000). Conspicuous consumption. In J. B. Schor & D. B. Holt (Eds.), *The consumer society reader* (pp. 187–204). New York: The New Press.

Willinsky, J. (1998). *Learning to divide the world: Education at empire's end.* Minneapolis: University of Minnesota Press.

Part I

Education, Consumption, and the Social, Economic, and Environmental Crises of Capitalism

2 Rootlessness, Reenchantment, and Educating Desire

A Brief History of the Pedagogy of Consumption

Michael Hoechsmann

> The merchandise itself is by no means available to all, but the vision of a seem-
> ingly unlimited profusion of commodities is . . . nearly unavoidable . . . We who
> have tasted the fruits of the consumer revolution have lost our innocence.
>
> (Raymond Williams, 1982, p. 3)

The process of historical change that resulted in the culture of consumption we know today has been for the most part a gradual one that defies the simplistic historiography of dates and events. To chart the emergence of a cultural ethos, a social practice, or an economic mode of production by isolating one element from a broader matrix is to obscure significant historical continuities that persist despite changing conditions. As Lipsitz (1994) remarks: "much of what seems new in contemporary culture carries within itself unresolved contradictions of the past" (p. 19). Nonetheless, major social, economic, and cultural innovations do carry with them the potential for radical transformations in the lives of people and communities. If a process such as consumption cannot be held accountable for all the changes apparent in a particular historical epoch, a careful analysis of it can, however, shed some new light on the nature of the historical changes occur-ring in that period. Ultimately, the study of consumption sites and practices is fertile ground for interdisciplinary work that focuses closely on the changing social, economic, and cultural conditions of our brave new world.

To track a genealogy of the development of a pedagogy of consumption requires attention to historical moments where consumer goods played an instructive role in people's everyday lives. This is less a story of shop-till-you-drop consumer fulfillment, but rather of those spaces that open up in the imaginary lives of real people who learn to dream of, and desire for, particular goods and the lifestyles associated with them. Ultimately, the emergence of consumer desire, and the cultural production of imaginary wants and needs, has been described by a variety of authors as involving a reenchantment of the world for populations undergoing tremendous and ruptural social, cultural, and economic change. For example, as Williams (1982) documents in *Dream Worlds: Mass Consumption in Late-Nineteenth Century France*, late-nineteenth-century department stores encouraged a dream world of participation in the culture of consumption for restless and uprooted populations, and world fairs taught a "lesson in things." The "lesson" these fairs provided was to demonstrate "the social benefit of [the] unprecedented material and intellectual progress" that was unsettling the established verities of cultural and social life (p. 58). The Paris world fairs not only played a pedagogical role in teaching people to adapt to the brave new world around them, but they also made the crucial link between pedagogy and commerce that is with us to this day.

There is a growing bibliography of works that tracks the increasing centrality of consumption to the cultures, societies, and economies of the global North.[1] Particularly in Northern nations, but increasingly on a global scale, consumption has become an important determinant of our social selves, a primary site of self- and group-identity. Consumption is not simply an act of compliance but is rather a complex mediation of self- and group-identity with everyday needs and desires. In other words, while consumption cannot be controlled or manipulated in any direct way, much consumer behavior is an attempt both to identify with an image—however illusory—and to belong to a community whose structures of identification include the purchasing of certain goods. The broad processes of consumption link together self- and group-identities as enacted in everyday life with both the powerful imagery and imaginary of the mass media and the cultural centrality of material goods as the symbolic means for self- and group-expression.

To describe consumption as a trope of contemporary culture is to suggest that the social and cultural conditions that exist in a consumer society are in many ways fundamentally different from those that preceded it. It is not to assert, however, that a total and absolute break with the past has occurred. Rather, it is to suggest that a new organizing principle for reflection and action has been overlaid on top of older ones, and that this new "trope," or shared figure of thought, has become hegemonic in contemporary cultures of the global North. A trope is a figure of thought that predisposes language and thought in particular ways. My working definition of trope is "a conceptual trigger underlying an entire discourse which conjures up associated meanings and narratives." Like metaphor, trope works on the vertical plane of associated meanings. The specific characteristics of the trope of consumption will be teased out in greater detail later in this chapter, but, at the risk of a reductive account, this trope sets the stage for new conceptions of fashion, style, and novelty, as well as the increased significance of material goods as markers of self- and group-identity.

The Romantic Spirit of Consumerism

Pinpointing the exact emergence of a cultural phenomenon such as consumption is an enterprise fraught with hazards. *The Birth of a Consumer Society: The Commercialization of Eighteenth-Century England* (McKendrick, Brewer, & Plumb, 1982), which situates the first "consumer revolution" in eighteenth-century England, attempts to respond to criticism, as McCracken (1988) puts it, that historical scholarship "has emphasized the 'supply' side of the transformation and ignored the 'demand' side" (p. 5). To focus attention to the demand side of the equation means having to muddle through histories of cultural change to seek answers for human behavior. Importantly, this involves the interrogation of existing and seemingly irreconcilable models of cultural change: on the one hand, models of restraint associated with asceticism and Puritanism, and, on the other, models of excess associated with hedonism and Romanticism. As well as beginning to focus attention to the other side of the consuming coin, McKendrick et al. challenged the orthodoxy of a view of consumption emerging spontaneously from the late-nineteenth-century streets and arcades of Paris. Rather, the authors stated that "no one in the future should doubt that the first of the world's consumer societies had unmistakably emerged by 1800" (quoted in Campbell, 1987, p. 6).

In fact, a middle-income market sensitive to changes in fashion fueled the growing demand in eighteenth-century England for textiles and clothing, crockery, metals, cutlery, books, journals, and toys. In the case of clothing, changes in fashion that had formerly taken generations to occur were now subject to a rapid pace of change in shape, material, and style. For example, purple was an "in" color in 1753, but white linen with a pink pattern was "de rigueur" by 1757. Similarly, the "couleur de noisette" was in fashion in 1767, only to be surpassed by dove gray the following year (Campbell, 1987, pp. 24–5). In other words, elements central to contemporary consumption patterns, the participation of middle-income groups, and the ongoing and rapid shifts in style were anticipated by this early flurry of consumer activity.

In search of the origins of modern consumption, other scholars have dug even deeper into the historical record. In *From Graven Images: Patterns of Modern Materialism*, Mukerji (1983) argues that a "consumerist culture" arose in the fifteenth and sixteenth centuries as printed materials and nontraditional fabrics began to circulate in Europe. In particular, Mukerji attempts to track the rise of "hedonistic consumerism" in the cultures of the early modern period. As another historian of consumption, McCracken (1988) argues, Mukerji tries to prove that "consumerism predates the rise of capitalism and, further, that consumerism helped to create the capitalism it is conventionally supposed to have followed" (p. 11). Central to Mukerji's approach is the supposition that the new worldview of consumerism was not simply an attempt by people to emulate the practices of high-status individuals, but that goods had "become a medium for the expression, transformation, and even the innovation of existing cultural ideas" (McCracken, p. 10). Thus, by attempting to uphold a distinction between the simple acquisition of goods and their adoption into everyday cultural life as defining elements of self- and group-identity formation, Mukerji provides an historical and theoretical point of departure for the analysis of the emergence of modern consumption.

McCracken (1988), argues that "a spectacular consumer boom" (p. 11) took place in the Elizabethan period of late-sixteenth-century England as nobles competed for the favors of the Queen. Elizabeth herself had created a spectacle of consumption in her own court, to which the nobility felt compelled to respond. Spending on "housing, hospitality, and clothing were staggering" (p. 11), but, more importantly, modern consumption patterns such as the demand for novelty and the diversification of "taste" had cultural impacts which reached down below the nobility to subordinate groups who were "now subject to styles and fashions from a larger court society" (p. 15). McCracken argues that events of this period hold great significance, as "this gradual shift helped prepare the way for later consumer explosions and the eventual participation of social groups that were now excluded" (p. 15).

For some theorists, the emergence of consumption within a capitalist framework, and not the example of unbridled consumptive excess, should be taken as the historical point of departure. Bocock (1993) argues that the early patterning of consumption within a distinctively capitalist economic structure can be discerned in England in the late seventeenth century. While Puritanism, well known for its ascetic qualities, had a moderating influence on consumer desire, the early bourgeoisie of agricultural and manufacturing capitalism "pursued the peaceful, systematic rational generation of profits through the sale of commodities produced for a free market" (p. 11) and spent some of this money maintaining a comfortable, though not ostentatious, lifestyle. Profits were reinvested into family businesses which would create the conditions for the successful development of British capitalism in the eighteenth century. With the restoration of the monarchy in 1688, cultural values associated with Puritanism were relaxed somewhat: clothing became subject to fashion among the well-to-do and theater became acceptable again. Thus, the growth of businesses, trade, and commodity circulation in this period helped create the infrastructure for modern consumption.

It does not require too deep a study of the literature of this early modern period to discover an almost irreconcilable divide between the Weberian ascetism described by Bocock and the consumptive excesses conjured up by both Mukerji's "hedonistic consumerism" and McCracken's account of the spectacular consumption of Queen Elizabeth, which helped pave the way for a stable infrastructure for consumption at the time of the Restoration. Troubled by some of the gaps presented by a Weberian historiography of the early modern period, Campbell (1987) sets out to investigate "an awkward time-shadow" which obscures "that crucial period between c. 1650 and 1850" (p. 11). According to Campbell, the transition from a pre-modern, feudal past where most socio-political and cultural worldviews were thought to be religious in nature, to the contemporary capitalist world where the opposite is thought to be true has not been adequately theorized. Weber's thesis of the Protestant ethic and its attributed worldviews of physical industriousness, material ascetism, sensual restraint, and economic parsimoniousness, combined with Enlightenment values of progress through rationality, materialism, and secularity have been too zealously adopted by generations of researchers to explain the rise of the "spirit of capitalism." Missing in this equation is an account of the rise of the social and cultural framework that has sustained and nourished this "spirit" right from its early beginnings.

In *The Romantic Ethic and the Spirit of Modern Consumerism*, Campbell (1987) set out to explore the cultural phenomenon of Romanticism, a cultural force antagonistic to the hegemonic influence of Puritanism. While Campbell agrees with the interpretation of McKendrick et al. that this revolution took place among "the middle or trading classes, together with artisans and sections of the yeomanry," which were "those sections of English society with the strongest Puritan traditions," he attempts to reconcile how the demand for luxury goods and the "pleasurable indulgences of dancing, sport and novel-reading" would arise given the dominant cultural currents of the times. The crux of Campbell's argument turns on the distinction between "traditional" and "modern hedonism," a "shift of primary concern from sensations to emotions" (p. 69). According to Campbell, "romanticism provided that philosophy of 'recreation' needed for a dynamic consumerism: a philosophy which legitimates the search for pleasure as a good in itself and not merely of value because it restores the individual to an optimum efficiency" (p. 201). The cultural link between romanticism and consumption is played out in everyday life with the development of fashion and fashion consciousness, as well as with the rise of the novel—itself a product of changing technologies—which is both an object of consumption and a vehicle for romantic values.

Combined with the disenchantment of nature associated with the "scepticism and optimistic rationalism of [the] Enlightenment" (p. 75), a "distinctive cultural complex" emerged which involved "the widespread adoption of the habit of covert daydreaming—individuals [did] not so much seek satisfaction from products, as pleasure from the self-illusory experiences which they construct from their associated meanings" (p. 89). Campbell argues that the increasing emphasis on novelty and insatiability, which can account for new popular practices such as window-shopping, show that the "spirit of modern consumerism is anything but materialistic" (p. 89). In sum, "the romantic ideal of character, together with its associated theory of moral renewal through art, functioned to stimulate and legitimate that form of autonomous, self-illusory hedonism which underlies modern consumer behaviour" (pp. 200–201).

From these accounts, it appears that much of the cultural groundwork was already laid for the emergence of mass consumption in the latter half of the nineteenth century. The trade in goods had been growing since the fifteenth and sixteenth centuries. This trade was not limited to an elite, but increasingly involved a middle-income market. Many items, but particularly clothes, were susceptible to rapid changes in fashion, and distinctive tastes emerged to differentiate consuming groups. Along with the acceptance of the dictates of fashion came the desire for—and pleasure in—novelty. Despite the moderating influence of Puritanism, insatiability and the desire for excess was not limited to the elite, and the ascetism associated with Puritanism helped provide the commercial infrastructure for the growth of consumption. A distinct cultural complex associated with Romanticism helped break down the restrictive social mores of Puritan orthodoxy. This both helped to contest Puritan ascetism and to channel popular pleasure—which goes back to the horizons of human history—from rituals to goods, and from communal practices to individual acts of consumption. These inheritances, and the central tension between consumptive release and economic restraint, set the stage for the tremendous social changes of the late nineteenth century and continue to impact cultural life to this day.

Modernism and the Rise of Mass Consumption

While consumption as a popular practice, a cultural ethos, and an economic relation has a long history which predates the second half of the nineteenth century, this is the historical period which is commonly credited for a dramatic rise in the cultural significance of consumption (Leiss, Kline, & Jhally, 1990). Leaving aside momentarily the details of this transformation, it is important to acknowledge that this period is significant for the development of the social, economic, political, and cultural practices and institutions which made up the modern conditions of the nations of the global North. This is a period of dramatic social change: it gives rise to the Industrial Revolution, to the massive growth of cities—not only in quantitative terms but in terms of cultural significance—and, significantly for our purposes, it is also the period which gives rise to compulsory mass education. Whereas the first two of these changes are of immediate significance to the cultural consolidation of consumption, for the purposes of this volume the latter must be kept in focus. If schooling and the didactic institution of consumption, the modern advertising industry, can be seen to arise out of the same historical setting, the differing "pedagogies" of these institutions can be submitted to rigorous comparative scrutiny.[2]

Several factors combined in the late nineteenth century to facilitate the growing cultural significance of consumption. While acknowledging that the rise of consumption predates the late nineteenth century, Leiss et al. (1990) signal the importance of the Industrial Revolution, arguing that it was "only when the market system was combined with industrialization and sustained technological innovation" that the "revolutionary effects" of consumption made "themselves felt in everyday life" (p. 65). The changes that swept through world metropolises—particularly those in the global North which were fat with the spoils of Empire—in the latter half of the nineteenth century were nothing short of dramatic. Xenos (1989) points out the significance of changes in urban life, such as the Haussmanization of Paris, a rationalization of urban space that enabled the construction of grand boulevards where shoppers could circulate and the growth of mass transportation to bring shoppers to large city-center department stores (p. 88). As Schudson (1984) remarks, these changes to urban centers "changed the spatial possibilities of daily life" (p. 152). Williams (1982) argues that major economic transformations in this period resulted in the growth of average discretionary income and that changes in commerce such as the introduction of credit and the bank check played a role in the new conditions of consumption. She also points out that the rapid changes in technology lowered the cost of existing consumer goods and created new ones. In fact, states Williams, "After 1850 many notable inventions were consumer products themselves—the bicycle, the automobile, chemical dyes, the telephone, electric lighting, photography, the phonograph" (p. 10). The radical nature of technological, economic, and social change in this historical period, combined with the consumptive seeds already sown in the early modern period, ushered in a set of historical changes that we are living with to this day.

Novelty has come to be known as a quintessential modern condition. An important feature of the modern world was the acceleration of technological, social, and cultural change. Technological innovation occurred at breakneck speed. One technology, the telegraph, enabled the movement of information across geographical boundaries, and the growth of the modern press resulted in the document of novelty, the newspaper. The newspaper quickly developed a symbiotic relationship with the department store. As advertising grew, newspapers informed people about department stores, and department stores helped prop up the revenues of newspapers (Schudson, 1984). Landscapes, particularly urban ones, changed rapidly and constantly. Communities were forever altered as people were thrown into new environments where they rubbed shoulders for the first time with strangers. In the midst of this disorienting speed-up of social and cultural change, the new department stores and a proliferation of new consumer goods attained a new cultural significance.

The resilience of popular cultural forms has always played a role in the ability of communities to withstand radical and ruptural change. For example, Bakhtin (1968) has documented the role of carnival and the banter of the marketplace as sites where European popular traditions were sustained even during the oppressive Middle Ages. As Gutman states: "Peasant parades and rituals . . . [were] natural and effective forms of self-assertion and self-protection" (quoted in Leiss et al., p. 54). However, in the face of the massive changes to social and cultural practices in Europe in the late nineteenth century "gradually . . . the older patterns of life and culture fell apart" (p. 54). As the preceding discussion on the early modern period documents, it is not necessary nor prudent to attribute too revolutionary a role in this historical period to changes that were gradually taking place. Nonetheless, it is apparent that the numbing extent of change was a lived reality of communities in the late nineteenth century. Many modern European writers of the era wistfully noted the breakdown of popular traditions which had offered communities a sense of wholeness and rootedness in the pre-modern world. In his essay, "Integrated Civilizations," Lukacs (1971) idealizes a past when people knew their place in the world:

> Happy are those ages when the starry sky is the map of all possible paths— ages whose paths are illuminated by the light of the stars. Everything in such ages is new and yet familiar, full of adventure and yet their own. The world is wide and yet it is like a home.
>
> (p. 29)

As Campbell (1987) explains, modern rootlessness is a corollary of the "disenchantment" of the world associated with the rationalism of Enlightenment values (p. 72), but the bewildering nature of change in the late nineteenth century is appropriately the era when this new condition becomes a lived feature of everyday life.

For the early-twentieth-century European intelligentsia, the search for answers was a philosophical question. Citing the adage of philosopher Novalis, "philosophy is really homesickness, it is the urge to be at home everywhere," Lukacs (1971) attempts to explain the anomie of the modern condition. States Lukacs: "the happy ages have no philosophy . . . all [people] in such ages are philosophers, sharing the utopian aim of every philosophy" (p. 29). In a dawning era of epistemological uncertainty, emergent cultural elements such as consumer goods and dreams were sources to be drawn upon for people and communities to replace social and cultural foundations which had sustained them through the ages. Consumption, which was staged as popular spectacle on city streets, in world expositions, and through nascent promotional forms such as department store catalogs and print advertisements, grew exponentially in this period as a defining social and cultural phenomenon.

Theorists of consumption have focused on late-nineteenth-century Paris as the laboratory of the modern consumer society for very good reasons. First, Paris held five significant world expositions in this period (1855–1900) which were popular spectacles of technology and consumption. Second, the world's first department store, the Bon Marché, opened in Paris in 1869. As well as standing as a temple of consumption in the city center, the Bon Marché also quickly integrated non-urban social space into the new urban culture of consumption by introducing catalog sales. Third, the urban reconstruction initiated by Baron Haussmann in 1850 provided the archetype for the consumption-oriented city center. Where this chapter privileges the historical developments in Paris, it was but a staging ground for the mass transformation of life in the new culture of consumption. As a significant moment in a sanctioned history, Paris might best be seen as a metonym for social and cultural histories which transcend the specificities of their time and place. While Paris led the global North in the introduction of the new culture of consumption, by the end of the century cities such as Berlin, London, Glasgow, New York, and Chicago had followed suit.

As Williams (1982) documents, the popular phrase of the time that described the purpose of early world fairs was to teach a "lesson of things." The "lesson" these fairs provided was to demonstrate "the social benefit of [the] unprecedented material and intellectual progress," which was unsettling the established verities of cultural and social life (p. 58). The Paris world fairs were instructive events that heralded the new, taught the value of material goods, and nurtured the link between pedagogy and commerce that would develop through the twentieth century. While the world fair of 1851 at the Crystal Palace of London had been ostensibly "innocent of commercial purpose," the Paris world fair of 1855 inaugurated the tradition of charging admission and placing price tags on exhibited objects. The world fairs provided a forum for the introduction of new technologies such as: industrial innovations (1855, 1867); scientific discoveries such as electricity and photography (1878); and meteorological, aeronautical, and communications research (1889). By the time of the 1900 world fair, however, "the sensual pleasures of consumption triumphed over the abstract intellectual enjoyment of contemplating the progress of knowledge" (p. 59). What was staged in 1900 was the spectacle of urban consumer culture itself: "the 'lesson of things' taught by the make-believe city of the 1900 expo was that a dream world of the consumer was emerging in real cities outside of its gates" (p. 66).

The significance of the sequence of events that culminated in the 1900 world fair was "the sheer emphasis on marketing," but also "how this marketing was accomplished—by appealing to the fantasies of the consumer" (Williams 1982, p. 64). "If the use of commodities to create a dreamworld was not a late 19th century innovation," states Williams, "what was new in that era was the great increase in the varieties of dreams appealed to by commerce" (p. 109). In historical retrospective, it is difficult to comprehend the significance of the introduction of electricity to the culture of consumption, but its role in illuminating the world fairs, the department stores, and the city itself—and eventually facilitating important vehicles of consumer culture such as radio and television—is of tremendous importance. Williams argues that with the introduction of electricity the whole city assumed "the character of an environment of mass consumption" (p. 89). That the spectacle of illumination coincided with the growth of the commercial display of commodities, allowed merchandisers to nurture new collective "structures of feeling" in the sphere of consumption. As Williams remarks, "electricity created a fairyland environment . . . a make believe place" (p. 84) which has "nurtured a collective sense of life in a dreamworld" (p. 85).

As mentioned, two other key factors played a role in the growth of the culture of consumption in the late nineteenth century: the emergence of department stores and the redevelopment of urban space. It is in the sites of everyday life that the spectacle of consumption is gradually incorporated into popular practice. Williams's (1982) oft-cited comment sums up the significance of department stores to the history of consumption:

> As environments of mass consumption, department stores were, and still are, places where consumers are an audience to be entertained by commodities, where selling is mingled with amusement, where arousal of free-floating desire is as important as immediate purchase of particular items.
>
> (p. 67)

While commodities were staged in department stores, so too were consumers. As Xenos (1989) points out, the spectacle of consumption enacted in the new retail environments also involves the display of the shoppers themselves. Xenos states that "people were placed on display along with commodities" and that part of the "enjoyable atmosphere was due as well to the ability . . . to gaze upon shoppers" (p. 87). Schudson (1984) remarks on the new social significance of department stores: "People thought of stores as social centers and dressed up to go shopping" (p. 151). Of course, the legacy of fashion and emulation from the early modern period presages this development, but it is argued that the ability to gaze, and be gazed upon, is institutionalized in the new consumer environments.

When the labyrinthine city streets of Paris were demolished and replaced with streamlined boulevards in the 1850s, new social spaces enabled new forms of social and cultural life to bloom. "The emergence of boulevards as sites of social display" (Xenos, 1989, p. 88) and the arcades that opened their doors to boulevard strollers became sites where the emerging modern consciousness was first staged. The arcades "presented the myriad products of a blossoming luxury industry for gazing, buying, flaunting and consuming" (p. 89), activities that literally spilled out the doors of these early shopping malls onto the boulevards. As people increasingly migrated to cities and traditional neighborhood distinctions broke down, the bewildering yet fascinating nature of walking shoulder to shoulder with strangers was played out. An emergent sensibility enabled people to adjust to the rapid nature of change in the new urban environments, in the words of Baudelaire, "to be away from home and yet to feel at home anywhere" (quoted in Xenos, 1989, p. 89). Thus, consumption in its broadest sense, the appropriation of goods to stage a performance of social identity, came to assume the mantle of social stability. Whereas such markers of identity as community (both in relation to people and land) and craft had provided the psycho-social conditions for grounding people, for giving people a sense of certainty where "the starry sky is the map of all possible paths," the mobilization of identity and desire in the new consumer spheres brought about the "reenchantment" of social life (Benjamin, quoted in Buck-Morss, 1989, p. 253). Whether the new plenitude offered by consumption was simply "compensatory fulfilment" (Fox, quoted in Leiss et al., 1990, p. 59), a surrogate sense of being in an era when "all that is solid melts into air,"[3] does not detract from the enormous significance of consumption to the social life of cultures of the global North since that time.

It is important to recognize that the expansion of consumption occurred in a period of industrial development in the North, a time when it appeared that the explosion of the productive capacities of Northern economies would permit unlimited growth in consumptive appetites. While, as Schudson (1984) argues, "luxury was not democratized so much as made markedly more visible, more public . . ." (p. 151), the abundant and shimmering display of goods played an important role in creating modern subjects from the newly displaced populations. As Williams (1982) points out, the dream world that emerged from the new environments of mass consumption was not limited to the actual purchase of goods, but it was also a site that offered people a chance to "indulge temporarily in the fantasy of wealth" (p. 91). This dream of wealth, states Williams, is the "long-term accomplishment of the consumer revolution" (p. 92).

As consumption became a way of life to a growing number of people, the struggle to define a social self became more complex. The nature of childhood as a family apprenticeship into adult life had already been displaced by the movement of the forces of production out of the home and into the factory, and just as compulsory public schooling was institutionalized to fill this void, the sphere of consumption emerged as another profound pedagogical site. Schudson (1984) argues that by the turn of the twentieth century "children learn[ed] to pay attention not just to their parents but to the peer group and to the mass media" (pp.153–154). According to Xenos (1989), those most affected by the social instability of this period were the middle class where social positions are "most precarious" and "where identity is poised uneasily between relationally defined extremes and where catching up to the styles previously adopted by those above instantaneously results in the debasement of those same styles" (p. 100). One of the stabilizing influences offered by early marketers were familiar brand names, which "provide people with some sense of identity and continuity in their lives" (Schudson, 1984, p. 156). Whether this commercial gesture compensates for a loss of stability or not, clearly the question of identity and belonging emerged as central concerns in this period.

The enhanced social significance of consumption did not escape the attention of contemporary critics. As Hirschman reports, from the beginning, fears have abounded that "new types of goods would corrupt society and individuals alike" and that "attacks on 'consumerism' are as old as the literature on economic development itself" (quoted in Leiss et al., 1990, p. 53). Simmel, a philosopher and sociologist whose career spans the turn of the century, argued that it was

> only by screening out the complex stimuli that stemmed from the rush of modern life that we could tolerate its extremes. Our only outlet . . . is to cultivate a sham individualism through the pursuit of signs of status, fashion or marks of individual eccentricity.
>
> (Quoted in Bocock, 1993, p. 16)

Williams (1982) develops this point, remarking that the new culture of consumption "diverts attention to merchandise of all kinds and away from other things, like colonialism [and] class structure . . ." (p. 91). States Williams: "The population explosion, the hunger crisis, the energy shortage, the environmental crisis, chronic inflation—all these central concerns of the present originate in our values and habits as consumers" (p. 4). Thus, from the beginning, the dream world of consumption can be seen to obfuscate real concerns of social justice and environmentalism.

Unlike Simmel, another social critic of the early twentieth century, Walter Benjamin, recognized the danger inherent in the new culture of consumption, but also the revolutionary potential. Buck-Morss (1989) comments that Benjamin "takes mass culture seriously not merely as the source of the phantasmagoria of false consciousness, but as the source of the collective energy to overcome it" (p. 253). The problem, for Benjamin, is how to transform the revolutionary potential offered by this period of rapid and radical change into a "materialist education." As products changed to meet the needs of the new mass market, and a new modernist aesthetic of function over form began to develop, Benjamin remarked on what he felt was a "tremendous social(ist) potential" (quoted in Buck-Morss, 1989, p. 303). Buck-Morss states, "as long as the 'present' still had revolutionary potential, Benjamin could conceive of it positively—indeed, teleologically—as 'the waking world towards which the past was dreaming'" (p. 304).

Thus, the dream world of consumption can be seen also as playing a key part in the rupturing of cultural verities, and opening up a space where new worldviews would be mobilized if a "collective 'awakening' . . . synonymous with revolutionary class consciousness" (p. 253) could occur. Berman, whose *All That is Solid Melts into Air* (1982) is a central text in the discussion of a modern consciousness, argues passionately, "modern society, although racked with pain and misery and riven with uncertainty, nevertheless enables men and women to become freer and more creative than men and women have ever been" (p. 33). In other words, some of the certainties which were let go of were oppressive in the first place. States Berman: "If everything must go, then let it go: modern people have the power to create a better world than the world they have lost" (p. 34). While twentieth-century developments have put such optimism into question, his statement does reflect the hope that some modern theorists, such as Benjamin, placed in the new social constellations.

By now, the dream world of modernity lies rusting in the rail yard, an optimism betrayed by warfare, exploitation, and greed. We remain committed to certain emancipation narratives, but they have been uncoupled from the cultural conditions of modernity. What remains from this era, however, is the staging and spectacle of the commodity, the consumer good as object of desire, the act of consumption as an identity performance, and the reenchantment of the spiritual and communal world in and through participation in consumerism. It would do injustice to the specificities of the twentieth century to try to encapsulate that history in the conclusion of this chapter. Suffice it to say that consumer culture reached an apex in the post-World War II era, when consumerism was elevated to a patriotic duty in countries of the North such as the United States, before becoming radically transformed in the post-OPEC, post-Fordist era of economic globalization after 1973. These histories have been taken up by other authors. What interests us, in this chapter, is how the cultural conditions of late-nineteenth-century consumption continue into the present, and to what extent they continue to play an instructive role in our lives.

At the outset of the twenty-first century, it is difficult to extricate the material realities of overconsumption—the ongoing economic exploitation of the majority of the world's populations and global environmental degradation—from the whimsical fulfillments of consumer desire on the part of individuals and groups in the overdeveloped global North. With the continual emergence of new consuming publics, as is the case in contemporary China and India, the sustainability of practices that have developed over centuries is questionable, at best. A critical pedagogy of consumption for new times must include the three Rs—reduce, recycle, reuse—but it must also reorient itself towards the reenchantment of the world in non-material practices. This trend has been building steam alongside the consumer revolutions of the past century in alternative communities, New Age and other forms of spiritual awakenings, and in some forms of artistic practice. These interventions are modest at best, but they are harbingers of sustainable social and cultural practices for new times. Consumer desire and fulfillment has always involved the imaginary resolution of real, material contradictions and circumstances. It is in the recognition of a sense of rootlessness and the desire for reenchantment, that a pedagogy oriented to non-material fulfillment can arise.

Notes

1 For the purposes of this chapter, the global North shall be taken to mean the societies and cultures of contemporary Europe and North America. While the social and cultural transformations associated with the consolidation of consumption in the global North in the latter half of the nineteenth century have effects that reach beyond this geographical and historical framework, it is a Eurocentric conceit to unilaterally impose them on the rest of the world.
2 For a discussion of the pedagogy of advertising, see Hoechsmann (2007).
3 This phrase of Karl Marx became the basis for Marshall Berman's (1982) historical account *All that is solid melts into air: The experience of modernity.*

References

Bakhtin, M. (1968). *Rabelais and his world.* Cambridge, MA: MIT Press.
Berman, M. (1982). *All that is solid melts into air: The experience of modernity.* New York: Simon and Schuster.
Bocock, R. (1993). *Consumption.* London: Routledge.

Buck-Morss, S. (1989). *The dialectics of seeing: Walter Benjamin and the arcades project.* Cambridge, MA: MIT Press.

Campbell, C. (1987). *The romantic ethic and the spirit of modern consumerism.* Oxford, UK: Basil Blackwell.

Hoechsmann, M. (2007). Advertising pedagogy: Teaching and learning consumption. In D. Macedo & S. Steinberg (Eds.) *Media literacy: A handbook* (pp. 653–666). New York: Peter Lang.

Leiss, W., Kline, S., & Jhally, S. (1990). *Social communication in advertising: Persons, products and images of well-being.* Scarborough, ON: Nelson Canada.

Lipsitz, G. (1994). We know what time it is: Race, class and youth culture in the nineties. In A. Ross & T. Rose (Eds.). *Microphone fiends: Youth music and youth culture* (pp. 17–28). New York: Routledge.

Lukacs, G. (1971). *The theory of the novel* (A. Bostock, Trans.). Cambridge, MA: MIT Press.

McCracken, G. (1988). *Culture and consumption.* Bloomington: Indiana University Press.

McKendrick, N., Brewer, N., & Plumb, J. H. (1982). *The birth of a consumer society: The commercialization of eighteenth-century England.* Bloomington: Indiana University Press.

Mukerji, C. (1983). *From graven images: Patterns of modern materialism.* New York: Columbia University Press.

Schudson, M. (1984). *Advertising: The uneasy persuasion.* New York: Basic Books.

Williams, R. (1982). *Dream worlds: Mass consumption in late-nineteenth century France.* Berkeley: University of California Press.

Xenos, N. (1989). *Scarcity and modernity.* New York: Routledge.

3 Consuming Learning

Robin Usher

We can't let terrorists stop us from shopping.

(George W. Bush, September, 2001)

In education, as in the social sciences generally, consumption is still a difficult and controversial topic despite the growing volume of scholarly literature on the subject. While it is now accepted that consumption figures importantly in the lives of people from all social strata, critical language still features strongly in accounting for its significance. In various brands of critical theory, the consumer as the dupe of capitalism assumes a central place. Critical theory provides influential paradigms of consumption, such as the Marxist, where consumption is seen as simply a reflex of production, and the Frankfurt School, where it is seen as alienated consciousness, the source of manipulation and passivity. Consumption is signified as ideology, with ideology critique the only appropriate response.

In contrast, at the other end of the spectrum, classical economic theory with its assumption of the rational hero maximizing utility through consumption is at the heart of contemporary economic rationalism and, in being so uncritical, it too is equally problematic. I want to argue that neither notions of consumers as rational utility maximizers nor as deluded or duped victims of capitalism are satisfactory. In any investigation of the place of consumption in education, we have to question both the language of manipulation and the language of rational action in order to tell a different story about the significance of consumption in people's lives, in a contemporary social order where, whatever we may feel about it, consumption has assumed a central status.

We are all affected in significant ways by contemporary consumer culture and consumerist discourse and images, even when resisting. They have become the motor of contemporary capitalism, generating the core values and sensibilities of the social order. They are multicultural and, with the impact of space–time compression, unconstrained by geographical boundaries. Furthermore, while readily conceding that not all consume equally, with continuing gulfs between rich and poor, I want to argue that consuming is not always, and of necessity, best understood as manipulative or mystifying. Equally, however, contra the economic rationalists, I would not want to argue that consuming is always a desirable thing.

My position is perhaps closer to one influenced by postmodern and post-structural theorizations. Writers drawing on these theorizations (for example, Featherstone, 1991; Urry, 1995; Usher, Bryant, & Johnstone 1997) have high-lighted the significance of consumption in the social order where it is seen as having a variety of effects. On the one hand, there is the notion of fragmented consumers who seek through consumption to stabilize, even if only temporarily, a confusion of identities. On the other, this fragmentation and identity confusion is seen as liberatory since the institutions that have hitherto defined identity no longer have the same defining—and often repressive—power. Identity, it is argued, can be constructed and expressed through consumption as a mode of becoming, the dominant mode through which individuals can creatively construct and express a fluid identity from a variety of possibilities now open to them.

In the "fast" culture of the contemporary moment, the experience of social participation is contingent on patterns of consumption rather than rooted in processes of production. It is what we consume rather than our work or our occupation that defines who we are. This shift points to a significant difference between classical capitalism and what I refer to as "fast" capitalism where the latter has cultural as well as economic and political effects. While classical capitalism fostered an ethic of production, fast capitalism fosters and indeed requires an ethic, and also an aesthetic, of consumption. For Marxists, labor was always the source of creativity and fulfillment; the argument now is that consumption fills this role. In the process, what Baudrillard (1988) refers to as "images circulating as true value," (p. 11) the bewildering circulation of signs that do not so much represent the real but *are* the real—what I have referred to as "fast" culture—has now become the most significant tendency in "fast" capitalism. As lives become shaped by signs that function without reference to a real outside themselves, identities combine and recombine in an apparent free play.

Consumption therefore has to be thought of not simply as the consuming of *goods*, but in a more semiotic way in terms of the signs and significations with which consuming is indelibly imbued. Here consuming becomes a *meaningful* activity where nothing is consumed purely and simply on a functional basis. Consumption always involves the giving and taking of meaning and is the means by which meanings are shared. What is consumed—be it goods, objects, or images—are *signs* that communicate something to others, that code behavior by structuring actions and interactions, and that *bring forth* individuals.

If we think of the consuming of *signs* rather than of *things* (although signs are themselves material) the implication is that goods of whatever kind only make sense in terms of their sign values. To say this about consumption is to say in effect that consumption is cultural because it always involves the giving and taking of meaning. For example, in order to experience a "need" and to act on it by consuming, we must be able to interpret or give meaning to our experiences and our situation, and these are socially constructed interpretations. Consumption is articulated within specific and meaningful ways of life—no one simply eats "food," they eat "bread" or "foie gras," no one simply buys a car, they buy a Ford or BMW, where owning the latter means something quite different from owning the former. Things are taken up as signs in order to *communicate*.

Consumer culture is therefore material and semiotic, an economy of signs, where individuals and groups through what and how they consume communicate messages about position and worth and where consumption is articulated within specific ways of life. Bourdieu and Passeron (1977) remind us that consumption is a set of socio-cultural practices that do not simply *express*, but rather actually *construct*; consumption establishes differences between and within social groups through defining both *how* and *what* to consume, and in the process linking identity with consumer practices. Consumption is thus a process for the cultural production, reproduction, and communication of social relations and social order.

What is consumed and how it is consumed function as *signs* of identity that both differentiate (signifying particular difference from others) and show solidarity (signifying the same as particular others). Consumption can do this because it is more flexible and dynamic than production or occupation in shaping identity. There is a greater fluidity in the cultural "supermarket" where choice and variety are multiple. Lifestyle choices are constantly and rapidly changing. In providing opportunities for self-expression, these choices then stimulate a desire for further consumption. Thus identities can be experimented with and with consequently less commitment than before to any singular fixed identity. This is an *aestheticization* of life that involves a whole range of practices of the aesthetic where the emphasis is on lifestyle and its enhancement.

Many sites have become centers of aesthetic consumption—urban areas, redeveloped and gentrified; shopping malls; museums; theme parks. These centers of consumption flourish where lifestyle concerns manifested through consumption rather than production become significant. The influence of fashion, image, and "taste" pervade an increasingly all-embracing consumer culture that affects all social groups, although some more than others. These are not simply physical sites. These centers of consumption are also semiotic, they *signify* and provide spaces for new experiences and the (re)formation of identities. This is why many argue that lifestyle has now replaced other forms of hierarchical social categorization where its practices have become significant in shaping people's subjectivity and, through that, their sense of identity.

A useful way of thinking about consumption in fast capitalism is as a common *language* through which cultural significations are expressed and interpreted, where individuals "buy" their identity or their "being" with each act of consumption. Baudrillard sees consumption not as a passive "using up" of produced items, but as a framework that enables active relationships within a cultural system (Baudrillard, 1996). This language or semiotic "system of objects" is a structural and differential logic of signs that defines the social order. He argues that everything exists within this logic, a logic that constitutes the *signifying fabric* of our everyday existence. Consumption is thus not located in the exotic but in the quotidian, carried out through the social practices of everyday life.

Baudrillard refers to *consumativity* as the "code" that structures the social order of fast capitalism. This code or structural force links together consumer culture and fast capitalism. Consumer culture projects a hyper-real world of constantly proliferating images, or what Baudrillard calls "simulacra," that are consumed as a desirable reality. Representation has become media-ted to the point where it becomes more real than the real. Baudrillard refers to *simulacra* as copies or models that nonetheless no longer have referents, that are reproduced as hyper-real, and where, although not without meaning, that meaning—given that it is not anchored to an external object or referent—becomes multiple and even undecidable. In other words, simulacra are weightless, decontextualized signifiers.[1] Although copies, they are nonetheless material because they shape the way the real is perceived, or to put it another way, they generate meanings in all spheres of everyday life.

With the proliferation and accelerated circulation of images, hyper-reality is now no longer a limited experience but rather the major condition of contemporary life. Consumerism, the motor of sign values, is the contributing factor in creating this hyper-reality, with hyper-reality in its turn reinforcing the sign economy of consumption. With the consumption of images as signs, thoughts and feelings intertwine with the desire induced by images. For Baudrillard, the code of consumativity marks a ceaseless movement such that the consumption of images is never satisfied—there is always a lack, an endless desire to possess the real but where there is no real, only its image or simulacra (Baudrillard, 1988). It is thus the desire to consume rather than the act of consumption that is significant. Consumption marks a move from the satisfying of necessity, which can be satisfied, to desire, which can never be satisfied. Desires are depthless, any fulfillment always temporary, with desire continually renewed.

Furthermore, as capitalism grows ever more competitive, meaning becomes dispersed and fragmented. It is not so much that each person desires a *specific* object or image, but that each desires what the other desires. People desire the desires of the other.[2] When *fulfillment* can only be found through a world of simulation, there will always be more sign images to be consumed and more desires to be attended to, with fulfillment indefinitely postponed. Commodification feeds an accelerating circulation of signs in the sphere of culture.

The consumption of signs in conditions of fast culture and fast capitalism must inevitably involve a constant, yet unstable, repositioning of subjectivity and a consequent re-forming of identity. As a result, subjectivity becomes a *task*, a performance, rather than a given—something always in process. *Becoming* rather than *being* becomes the ontological priority. Experience becomes contingent and flow-like rather than coherent and determinate. New forms of experience proliferate, with experience generating further experience. Sensibilities are attuned to the pleasure of constant and new experiencing, where the flow of experiencing becomes its own end rather than a means to an end, part of a constant making and remaking of a lifestyle. The unified, coherent, and sovereign self of modernity, the firm ground for the fixing of identity, becomes a multiple discontinuous self traversed by multiple meanings and whose identity is continually in a process of re-formation.

In his influential characterization of late modernity, Giddens (1991) argues that matters of identity become urgent questions in need of an answer rather than answers that can be drawn from meanings that are already available in a pre-given social order. With a greater range of decisions people have to make in relation to identity formation, an existentially and semiotically troubling situation arises where the very uncertainty and ambivalence which give rise to the need to make such decisions actually makes decision-making less secure and therefore troubled. Here Giddens fashions contemporary times as entailing a troubling "risk" with a consequent stress in coping with this risk but where the need to cope is the source of *learning* which—since risk is always present—is therefore lifelong. However, while broadly agreeing with Giddens' argument, I would like to put forward a qualification. Following the thread of my argument so far, the proliferation and consumption of signs, far from being simply existentially troubling can also be existentially pleasurable, as is the need to continually remake identity. There is risk but it is one of not being able to signify oneself in desirable ways, of not being able to respond to lack and desire—the pursuit of which involves learning that never reaches an end. Learning here can be about pleasure and creativity, a point to which I shall return below.

From this we can highlight three significant features of consumption. First, it is always incomplete—it always precipitates an absence. Second, it neither knows any bounds nor respects existing boundaries.[3] Third, meaning or signification, although reaching a temporary anchoring-point, is ultimately always deferred. Relating this to the economy of fast capitalism, the cultural economy of signs bears a structural resemblance to the conventional economy of commodities that gave birth to it. Goods and services are invested with iconic difference and value to make them stand out, to signify difference. What emerges very clearly and very significantly is that consumption has to be seen as a complex and multidimensional semiotic as well as material process.

The implication I want to draw is that consumers should not be seen as passive victims or as rational utility maximizers but rather as actors within a social system that is perpetuated by its use no matter for what end. Consumption and its attendant social order survive as a language or logic through which consumers choose to "speak" and which they perpetuate in so doing. That consumers "speak" in this way is not to be accounted for simply by pointing to the usual paradigms of consumption, since these neglect the dimension of desire that is manifested in consumption and to which even oppressed groups are not immune.

Furthermore, there is plenty of evidence to suggest that rather than always being victims and dupes of consumer culture "consumers can resist the dominant economic order, even as they consume its outputs, its commodities and its images" (Gabriel & Lang, 1995, p. 139). In the practices of everyday life, people can transgress economic rationality and subvert the existing order by using consumer objects for purposes different to those intended for them by their producers—in effect, resisting through consuming—and this is itself a mode of self-expression (de Certeau, 1984). In other words, through consumption one can engage in meaning-making of one's own, which does not simply reflect the meanings of those who produced that which is consumed. Baudrillard (1996, 1988) argues in his usual fatalistic way that consumer society is specifically designed to deflect and incorporate resistance to the extent that everything is consumed, including resistance to consumption. There is some merit in this argument given that resistance is itself semiotic, a lifestyle practice, a means of identity seeking and formation. Bourdieu (1984) points out that so much meaning has become so heavily invested in consumption because the very existence of the bourgeoisie is at stake. On the other hand, it is also the case that consumers *do* manage to evade mechanisms of discipline and they *can* take advantage of opportunities to trace out unforeseeable and unreadable paths.

It is perhaps too much to expect that consumers, even if they desired to, can subvert the market or circumvent its power. Social transformation in the contemporary moment is more likely to occur through pockets of resistance such as ecological and counter-cultural movements, as well as gay, lesbian, and cyber-communities. Globalization and electronic media enable rather than hinder this kind of resistance.

What Does All This Mean for Learning?

How do fast capitalism and signifying consumption impact learning and knowledge? What Baudrillard (1996, 1988) is pointing to with his notions of hyper-reality and simulation is a loss of finalities, or to put it another way, the loss of the foundations of knowledge. Knowledge therefore has to be seen as decentered with a consequent valorization of multiple forms of knowledge and ways of knowing. And with this comes a re-signification of learning. Finalities lose their meaning because they have to assume the existence of an unmediated real. Baudrillard's argument is precisely that there is no unmediated real. There is a real, but it is a hyper-real,[4] and with the hyper-real there can be no finalities. Consequently, learning is more rhizomatic than arboreal, taking off in a variety of directions rather than being bound by the pre-defined goals of modernity's educational project (Deleuze & Guattari, 1988).

In this condition, rather than the search for truth or deep meaning—the pursuit of *a* truth—learning becomes instead a response to desire in the pursuit and consumption of a *range* of truths and an involvement in truth-making practices. In some ways this is bad news for education. I shall say more about this later. In this situation, experience comes to be seen "not as an unmediated guide to 'truth' but as a practice of making sense, both symbolically and narratively, as a struggle over material conditions and meaning" (Brah, 1996, p. 116). Given the proliferation of signs and meaning-making possibilities, it is little wonder that practices of signification, such as those to do with lifestyle, have assumed such a significant place.

At the same time, none of this need be understood as a *refusal* of knowledge, even though it may not signify "learning" as conventionally understood. It is perhaps better seen as "a reformulation of what the desire for knowledge might be about" (Game, 1991, p. 18). These reformulations may include a desire for truth as revelation, truth as advocacy, truth as resonance as well as truth as correspondence, and even for truth as the renewed search for foundations.[5] The point is that no one of these truths can claim to speak the *whole* truth, and it is recognized that they cannot, even though many would still wish them to do so. The possibility and the recognition of multiple truths is disturbing for some while for others it may be a pleasure, as are the multiple possibilities for the re-formation of identity that underpins the desire to seek out multiple forms and sites of knowledge.

What all this signifies is an openness rather than a closure, the desire to assert a definitive truth, even though in a time of openness many will still desire definitive truths and will continue to seek them. This bears significantly on a point made earlier about the aesthetics of the sign value economy and culture. In this social order, learning is energized by desire that can follow many paths, rather than learning governed solely by the pursuit of universal truth (science), unproblematic democracy (citizenship), self-realization (personal development), spirituality (religion), or even the more obvious learning demands of the market. It is not so much that these latter disappear, far from it, rather it is that they no longer constitute quite the dominant and exclusive significations of learning that are foregrounded as "worthwhile" and valuable. These become just a part of the desire to learn which can take multiple forms.

Given this, it is perhaps not coincidental that there has occurred a continually growing trend characterized by the increasing ubiquity and multidirectionality of learning and with a corresponding lessening of the centrality of institutional education. The practices of the quotidian are themselves foregrounded as learning activities. There is an increasing diversity, multiplicity, and de-differentiation characterizing the landscape of learning, and a reconfiguring of learning opportunities away from what educators think is good for learners to what learners themselves consider valuable and value-adding: "Educational practitioners . . . become part of the 'culture' industry, vendors in the educational hypermarket. In a reversal of modernist education, the consumer (the learner) rather than the producer (educator) is articulated as having greater significance and power" (Usher et al., 1997, pp. 107–108).

Thus as people become increasingly positioned as consumers, they also become signified as consumers of learning. My argument is that participation in learning activities, coupled with the increased significance of non-institutional learning, cannot be understood by contemporary educators without reference to consumption. To follow Baudrillard (1996, 1988), learning is now coded by consumption—or to put it another way, to learn is to consume and to consume is to learn. Linked to this is the widespread and continuing impact of a variety of forms of electronic media that at one and the same time are becoming increasingly sophisticated and increasingly accessible and available. This increases the range of learning options, catering to all tastes and interests and previously unavailable, now waiting to be consumed. Indeed one could argue that learning activities have become consumer goods in themselves, purchased as the result of choice within a marketplace where learning products compete with those of leisure and entertainment and are often indistinguishable from these.

As I noted earlier, unlike the mass consumption of modernity, consumption now signifies a choice for difference and difference as choice, the different and distinctive within a signifying culture that stimulates dreams, desires, and fantasies in developing the life project of the self. It is in this sense that learning comes to be signified in terms of lifestyle practices:

> [K]nowledge becomes important: knowledge of new goods, their social and cultural value, and how to use them appropriately. This is particularly the case with aspiring groups who adopt a learning mode towards consumption and the cultivation of a lifestyle. It is for groups such as the new middle

class, the new working class and the new rich or upper class, that the consumer culture of magazines, newspapers, books television and radio programs which stress self-improvement, self-development, personal transformation, how to manage property, relationships and ambitions, how to construct a fulfilling lifestyle, are most relevant.

(Featherstone, 1991, p. 19)

Knowledge (what is learned) has itself become a sign, a commodity, a product in its own right, that can be purchased and consumed for its economic and cultural value—capital which can confer competitive advantage and/or status or at least alleviate the fear of falling behind, either economically or culturally. One implication is that knowledge needs to be made readily consumable—it must have the appropriate signifiers for learners, and what constitutes "appropriate" will vary with the variety of lifestyle practices concerned.

Learning then is integral to lifestyle practices, and within these practices works through an expressive mode. It is individuated with an emphasis on self-expression and marked by a stylistic self-consciousness. Aestheticization, the self-referential concern with image and the constant and pleasurable remaking of identity, necessitates a learning stance towards life as a means of self-expression and identity. In the process individuals are themselves positioned as meaning-makers, as "designers" (Kress, 2003). From this perspective, the semiotic view of people as makers of meaning recodes the cognitive view of people as mentalistic learners.

With lifestyle practices, every aspect of life, like every commodity, is imbued with self-referential meaning, a message to ourselves and to others of the sort of person we are. A good case in point is the contemporary emphasis on the body as a focus for identity. The body is itself now a commodity to be consumed, the youthful, fit body, an image that signifies (Watson, 2005). Here, consumption is a signifier of the need to make oneself different and to identify with those aspired to, where everything consumed signifies an aspect of an aspiration. We witness also the growth of activities related to the fashioning of a new identity—assertiveness training, slimming, bodily well-being, creative writing, interpersonal skills, counseling, rebirthing, makeovers, and spirituality. All of these can now be seen to be embedded in practices that are signified as "learning."

These lifestyle practices, then, are practices of signifying consumption and, moreover, of consumption that is potentially unending because, although deniable, desire—based on lack—is never satisfied. There is always the need for new experiences and hence more learning. It is the very openness or multiple significations of experience, rather than its potential for classification and closure or fixed signification into pre-defined learning, that provides the vehicle for the fueling of desire. There is an endlessness to learning therefore, lifelong and lifewide.

Lifestyle practices are not confined to any one particular social or age group, nor are they purely a matter of economic determination. Economic capital certainly plays a part in influencing the capacity of individuals to be more or less active in their lifestyle practices, but cultural capital is just as significant. Indeed, as Bourdieu and Passeron (1977) argue, cultural capital is as—if not more—important for identity and social positioning. These practices are themselves ways of acquiring and enhancing cultural capital. The significant characteristic of life-style practices is a self-conscious and reflexive adoption of what can be termed a learning mode, a disposition or *stance* towards life, a "lifelong" learning integral to the sensibilities, values, and assumptions embedded in these practices that provide the means of expressing identity. Thus as well as the economic imperative there are other equally significant aspects of contemporary learning, now more akin to a discourse for the governing of life, where the "conduct of conduct" entails the adoption of a design sensibility to one's life and self.

Relating learning to consumption means locating learning in a cultural economy of signs in which consumer choices are communicative practices and learning becomes a marker, an expressive means of self-development. In this sense, learning does not necessarily signify education. With the play of desire and with learning as the fulfillment of desire, learning becomes oriented to specific learner-defined ends, rather than being tied to the educational project's search for enlightenment, truth, deep meanings, or some end pre-defined by the educational system, unless of course these too are recognized as desirable. Equally, education need not necessarily signify learning, unless being signified an "educated person," usually through credentials, is considered desirable, an important aspect of identity formation, or if it acts as a means of distinguishing self from others and a means of desirably identifying with other educated/credentialized persons.

Bad News for (Adult) Education?

There is a certain irony in the fact that learning in the midst of a consumer society should be blossoming throughout the social order. As far as learning is concerned, this is something for which adult educators have long wanted and worked hard. With the help of ubiquitous, time–space-compressing electronic media the dream of learning that is just-in-time, just-when-needed, and always-there is now capable of realization. Yet there is not the contentment one would have expected, mainly because many doubt whether much of the learning taking place is "worthwhile." But that poses the question—who is to define what is worthwhile? And therein lies the problem, for institutionalized education of all types and all levels no longer has the authoritative last word and therefore while it can keep on trying to be the gatekeeper and patrol boundaries its success is likely to be fairly limited. This situation is a feature of postmodernity and is probably why education has found it so hard to come to terms with it.

Earlier I spoke of postmodernity as a condition where learning was not the pursuit of *a* truth, but rather a response to the desire to consume a *range* of truths. I commented there that this was bad news for education, and I meant by this that education has traditionally been about the pursuit of *a* truth. Once that goes the stability, solidity, and rigor of learning goes also, and that is probably why many educators question the worthwhileness and indeed legitimacy of much of the learning embedded in consumer society's lifestyle practices.

Postmodernity has a double aspect. On the one hand, virtually anything is acceptable, and in this sense postmodernity is liberating, happily accommodating the learning embedded in the lifestyle practices of the consumer society.

On the other hand, however, anything is also suspect, and this is extraordinarily frustrating for those seeking social justice and transformation because nothing is sufficiently credible to merit the commitment necessary to achieve those goals. Lifestyle practices are difficult to work with in achieving those goals in a hyper-real consumer culture, and so to organize action for political and social change and, furthermore, to do this through education is consequently also very difficult.

We are all now painfully aware of the downside of consumption—pollution and conspicuous waste being the least of it. There is plenty of scope here for education programs. Having said this, however, no one, least of all educators, has the power to wish it away. As McCracken (1990) points out, "the meaning of what is accomplished by consumer processes are important parts of the scaffolding of our present realities. Without consumer goods, certain acts of self definition and collective definition in this culture would be impossible" (p. 72).

In this situation it is difficult to see a clear way forward in program terms. Of course, educating for and in lifestyle practices offers, and indeed is providing, great scope for education provision, as indeed does the vocational market. For those who see adult education as a dollar-making enterprise, consumer society provides unparalleled opportunities. But obviously that is not to the taste and sensibilities of critical educators. Perhaps the way ahead here is to work with the pockets of resistance to the consumer society that I referred to earlier and that involve learning on the part of those participating, but a learning that is more rhizomatic than arboreal, a learning that takes off in a variety directions. This kind of learning, driven to a very large extent by the continuing development of the electronic media, offers significant scope and new opportunities for education.

Notes

1 A copy of a copy that has been so dissipated in its relation to the original that it can no longer be said to be a copy. The *simulacrum*, therefore, stands on its own as a copy without a model.
2 Baudrillard has also argued that ultimately people desire and seek to consume the myth of consumption.
3 In this, it is a mirror of a fast capitalism, which is characterized by a de-territorializing fluidity and mobility.
4 Consumerism is the contributing factor in creating hyper-reality. The hyper-real is a world of constantly proliferating images or "simulacra" that are *consumed* as a desirable reality.
5 It could be argued that fundamentalists of all religions are embarked on such a renewed search.

References

Baudrillard, J. (1988). *The ecstasy of communication.* New York: Semiotext(e).

Baudrillard, J. (1996). *Selected writings.* Cambridge, UK: Polity Press.

Bourdieu, P. (1984). *Distinction: A social critique of the judgement of taste.* London: Routledge.

Bourdieu, P., & Passeron, J. (1977). *Reproduction in education, society and culture.* London: Sage.

Brah, A. (1996). *Cartographies of diaspora: Contesting identities.* London: Routledge.

de Certeau, M. (1984). *The practice of everyday life.* Berkeley: University of California Press.

Deleuze, G., & Guattari, F. (1988). *A thousand plateaus.* London: Athlone Press.

Featherstone, M. (1991). *Consumer culture and postmodernism.* London: Sage.

Gabriel, Y., & Lang, T. (1995). *The unmanageable consumer.* London: Sage.

Game, A. (1991). *Undoing the social.* Buckingham, UK: Open University Press.

Giddens, A. (1991). *Modernity and self-identity: Self and society in the late modern age.* Cambridge, UK: Polity Press.

Kress, G. (2003). *Literacy in the new media age.* London: Routledge.

McCracken, G. (1990). *Culture and consumption: New approaches to the symbolic character of consumer goods and activities.* Bloomington, IN: Indiana University Press.

Urry, J. (1995). *Consuming places.* London: Routledge.

Usher, R., Bryant, I., & Johnston, J. (1997). *Adult education and the postmodern challenge.* London: Routledge.

Watson, N. (2005). Postmodernism and lifestyles. In S. Sim, (Ed.), *The Routledge companion to postmodernism* (pp. 35–44). London: Routledge.

4 Producing Crisis

Green Consumerism as an Ecopedagogical Issue

Richard Kahn

> The junk merchant doesn't sell his product to the consumer, he sells the consumer to the product. He does not improve and simplify his merchandise. He degrades and simplifies the client.
>
> (William S. Burroughs, 2003, p. 224)

In medieval times, the socially condoned form of responding to one's sinful behavior was to purchase an indulgence from the Church, a kind of pardon issued by the clergy that said all was well once again between the kingdoms of Heaven and Earth for the monetary contributor. Today, when the megamachinery of society regularly results in the blowback of political and economic upheaval, the public is routinely told by the state (e.g., Bush, 2001, 2006) and its neoliberal ideologues (e.g., Friedman, 2008) that the smart person's solution to these problems is simply to spend and shop. This amounts to more than just the strings of people's everyday lives being pulled and persuaded by greedy capitalist puppet masters; it is symptomatic evidence of the affluent society's generally insane commitment to what has been termed "fundamentalist consumerism" (Levine, 2009). This fundamentalism's ruling idea—that larger structural disorders can be properly rectified through acts of individual consumer choice—has become particularly ubiquitous in connection to our planet's burgeoning ecological crisis. Here, an ostensibly enlightened buying public concerned with the degradation of the Earth's limited natural resources, practices "boycotts" that signal to business and government alike that society is ready to pay for the sustainable production of goods and services in specific market sectors. Thus hailed by consumers, it is the green consumerist belief that businesses then respond by adding corporate social responsibility to their missions, opening production lines of "green" market goods, and by becoming less ecologically rapacious forces in the world.

Emerging from the legacies of Reaganomics and Thatcherism, green consumerist ideology entered into the mass consciousness on both sides of the Atlantic through widely popular self-help environmentalist bibles like *The Green Consumer Guide* (Elkington & Hailes, 1988) and *50 Simple Things You Can Do to Save the Earth* (EarthWorks Group, 1989). In 1992, the idea of green consumerism additionally gained traction in policy debates with the publication of *Agenda 21* (United Nations Conference on Environment and Development, 1992), a document that pointed to the developed world's extreme over-consumption of natural resources as a primary sustainability issue requiring the development of eco-efficiency strategies and market instruments capable of shifting consumption patterns.[1] Importantly, *Agenda 21* also called for sustainable consumption through "a radical realignment of social and economic institutions" (Seyfang, 2005, pp. 292–293), imploring governments to employ and integrate qualitatively different visions of wealth and prosperity that would serve the public good. This form of alternative, possibly non-capitalist, sustainable development remains extant today as a critical cultural potential exerting opposition-from-below on mainstream forms of policy and social practice. However, the current majority of sustainable development initiatives undeniably find themselves folded into the interests of global neoliberals in either their aggressive corporatist or Third Way welfarist varieties (Kahn, 2008a).

Since green consumerism's modest beginnings in the late 1980s and early 1990s, the last two decades have seen a steady proliferation of popular books, as well as television shows (and now an entire cable channel), films, Internet sites, and advertisements, all encouraging people to "vote with their dollar" on behalf of supposedly sustainable commodities. Sometimes these votes are indirect as well, as evidenced by the recently inaugurated Obama administration's assertion that its election victory amounted to a vote for the governmental investment of hundreds of billions of tax dollars into Big Auto, Energy, and Construction towards the creation of millions of "Green Collar Jobs" over the next decade (Schneider, 2009). Therefore, while significant financial investment reports such as GreenBiz.com's *The State of Green Business 2009* continue to forecast that a green economy remains for the time-being more talk than actual walk, it is undeniable that sustainability as a capitalist development paradigm has become an ever-more dominant trend over the last decade in both policy and products.

As we have known since Marx, capitalism both breeds and loves crisis. Pervasive ecological calamity, then, allows for green consumerism to emerge as perhaps the ultimate form of "disaster capitalism" (Klein, 2008) seen to date.[2] It is an opportunity for corporations to turn the very crisis that they generate through their accumulation of capital via the exploitation of nature into myriad streams of emergent profit and investment revenue.

Green Consumerism as Public Pedagogy

> "Consum-ere," the Latin root for consuming, means to take up completely, make away with, devour, waste, destroy, spend . . .. "Good consumerism" simply extends and legitimates our impulses to destroy, to ruin ourselves and our environments, to waste away our natural and social inheritance, to produce decay and rot.
>
> (Gustavo Esteva & Madhu Suri Prakash, 1998, p. 17)

Whether it is a hybrid vehicle, organic food, an energy-efficient light bulb, shade-grown coffee and fairly traded chocolate, non-toxic housecleaning supplies, or a properly "greened" ethical investment stock portfolio, all manner of consumer life has begun to offer options for people seeking to be more socially and environmentally conscious in their lifestyles. Moreover, some or all of these may be appropriate responses to our historical moment as people attempt to live more sustainably in a highly capitalized society. Yet, critical due diligence is also required of them. For our educational relationship with the ecological issues that these products purport to help solve is reduced and cheapened when we accept that buying the new "eco-friendly" formula thereby absolves us of deeper levels of social inquiry and political action.

Certainly, it is true that no product in itself necessarily prevents our further commitment to establishing a transformative relationship to the world. However, when taken as a whole, the culture of green consumerism can easily serve as a way to reproduce socially the dominant social order through a wide variety of narcoleptic shopping exercises that profess our collective salvation via the growth of individuals' mounting credit debt. In this respect, Giroux (2005) has written of the ways in which corporations and the dominant business discourse today mark

> the space of a new kind of public pedagogy, one in which the production, dissemination, and circulation of ideas emerge from the educational force of the larger culture. Public pedagogy in this sense refers to a powerful ensemble of ideological and institutional forces whose aim is to produce competitive, self-interested individuals vying for their own material and ideological gain. Under neoliberalism, pedagogy has become thoroughly reactionary as it operates from a variety of education sites producing forms of pedagogical address in which matters of personal agency, social freedom, and the obligations of citizenship conceive of political and social democracy as a burden, an unfortunate constraint on market relations, profit making, and a consumer democracy.
>
> (¶ 10)

Mainstream green consumerism should be conceived of as public pedagogy in exactly this manner, for it serves to weaken robust ideas of political and social democracy, as personal agency, social freedom, and the obligations of citizenship are ideologically tethered to capitalist market relations and renewed profiteering.[3] In the form of a feel-good catharsis, the take-home message of green consumerism is largely to stop worrying about the big problems and to instead do one's little part for sustainability through endless repetitions of spending on behalf of "the planetary good." Of course, it is far from clear how increasing one's acquisition of sustainable commodities in any way represents real opposition to either a culture defined by hyperconsumption or an economic structure that demands it.

Global Psychosis?

> Our complex global economy is built upon millions of small, private acts of psychological surrender, the willingness of people to acquiesce in playing their assigned parts as cogs in the great social machine that encompasses all other machines. They must shape themselves to the prefabricated identities that make efficient coordination possible . . . that capacity for self-enslavement must be broken.
>
> (Theodore Roszak, 1995, p. 16)

In 1961, the psychologist Stanley Milgram conducted the first in a famous series of experiments in which test subjects assigned the role of "teacher" believed that they administered electroshocks in 15-volt increments to a remote "learner," supposedly in order to evaluate the role of punishment as a pedagogical technique for improving poor performance (see Milgram, 1963). Unaware that the experiments' stated aims were a hoax in which the "learner" was in fact an actor who would consistently broadcast tape-recorded cries of pain beginning at 75 faux volts of shock, the "teachers" of the research study assumed that they were causing (potentially grave) injury to their fellow research participant. Video footage of the experiments reveals the "teachers" as initially concerned, and then increasingly resistant and demonstrably upset, by the apparent effects of their sadistic activity when the voltage they believed that they discharged grew steadily higher. Still, upon being encouraged to persist with the research by an overseeing expert, at 150 volts, over 82% of the "teachers" continued to deliver what they believed to be additional electric shock to the "learner," and startlingly some 65% did so all the way until 450 volts—the experiment's highest electricity register.[4]

One participant, after repeatedly begging to check on the "learner" (who had stopped responding after complaining about heart trouble at 300 volts), found his demands casually rebuffed by those in charge, which resulted in his asking nervously multiple times, "Who is going to take responsibility for this?" Upon being told that the lead investigator would take full responsibility and that he as "teacher" would be absolved of any, despite showing signs of severe psychological agitation, this "teacher" then continued to complete the experiment and administer numerous shocks at 450 volts to the "learner." Finally, he had to be stopped from doing so through external intervention. Thus, the Milgram experiments were stunning rituals of duty to perceived power norms that served to reveal how even well-meaning people would continue in the large to be obedient agents for a dehumanizing system, if they believed it to be under the control of responsible authorities. Faced with moments of personal crisis, the majority of test subjects responded by repressing the moral demand that they transform their relationship to the crisis situation by radically opposing the structure that supported it. Buoyed in this response by the belief that their hierarchical superiors would shoulder the accountability for their actions, Milgram's "teachers" instead demonstrated how aggravated social crisis could easily result in the ongoing reproduction of overt status quo expectations in individuals' lives.

In many respects, Milgram's 450 volts is our contemporary threat limit of 450 parts per million (ppm) of atmospheric carbon dioxide (CO_2), a tipping point at which leading climatologists now believe planetary global warming will hurtle out of humanity's control and engender a worldwide ice-free state of dynamic cataclysm (Hansen, et al., 2008). Whereas Milgram's test subjects repeatedly added 15 volts of pain far past the point when they consciously desired to do so, as a global society we collectively add 2 ppm of CO_2 annually to our planet's atmosphere despite it being publicly known that our present level of 385 ppm is considered dangerous such that it must be reduced immediately by significant amounts. While there are many sources that contribute to global warming (including nonanthropogenic sources), some of the chief causes for our present climate crisis are the globalization of industrial forms of energy delivery, goods manufacture, transportation, and agriculture/livestock production as the core staples of modern life (Food and Agriculture Organization of the United Nations, 2007; Intergovernmental Panel on Climate Change, 2007, p. 105). Each of us, then, who is a participating member of the global consumer society that is constituted by the hyperconsumption of such staples, is in a sense responsible for its terrible consequences, as we daily help to produce them through our tacit consent of the socio-economic order.

Ecological High Noon

> Trouble in the wild waves, Trouble in the wind sprays, Trouble on the green things, Trouble on the housetops, Trouble in the mountain, Trouble at the river: Going to see trouble all around this world.
>
> (Woody Guthrie, 1963, p. 190)

Although global warming has been christened *the* mega-challenge of our time, of such a magnitude that even the combined and timely cooperation of all the world's nations may no longer be able to prevent its long-term effects (Solomon, Plattner, Knutti, & Friedlingstein, 2009), the continued expansion of corporate globalization must be linked to another nightmarish set of related but differing ecological catastrophes. In 2005, the UN-funded Millennium Ecosystem Assessment (MEA) released the most encompassing study to date about the state of the planet's ecology. The report's findings were alarming for the present and dire as regards the future.

To summarize, the report found that during the last 50 years, humanity has altered (and mainly degraded) the Earth's ecosystems "more rapidly and extensively than in any comparable time of human history" (MEA, 2005, p. 2). This was done largely on behalf of an exponential demand for primary natural resources that coincides with the social and economic changes wrought by corporate globalization. For instance, between 1960 and 2000, the world's population doubled and the global economy increased by more than six-fold, resulting in more land (e.g., forests, wetlands, prairies, savannahs) being converted for agricultural uses than had taken place during the 150 years prior combined (p. 2). While the majority of the world's farming practices (e.g., industrial monocropping, slash-and-burn) continue to debase soil quality towards desertification, short-term food production via these methods increased by a factor of nearly three, water use doubled (nearly 70% of used water goes to agriculture), half of all wetlands were developed, timber pulping and paper production tripled while 50% of the forests disappeared, and the damming of flowing waterways doubled hydropower (p. 5). Moreover, over the same time period, unsustainable fishing contributed to grave losses of global mangroves, which were reduced by approximately 35%, as well as of coral reef biomes—our underwater tropical rain forests—which have suffered extinction and damage rates of 20% each respectively (p. 5).

This has led (and will continue to lead) to unthinkable levels of marine species extinction. The rise of commercial fishing has eradicated some 90% of the ocean's largest fish varieties and it is expected that no commercial fishery will be left active in the world by 2048 based on present rates of catch (Worm et al., 2006). The effects of post-World War II globalization have been equally profound on other species, as we have experienced 1,000 times the historical rate of normal background extinction, with upwards of 30% of all mammals, birds, and amphibians currently threatened with permanent disappearance (MEA, 2005, p. 4). In other words, over the last half-century we have been involved in a mass die-off of non-human animals such as we have not witnessed for 65 million years, and worse yet, predictions for the future expect these rates of extinction to increase ten-fold (p. 5).

This unfolding natural disaster is also a social disaster for huge numbers of the population—those that do not generally serve to benefit from the World Bank, International Monetary Fund, and multinational corporations: the global destitute, poor, and working classes who cannot meaningfully partake of the consumer society's living standard improvements (see Kahn, 2008a, 2008b). People, especially in the Global South, depend directly upon ecosystem services—a wide range of natural resources and processes—in order to survive. These services, while freely provided by nature, contributed some \$33 trillion of global economic value in 1997 (Wilson, 2002, p. 106). It is now known that over the last half-century of globalization at least 60% of ecosystem services have been damagingly overused, with trends growing continually worse, especially for those who can least afford to compensate for such environmental disruption (MEA, 2005, p. 1). In the face of such staggering statistics, we should remain skeptical of green consumerism's connotations of sustainability.

Running on the Treadmill

> The Chairman of the board will always tell you that he spends his every waking hour laboring so that people will get the best possible products at the cheapest possible price and work in the best possible conditions. But it is an institutional fact, independent of who the chairman of the board is, that he'd better be trying to maximize profit and market share, and if he doesn't do that, he's not going to be chairman of the board any more. If he were ever to succumb to the delusions that he expresses, he'd be out.
>
> (Noam Chomsky, quoted in Moyers, 1989, p. 42)

Green consumerism is a particularly limited pedagogy in as much as it suggests an inflated sense of individual agency over the world's industrial processes, when in fact people are often systematically denied critical knowledge and control over the means of the production for the goods they are encouraged to buy. Just as Milgram's research participants almost never awoke to ask the most relevant questions of the experiment's structure itself, so too do informed consumers often fail to recognize that "green" products (if they are that) do not arise in the world as retail commodities *ex nihilo*. Green consumer goods are first and foremost products of a particular form of economic system that, according to Eastwood (2006), "has little to do with the fiction of rational choice and far more to do with psychological manipulation . . .. Capital accumulation relies not only on the production of goods, but also . . . on the production of the willing consumer" (pp. 118–119).

In other words, green consumerism often occludes the "treadmill of production" (Gould, Pellow, & Schnaiberg, 2008) of which it is a part. Per treadmill theory, over the last 60 years, capital investment has continually sought to augment profits from goods production by lessening the role of human labor in favor of the increased use of industrial technologies. In contrast with manual labor, these technologies have required vast amounts of energy and chemicals to work and have thus caused historically unprecedented amounts of ecological degradation as a result. Further, industrial technology amounts to sunk capital that imposes fixed costs on production owners, thereby requiring a continual increase in the rate of manufacturing to maximize revenue. This itself demands an army of enthusiastic consumers that is guaranteed through marketing and educational strategies (Foster, 1999), as well as the complicity of government in order to deregulate production standards, subsidize increased natural resource extraction, and ensure that the environmental effects of industrial mass production are borne by the public even as profit remains privatized.[5]

Sustainability education, then, must move beyond training people for membership in the green economy. Rather, it must relate critiques of consumption to production as part of a larger reconstructive political project concerned with the radical democratization of the workplace and the larger society. Such a Reddish-Blue/Green pedagogical alliance as I envision emerges out of a dialectic of absolute negation (McLaren, 2003) and involves learning how the domination of nature proper is prototypical of all other forms of social alienation and dehumanization.

For Critical Ecopedagogy

> Today, we can easily imagine the extinction of the human race, but it is impossible to imagine a radical change of the social system—even if life on earth disappears, capitalism will somehow remain intact.
>
> (Slovoj Žižek, 1999, ¶ 36)

Change may have come to America with the ascension of Barack Obama to the throne of *Prima Imperator* but then let us all hope that such change trickles down to the head of the White House's National Economic Council, Lawrence Summers. It is nothing short of ominous that the person fronting America's present economic agenda is the same individual who as the Chief Economist of the World Bank argued in 1991 that:

> There are no . . . limits to the carrying capacity of the Earth that are likely to bind any time in the foreseeable future. There isn't a risk of an apocalypse due to global warming or anything else. The idea that we should put limits on growth because of some natural limit, is a profound error and one that, were it ever to prove influential, would have staggering social costs.
>
> (Quoted in George & Sabelli, 1994, p. 109)

During the same period, a then-confidential memo from Summers contained this ecological wisdom:

> Just between you and me, shouldn't the World Bank be encouraging more migration of the dirty industries to the LDCs [less developed countries]? I think the economic logic behind dumping a load of toxic waste in the lowest wage country is impeccable.
>
> (Quoted in Foster, 2002, p. 60)

This decade, while serving as Secretary of the Treasury under Bill Clinton, Summers (along with Alan Greenspan) intervened on behalf of Kenneth Lay and Enron in the energy crisis that the corporation was secretly manufacturing throughout the state of California. Despite then-Governor Gray Davis's contention that corporate malfeasance was the primary cause of the state's electricity woes, Summers instead urged him that they were more properly analyzed as resulting from a market crisis that would be best addressed by the immediate removal of consumer rate caps and a rapid environmental deregulation of the energy sector (Eichenwald, 2005). The ideology voiced by Summers—in essence, Neoliberalism 101—represents everything we must whole-heartedly oppose and educate against if sustainability is to be more than a noxious greenwash in our lifetimes.

While I am certainly not hostile to popular educational calls to rethink the ecological design of schools or champion increased outdoor experiences for children, such as sponsored by the *No Child Left Inside Coalition*,[6] these initiatives profoundly block eco-literacy to the degree that they leave robust structural critique and learning how to organize collective opposition to capitalist social relations off the agenda. To work in a community garden can teach the sort of core values about the cultural commons, care, self-sufficiency, and biophilia that are the likely pathways to a sustainable future. However, there is nothing in this work that necessarily entails knowledge about the political economy of the transnational class or the bludgeoning militarism of the plutocratic super-elite. This dangerous insufficiency is more evident still in green consumerist acts.

Mumford (1970) wrote:

> Once an organic world picture is in the ascendant, the working aim of an economy of plenitude will be not to feed more human functions into the machine, but to develop further man's incalculable potentialities for self-actualization and self-transcendence, taking back into himself deliberately many of the activities he has too supinely surrendered into the mechanical system.
>
> (p. 395)

Part of ecopedagogy for sustainability, as I envision it, is taking back our humanity by learning about the dehumanizing capitalist system: its history, how it operates, for whom, and what potentials it holds. This form of study is part of what Best and Kellner (2001) call the articulation of a critical, multiperspectival, and reconstructive social theory. Due to our present age's heightened sense of danger and complex manifestations of power, environmental education of any kind that operates devoid of such a critical theory crosses a bridge to nowhere at the edge of the world. Still, social theory without a literacy foundation of sustainable practice is itself a barrier preventing the autochthonic liberation of human instincts for peace, beauty, and joy. Just as there is no sense in homesteading in a forest beseeched by a Weyerhaeuser clearcut, so too ranting about capitalism without putting daily foot to the production of its alternative is symptomatic more of nihilism than planetary emancipation.

As Panitch and Leys (2007) argue, we must make multiple moves in our political education: from blind consumerism to a mobilization against specific corporations to an organized understanding of the unsustainable logic of the capitalist system *in toto*. Then, we must go further still by pushing past the imaginative inertia that can easily set in when we daily confront the juggernaut of global neoliberalism and all its ecological perils in the abstract. Sustainability will not come as easy as a grocery aisle, but it is not impossible either. By contrast, its very possibility becomes ever more manifest as we participate in the ongoing struggle for another world. All power to the imagination!

Notes

1 Regarding the hyperconsumption of the global North, the WorldWatch Institute (2006) has reported that 60% of private consumption takes place amongst the 12% of the world's population that lives in North America and western Europe, while the peoples of south Asia, sub-Saharan Africa (who constitute one-third of the global population) account for only 3.2% of private consumer spending.

2 Again, we must here distinguish between mainstream forms of green consumerism and counterhegemonic varieties extant in at least some vegan, slow food, DIY, permacultural, and other subcultures.

3 As watchdogs of school commercialism point out, corporations also seek to use school curricula as another pedagogical avenue for rooting green consumer ideology to their benefit. For instance, Molnar (2006) describes a 1983 visit to the Association for Supervision and Curriculum Development where he encountered free curricular materials from McDonald's on nutrition and the environment (pp. 65–66). He goes on to write that, in addition to McDonald's, he has learned that "the pork farmers, the plastic bag manufacturers, the Dairy Council, the timber industry, the oil industry . . . and many, many more have a curriculum to offer" (p. 66). In Kahn (forthcoming), I document the story of a Chicago-area vegan teacher who was fired in part for educating in opposition to the crass eco-commercialism of the Dairy Council in his school.

4 In Milgram's first experiment all test subjects deployed the maximum 450 volts to the "learner" without question. So Milgram devised additional factors that he thought should make it less likely that they would do so for additional tests. For instance, the final three levers of over 400 volts were labeled "Danger severe shock XXX" and the "learner" began to express increasingly vociferous demands to end the experiment starting at 150 volts.

5 A great interactive lesson in the treadmill is at: http://thestoryofstuff.com.

6 For more on the Coalition and its aims, see http://nclicoalition.org.

References

Best, S., & Kellner, D. (2001). *The postmodern adventure: Science, technology and cultural studies at the third millennium*. New York: The Guilford Press.

Burroughs, W. S. (2003). *Naked lunch*. New York: Grove Press.

Bush, G. W. (2001, October 11). Bush on state of war. Retrieved February 6, 2009, from http://www.washingtonpost.com/wp-srv/nation/specials/attacked/transcripts/bush_text101101.html

Bush, G. W. (2006, December 20). Remarks at press conference. Retrieved February 6, 2009, from http://thinkprogress.org/2006/12/20/bush-shopping/

EarthWorks Group. (1989). *50 simple things you can do to save the earth.* Berkeley, CA: Earthworks Press.

Eastwood, L. (2006). Contesting the economic order and media construction of reality. In S. Best & A. J. Nocella, II (Eds.), *Igniting a revolution: Voices in defense of the earth,* (pp. 114–126). Oakland, CA: AK Press.

Eichenwald, K. (2005). *Conspiracy of fools: A true story.* New York: Broadway Books.

Elkington, J., & Hailes, J. (1988). *The green consumer guide.* London: Victor Gollancz.

Esteva, G., & Prakash, M. S. (1998). *Grassroots post-modernism: Remaking the soil of cultures.* New York: Macmillan.

Food and Agriculture Organization of the United Nations [UNFAO]. (2007). *Livestock's long shadow: Environmental issues and options.* Rome: UNFAO. Available: ftp://ftp.fao.org/docrep/fao/010/a0701e/a0701e.pdf

Foster, J. B. (1999). Global ecology and the common good. *Cultural Logic, 3*(1). Retrieved February 6, 2009 from http://eserver.org/clogic/3-1&2/foster.html

Foster, J. B. (2002). *Ecology against capitalism.* New York: Monthly Review Press.

Friedman, T. L. (2008, November 16). Gonna need a bigger boat. *New York Times.* Retrieved from http://www.nytimes.com/2008/11/16/opinion/16friedman.html?_r=1&hp

George, S., & Sabelli, F. (1994). *Faith and credit: The World Bank's secular empire.* Boulder, CO: Westview Press.

Giroux, H. (2005). Cultural studies in dark times: Public pedagogy and the challenge of neoliberalism. *Fast capitalism, 1*(2). Retrieved February 6, 2009 from http://www.uta.edu/huma/agger/fastcapitalism/1_2/giroux.html

Gould, K, Pellow, D. N., & Schnaiberg, A. (2008). *The treadmill of production: Injustice & unsustainability in the global economy.* Boulder, CO: Paradigm Publishers.

Guthrie, W. (1963). Trouble at Redondo. *Woody Guthrie folk songs.* New York: Ludlow Music.

Hansen, J., Sato, M., Kharecha, P., Beerling, D., Masson-Delmotte, V., Pagani, M., Raymo, M., Royer, D. L., et al. (2008). Target atmospheric CO2: Where should humanity aim? *The Open Atmospheric Science Journal, 2,* 217–231.

Intergovernmental Panel on Climate Change. (2007). *Climate change 2007: Mitigation of climate change.* Cambridge, UK: Cambridge University Press.

Kahn, R. (2008a). From education for sustainable development to ecopedagogy: Sustaining capitalism or sustaining life? *Green Theory & Praxis: The Journal of Ecopedagogy, 4*(1), 1–14.

Kahn, R. (2008b). Towards ecopedagogy: Weaving a broad-based pedagogy of liberation for animals, nature and the oppressed people of the earth. In A. Darder, R. Torres & M. Baltodano (Eds.), *The critical pedagogy reader* (2nd ed.). New York: Taylor & Francis.

Kahn, R. (Forthcoming). Towards an animal standpoint: Vegan education and the epistemology of ignorance. In E. Malewski & N. Jaramillo (Eds.), *Epistemologies of ignorance and the studies of limits in education.* Charlotte, NC: Information Age Publishing.

Klein, N. (2008). *The shock doctrine: The rise of disaster capitalism.* New York: Picador Press.

Levine, B. E. (2009). Fundamentalist consumerism and an insane society. *Z-Mag.* Retrieved February 6, 2009, from http://www.zmag.org/zmag/viewArticle/20446

McLaren, P. (2003). Critical pedagogy and class struggle in the age of neoliberal globalization. *Democracy and Nature, 9*(1), 65–90.

Milgram, S. (1963). Behavioral study of obedience. *Journal of Abnormal Social Psychology, 67*, 371–378.

Millennium Ecosystem Assessment [MEA]. (2005). *Ecosystems and human well-being: Synthesis.* Washington, DC: Island Press.

Molnar, A. (2006). Public intellectuals and the university. In G. Ladson-Billings & W. F. Tate (Eds.), *Education research in the public interest* (pp. 64–80). New York: Teachers College Press.

Moyers, B. (Ed.). (1989). *A world of ideas.* New York: Doubleday.

Mumford, L. (1970). *The myth of the machine: The pentagon of power.* New York: Harcourt.

Panich, L., & Leys, C. (Eds.). (2007). *Coming to terms with nature: Socialist register 2007.* New York: Monthly Review Press.

Roszak, T. (1995). The greening of psychology: Exploring the ecological unconscious. *The Gestalt Journal, 18*(1). Retrieved February 6, 2009, from http://www.igjournal.org/guests/Roszak.pdf

Schneider, K. (2009, January 19). What Barack Obama's inauguration means for green energy. *Guardian UK.* Available: http://www.guardian.co.uk/environment/2009/jan/19/obama-green-energy-economy

Seyfang, G. (2005). Shopping for sustainability: Can sustainable consumption promote ecological citizenship? *Environmental Politics, 14*(2), 290–306.

Solomon, S., Plattner, G. K., Knutti, R., & Friedlingstein, P. (2009). Irreversible climate change due to carbon dioxide emissions. *Proceedings of the National Academy of Sciences of the United States of America.* Available: http://www.pnas.org/content/early/2009/01/28/0812721106.abstract

United Nations Conference on Environment and Development. (1992). *Agenda 21: The United Nations program of action from Rio.* New York: UN Publications.

Wilson, E. O. (2002). *The future of life.* New York: Alfred A. Knopf.

WorldWatch Institute. (2006). *State of the world trends and facts: The state of consumption today.* Retrieved from http://www.worldwatch.org

Worm, B., Barbier, E. B., Beaumont, N., Duffy, J. E., Folke, C., Halpern, B. S., et al. (2006). Impacts of biodiversity loss on ocean ecosystem services. *Science, 314*(5800), 787–790.

Žižek, S. (1999). Attempts to escape the logic of capitalism. *London Review of Books, 21*(21). Retrieved February 6, 2009, from http://www.lrb.co.uk/v21/n21/zize01_.html

5   Teaching Against Consumer Capitalism in the Age of Commercialization and Corporatization of Public Education[1]

Ramin Farahmandpur

> I thought communism was s*** but capitalism is even worse.
> (Herman Haibel, retired blacksmith, East Berlin.
> Cited in Kirschbaum, 2009, ¶ 12)

As the ticker-tape parades on Wall Street subside, and as the ideological smoke-screen of free market fundamentalism finally clears, we find ourselves bearing witness to the "shock and awe" of the worst economic and financial crisis since the Great Depression. All this comes after three decades of unprecedented record-breaking corporate profits engineered by neoliberal social and economic reforms that included deregulation, privatization, anti-labor and anti-union legislations, outsourcing, and downsizing of labor. The outcome of these economic reforms has been the upward redistribution of wealth for the richest 1% of Americans and the downward distribution of consumer and financial debt for the working men and women whose wages have remained stagnant since the late 1970s. As we all know by now, capitalism does not come equipped with airbags, not even for an A-list of real-estate magnates, private investors, and foundations who were recently defrauded of millions of dollars by Bernard Madoff's $50 billion Ponzi-scheme scandal.

With the economic and financial meltdown in full swing, an increasing number of working men and women find themselves standing in long unemployment lines, public schools across the nation are forced to cut back on educational programs and services, and working-class and underrepresented first-generation college students are faced with rising tuition and growing class sizes often taught by a contingent and flexible workforce of adjunct and part-time professors who must often teach three or more classes each term merely to make ends meet. Working-class families, unable to pay their subprime and adjustable-rate mortgages, are recognizing that owning a piece of the American dream is now far from within their reach. According to David Leonhardt (2009) of the *New York Times*, the collapse of the housing market has forced more than three million foreclosures and a significant decline in the real-estate values of ten million other homeowners.

As we speak, most—if not all—states are experiencing the devastating effects of the economic and financial crisis. Ranked as the eighth largest economy in the world, surpassing most Western industrial nations, California, for instance, is now on the brink of economic collapse. More than 20,000 state employees, including schoolteachers, are at risk of losing their jobs as the state struggles to overcome a $40 billion budget deficit. In Detroit, Michigan, after General Motors lost more than $20 billion in 2008, negotiations are underway between the automobile company and the United Auto Workers (UAW) to reduce its retiree healthcare benefits. Finally, in Oregon, in 2009 alone, the recession has created an $855 million deficit in the state's budget, and possibly another $3 billion for the 2009–2011 biennium. One of the proposals suggested to balance the state's budget crisis includes reducing the number of instructional days at public schools, slashing the state's university system and community college budgets, and rolling back social services, including daycare for working-class families.

In this chapter, I examine consumption practices insofar as they are linked to the commercialization and corporatization of public education. I begin with a brief overview and analysis of the current social, political and economic crisis facing U.S. imperialism. In the second section of this chapter, I argue that, with the deepening crisis of global capitalism, Marx and Marxist analysis are far more urgent today than at any other time in history, and I explicate how activists across the globe are engaged in anti-capitalist struggles. In the third section, I discuss and provide examples of commercialization of school programs and classroom curricula due to budget shortfalls in school districts across the nation. In the concluding section, I sketch out in broad strokes a number of fundamental steps teachers and educators can undertake to help students develop consumer literacy skills, which I locate within the broader framework of critical literacy.

Clear and Present Danger: The Crisis of U.S. Imperialism

By the late 1980s and the early 1990s, with the demise of its main ideological and political rival—the former Soviet Union—the United States pursued a "unilateralist" foreign policy that included the expansion of its geopolitical interests in the Middle East and in Central Asia by establishing an unprecedented military presence in the region. However, at the same time, the United States faced economic, ideological, and military-political crises (Bello & Rees, 2005).

With the decline of the post-war economic boom in the late 1970s, the United States and its main Western industrial capitalist allies experienced a crisis of overproduction of consumer goods that flooded the global markets. The present crisis of overproduction has moved towards the intensification of competition among transnational corporations, causing what some economists have identified as a "crisis of profitability" (Brenner, 2006). As early as the 1980s, the response of the leading Western capitalist economies to overcapacity and overproduction was to introduce neoliberal social and economic reforms. These reforms encouraged investment in finance and speculative capital that involved "squeezing value out of already created value" (Bello & Rees, 2005, ¶ 3). A second response to the crisis of overcapacity and overproduction was to move the manufacturing industry abroad to Third World and developing nations, including China, where labor costs are lower than in any other labor market in the world.

In addition to the economic crisis, the invasion and occupation of Iraq in spring of 2003 deepened the military-political crisis of U.S. imperialism. The imperial ambitions of the United States, which included becoming the sole global economic and military power in the absence of its geopolitical and ideological rival, the former Soviet Union, has caused what Bello and Rees (2005) identify as the "crisis of overextension" (¶ 1), which can be described as the "gap between goals and resources" (¶ 2). To achieve its foreign policy objectives, U.S. imperialism has resorted to its brutal military might to overthrow forcefully any nation or government foolish enough to challenge its hegemony and threaten its economic and political interests. The first series of post-Soviet era military interventions in Iraq (in 1991), Somalia (in 1993), and Yugoslavia (in 1999) served as experiments for what was to follow in future large-scale military operations and interventions, including the invasion and military occupation of Iraq and Afghanistan.

Despite the political and military fiasco in Iraq, the United States is not deterred from further escalating the likelihood of a military confrontation with Iran or Korea over their nuclear programs. Many political analysts, including Chomsky (2005), note that Iran may be the next target of U.S. imperial aggression. There are reports of growing military build-up of Israeli and American forces on the border between Turkey and Iran, including an increasing number of reconnaissance missions flown over the Iranian airspace to collect military and non-military intelligence. Both the United States and Israel have publicly declared Iran as a major military and economic threat to their geopolitical interests in the region. However, they are also aware that a military attack on Iran will further destabilize the Middle East.

The third crisis Bello and Rees (2005) identify is the crisis of legitimacy. In the United States as well as in many other nations around the world, millions of workers, students, farmers, and even some segments of the disfranchised middle class have participated in protests and marches against U.S. foreign policy. In November 2005, massive protests erupted as a reaction to Bush's participation in the Summit of the Americas in Argentina. Similar protests followed in Venezuela in which demonstrators demanded the immediate withdrawal of U.S. forces from Iraq and Afghanistan. Back in the Homeland, a growing number of organizations and grassroots movements opposed to the occupation of Iraq, including Military Families Speak Out, Gold Star Families for Peace, and the Iraq Veterans Against the War, are demanding the safe return of U.S. troops back home and an immediate end to the war.

Marx Reloaded

The current crisis of global capitalism has set the stage for the return of Marx. Even the fall of the Berlin Wall and the breakup of the former Soviet Union and Eastern European socialist countries have not deterred the old bearded devil from making a comeback. Marx made the cover of the February 2, 2009 European edition of *Time Magazine*. A digitized reproduction of Marx's famous photograph with the question "What would Marx think?" is printed beneath it. In the edition, Peter Gumbel's cover story "Rethinking Marx," may at first appear to be a tribute to and an acknowledgement of Marx's contributions to economic theory, but a careful reading of the essay reveals that it is an outright refutation of Marxism. By juxtaposing Marxism with bureaucratic forms of socialism in the former Soviet Union and Eastern European countries, Gumbel suggests that there is no alternative to capitalism, and that Marx was dead wrong. On the contrary, the current social and economic climate in Germany has once again resurrected the specter of Marx. Consider the academic publisher Karl-Dietz-Verlag who reports that its sales of Marx's *Das Kapital* has increased threefold thanks to a growing interest of students, workers, teachers, and intellectuals who are rediscovering the importance and relevancy of Marx in an age of rampant exploitation, geopolitical domination, and imperial conquest. Kirschbaum (2009) reports that in a recent poll, 52% of former East Germans expressed their disillusionment with capitalism and another 43% longed for a return to socialism. As one interviewee in the study pointed out, at least socialism provided their basic necessities such as food, healthcare, and employment. This sentiment should come as little surprise, given that the former East German region has been ravaged by deindustrialization, depopulation, and underemployment—which has swelled to 14% as West German corporations and banks moved to purchase former East German factories at bargain-basement prices only to close them down in favor of cheaper labor markets overseas.

If there is any indication that capitalism has finally succeeded in defeating socialism, burying it alongside Lenin's tomb in Red Square, then we need to question why millions of former Soviet citizens continue to dream about socialism? A nationwide survey of 1,600 Russians found a growing discontent among Russians with the mafiocracy that now rules over much of Russia and its former republics. The nationwide poll, published back in November 2002, concluded that between 1990 and 2002 the number of Russians who believed that the Bolshevik revolution had a "positive" impact on Russia had jumped from 49% to 60%. In addition, 33% of the Russians surveyed believed that communism had improved living standards. Finally, 43% of Russians surveyed expressed that they would have "actively" supported the Bolsheviks (Nedbayeva, 2002).

The explanatory power of Marx's insights and analysis of capitalism and the workings of the free market is far from exhausted. In fact, Marx is more relevant today than at any other time in history, especially when there is no end in sight to the growing social and economic polarization caused by the recent neoliberal social and economic reforms. Consider a recent survey conducted by Britain's Radio 4 that hosts the morning program *In Our Time*. Radio listeners who participated in the survey voted Karl Marx as the greatest philosopher of all time. The second and third place votes went to David Hume and to Ludwig Wittgenstein, respectively. Even a growing number of colleges and universities across the United States are showing a renewed interest in the work of Marx. The University of Rhode Island now offers a new honors course to undergraduate students which focuses on the ideas and theories of Karl Marx. The topics covered in the class include the history of capitalism and the study of Marx's *Capital*.

Not surprisingly, Marx has become unfashionable among, if not anathema to, most academics in higher education in the United States and abroad. While universities and colleges are too eager to offer courses on post-colonialism, postmodernism, post-structuralism, and cultural studies, they are far less willing to provide any serious forums or seminars in which Marx can be critically discussed, debated, and studied. And while most armchair academics on the left of various stripes in North America—especially proponents of postmodernism and post-structuralism—continue to dismiss Marxism outright for its failure to fulfill its promise of bringing forth the necessary social and political conditions for the development of a socialist utopia and to ignore willfully the powerful effects social class has on the life chances of the working poor, the debates over class, especially in the media, have only intensified. The *New York Times* devoted a series of articles on social class in America, which was published later by a group of its correspondents as a book entitled *Class Matters* (Correspondents of the New York Times, 2005). The book focuses on how social class shapes and determines many aspects of our lives including access to health care, education and housing. While the authors of the book should be praised for raising public awareness on the taboo subject of social class, regrettably most of their analysis draws upon neo-Weberian interpretations of social class. For example, the authors fail, in the main, to include key Marxist concepts such as "exploitation," "alienation," "commodity-production," "wage-labor," "ownership of the means of production," and "the forces of production," all of which illuminate and enrich our understanding of social class. They dilute the concrete experiences associated with class by focusing instead on consumption patterns and practices of individuals and groups in society. They admit that the concept of class is an elusive construct because it encompasses culture, rank, identity, attitudes, taste, and wealth. Navarre (2006) offers a compelling argument for why scholars on the left should not abandon key Marxist concepts such as *class struggle, class, class power*, and *class structure*, all important to understanding the workings of capitalism, imperialism and neoliberalism. These key concepts and categories enable us to decode the DNA of capitalism as a social, economic, political, and cultural system, from the invasion and occupation of Iraq to the defeat of the European constitution.

The Future of Anti-Capitalist Struggles

The anti-WTO protests in Seattle in 1999, and the widespread demonstrations against the G8 summit in Genoa, Italy in 2001, have generated a growing resurgence of coalitions comprising social movements, progressive organizations, labor unions, community activists, and ordinary citizens who are collectively engaged in various forms of struggles and resistance against global capitalism and U.S. imperialism. The recent anti-immigration Sensenbrenner bill, named after its author and leading sponsor Rep. James Sensenbrenner, which criminalizes undocumented immigrants who are illegally living and working in the United States at a felony level, has outraged and angered many immigrant communities across the United States. In Los Angeles, for example, more than 500,000 demonstrators poured into the city streets and protested against the anti-immigration legislature on March 25, 2005. The following day, more than 36,000 students in the Los Angeles Unified School District walked out of their classrooms and marched into the streets protesting against the bill. Similar student demonstrations and walkouts were reported in Dallas, Detroit, and Phoenix.

Along with the recent mass protests in the United States against the domestic policies of the Bush Administration and its cronies, there has been a growing and visible international movement against neoliberal social and economic policies. In France, for example, over a million workers clashed with police over the new labor laws that allow private corporations more flexibility to release or fire workers under age 26. In Argentina, the workers' autonomous movement has emerged as a response to the country's recent financial downfall. More than 20,000 unemployed workers organized themselves and took over and reopened factories that were closed down and abandoned by companies that moved their operations abroad to China where labor costs are much lower and profits are much higher. In Bolivia, the victory of Evo Morales, the first indigenous president in the country's history, is a sure sign of hope for the millions of indigenous people who make up 75% of the Bolivian population. In recent years, the enforcement of neoliberal social and economic policies in Bolivia spearheaded by such international bodies and organizations as the IMF have only contributed to the acceleration of social and economic polarization. In the case of Bolivia, free trade has downsized the standard of living of more than 66% of Bolivians, who have been forced to survive on two dollars a day. Recently, in a symbolic gesture of solidarity with the Bolivian people, President Morales announced he would cut his salary by half in order to hire more teachers.

Given the current global economic and political crisis we face today, why should teachers be concerned with the political economy of schooling under global capitalism and the new imperialism? How can they recognize their role in the ensuing battle between labor and capital? Why should teachers be troubled with the growing class polarization and the maquiladorization of the global economy? What lasting impact, if any, will the persistent wave of attacks of neoliberal social and economic policies have on the working conditions of teachers? Can teachers join workers and resist the corporatization and privatization of schools? These questions along with others can be answered only in the course of revolutionizing educational practices, which largely depends on the willingness of teachers to join anti-capitalist struggles.

Commercialization and Corporatization of Public Education

As the "war on terror" (and we might add to this the economic terror spawned by global capitalism) extends its tentacles to all corners of the globe, and as U.S. imperialism spreads so-called "democracy" and "freedom" amongst the people in Iraq and Afghanistan (with bullets and smart bombs targeting innocent men, women, and children), the military defense budget continues to swell at the expense of more drastic cuts in funding of public education. A significant part of the neoliberal agenda has been directed at the "business" of education—literally. Here I am referring to the growing commercialization and corporatization of public schools, which is now at the center of much-heated public debate and controversy. Coca-Cola, McDonald's, and Exxon are among a long list of corporations who are providing financial help to some of the nation's 80,000 public schools. Indeed, this is the case for many urban school districts forced to accept corporate funding because of a shortage of qualified teachers, school textbooks, resources, and materials.

It is not uncommon these days to see school buses in certain states covered with advertisements for Burger King and Wendy's fast-food chain restaurants. It has become fashionable for elementary schoolchildren to carry books wrapped in free book covers plastered with ads for Kellogg's Pop-Tarts and Fox TV personalities. School districts have granted Coca-Cola and Pepsi exclusive contracts to sell their products in schools. In health education classes students are taught nutrition by the Hershey Corporation that includes a discussion on the important place of chocolate in a balanced diet. A classroom business course teaches students to value work by exploring how McDonald's restaurants are operated, what skills are needed to become a successful McDonald's manager, and instructions on how to apply for a job at McDonald's. Ecological and environmental education now involves students learning ecology from a "Life of an Ant" poster sponsored by Skittles candy and an environmental curriculum video produced by Shell Oil that concentrates on the virtues of the external combustion engine.

Faced with the shortage of revenues to support existing educational services and programs, many school districts have forged partnerships with corporations eager to step into the lucrative education market. Consider McDonald's recent adoption of a new strategy to promote its products in the highly profitable market dominated by children. This comes after the much highly publicized libel suit now famously referred to as the McLibel Case, and the recent film, *Super Size Me* (Spurlock, 2004), which raised ethical and moral questions regarding McDonald's food processing and preparing practices that many believe have significantly contributed to the increasing obesity and other health risks among children. Hellmich (2005) writes that in an effort to restore its much-tarnished public image as the family-friendly fast-food chain, and to further protect its market shares, McDonald's has decided to capitalize on physical education programs in public schools. Over seven million students in 31,000 public schools have agreed to participate in McDonald's "Passport to Play" program. The program consists of a number of multicultural physical education activities including "boomerang golf" from Australia, "Mr. Daruma Fell Down" from Japan, and Holland's "Korfball." Students who complete each of these activities receive a stamp in their "passport" issued by McDonald's. According to Bill Lama, McDonald's chief marketing officer, the objective of the Passport to Play program is to educate students on the "importance of eating right" and "staying active." Such a strategically calculated move allows McDonald's not only to restore its image in light of the negative publicity it has received in the past few years, but it also helps McDonald's to have a greater presence and visibility in public schools (Hellmich, 2005). If the previous examples do not raise any concerns, then consider Tom Farber, a high-school teacher in the Poway Unified School District in Rancho Bernardo, California who decided to sell advertising spaces on tests, quizzes, and exams to pay for supplies that the school could not afford to purchase due to California's recent budget crisis. Advertising space for sponsors could run between $10 and $30 (Toppo & Kornblum, 2008).

These examples and others illustrate that corporations are not so much interested in preparing students for critical citizenship and civic engagement as they are in developing future consumer-citizens. Whereas the former encourages students to question, conceptualize, analyze, theorize, and reflect critically upon their experiences in the world, the latter lures students into an uncritical and blind acceptance of market values and practices designed to reinforce and maintain capitalist social relations of production. As Charles Sullivan (2003) eloquently notes:

> Of course it is not in the self-interest of capitalism to educate people who can see capitalism for what it is, to think critically about it, and perhaps even do something to change it. Corporate education exists to promote programming consumers and providing an obedient work force to an unfair slave wage system, not to provide society with a well-informed and politically active citizenry. In fact these are the things that pose the greatest threat to America's corporate oligarchy.
>
> (¶ 11)

In spite of the daunting challenge that educators face, we should encourage students to question and deconstruct the role of consumer capitalism in the commercialization and corporatization of education and schooling.

Teaching Against Consumer Capitalism

In the wake of the widespread corporate assault on public education, teachers and educators can offer students a pedagogy that enables them to challenge and contest consumerism and consumption practices within public schools. Below, I sketch out in broad strokes a number of fundamental steps teachers and educators can undertake to help students develop critical consumer literacy skills, which I locate within the broader framework of critical literacy.

A major step in preparing students to develop critical consumer literacy is to provide them with meaningful learning experiences (i.e., through the use of media literacy, cultural literacy, etc.) and to validate the experiences that students bring into the classroom from their everyday lives. Student experiences can be linked to theme-based curricula designed to facilitate economic literacy, media literacy, eco-literacy, consumer literacy, and other forms of literacies linked to a critique of social and economic policies motored by unregulated global capitalism.

Second, educators can offer students a "language of critique" and a "language of possibility" to help them to conceptualize, analyze, theorize, and reflect critically upon their experiences. Giroux (1988) uses the term "language of critique" to refer to developing a theoretical vocabulary and a set of analytical skills drawn from mainly the disciplines of sociology, critical theory, and cultural studies. The term "language of possibility" refers to developing a vision of a better world by bringing theory into practice (praxis). In other words, it refers to using the new sets of analytical skills from the social sciences to interrogate and transform the social conditions that have socially, culturally, and historically produced one's individual and collective experiences.

The recognition of the dialectical unity between theory and practice and action and reflection is a third step educators can undertake to empower students. Here

I make a distinction between reflection and critical reflection. While the former is related to students' awareness of their concrete social and economic circumstances, the latter deals with the investigation of their social location in the world as well as their relationship to the world. Freire (1978) refers to this as a "radical form of being," which he associates with "beings that not only know, but know that they know" (p. 24).

This brings us to the action dimension of critical literacy—what I refer to as praxis-oriented pedagogy. Praxis-oriented pedagogy bridges the gap between critical knowledge and social practice. This involves bringing theory into the streets. It includes organizing and mobilizing students, parents, and teachers at the community level, and linking their struggles to larger national and international struggles.

Preparing students for critical consumer literacy deepens the roots of democracy by encouraging students to actively participate in public discourses and debates over social, economic, and political issues that affect everyday life in their own and neighboring communities. In this way, students can acquire the civic courage and moral responsibility to participate in democratic life as critical social agents, becoming authors of their own history rather than being written off by history.

Note

1   This is a substantially revised version of a previous essay:
   Farahmandpur, R. (2006). A critical pedagogy of hope in times of despair: Teaching against global capitalism and the new imperialism. *Social Change, 36*(3), 77–91.

References

Bello, W., & Rees, J. (2005). U.S. imperialism: The cracks in the U.S. machine. *Socialist Review*. Available: http://www.socialistreview.org.uk/article.php?articlenumber=9501.

Brenner, R. (2006). *The economics of global turbulence.* London: Verso.

Chomsky, N. (2005). *Imperial ambitions: Conversations on the post-9/11 world.* New York: Metropolitan Books.

Correspondents of the New York Times. (2005). *Class matters.* New York: Times Books.

Freire, P. (1978). *Pedagogy as process: The letters to Guinea-Bissau* (trans. C. St. John Hunter). New York: The Seabury Press.

Giroux, H. A. (1988). *Teachers as intellectuals: Toward a critical pedagogy of learning.* South Hadley, MA: Bergin and Garvey.

Hellmich, N. (2005). McDonald's kicks off school PE program. *USA Today*, September 12.

Kirschbaum, E. (2009). Global crisis sends East Germans flocking to Marx. *Reuters*. Available: http://www.reuters.com/article/artsNews/idUSTRE49F5MX20081016

Leonhardt, D. (2009). Bailout likely to focus on most afflicted homeowners. *The New York Times*, Section A, p. 1.

Navarre, V. (2006). The worldwide class struggle. *Monthly Review, 58*(4), 18–33.

Nedbayeva, O. (2002). Putin's Russia seeks role model in Tsarist past. *AFP* (Moscow).

Spurlock, M. (2004). *Super Size Me!* USA: Showtime Networks.

Sullivan, C. (2003). Programming the work force: The failure of mass education. *Counterpunch*. Available: http://counterpunch.org/sullivan02252003.html

Toppo, G., & Kornblum, J. (2008). Ads on tests add up for teacher. *USA Today*. Available: http://www.usatoday.com/news/education/2008-12-01-test-ads_N.htm

Part II

Schooling the Consumer Citizen

6 Schooling for Consumption

Joel Spring

"Go Red for China," proclaimed ads for Pepsi soft drinks being sold in red instead of the traditional blue cans for the 2008 Beijing Olympics (Barboza, 2008). The advertising slogan played on the association between "Red" and communism. Regardless of the ideology or political organization, however, consumerism triumphs (Spring, 2009). Today, communist China is the second largest advertising market after the United States (Barboza, 2008). How did consumerism triumph over economic and political differences? And what roles do schools play in promoting consumerism? In this chapter I focus on how schools historically promoted the ideology of consumerism and currently keep it alive.[1]

The story of schooling and consumerism begins in the United States in the 1890s and early twentieth century when U.S. economists articulated the need for a consumerist society, professional advertising was born, and U.S. schools began to teach consumerist values in home economics courses and in planned eating experiences in school cafeterias. Consumerist ideology emerged in the twentieth century as a mixture of earlier ideas about the value of work, the accumulation of wealth, and equality of opportunity; and later, notions that progress should be measured by economic growth development of new products, and consumer spending. Consumerism, as expressed by economists like Patten in the early twentieth century, was the answer to a Puritan concern that industrial expansion and mechanized agriculture would result in less work, more leisure time, and eventual moral decay. In the aptly titled 1907 book, *The New Basis of Civilization*, Patten argued that the desire to buy the new products of technological advances and commodified leisure would spur people to work harder. Patten (1968) argued, "the new morality does not consist in saving, but in expanding consumption" (p. 215). He explained:

> In the course of consumption . . . the new wants become complex . . . [thus] the worker steadily and cheerfully chooses the deprivations of this week . . . Their investment in to-morrow's goods enables society to increase its output and to broaden its productive areas.
>
> (p. 141)

Thus the potential for more leisure time through advancements in technology was negated by creating desires for endless consumption of goods.

Educating Women as Consumers

Women were targeted early by both schools and professional advertisers who sought to foster consumerism. Key to the image of the "new woman" of the early twentieth century was the introduction of home economics courses and cafeterias in public schools, the development of the food industry, and the focus on brand loyalty. The new consumer woman emerged as brand names became central to advertising, after the passage of the 1870 federal trademark law.

The introduction of home economics in schools was based on the promise of freeing women from household drudgery through the purchase of products, particularly prepared brand-name foods. While advertisers fostered consumerism by attempting to manipulate desire, home economists thought of themselves as rational and scientific. Through the purchase of prepared foods and new cleaning technologies, housewives—home economists hoped—would have more time available to seek education and help improve society. Early home economists were career scientists who, unable to find employment in existing scientific fields, created departments of domestic science in universities; they were thus models for their own visions of the new woman who was highly educated and interested in social improvement. Home economics courses spread through public schools and universities after passage of the Smith–Hughes Act of 1917, federal legislation which provided support for home economics teachers in public schools and required the hiring of home economics instructors on college campuses to train teachers (Apple, 1997).

Shapiro (2001) credits home economists with the development of a distinctive American cuisine during the latter part of the nineteenth century, as they transformed "a nation of honest appetites into an obedient market for instant mashed potatoes" (p. 152). Home economists helped develop and sell the new American diet of prepackaged foods; in public schools and college classes they taught how to prepare this diet, how to handle fashion trends and consumer credit, and how to manage household budgets. They conducted pioneering research in food technology, which resulted in the development of new food products and made possible the proliferation of fast-food chains. They helped manufacturers develop and sell new gadgetry for the home, including refrigerators and washing machines (Goldstein, 1997). And they helped make school and hospital cafeteria food healthy, inexpensive, and bland. Through school cafeterias, they hoped to persuade immigrant children to abandon their parents' diets for the new American cuisine.

The profession of home economics evolved from an annual series of conferences held at Lake Placid, New York beginning in 1899 under the leadership of Ellen Richards. Richards, founder of the American Home Economics Association and the first woman to receive a degree from the Massachusetts Institute of Technology (MIT), brought together a faith in the ability of science to improve human existence, a desire to improve women's education, and a belief that the home was the central institution for reforming society. In 1883, Richards became the first female instructor at MIT, teaching courses on sanitary and household chemistry that focused on cooking and cleaning (Stage, 1997). In 1887, Richards conducted a study of municipal sewage treatment systems and developed the first water purity standards (Vincenti, 1997).

Portending the future marketing of packaged and frozen dinners, Richards helped found the New England Kitchen in Boston in 1890. The founders hoped to improve the lives of working and poor people by providing pre-prepared, pre-packaged, sanitary, and economical food; because the food was cooked under scientific conditions, buyers would also learn to expect consistent flavor and texture. Richards envisioned a neighborhood establishment that would prepare and sell food, and educate buyers about sanitary conditions and cooking methods.

Richards's dream spread across the country. Jane Addams sent a settlement worker from Chicago to learn Richards's method and created a similar kitchen at Hull House. Another kitchen opened in Providence, and Richards was invited to create a New England Kitchen at the 1893 Chicago World's Fair. Afterwards, the New England Kitchen focused on selling prepared foods to Boston's nine public schools. In 1895, Richards helped create a model program for Boston's public school cafeterias. Prior to 1895, janitors in Boston schools were responsible for the lunch program. Using new theories on nutrition, sanitation, and food preparation, Richards and her colleagues introduced the new American diet to Boston school children (Vincenti, 1997). These efforts set the stage for trained domestic scientists to take over school cafeterias to ensure students received healthy and sanitary food.

Richards projected a liberating role for prepared food. In her dream home where the purchase of cheap mass-produced furniture allowed more money for intellectual pleasures, the pantry was filled with a large stock of prepared foods—mainly canned foods and bakery products. Richards's dream pantry was based on the reality of a growing industry for canned foods; by the beginning of the twentieth century, "canned goods were a standard feature of the American diet . . . [including] processed foods of all kinds—packed dry cereals, pancake mixes, crackers and cookies machine-wrapped in paper containers, canned hams, and bottled corned beef" (Cowan, 1983, p. 73). In 1900, Richards provided her vision of the commodification of housework:

> Housekeeping no longer means washing dishes, scrubbing floors, making soap and candles; it means spending a given amount of money for a great variety of ready-prepared articles and so using commodities as to produce the greatest satisfaction and the best possible mental, moral, and physical results.
>
> (Quoted in Heinze, 2000, p. 22)

The so-called philosopher of home economics, Caroline Hunt, clearly delineated the new role of women as consumers. Like Richards, Hunt equated women's freedom with a change in household roles from producer to consumer. Women would have more free time for education, she argued, if they bought factory-made products rather than producing them at home. She argued that a woman who "shall insist upon carrying the home-making methods of today into the tomorrow will fail to lay hold of the possible quota of freedom which the future has in store for her" (Hunt, 2001a, p. 56).

Hunt consistently highlighted the importance of transitioning household tasks from production to consumption, a transition she viewed as part of larger processes of industrialization and job specialization. In a paper she read at the 1904 Lake Placid Home Economics Conference, she argued, "The home has delegated to the school not only the technical but also the general education of the child; to the factory the manufacture of clothing, of furniture, and of house furnishings" (Hunt, 2001b, p. 71). While the responsibilities of the household were changing, she contended, they still played an important role in society. Households were still responsible for raising children to school age, teaching morality, and educating about beauty and "rational sociability."

Hunt linked intelligent consumption to a concern for the general welfare of society. At the 1906 Lake Placid Conference, she stated, "The wise consumer has in mind not only his own advantage, but the welfare of those who make, transport and care for the commodities he uses" (Hunt, 2001c, p. 76). Hunt continued:

> There is . . . an important way, other than thru [sic] purchase of food, in which women control a large amount of human energy, and that is thru [sic] buying and using what may be called art products including clothing and house furnishing . . . . The college should give students an intelligent attitude with reference to the responsibilities arising from their consumption of these products.
> (Hunt, 2001c, p. 78)

Hunt envisioned college-educated women finding time for engaging in social reform movements—or "municipal housekeeping"—by consuming rather than producing household goods.

In summary, through home economics courses U.S. schools promoted the idea that women were central consumers of the household and that household work should be facilitated through the purchase of goods and products. Additionally, planned obsolescence was introduced as part of the new ready-to-wear industry. As I discuss below, students were taught to purchase new products based on changes in design rather than the failure of an already owned product.

Teaching Planned Obsolescence

Early ideologue of consumerism Simon Patten argued in 1889 that maintaining consumer dissatisfaction was key to economic growth:

> It is not the increase of goods for consumption that raises the standard of life . . . [but] the rapidity with which [the consumer] tires of any one pleasure. To have a high standard of life means to enjoy a pleasure intensely and to tire of it quickly.
> (Quoted in Marchand, 1985, p. 51)

Producers feared that satisfied consumers might stop consuming and sought to keep them in constant states of desire to purchase more goods.

Changing designs were central to spurring the purchase of new clothing being manufactured by the early ready-to-wear industry. In the nineteenth century, most people except the rich had few articles of clothing because they were mainly handmade. With the development of the ready-to-wear industry in the late nineteenth century, average consumers could afford a wide range of clothing. Manufacturers learned to change designs, forcing previously purchased products out of fashion, and spurring consumer desires to buy new products. Fashion became a form of built-in obsolescence that eventually spread to other products such as automobiles and appliances.

Schools and home economists played an important role in promoting consumption based on fashion. During the 1920s, home economists promoted high-school fashion shows that used live models and music. The home economists' goal was to prepare girls for the modern role of consumer. Joselit (2001) states that through these shows, home economists hoped to "transform high school students into surefooted consumers by teaching them 'buymanship'" (p. 29).

The bombarding of the public with brand names and new fashion that promised personal transformation sparked a public debate. Joselit (2001) argues that the growing ready-to-wear industry caused, "A broad swath of Americans, from self-styled aesthetes to certified domestic scientists . . . to [worry] about the social and moral consequences of a nation now at liberty to change its clothes—and its image—at will" (p. 30). Before World War I, critics in popular magazines called the use of fashion to control the public a new form of tyranny that caused addictive consumer behaviors comparable to opium or alcohol.

Working in high schools and youth clubs, home economists in the 1920s tried to turn fashion-conscious shoppers into "wise" consumers. High-school and 4-H club members participated in contests where they modeled clothing before panels of home economists. Prizes were given for the most "economical" and "sensible" clothing. Working with the U.S. Department of Agriculture, home economists published and distributed a series of scorecards to teach students how to evaluate clothing purchases. These scorecards contained points for "general appearance," "suitability," "economic factors," "health aspects," and "social influence" (Joselit, 2001, p. 30).

Like the new American cuisine, clothing fashions promised democratization of consumption. With inexpensive ready-to-wear clothing, everyone could participate in fashion changes. In the nineteenth century, social class distinctions were obvious between those who could and could not afford to have clothes made by professional tailors. In the twentieth century, the mass appeal of blue jeans blurred social class distinctions in dress. However, designer names and logos began to identify the cost of clothing, and social class distinctions in fashion were clearly re-established in the later part of the twentieth century.

Educating for Civic Consumerism

The development in the 1930s of the high school as a mass institution created a new consumer market. Between 1900 and 1940, the percentage in high school of youth aged 14 to 17 increased from 11% to 88% (Schrum, 1998). After World War II, the "American Way of Life" became a major theme in the Cold War between the United

States and the Soviet Union. The Cold War was portrayed as a clash between free enterprise and Communist economic systems under the banner of American and Soviet nationalism. The winner would be the system producing the most consumer goods. The growth of the teenage consumer market meant teens were learning early how to be good consumers. Many affluent teens were growing up in new suburban developments where shopping malls were becoming centers of consumer desires.

World War II set the stage for schools to promote consumption as an integral part of the "American Way of Life." During the war, public relations efforts promoted consumer messages, especially the idea that the American economic system provided the highest *economic* standard of living—that is, the highest level of consumption. The Secretary of NEA's Educational Policies Commission, William Carr, declared in March 1941 that public schools would cooperate with business in teaching "Americanism," "economic literacy," and "personal economics," while preparing "youth for personal work" (Carr, 1941, pp. 19–20). Local Chambers of Commerce also promoted consumer education in schools, emphasizing the management of personal buying power and promoting an understanding of the American economic system. These programs sought to create an instinctive association of business with patriotic Americanism. Linking consumption, Americanism, and business, Carr (1941) wrote, schools "provided a highly literate and educated population . . . constituting the world's greatest consuming markets" (pp. 96–97).

After WWII, advertisers directed their attention to the consuming habits of high-school students. The 1930s teenage culture, spawned by the mass institutionalization of youth in high school, lacked spending power. But after WWII, spending among youth increased, as symbolized by *Seventeen* magazine with its slogan, "Teena means business" (Schrum, 1998). The word "teenager" was invented by marketers during the 1940s to mean a group defined by high-school attendance (Schrum, 1998). In a crass commercial effort, *Seventeen* magazine advertised the potential teenage market with slogans such as "When is a girl worth $11,690,499"? (Schrum, 1998, p. 143), which referred to the amount of money spent on teenage advertisements in *Seventeen*.

Like their mothers, teenage girls were primary targets of marketers. Schrum (1998) describes *Seventeen*'s editorial message for teenagers in the late 1940s and early 1950s as "civic consumerism," an idea that combines "one's democratic role as active citizen with one's duty as a responsible and active consumer" (p. 149). During this time, "voting and democracy, as well as pride in America and the right to buy goods, were common themes . . . a reflection of both lingering war rhetoric and the beginning of the Cold War" (Schrum, 1998, p. 156). Corresponding to earlier concerns with controlling adolescent sexuality through high-school activities, advertisers hoped to channel teenage sexuality into consumerism. Ads for girls displayed clothing and other products that would enhance their dating potential. Boys directed their consumer sexuality at cars, hoping that the hot car, or "hot rod," would result in the hot date.

Integrating Schools and Consumption

The civil rights movements of the 1950s and 1960s not only ended legal school segregation but also integrated textbooks, mass media, advertising, and the consumer market. While issues of political equality, voting rights, and school integration were central to the civil rights movement, the theme of equality of consumption, as embodied in the concept of equality of opportunity, became a goal. Equality of opportunity meant all citizens should have equal opportunity to pursue wealth, including equal opportunity to training, jobs, and benefits. This implied that equality of opportunity, if it existed, would lead to equality of consumption.

Prior to the 1950s and 1960s, a separate consumer market existed for African Americans, with separate products, ads, and magazines. In contrast, national advertising and magazines like *Seventeen* were directed to a white audience. Ads produced by African-American-owned companies emphasized the new black woman and enhancement of racial pride. C. J. Walker, a pioneer developer of African-American cosmetics, supported equal rights for both women and African Americans, and promoted the use of cosmetics as a matter of racial pride. Black women, she felt, should look good and project a positive social image. Using sales-women, Walker hoped to create a new career route for African-American women. One of her sales force claimed Walker had enabled "hundreds of colored women to make an honest and profitable living" (Peiss, 1998, p. 91).

Some critics suggested advertisements directed at black consumers promoted white standards of beauty as exemplified in ads such as: "New 3-way Skin discovery Gives You WHITE SKIN OVERNIGHT," and "MAKE YOUR HAIR STRAIGHT AND BEAUTIFUL" (Weems, 2000, pp. 167–168). Ads for such products were the richest source of revenue for the black press (Weems, 2000). In the 1950s, Black Power advocates condemned whiteners and straighteners for reflecting beauty standards imposed by the white community. Black pride was part of a wider movement, which included Native Americans and Chicanos, to embrace beauty standards based on racial pride. Among these groups, traditional dress, jewelry, and hairstyles became symbols of rebellion against white images in textbooks, ads, and media. Black pride championed natural beauty fashioned by Afro hairstyles and acceptance of natural skin color, resulting in a decrease in the use of whiteners and straighteners; a study of *Ebony* magazine between 1949 and 1972 found a rapid decline in ads for straighteners and skin whiteners and the appearance of ads for Afro hairstyles (Weems, 2000).

Weems (2000) argues the revolution in black female identity was not accompanied by the same loyalty to black businesses as had previously existed. Recognizing the spending power of the black community, white-owned businesses gained control of the black cosmetic market. In 1991, the Maybelline Company introduced "Shades of You" cosmetics for black women. At the time its major competitor in the general cosmetics market was Cover Girl. Industry consultant Allan Motus said this was a smart move: "Instead of going eyeball to eyeball with Cover Girl, they can go for a specific segment for incremental market share" (Weems, 2000, p. 175). Also in 1991, Estée Lauder created "Prescriptives for All Skins," with 100 makeup shades; Prescriptives attracted 50,000 black buyers in its first year (Weems, 2000).

Ironically, the black pride movement integrated African Americans into the general consumer market while undermining traditional black businesses. For some African Americans, the civil rights movement meant equal opportunity to pursue the American dream within the framework of a specific racial identity. Freedom to consume did not mean having to take on a white identity. However, for many African Americans, equality of educational opportunity and equality of opportunity meant an equal chance to earn and consume.

An important advertising goal was creating images that would "integrate" the consumer market, which meant creating advertising images designed to appeal to all racial audiences. This step established a certain level of interracial camaraderie about consumer products. According to *New York* magazine columnist Bernice Kanner, one of the best 100 TV ads showed black football player Mean Joe Greene drinking a bottle of Coca-Cola. Kanner (1999), describing then-vice president of marketing operations at Coca-Cola Bill Van Loan's reaction to the ad, states,

> Just as Marlboro owned macho cowboys, Coca-Cola thought it could 'own the world of smiling Americans,' said Bill Van Loan . . .. Unlike Pepsi advertising, which invited people 'to join some mythical group, Coke spots featured product as hero, causing the smile,' he said.
>
> (p. 137)

The integration of the consumer market was also noted by *Village Voice* advertising columnist Leslie Savan (1994), who argued that white males were attracted to Nike's black advertising images out of a desire to be hip.

From Home Economics to Family and Consumer Sciences

By the twenty-first century, schools were consumer sites and, symbolically, "Home Economics" was renamed "Family and Consumer Sciences." Molnar (1996) details the extremes companies use to advertise and sell products in schools. In 2000, the U.S. General Accounting Office released a report on the commercialization of schools, stating, "Marketing professionals are increasingly targeting children in schools, companies are becoming known for their success in negotiating contracts between school districts and beverage companies, and both educators and corporate managers are attending conferences to learn how to increase revenue from in-school marketing for their schools and companies" (Hays, 2000, ¶ 2).

While consumerism invaded schools, classrooms became sites for teaching consumer values. "Functioning effectively as providers and consumers of goods and services" is an instructional goal for students in high-school Family and Consumer Sciences courses, formerly known as Home Economics (National Association of State Administrators for Family and Consumer Sciences [NASAFACS], 1998, p. 2). The historic role of home economics courses in teaching women to be scientific producers of food and clothing in the home, and household managers, was transformed into career-oriented courses for females and males as preparation for work in the food and textile industries. In addition, these courses now stress different aspects of consumerism. The underlying assumption of these courses is that people will primarily be consumers of manufactured goods.

Symbolic of these changes is the new name *Family and Consumer Sciences*. The earlier American Home Economics Association was founded by Ellen Richards who dreamed of household science freeing women from housework to pursue higher levels of education. In 1994, the organization changed its name to the American Association of Family and Consumer Sciences (AAFCS). The core values of the newly named organization included preserving the family as the fundamental social unit, supporting diversity and human rights, and protecting the environment. Regarding consumerism, the core values include, "Holistic, interdisciplinary, integrative and preventative perspectives in addressing the issues of individuals and families as consumers" (AAFCS, 2001, cited in Bull & Cummings, 2002, p. 31).

While early home economics courses focused on teaching cooking, sewing, and household management to girls, new national standards created by AAFCS in 1998 were directed at teaching females and males career, family, and consumer roles.[2] Cooking classes were replaced with the study of careers in "food production and services" and "food science, dietetics, and nutrition" (NASAFACS, 1998, p. 10). In the early twentieth century, the goals of cooking classes for young women were to Americanize immigrants, reform home diets, and turn housewives into scientific workers. The 1998 standards were more geared to Richards's vision of processed and packaged food production creating a healthy, sanitary, and liberating diet. And, unlike early sewing instruction, the new standards were geared to careers in the ready-to-wear and related industries, or careers in "textiles and apparel" (NASAFACS, 1998, p. 10). Whereas early home economics courses sometimes focused on family leisure time activities, the new standards introduced students to careers in "hospitality, tourism, and recreation" (p. 10). And finally, household management became a study of careers in "housing, interiors, and furnishings" (p. 10).

Changing instruction from *how to* sew and cook to information on possible careers in food and textile production conveys the message that households should rely on prepared food and ready-to-wear clothing. In addition, informing students about careers in tourism and recreation prepares students to think about leisure activities as commodities. The 1998 standards reinforce these attitudes. For instance, the goal for "Consumer and Family Resources" is: "Demonstrate management of individual and family resources including food, clothing, shelter, health care, recreation, and transportation" (NASAFACS, 1998, p. 45). This goal simply means learning to budget for the purchase of these items. In other words, the goal is to teach students to consume within their financial limits.

There is a potential critical edge in these standards, however. Ideally, courses do not simply teach students how to shop within their means. Students are also supposed to be taught the "relationship of the environment to family and consumer resources" and to "analyze policies that support consumer rights and responsibilities" (NASAFACS, 1998, p. 45), in addition to analyzing "consumer advocacy" and "resource consumption for conservation and waste management practices" (p. 59). Taken to its critical limits, the implementation of these goals would teach students about the potentially detrimental effects of consumerism through environmental pollution and the depletion of natural resources. In addition, education about consumer rights could result in consumer activists concerned about product quality and safety. In either case, the goal is to educate responsible consumer citizens.

However, the commitment to consumerism is highlighted in the 1998 national standards' goal: "Analyze interrelationships between the economic system and consumer actions" (NASAFACS, 1998, p. 45). This represents the triumph of Patten's economic views. It suggests the economy should be examined from the standpoint of consumer actions, such as consumer confidence and spending. For instance, students learn why retailers and economists worry about holiday purchases, future consumer spending, and measures of consumer confidence. This view of the economy results in attitudes that the major news about the Christmas season is how much shoppers are spending.

While schools teach consumerism through conveying the message that education is a form of consumption, in-school ads, and consumerism-oriented courses, a new global peer group of teens is being created that relates through brand names and consumer activities. These "new world teens . . . all speak the same language of global brand consumption" (Moses, 2000, p. 4). Moses argues, "Teens love brands . . . .. Brands are passports to global culture" (p. 10). Asking teens worldwide to identify 75 brand icons, Moses (2000) found the five most popular are Coca-Cola, Sony, Adidas, Nike, and Kodak. "Unabashed consumerism" is the number one unifier of global teen culture (Moses, 2000). In the upbeat language of advertising, she writes, "In an age of abundance for much of the world's growing middle class, teens see consumer products as one of the limitless joys of life" (p. 37).

The very existence of a global teen market suggests that most countries, through schooling, have separated teenagers as a distinct cohort group from children and adults. By indirectly creating a segregated cohort group, secondary schools have allowed for specific marketing techniques to be directed at the global consumer-oriented adolescent. Moses (2000) suggests there is a relationship between the unstable period of adolescence and brand affiliation—brands promise a reliable and standard product and provide an anchor in the uncertain world of adolescence.

Connecting Schools to the Consumer Market: Fast-Food Education

The invasion of fast-food franchises into schools symbolizes an educational acceptance of consumerism. As discussed earlier, home economists embraced packaged and prepared foods, and set a standard for American tastes in school and hospital cafeterias. The manufacturing of an American cuisine reached new heights in the 1950s when the automobile and suburban living created a mobile population looking for a quick meal. To some extent, fast food realized home economist Ellen Richards's dream of community kitchens and convenience food freeing women from cooking. Of course, Richards might criticize the quality of franchise food and their educational undertakings.

Fast-food franchises' involvement in schools is linked to their efforts to project an impression of fast-food outlets being friendly and clean places for families to eat, and acts as a public relations gimmick to create positive community images. Their themed environments are meant to identify them as family friendly. Their logos and architecture identify their particular franchise. Those familiar with the differing franchise designs and logos can easily identify them even when speeding down the highway in a car (Schlosser, 2001).

McDonald's has ventured directly into the education business by distributing a Black History curriculum. Jumping on the Charter School bandwagon, Burger King, in cooperation with Communities in Schools, Inc. (CIS) has opened 24 CIS/ Burger King Academies across the nation for students facing problems of "poor school attendance, illiteracy, teen pregnancy, drug and alcohol abuse, school violence, and lack of self-esteem" (Burger King, 2001). The Burger King Academies, serving as both advertising and public relations, work with local social services, public schools, and universities. Bearing the appellation "Burger King Scholars," needy students can attend college or post-secondary vocational schools with scholarships from the Burger King/McLamore Foundation's North American Scholarship Program, which in 2006 provided almost $1.8 million dollars (Burger King, 2008).

Perhaps most involved in education is Yum! Brands corporation, which owns Taco Bell, A&W, KFC, Long John Silver's, and Pizza Hut. Three of these—Taco Bell, Pizza Hut, and KFC—are directly involved in educational activities. As sponsor of the Discovery Science Center in Santa Ana, California, Taco Bell provides science programs aligned to the requirements of California State Science Content Standards (Discovery Science Center, 2006). Taco Bell Foundation, in partnership with Boys & Girls Clubs of America, operates TEENSupreme programs throughout the United States and on worldwide military installations. The programs are "committed to inspiring teenagers to graduate from high school and become caring, educated and productive adults" and seek to "foster educational, career, and service opportunities for teens" (Taco Bell, 2009, ¶ 1). To build a positive public image, Taco Bell restaurants have in-store canisters so patrons can make donations to support the program (Taco Bell, 2009).

In 1988, President Ronald Reagan awarded Pizza Hut's president Art Gunter a Private Initiative Citation for its educational program BOOK IT! (Spring, 2003). This national reading incentive program began in 1984 with an enrollment of 200,000 elementary school students. By the 1998–1999 school year, 22 million children in 895,000 classrooms were enrolled. The program serves as a public relations project and as advertising. Under the program, children who achieve monthly reading goals are rewarded with a Personal Pan Pizza and a button from the manager of the local Pizza Hut restaurant. Achieving six-month goals earns an All-Star Medallion at a local Pizza Hut. In 1998, the BOOK IT! BEGINNERS PROGRAM was started for pre-school and kindergarten students with the monthly Personal Pan Pizza award, and currently reaches over 1.7 million children (Pizza Hut, 2009).

While Burger King Academies serve high-school students, KFC has entered the day-care business for younger children. On August 4, 2001, the nation's first Colonel's Kids Child Care Center opened in Columbus Junction, Iowa; the center offers infant care, day care, crisis care, before and after school care, and summer care for infants through children aged 12 (KFC, 2001). KFC has staked out its part of the contribution to education day-care and afterschool programs, with its "Colonel's Kids Charity," which was established as a non-profit in 1999. Its mission is "to help provide nationwide access to high-quality child care and assist families who could otherwise not afford it . . . KFC's Colonel's Kids funds grants through the YMCA in extended-hour and infant/toddler child-care programs" (Yum! Corporate Responsibility, 2008, ¶ 1).

It is fitting that I end this brief review of fast-food education with KFC's support of day-care centers. It could be suggested that the need for Colonel's Kids Child Care Centers and Burger King Academies for troubled adolescents is a product of the mobile and frantic family life that made fast food successful. Contrary to the 1950s myth of the traditional family, the harried lives of two-wage-earner households might create a dependence on fast food. It certainly is a distortion of Richards's dream of saving time from cooking so that women could have more freedom. Would she have approved of a quick and cheap family dinner at McDonald's or Burger King so the kids could use the franchise's playgrounds?

Conclusion

The wedding of education, advertising, and media resulted from efforts to redefine femininity and masculinity in the corporate age, reform the American family, control American youth, resolve conflicts between schools and media over cultural control, use media and schools as part of national defense in the Cold War, create efficiency in food production, and maintain the ideology of consumerism, which makes increased production dependent on increased consumption. Within this framework, increased consumption requires motivating consumer desires through advertising, which becomes the driving force of the economy. Every space, including public spaces, becomes an advertising opportunity. The promise of increased levels of schooling is not greater happiness but increased levels of consumption. Equality of opportunity means equality of opportunity to consume. America's cuisine, advertising, and media are its most important contributions to world culture. Schools help prepare future citizens to think of education as a means to a high income, which will ensure high levels of consumption. Consumerism now dominates global educational policies as policymakers claim education will increase economic growth and equalize global spending on consumer items (Spring, 2009).

Notes

1 This chapter is based on my book _Educating the Consumer-Citizen: A History of the Marriage of Schools, Advertising, and Media_ (Mahwah, N.J.: Lawrence Erlbaum Associates, 2003).

2 In 2008 NASAFACS and AAFCS revised these 1998 standards; these newest standards continue

the proud tradition of providing the framework for national, state, and local programs that prepare students for family life, work life, and careers in Family and

Consumer Sciences by empowering individuals and families across the life span to manage the challenges of living and working in a diverse global society.

(NASAFACS, 2008, ¶ 3, http://www.aafcs.org/FCSstandards/)

References

Apple, R. D. (1997). Liberal arts or vocational training? Home economics education for girls. In S. Stage & V. B. Vincenti (Eds.), *Rethinking home economics: Women and the history of a profession* (pp. 79–95). Ithaca, NY: Cornell.

Barboza, D. (2008). Seeking to tap Olympic pride, Western ads cheerlead for China. *New York Times*, July 20, pp. 1, 8.

Bull, N. H., & Cummings, M. N. (2002). Taking steps for family and consumer sciences educators in Connecticut: A model for change. *Journal of Family and Consumer Sciences Education, 20*(2), 30–36.

Burger King. (2001). BK Academies. Retrieved March 21, 2001 from: http://www.burgerking.com

Burger King. (2008). Burger King reaches $10 million donation milestone with 2006 award of 1,572 scholarships to high school graduates. Available: http://www.bk.com/company-info/community/news.aspx

Carr, W. (1941). An educator bids for partners. *Nation's Business*, March 1941, pp. 19–20, 96–97.

Cowan, R. S. (1983). *More work for mother: The ironies of household technology from the open hearth to the microwave.* New York: Basic Books.

Discovery Science Center. (2006). Taco Bell Discover Science Center celebrates successful year. Available: http://www.discoverycube.org/press.aspx?a=4

Goldstein, C. M. (1997). Part of the package: Home economists in the consumer product industries, 1920–1940. In S. Stage & V. B. Vincenti (Eds.), *Rethinking home economics: Women and the history of a profession* (pp. 271–296). Ithaca, NY: Cornell.

Hays, C. L. (2000). Commercialism in U.S. schools is examined in new report. *The New York Times*, September 14, 2000, available: http://query.nytimes.com/gst/fullpage.html?res=9D0DE1D71538F937A2575AC0A9669C8B63&sec=&spon=&pagewanted=1

Heinze, A. (2000). Jewish women and the making of an American home. In J. Scanlon (Ed.), *The gender and consumer culture reader* (pp. 19–29). New York: New York University Press.

Hunt, C. (2001a). Revaluations. In M. East, *Caroline Hunt: Philosopher for home economics* (pp. 50–65). College Park: Pennsylvania State University.

Hunt, C. (2001b). Home economics at the University of Wisconsin, A housekeeper Conference, from the Sixth Lake Placid Conference on Home Economics, 1904. In M. East, *Caroline Hunt: Philosopher for home economics* (pp. 65–75). College Park: Pennsylvania State University.

Hunt, C. (2001c). Higher education symposium, Eighth Lake Placid Conference on Home Economics. In M. East, *Caroline Hunt: Philosopher for home economics* (pp. 76–85). College Park: Pennsylvania State University.

Joselit, J. W. (2001). *A perfect fit: Clothes, character, and the promise of America.* New York: Henry Holt and Company.

Kanner, B. (1999). *The 100 best TV commercials . . . and why they worked.* New York: Random House.

KFC. (2001). Columbus Junction celebrates grand opening of nation's first Colonel's Kids childcare center. Available: https://www.kfc.com/about/pr/080401.htm

Marchand, R. (1985). *Advertising the American dream: Making way for modernity, 1920–1940.* Berkeley: University of California Press.

Molnar, A. (1996). *Giving kids the business: The commercialization of America's schools.* Boulder, CO: Westview Press.

Moses, E. (2000). *The $100 billion allowance: Accessing the global teen market.* New York: John Wiley & Sons.

National Association of State Administrators for Family and Consumer Sciences (NASAFACS). (1998). National standards for family and consumer sciences. Decatur, GA: Vocational-Technical Education Consortium of States. Available: http://www.montana.edu/hhunts/FCS%20Education%20Extension%20Curriculum%20Forum/FACS_Standards_1_%5B1%5D.pdf

Patten, S. (1968). *The new basis of civilization.* Cambridge, MA: Harvard University Press.

Peiss, K. (1998). *Hope in a jar: The making of America's beauty culture.* New York: Henry Holt & Company.

Pizza Hut (2009). About Book it! Beginners. Available: http://www.bookitprogram.com/beginners/

Savan, L. (1994). *The sponsored life: Ads, TV, and American culture.* Philadelphia: Tempe University Press.

Schlosser, E. (2001). *Fast food nation.* New York: Houghton Miffler.

Schrum, K. (1998). "Teena means business": Teenage girls' culture and Seventeen magazine, 1944–1950. In S. A. Inness (Ed.), *Delinquents and debutantes: Twentieth-century American girls' cultures* (pp. 134–163). New York: NYU Press.

Shapiro, L. (2001). *Perfection salad: Women and cooking at the turn of the century.* New York: Random House.

Spring, J. (2003). *Educating the consumer-citizen.* Mahwah, NJ: Lawrence Erlbaum Associates, Inc.

Spring, J. (2009). *Globalization of education: An introduction.* New York: Routledge.

Stage, S. (1997). Ellen Richards and the social significance of the home economics movement. In S. Stage & V. B. Vincenti (Eds.), *Rethinking home economics: Women and the history of a profession* (pp. 17–33). Ithaca, NY: Cornell.

Taco Bell. (2009) Taco Bell Foundation for Teens: About us. Available: http://www.teensupreme.org/AboutUs.htm

Vincenti, V. B. (1997). Chronology of events and movements which have defined and shaped home economics. In S. Stage & V. B. Vincenti (Eds.), *Rethinking home economics: Women and the history of a profession* (pp. 321–330). Ithaca, NY: Cornell.

Weems Jr, R. E. (2000). Consumerism and the construction of black female identity in twentieth-century America. In J. Scanlon (Ed.), *The gender and consumer culture reader* (pp. 166–178). New York: NYU Press.

Yum! Corporate responsibility. (2008). The KFC Colonel's Kids Charity. Available: http://www.yum.com/responsibility/colkids.asp

7 Schools Inundated in a Marketing-Saturated World

Alex Molnar, Faith Boninger, Gary Wilkinson, and Joseph Fogarty

Today's children have more spending money at their disposal than ever before, and they also influence their parents' spending (McNeal, 1998). With average life expectancy reaching into the seventies, these children have many years of buying ahead of them. For these reasons, just about anyone who sells anything is eager to reach children. And they do: everywhere and anywhere they can.

Marketers reach children in the context of a global marketing environment that recognizes fewer and fewer boundaries (Molnar, Boninger, Wilkinson, & Fogarty, 2008). This "total environment" of marketing is enabled in part by new technologies that allow advertisements to appear in places they could not have been before, such as video games, social networking websites, and cell phones. It is also the result of greater cultural acceptance of marketing as an everyday fact of life, a friendly political environment, and a willingness on the part of marketers and advertisers to breach boundaries that previously limited their activities (Molnar et al. 2008).

Trends in and Implications of Marketing to Children

Three trends characterize how marketing and advertising are changing the social environment of childhood: advertising is becoming ever more pervasive, the boundary line between advertising and editorial content is becoming less distinct, and the relationship between marketers and consumers is becoming more interactive. Our review of advertising and marketing publications and the popular press suggests that as these three trends continue to develop, they are intertwining in increasingly complex and sophisticated ways. In the United States, England, and Ireland, corporations are striving not only to make their products as visible and appealing to children as they can, but more importantly, to generate as much interaction as possible between children and products in games, contests, and other activities—both at home and in school.

Advertising Is Increasingly Pervasive, Insidious, and Interactive

Marketing and advertising exist within and help shape our cultural, economic, political, and social contexts. The language and values of commerce are, for example, slowly becoming accepted as the standard filter through which people read, interpret, understand, and behave in the world (Wieseltier, 2008). In commercial culture, business practices are generally evaluated not in terms of right or wrong, but in terms of their money-making potential. For example, everyone knows that if McDonald's sponsors a "McTeacher's Night" and returns some of the evening's receipts to a local school, McDonald's is getting something from the deal—probably more than the school is. But because the public is savvy about how business works, most observers do not criticize McDonald's; instead, they are likely to endorse how effectively "one hand washes the other" (for example, see Goodyear, 2008).

Materialism and debt are part and parcel of the culture of commercialism. With products to sell—some of them necessities, many surely not—marketers do everything they can to create demand. Psychologist Allen Kanner points out the underlying message that cuts across almost all advertising: that the purchase of material goods is the key to happiness. Even ads for "good" products, he notes, contribute to the materialist message: the more people believe they need material goods to be happy, the more time they devote to all aspects of consuming, and the less time they devote to activities that satisfy non-material needs (Kanner, 2007). Research has found that higher materialistic values are related to lower self-esteem, chronic physical symptoms, and higher rates of anxiety, depression, and psychological distress (Schor, 2004). In teenage children, higher materialistic values also correlate with increased smoking, drinking, drug use, weapon carrying, vandalism, and truancy (Kasser, 2002).

Marketing Strategies: Stealth and Engagement

As advertising becomes more pervasive, consumers' attention is ever more a commodity. Advertisers, struggling to grab their share of a finite resource, try to pull attention to their ads by seemingly contradictory means. On the one hand, *stealth strategies* hide marketing in editorial content. Consumers expose themselves to this type of marketing by accident, while they believe they are encountering only the content of a television show or article. From a persuasion perspective, stealth marketing works by sliding under the radar of targets who don't realize they are being exposed to brands (McCarty, 2004). On the other hand, *engagement strategies* actively engage consumers in marketing. Such strategies as encouraging consumers to post product reviews on social networking sites build brand loyalty and sales by turning consumers' initial interest in the product or advertisement into active cognitive and behavioral involvement with it.

When people are induced to persuade *themselves* about something, they are more likely to be persuaded—and to be powerfully persuaded over a long period of time—than when someone else tries to persuade them (Petty & Cacioppo, 1986). Moreover, successful persuasion is created when people—both adults and children—are induced to take some action regarding an issue or product (Festinger & Carlsmith, 1959). Thus, when consumers interact with marketing materials, they are more likely to develop positive attitudes toward, and then buy, the brands promoted. Sometimes stealth and engagement strategies merge, as potential consumers unwittingly engage by passing along to their friends advertisements that were designed to "go viral."

Of course, advertisers have always tried to grab consumers' attention. What is different now is that the grab is more subtle and subversive, so much so that consumers—especially children—do not even realize their attention has been hijacked. They define their activity as "watching TV," "downloading a video," or "playing a video game" without realizing they are simultaneously exposing themselves to brand marketing.

The Implications of Marketing to Children

With the proliferation of competing brands, the stakes for developing brand loyalty at an early age are getting higher. As a result, even the youngest children are being exposed to even *more* advertising, in every medium and every location. These include all media that children employ: television and radio as well as computers, video games, and cell phones. Schools, although low-tech, are more valuable to advertisers than ever because of the captive audience they provide.

The ubiquity of advertising and the strategizing behind it may make it seem that advertisers and marketers have consumers all figured out, but that is not necessarily the case (Donation, 2007). Marketers' data is more plentiful than it is interpretable, and technology is developing faster than marketers can figure out how to use it (Neff, 2008; Steinberg & Hampp, 2007). The sheer mass of advertising evident is at least partly a result of advertisers casting a wide net, trying everything and hoping something works (Steinberg, 2007; Steinberg & Hampp, 2007). In this context, let us consider what children found in 2008 on their televisions and computers.

On television, product placement and integration have reached a new high. Product placement "involves the physical appearance of a product in a television show," whereas product integration "is the embedding of a commercial product or service into the very plot of a show" (Markey & Waxman, 2007, ¶ 2). The Nielsen Company reported in March 2008 an overall 13% increase in the number of product placement occurrences in prime-time broadcast network programming for 2007. The Top 10 programs featured 25,950 occurrences in 2007, compared with 22,553 occurrences in 2006. Cable TV is even more saturated with placements than the broadcast networks: the Top 10 programs featured 163,737 occurrences for 2007 (Neilsen Company, 2008).

It is unclear how viewers respond to product placement. Sometimes they respond critically, especially when the placement is too blatant or frequent, or if the particular viewer is sensitive to the technique (Grover, 2008; McCarty, 2004; Petty & Cacioppo, 1986). Young children, especially, would not be expected to be aware of product placement, given their lack of cognitive sophistication (Wilcox et al., 2004). Even college-age youth may not be aware of its prevalence. Phillips (2007), for example, reported that her marketing students at the University of Notre Dame were surprised when she informed them that products do not just appear in movies and TV shows for free. What's worse, she noted that her students "pay attention to who is wearing and using which items" (p. 4).

Product integration, in which commercial products are intertwined in the story lines of television shows, is also common. For example, after writers for the soap opera *All My Children* worked for days on an emotional hospital scene, they were told at the last minute that they had to integrate a new perfume being sold by Wal-Mart. So they did: in the final product, the emotionally distraught wife took a moment to talk about the Wal-Mart scent on the way to her comatose husband's bedside (Writers Guild of America, West & Writers Guild of America, East, 2005).

Television shows created from marketing material exemplify a blurring of the line between advertising and editorial content. Another kind of blurring occurs on the "second," computer screen, where young people engage in social networking, gaming, and e-mail. Teens are among the most active users of social networking sites such as MySpace and Facebook (Bulik, 2007a). Preteens are active in social networking as part of their activity in virtual worlds designed for them (Hall, 2007; Ho, 2008).[1] Even aside from the obvious advertising and behavior tracking now happening on social networking sites, these sites provide an opportunity for friends to communicate about products and brands and to share marketing materials.

According to Rob Norman, CEO of Group M Interaction, "The more you enable person-to-person communication, the more opportunities there are for individuals to influence each other" (Klaassen, 2007). One way companies try to enable communication is by providing "viral" material for people to pass among one another. The company Competitrak identified more than 4,000 pieces of viral content in the past four years, with "viral" defined as content that is intended to attract or engage an audience and that involves mention of a brand (Advertising Age, 2007). Although not all material meant to "go viral" does, it is relatively inexpensive to produce viral content to be shared on YouTube and to be e-mailed within social networks, and when that material does "go viral," its effectiveness is likely to be higher than that of a high-priced commercial (Hein, 2007).

For example, in December 2007, Burger King posted an eight-minute, documentary-style video about a day without Whoppers (Burger King Whopper Freakout Commercial, 2007). The video drew 250,000 unique visitors in December and was the most-recalled advertisement in the first two weeks of 2008 (York, 2008). The video also spurred viewers to comment on it on YouTube, to blog about it, and to create and post their own spoofs (Whopper Freakout Ghetto Vrs. (uncut-R), 2008). The "Whopper Freakout" phenomenon is fascinating for two reasons. First, it exemplifies how modern technology and advertising foster the blending of entertainment, social communication, and networking. Second, every consumer interaction with "Whopper Freakout" is intentional.

Another way kids interact with marketing materials is via games. A survey of 3,376 mothers found that 84% of children in surveyed families played video games (NPD Group, 2007). This prevalence explains the explosion of "advergaming," in-game advertisements, and cross-merchandising involving video-game brands. Advergames are designed to promote repeat traffic to websites and reinforce brands. Advergaming sites tend not to pressure visitors directly to buy their product, but do encourage visitors to register and to invite their friends to participate, thereby promoting the sites (and associated brands) virally (Dahl, Eagle, & Baez, 2003). "Candystand," "Millsberry," "Postopia," and "Nabiscoworld" are examples of advergaming websites that have been created to market to children.[2]

Webkinz provides the prototype for another model of internet gaming popular with children.[3] Webkinz are stuffed animals tied to a virtual world that children can enter in order to play with their pets' virtual presence there. The virtual pets need to be fed and played with, so kids have to log on often to keep their pets happy. Whereas child viewers may or may not pay attention to a 30- or 60-second TV commercial spot, they can spend hours on Webkinz World playing games, decorating their pets' rooms, and chatting with friends who are doing the same. Webkinz, like other virtual worlds for kids, engages children in advertisement for itself for however long children play on the site (Vu, 2007).

What is the impact of all this advertising on children? Marketers intend it to be brand awareness, which they are in fact cultivating. Children in 2008 know the difference between iPod and Zune, between Wii and Playstation, and between Webkinz and Shining Star stuffed animals (for example, Bulik, 2007b). More fundamentally, however, the sophistication and ubiquity of marketing legitimizes and reinforces the underlying ideology of consumption. Virtual worlds like Webkinz, Webkinz wannabes (such as Shining Stars and My E-Pets), and Club Penguin set up virtual economies for their players, so that by playing games or meeting challenges, children win virtual money that they are encouraged to spend to buy virtual rewards.[4] This type of virtual economy accustoms children to a consumerist mentality (Olsen, 2007).

How Commercialism Manifests Itself in Schools

We have tracked commercial activities in the schools between 1990 and 2008 and organized our findings into categories (Molnar et al., 2008).[5] Here we discuss seven categories that demonstrate the extent and variety of commercial activities present in schools: (1) fundraising activities, (2) incentive programs, (3) exclusive agreements, (4) appropriation of space, (5) sponsorship of programs and activities, (6) sponsored educational materials, and (7) electronic marketing. We define each of these briefly below, and discuss recent examples of each category in the context of "stealth" and "engagement" strategies in advertising and marketing as a whole. There is not a complete overlap between the categories of commercial activity and whether they entail embedding brands in neutral material or involving students in activity around the brand. In fact, some marketing strategies, like creating humorous viral videos, do both; and others, such as General Mills' fundraising program BoxTops for Education, are more or less engaging depending on how much a given school and its parents adopt General Mills' encouragement to involve children fully in the program. However, most of the categories tend to fall primarily on one side or the other, and considering them in this context helps elucidate the impact various commercial activities may have on children.

School-Based Marketing Strategies: Fundraising

Fundraising programs are commercial programs marketed to schools to raise funds for school programs and activities, including door-to-door sales, affinity marketing programs, and similar ventures. In a national study we conducted of the marketing of foods of minimal nutritional value in schools, we found fundraising to be the most prevalent form of advertising for food products in American primary schools, with 37.7% of schools participating (Molnar, Garcia, Boninger, & Merrill, 2008). The Center for Science in the Public Interest conducted a study of food marketing in Montgomery County (MD) schools, and likewise found that all the high schools, half the middle schools, and about 30% of the elementary schools conducted fundraisers with sales of candy, baked goods, soda, fast food, or other restaurant food; the most common fundraising activity involving food was school fundraising nights at restaurants, usually at fast-food or chain restaurants (Batada & Wootan, 2008).

The second most popular type of fundraising in Montgomery County was proof-of-purchase (typically General Mills' Box Tops for Education or Campbell's Labels for Education) and receipt-redemption programs (at Target, and at Giant and Safeway supermarkets) (Batada & Wootan, 2008). According to the Box Tops website, by 2006, more than 90,000 schools participated in the program; and by 2008, General Mills' total giving to schools topped $250,000 (General Mills, 2008a).

Fundraising programs vary both by program and by school in terms of how engaging they are. As mentioned above, schools vary in their level of engagement in the Box Tops for Education program. General Mills encourages involvement of all kinds, providing recipes, product coupons, and project ideas for kids (General Mills, 2008b, 2008c). At Boston Valley Elementary School, progress of the Box Tops program is tracked on a large chart in the cafeteria and a collection bin is housed in every classroom. Students empty the bins every Friday, then count and bundle the box tops, checking to see how quickly they'll win a popcorn or a sno-cone party (the former a reward for 1,000 box tops, and the latter for 2,000) (General Mills, 2008b). The more they are actively involved in the collection of box tops and in activities surrounding them, the more familiar children become with participating brands, and the more loyal they become to these brands. The brands become more than "what mom always bought"; the children develop a positive attitude toward them because they are associated with their school activities, including parties and contests.

School-Based Marketing Strategies: Incentive Programs

We define corporate-sponsored incentive programs as programs that provide money, goods, or services to a student, school, or school district when its students, parents, or staff engage in specified activities. Our food marketing survey found incentive programs to be the second-most prevalent form of food marketing in schools, with 31.6% of American primary schools participating (Molnar, Garcia, Boninger, & Merrill, 2008).

The advertising company Droga5 piloted a non-food-related program in the spring of 2008 that distributed free cell phones to New York City school students (The Million, 2008). Students were rewarded for their performance in school with what they care about outside of school: they got points on their phone for attendance, behavior, and class performance. The points "paid" for talk time, text messaging, and/or downloading on their phones. Brands were embedded into the structure of the program: Verizon provided the service on Samsung phones. As the program expands, other brands will be able to provide "responsible sponsorships" (McConnell, 2007).

School-Based Marketing Strategies: Exclusive Agreements

Exclusive agreements between schools and corporations give corporations the exclusive right to sell and promote their goods or services in the school district. In return, the district or school receives a percentage of the resulting profits. In our food marketing survey, exclusive agreements were the third most prevalent food marketing activity in which schools participated, with 16.3% of primary schools involved in such programs (Molnar, Garcia, Boninger, & Merrill, 2008). The Government Accountability Office found even higher numbers: of the schools they studied, almost 75% of high schools, 65% of middle schools, and 30% of elementary schools have exclusive contracts with soft drink companies (Government Accountability Office, 2005).

In May 2006, the Coca Cola Company, PepsiCo, Inc., and Cadbury Schweppes Americas Beverages, along with the American Beverage Association (ABA), entered into a voluntary agreement to reduce the caloric content of drinks sold in schools (American Beverage Association, 2008). The ABA reports significant progress in implementing the new school beverage guidelines in 75% of schools for the 2008–2009 school year, with shipments of full-calorie carbonated soft drinks to schools 45% lower during the 2006–2007 school year than they were in 2004 (Johanson, Smith, & Wootan, 2006).

Although any reduction in sales of sugared soft drinks is commendable, the nature of drinks being sold is the only change in exclusive beverage agreements. These contracts continue to provide for brand promotion through signage, book covers, front and side panels on vending machines, and logos on sports equipment, scoreboards, and cups (all of which are examples of appropriation of space, described below). This type of exclusive agreement is also mostly stealth marketing: students are exposed to branded material in the course of doing something else, such as getting something to drink (which could be anything, but only the one brand is ever available) or participating in a school sporting event.

School-Based Marketing Strategies: Appropriation of Space

"Appropriation of space" occurs when corporations place their names, logos, or advertising messages in school space, such as on scoreboards, rooftops, bulletin boards, walls, or textbooks. This category includes the awarding of "naming rights" to corporate entities in return for their sponsorship of capital projects or other school operations. It also overlaps with other categories, such as when schools receive branded cups, vending machines, and scoreboards as part of an exclusive agreement (Batada & Wootan, 2008), or when they hang posters advertising a corporate-sponsored fundraising effort. Appropriation of space strategies are often stealth strategies, in which the brand name becomes associated with a gym, for instance; or they simply may be straightforward advertisements.

For example, kids on their way to school may see print advertisements in their school buses (Pries, 2008; School Bus Media, 2008). And as of Fall 2006, kids in subscribing districts also "get to" listen to up to eight minutes of commercials per hour on BusRadio (Campaign for a Commercial-Free Childhood, 2008a).

According to the company, as of July 2008 BusRadio was reaching more than 1.5 million listeners on 14,000 buses; the organization Campaign for a Commercial Free Childhood (CCFC) lists 132 adopting districts across the United States (Campaign for a Commercial-Free Childhood, 2008b; Van Voorhis, 2008). The company promises a small percentage to participating school districts in addition to "a better alternative to inappropriate FM radio programming" that keeps "students seated, well-behaved and occupied in a positive way" (BusRadio, 2007). In addition to its appropriation of space, BusRadio requires an exclusive five-year contract with its participant districts (Exhibit A: Terms and Conditions, n.d.).

School-Based Marketing Strategies: Sponsorship of Programs and Activities

Corporations can pay for or subsidize school events or one-time activities in return for the right to associate their names with those events and activities. Schools provide an ideal opportunity for companies to sponsor programs and activities that allow them to create positive images for their brands. Junior Achievement (JA), a non-profit organization dating from the 1940s that is supported by partnerships with businesses, has long sought to educate young people to value free enterprise and to understand business and economics (Junior Achievement, 2008a). Its programs for students in kindergarten through twelfth grade intend to teach them how capitalism works and how they can succeed in the capitalist system. In 2007, the organization introduced JA Biztown, a simulated town school groups can visit and where children can try on adult working roles (Junior Achievement, 2008b).

In preparation for their visit, classes are provided with materials that teach about the economic system, about jobs that will be available to students, and about how to interview for those jobs. The real sponsoring corporations stock the Biztown shop with their products and are embedded as employers in the mock economy: students might work, for example, as CEO, CFO, news anchor, or camera operator at a Cox cable television station, or as CEO, marketing manager, or flight attendant at US Airways (Junior Achievement, 2008c). Children thus learn both about how the larger economy works and about specific partner corporations and their products. Biztown is an example of both stealth marketing (i.e., children unintentionally are exposed to and learn about brands and about capitalism more generally) and engagement marketing (i.e., they become behaviorally involved with a given corporation by "working" there for a day).

School-Based Marketing Strategies: Sponsored Educational Materials

Sometimes, corporations or trade associations provide schools with materials that claim to have instructional content. In the early twentieth century these materials were labeled, we think accurately, "propaganda." They are now commonly referred to using the more benign term "sponsored educational materials." Usually, these materials promote a company, or values consistent with a company's mission, in the context of an educational lesson. In 2007, Hidden Valley, the salad dressing company, instituted a pilot program that provided grant money and a salad bar to six elementary schools. The program expanded nationwide in 2008 (Hidden Valley Ranch, 2007). Hidden Valley partnered with Weekly Reader Custom Publishing to distribute classroom kits containing math, language arts, and science activities emphasizing the importance of eating vegetables to 30,000 elementary schools nationwide (Hidden Valley Ranch, 2007). This stealth campaign promotes salad dressing as a complement to vegetables.

Sponsored educational materials are not always delivered directly by companies. As mentioned earlier, the nonprofit organization Junior Achievement provides classroom materials to help prepare students for their visit to JA Biztown (Junior Achievement, 2008b). In Ireland, the country's Road Safety Authority has been an enthusiastic supporter of sponsored educational material. Its "Seatbelt Sherriff" campaign is sponsored by Renault and carries the Renault name and logo on the posters, certificates and badges given to children in second class (8-year-olds). The logo even appears on the cartoon Sherriff's clothing (Road Safety Authority and Renault Ireland, 2008).

School-Based Marketing Strategies: Electronic Marketing

We use the term "electronic marketing" to refer to marketing done via electronic channels. Corporations provide electronic programming, equipment, or both in return for the right to advertise to students, their families, and/or community members in the school or during their contacts with the school or district. For example, a new web-based service, HotChalk (2008), links students, teachers, and parents by providing a hub for communication among them. Teachers create a class website that serves as a clearinghouse for class information and materials, promoting web-based communication among all the "players." Hotchalk's funding comes from the ads it shows to after-school users over the age of thirteen (Springwise, 2007). In other words, although student users view straightforward ads when they access Hotchalk, they do so in the context of communicating about their classwork.

Prognosis for Commercialism in Schools

Children live, breathe, and play with brands. Advertising is everywhere, integrated into products, games, books, movies, the internet, and television. In addition to passively experiencing the advertising saturating their environments, children actively engage with it by playing branded videogames and by passing viral marketing videos among their friends. Corporations use such outlets as BusRadio to encourage children to visit branded websites to play, make requests, and offer opinions about anything that might keep them active on the site—and exposed to marketing messages. While advertising's pervasiveness in the world outside of school seems to make it almost unnecessary in school, that pervasiveness serves instead to legitimize and normalize it in school as well. In the intense competition for young consumers' attention, school remains a desirable marketing environment because children spend so many of their waking hours there as a captive audience.

For these reasons, we can expect current school marketing efforts to continue and new forms to evolve. School-based marketing in the near future is likely to share the dominant characteristics of other marketing efforts directed at children. Specifically, advertising is likely to be entwined with content, and to demand engagement, thereby winning children over by involving them behaviorally with the brand.

Conclusion

Marketing activities in school are but one manifestation of the "total environment" of advertising the marketing and advertising industries create. In this environment, advertising has become a dynamic tool for interactively engaging consumers, in as many ways, with as many technologies, and for as long a time as feasibly possible. Children, much like adult consumers but more so because of their vulnerability, are so heavily and so shrewdly targeted that they happily seek out and participate in marketing.

Children brought up in a total advertising environment don't recognize the subtle effect of an ever more materialistic culture on their perception of what is right, normal, and true. Children who play popular internet-based games with virtual economies, such as Webkinz, Millsberry, or Club Penguin, learn to assume a materialistic culture where securing money is a goal because it can be exchanged for goods. Of course, in these virtual economies they exchange virtual money for virtual goods, but this pretend play teaches them a materialistic understanding of success. As they practice earning money, they practice buying. By decorating avatars' or pets' rooms, for example, they learn that they, too, can and should buy things to decorate their own rooms. As psychologists have indicated, not only are higher materialistic values correlated with greater psychological distress and chronic physical symptoms, but the more time that is spent focused on buying, the less time is available for other, non-material pursuits like sports and volunteerism.

That children are used to wading in advertising in all areas of their lives, including school, leads some to propose that children are becoming so hardened to advertising that it is less effective—or less threatening, depending on your perspective. Nevertheless, although children may ignore or dismiss a particular message, in the larger scheme of things, the total advertising environment creates a materialistic atmosphere that encourages more buying, more identification with brands, and more commercialized values.

Some of the more egregious examples of commercialism in schools may fade in the coming years as a result of anti-commercial activism, legislation, and corporate self-regulation. BusRadio, targeted by activist groups such as Commercial Alert and Campaign for a Commercial-Free Childhood, may be one of these. The beverage companies are limiting their sales of high-calorie soft drinks in schools. However, we are likely to see more of the understated variants of school-based commercialism: the building of brand awareness through such approaches as sponsored educational materials and advertising panels on vending machines selling mostly branded water. As schools struggle to make ends meet, we are also likely to see businesses expanding the popular approach of "working in partnership" with schools to help with fundraising. This builds public goodwill and a positive brand image through marketing dressed as "corporate responsibility." These types of activities are especially effective marketing tools because even as corporations can sincerely deny that they constitute "advertising," they increase the effectiveness of out-of-school, overt, advertising.

Children's actual and potential purchasing power makes them a prized market for anyone with products to sell. In the absence of legal or cultural prohibitions on their activities, advertisers will therefore continue to exploit schools as marketing venues. As a result, for the foreseeable future, children's experiences in school will be shaped to some considerable degree by marketing values.

Notes

1 Find Webkinz World at http://www.webkinz.com/us_en/, Club Penguin at http://www.clubpenguin.com/, Barbie Girls at http://www.barbiegirls.com/homeMtl.html, Bebo at http://www.bebo.com/, and Habbo Hotel at http://www.habbo.com/
2 Find these at www.candystand.com, www.millsberry.com, www.postopia.com, and www.nabiscoworld.com
3 See www.webkinz.com and www.webkinzworld.com
4 See www.shiningstarz.com, www.myepets.com, and www.clubpenguin.com
5 Eight categories were originally defined, but in this chapter we do not discuss the eighth category, privatization, because although it is clearly commercial, it differs substantially from the other categories in that it does not entail advertising or marketing. Privatization refers to the management of schools or school programs by private, for-profit corporations or other non-public entities.

References

Advertising Age (2007, September 24). These brands aren't sick of viral. (Sidebar to Klaassen, A. The key to web video advertising.) *Advertising Age.* Retrieved September 18, 2008 from http://adage.com/digital/article?article_id=120616 (subscription required).

American Beverage Association (2008). Fact sheet: Beverages in schools. Retrieved July 12, 2008 from http://www.ameribev.org/industry-issues/school-beverage-guidelines/fact-sheets/index.aspx

Batada, A., & Wootan, M. G. (2008, January). Food and beverage marketing survey: Montgomery County public schools. Center for Science in the Public Interest. Retrieved July 12, 2008 from http://www.cspinet.org/new/pdf/mcpssurvey.pdf

Bulik, B. S. (2007a, October 8). Apple, Facebook tops for college students: Social networking twice as popular among young women in annual survey. *Advertising Age,* p. 12.

Bulik, B. S. (2007b, January 21). Little ears are big bucks for music players: Why marketers should care that almost one-third of users are kids 10 or younger. *Advertising Age,* p. 10.

Burger King Whopper freakout commercial (2007, December 17). Video posted on YouTube. Retrieved January 28, 2008, from http://uk.youtube.com/watch?v=IhF6Kr4ITNQ

BusRadio (2007). BusRadio™: Let's hear it! Frequently asked questions (website). Retrieved July 12, 2008 from http://www.busradio.net/faq.html

Campaign for a Commercial-Free Childhood (2008a). Turn off BusRadio (website). Retrieved September 12, 2008 from http://commercialfreechildhood.org/actions/busradio.htm

Campaign for a Commercial-Free Childhood (2008b). Campaign for a Commercial-Free Childhood: BusRadio districts (website). Retrieved July 12, 2008 from http://www.commercialfreechildhood.org/actions/busradiodistricts.htm

Dahl, S., Eagle, L. C., & Baez, C. (2003). *Analyzing advergames: Active diversions or actually deception.* Presented at the Helsinki meetings of the European Financial Management Association. Retrieved February 26, 2008 from http://ssrn.com/abstract=907841

Donation, S. (2007, October 1). Great Scott! Donation has his say. *Advertising Age,* p. 14.

Exhibit A: Terms and Conditions (n.d.). BusRadio contract posted online by Commercial Alert. Retrieved July 28, 2008 from http://www.commercialalert.org/busradiocontract.pdf

Festinger, L., & Carlsmith, J. M. (1959). Cognitive consequences of forced compliance. *Journal of Abnormal and Social Psychology, 58,* 203–210.

General Mills (2008a). All about box tops—History. Retrieved October 3, 2008 from http://www.boxtops4education.com/AboutBoxTops/History.aspx

General Mills (2008b). All about box tops—Box tops stories. Retrieved April 24, 2008, from http://www.boxtops4education.com/AboutBoxTops/StoryDetail.aspx?id=0

General Mills (2008c). Activity center. Retrieved April 24, 2008 from http://www.boxtops4education/Activitycenter/

Goodyear, L. P. (2008, February 5). McDonald's aiding elementary schools. *Arizona Republic.* Retrieved February 6, 2008, from http://www.azcentral.com/community/swvalley/articles/0205swv-fundraisers0206.html [Original link now expired. Article can be purchased at http://tinyurl.com/Trend-09-01]

Government Accountability Office (GAO). (2005, August). School meal programs: Competitive foods are widely available and generate substantial revenues for schools. Washington, DC: Author.

Grover, R. (2008, May 22). American Idol's ads infinitum. *Business Week.* Retrieved July 9, 2008 from http://www.businessweek.com/magazine/content/08_22/b4086038607130.htm

Hall, E. (2007, November 13). Look out, YouTube: Here comes Bebo: CBS, MTV set up channels on social net—and keep all the resulting ad revenue. *Advertising Age.* Retrieved November 14, 2007 from http://adage.com/digital/article?article_id=121989&search_phrase=%22look+out%2C+youtube%22

Hein, K. (2007, December 3). Putting the "I" in viral makes web ads infectious. *Brandweek.* Retrieved December 4, 2007 from http://commercialfreechildhood.org/news/puttiongthei.html

Hidden Valley Ranch. (2007, July 23). Hidden Valley® announces expanded Love Your VeggiesTM grant campaign: Elementary school in every state to receive $10,000 grant to promote fresh vegetable consumption (press release). Chicago, IL: Author. Retrieved August 6, 2007, from http://www.hiddenvalleyranch.com/pdf/lyv_grant_release.pdf

Ho, D. (2008, July 7). What teens want. *Sydney Morning Herald.* Retrieved July 7, 2008 from http://commercialfreechildhood.org/news/2008/07/what.htm

HotChalk (2008) (website). Retrieved July 12, 2008 from http://www.hotchalk.com/mydesk/

Johanson, J., Smith, J., & Wootan, M. G. (2006, December). *Raw Deal: School beverage contracts less lucrative than they seem.* Washington, DC: Center for Science in the Public Interest & Public Health Institute.

Junior Achievement (2008a). Junior achievement programs (website). Retrieved March 25, 2008 from http://www.jaaz.org/programs/

Junior Achievement (2008b). Our history (website). Retrieved March 25, 2008 from http://www.jaaz.org/about/history/

Junior Achievement (2008c). JA Biztown Shop. Retrieved March 25, 2008 from http://www.jaaz.org/support/biztown-shop/

Kanner, A. D. (2007, June 8). The corporatized child (p. 3). Paper presented at the Psychology-Ecology-Sustainability Conference, Lewis and Clark University, Portland, Oregon.

Kasser, T. (2002). *The high price of materialism.* Cambridge, MA: MIT Press.

Klaassen, A. (2007, November 12). Real revolution isn't Facebook's ad plan: Zuckerberg makes big claims, but future lies in power of peer-to-peer. *Advertising Age*. Retrieved November 13, 2007 from http://adage.com/digital/article?article_id=121929&search_phrase=%22real+revolution+isn%27t+facebook%27s%22

Markey, E. J. & Waxman, H. A. (2007, September 26). Letter to Kevin J. Martin, Chairman of the Federal Communications Commission. Retrieved July 7, 2008 from http://markey.house.gov/docs/telecomm/Letter%20with%20Waxman%20to%20FCC%20re%20product%20placement.pdf

McCarty, J. A. (2004). Product placement: The nature of the practice and potential avenues of inquiry. In L. J. Shrum (Ed.), *The psychology of entertainment media: Blurring the lines between entertainment and persuasion* (pp. 45–62). Mahwah, NJ: Lawrence Erlbaum Associates.

McConnell, R. (2007, November 19). NYC schools: Chattering classes? *Advertising Age*. Retrieved November 19, 2007 from http://adage.com/article?article_id=122090&search_phrase=ryan+mcconnell

McNeal, J.U. (1998, April). Tapping the three kids' markets. *American Demographics*. Retrieved July 12, 2008 from http://findarticles.com/p/articles/mi_m4021/is_n4_v20/ai_2Ø497111

Molnar, A., Boninger, F., Wilkinson, G., & Fogarty, J. (2008). Schools inundated in a marketing-saturated world: The Eleventh Annual Report on Schoolhouse Commercialism Trends: 2007–2008. Tempe, AZ: Commercialism in Education Research Unit, Education Policy Studies Laboratory, Arizona State University.

Molnar, A., Garcia, D. R., Boninger, F., & Merrill, B. (2008). Marketing of foods of minimal nutritional value to children in schools. *Preventive Medicine, 47*, 504–507.

Neff, J. (2008, February 7). The Super Bowl spot that got inside consumers' heads: Brain activity spiked for Coke, Bud Light, but minds were nearly numb to Drug Office. *Advertising Age*. Retrieved February 25, 2008 from http://adage.com/superbowl08/article?article_id=124942&search_phrase=brain

Neilsen Company (2008, March 31). U.S. advertising spending rose 0.6% in 2007, Nielsen reports. *www.neilsonmedia.com*. Retrieved July 9, 2008 from http://www.nielsenmedia.com/nc/portal/site/Public/menuitem.55dc65b4a7d5adff3f65936147a062a0/?vgnextoid=79334914a4409110VgnVCM100000ac0a260aRCRD

NPD Group (2007, October 16). Kids ages 2-to-14 consume digital content on a device between three and seven times per month. Press release (Author). Retrieved February 25, 2008 from http://www.npd.com/press/releases/press_080115.html

Olsen, S. (2007, November 15). What kids learn in virtual worlds. *C-Net News*. Retrieved December 27, 2007 from http://www.commercialfreechildhood.org/news/whatkidslearn.htm

Petty, R. E., & Cacioppo, J. T. (1986). *Communication and persuasion: Central and peripheral routes to attitude change*. New York: Springer.

Phillips, C. (2007, November 19). Millennials: Clued in or clueless?: Failing grade: The 10 things college students don't know about marketing. *Advertising Age*. Retrieved December 11, 2007 from http://www.brandamplitude.com/whitepapers/clueless.pdf

Pries, A. (2008, February 22). School bus ads generate cash, criticism. *New Jersey Record*. Retrieved February 25, 2008 from http://www.commercialfreechildhood.org/news/schoolbus.htm

Road Safety Authority and Renault Ireland (2008). The seatbelt sheriff. Retrieved March 30, 2008, from http://www.seatbeltsheriff.ie/

School Bus Media (2008). School Bus Media advertising. Retrieved February 24, 2008 from http://www.schoolbusmedia.org/SBMadvertisers.html

Schor, J. B. (2004). *Born to buy*. New York: Scribner.

Springwise (2007, November 19). Online space for kids, teachers and parents. Springwise.com. Retrieved November 19, 2007 from http://springwise.com/weekly/2007-11-14.htm#hotchalk

Steinberg, B. (2007, July 30). CW shatters the TV-ad-as-usual mold: Ten-second "cwickies" give marketers realistic option beyond the standard spot. *Advertising Age*, p. 1.

Steinberg, B. & Hampp, A. (2007, May 31). DVR ad skipping happens, but not always: First look at Nielsen's just-released commercial-ratings data. *Advertising Age*. Retrieved December 4, 2007 from http://adage.com/mediaworks/article?article_id=117Ø23&search_phrase=%22DVR+Ad+Skipping+Happens%22

The Million (2008). (website) Retrieved July 11, 2008 from http://www.millionnyc.com/indexfl.html

Van Voorhis, B. (2008, July 8). BusRadio gains industry ratings, criticism for pushing ads on kids. *Boston Herald*. Retrieved July 12, 2008 from http://www.commercialfreechildhood.org/news/2ØØ8/Ø7/busradio.htm

Vu, T. (2007, November 3). Stealth marketing concerns over kids' online sites. CBSS, kpix tv. Retrieved December 4, 2007 from http://www.commercialfreechildhood.org/news/stealthmarketing.html

Whopper Freakout Ghetto Vrs. (uncut-R) (2008, January 5). Video posted on YouTube. Retrieved January 28, 2008, from http://uk.youtube.com/watch?v=Jqgr4UUqdNg

Wieseltier, L. (2008, March 12). Branded. *The New Republic*, p. 56.

Wilcox B., Cantor J., Dowrick P., Kunkel D., Linn S., & Palmer E. (2004). Report of the APA Task Force on Advertising and Children. Washington, DC: American Psychological Association. Retrieved May 6, 2005 from http://www.asu.edu/educ/epsl/CERU/Guidelines/CERU-0402-201-RCC.pdf

Writers Guild of America, West, and Writers Guild of America, East (2005, November 14). "Are you SELLING to me?": Stealth advertising in the entertainment industry. Author. Retrieved July 8, 2008 from http://www.macleans.ca/culture/media/article.jsp?content=20050221_100566_100566

York, E. B. (2008, January 14). Did telling a whopper sell the whopper? The jury is still out, but BK's burger-denial ads rake in big recall numbers. *Advertising Age*. Retrieved January 28, 2008 from http://adage.com/article?article_id=123046&search_phrase=whopper+freakout

8 Exploring the Privatized Dimension of Entrepreneurship Education and Its Link to the Emergence of the College Student Entrepreneur

Matthew M. Mars

In developing the theory of academic capitalism, Slaughter and Rhoades (2004) argued that the notable shift in higher education toward the private marketplace that began in the late 1970s has been a response to both resource dependencies (see Pfeffer & Salancik, 2003) and neoliberal policy environments (see Harvey, 2005). Accordingly, these theorists illuminated and analyzed the organizational restructuring that has enhanced the abilities of post-secondary institutions and those within to engage in market and market-like activities. The pervasiveness of such organizational change has resulted in the emergence of a new regime within higher education: the academic capitalist knowledge/learning regime (Slaughter & Rhoades, 2004). This new regime co-exists with the longstanding public good knowledge/learning regime that is largely predicated on the freedom of professors and students to create and exchange knowledge and provide social critique in isolation of market and political pressures. Altbach (1997) has indicated, however, that market permeation in higher education has contributed to student disengagement in the kinds of social and political activism characteristic of the public good regime. Educators who are interested in pedagogy for social justice and the betterment of society are likely to share Altbach's concern over the dilution of the public good regime due to the rise of academic capitalism in the post-secondary academy.

In the context of academic capitalism, Slaughter and Rhoades (2004) identified students as captive markets—enrollment counts with associated monetary values and consumers of high-end institutional products and services (i.e., athletic gear, luxury campus housing). More recently, Mars, Slaughter, and Rhoades (2008) have argued that academic capitalism has provided some student entrepreneurs with increased market agency and the enhanced capacities to utilize institutional resources during the creation of independent entrepreneurial ventures. The implications of what Mars et al. termed *state-sponsored student entrepreneurship* include (1) the reshaping of the faculty/student relationship based on students and professors forming entrepreneurial partnerships; (2) the withholding of new knowledge during classroom exchanges in order to protect ownership of intellectual properties that have potential commercial value; (3) the further blurring of the boundaries separating higher education as a public domain from the private sector marketplace; and (4) the privileging of student entrepreneurs in the science and technology fields based on the perceived market value of their work relevant to the knowledge-based economy. In this chapter I advance the line of inquiry into state-sponsored student entrepreneurship through an exploration of the relationship between the private marketplace and the emergence and establishment of entrepreneurship education at the post-secondary level in the United States. Descriptive data reflecting the trends of naming endowed professorships (Katz, 2004) and entrepreneurship centers after private donors guided my empirical analysis. The primary conceptual contribution of this exploration is the development of key propositions on the effects of entrepreneurship education as a privatized academic trend on the emergence of state-sponsored student entrepreneurship.

Entrepreneurship Education

Entrepreneurship education has been documented to be one of the fastest-growing academic movements within higher education (Safranski, 2004). In a study of the growth of entrepreneurship education in the United States, Katz (2003) indicated that in 1999 there were over 2,200 entrepreneurship and small business courses being offered to approximately 120,000 students in over 1,600 colleges and universities. Entrepreneurship education has also experienced similar growth in Canada (Menzie, 2004), Europe (Bell, Callaghan, Demick, & Scharf, 2004; Garavan & O'Cinneide, 1994; Hytti & O'Gorman, 2004; Jack & Anderson, 1999), Asia (Dana, 2001), and Australia (Jones & English, 2004; Peterman & Kennedy, 2003). Furthermore, entrepreneurship education has been institutionalized across the disciplinary landscape of higher education with curricular offerings now being commonly offered to students pursuing degrees in a wide range of academic areas of study (Kuratko, 2005; Mars, 2007).

The activities of college and university entrepreneurship centers have not been limited to teaching and research. Consistent with the description by Slaughter and Rhoades (2004) of the interstitial organizations that in part characterize the academic capitalist learning/knowledge regime, entrepreneurship centers often link entrepreneurial actors from otherwise disconnected areas within the academy under the common goal of moving innovations out of laboratories and into commercial markets. For example, entrepreneurship centers can assist students (and professors) in developing business plans that, in combination with the support from units such as technology transfer offices, can effectively transform knowledge into intellectual properties and eventual commercialized innovations. Entrepreneurship centers also provide some students with access to the capital needed to act on entrepreneurial opportunities that have been identified through the commercial assessment of knowledge (Mars et al., 2008).

In *No Logo*, Klein (2002) argued private sector sponsors are increasingly aligning their brands with schools through sponsorships and exclusively contracted services. King and Slaughter (2004) described notable branding activities along the peripheral (non-academic) boundaries of colleges and universities that through exclusive contracts with athletic-gear corporations, fast-food franchises, soft-drink companies, etc., create captive student consumer markets. The similar trend of naming faculty positions and academic units after private market funding sources, however, has not attracted the attention of scholars. The description of the robust privatized dimension of entrepreneurship education that I outline in this chapter helps introduce this line of inquiry to the higher education literature.

Exploratory Platform

Two sources of descriptive data guided my exploration of the privatized dimension of entrepreneurship education. First, I drew upon existing descriptive data particular to privately endowed faculty positions in or directly related to entrepreneurship, which was provided by Katz (2004). Second, through a scan of the websites of the 142 U.S. collegiate entrepreneurship centers belonging to the Global Consortium of Entrepreneurship Centers (GCEC) as of July 1, 2008, I gathered descriptive data capable of capturing any trends specific to the naming of entrepreneurship centers after private sector benefactors[1] (Global Consortium of Entrepreneurship Centers, 2008). In conducting this scan, I recorded the number of GCEC-affiliated centers that were named in recognition of a private sector benefactor, which I argue is a reliable indicator of the privatized dimension of entrepreneurship education. I then disaggregated the named centers according to institutional type (public or private) and by classification based on the Carnegie Classification of Institutions of Higher Education system (Carnegie Foundation for the Advancement of Teaching, 2008). When public data was available I also tracked and compared the year in which namesake funding was gifted to specific entrepreneurship centers and when the respective centers were created. This comparison provided me with insight into the connection between private sector contributions and the expansion and institutionalization of entrepreneurship education.

Endowed Entrepreneurship Faculty Chairs

In a research project funded and published by the Ewing Marion Kauffman Foundation, Katz (2004) collected and categorized the number of and the monetary amounts linked to endowed faculty positions associated with or closely related to entrepreneurship. Katz defined endowed positions as

> a particular type of professorial job in a post-secondary institution. What makes endowed positions special is the attachment of some form of dedicated funding—an endowment—to the regular professorial position. Endowing a position is a way to make it distinctive in academic circles, and it is a way to confer additional status on the position holder.
>
> (p. 29)

Based on this definition, endowed faculty positions provide to entrepreneurship centers *human capital* in the form of highly sought-after academics who are attracted by the opportunities linked to endowment dollars, and *social capital* in the form of prestige and legitimacy. Important to my argument is the near inherency that endowed positions are the result of gifts made by benefactors (individuals or organizations) external to the academy. Also, endowed positions commonly carry the names of benefactors and thereby signal a formal relationship between holders, centers, institutions, and external constituents. This formalization of the public–private relationship is an indicator of the privatization of entrepreneurship education.

Katz's (2004) data showed the endowment of faculty positions to be a prevalent activity across entrepreneurship education. In 2003 there were 406 endowed faculty positions in or closely related to entrepreneurship within the United States, which is a rise from 237 such positions in 1999 and 97 in 1991.[2] Thus, there was a 41.6% increase in the number of endowed faculty positions in or closely related to entrepreneurship between 1999 and 2003, and a 76.1% increase between 1991 and 2003. These data clearly indicate that the endowment of faculty positions is a normative activity within the area of entrepreneurship education.

The monetary amounts of endowed faculty positions in or closely related to entrepreneurship are also noteworthy. According to Katz (2004), the mean annual salary of such an endowed faculty position was $162,018, with a range of $50,000 to $350,000. Additionally, endowed positions include annual research and travel budgets averaging $19,023. The data related to sizes of the endowments were equally compelling. The average size of faculty endowments in or closely related to entrepreneurship was $2,256,096. Thus, endowed faculty chairs in or closely related to entrepreneurship have included notable financial commitments from benefactors outside of the academy and financial incentives to those professors on the receiving end of such transactions.

Named Entrepreneurship Centers

Private sector gifts and funding have also contributed to the creation or expansion of entrepreneurship education centers and research institutes. My exploration of the naming patterns across the body of collegiate entrepreneurship centers belonging to the GCEC illustrated this trend. As shown in Table 8.1, 63 of the 142 (44.4%) GCEC member organizations were named based on private sector gifts. This naming trend was not distinct to either public or private colleges or universities. Instead, a near equal number of each institutional type (30 public versus 33 private) composed the sub-set of GCEC member organizations that carried the name of a private sector donor. The namesake trend was, however, noticeably clustered between three institutional classifications: research universities with very high research activity (36.5%), research universities with high research activity (22.2%), and master's colleges and universities with larger programs (19%). Despite this heavy concentration of research universities and larger master's degree granting colleges and universities, there were six additional institutional classifications represented within the GCEC named membership sub-set. Thus, the trend of naming entrepreneurship centers in recognition of private sector benefactors was both notable and institutionally diverse.

My exploration of named entrepreneurship centers belonging to the GCEC also revealed observable trends related to the timing of corresponding gifts and the creation of centers. First, 58 of the 63 named centers were named after 1980. This finding suggests the namesake trend has occurred concurrent to the emergence and establishment of the academic capitalist knowledge/learning regime, which Slaughter

Table 8.1 Namesake Trend Across Member Institutions of the Global Consortium of Entrepreneurship Centers (as of July 1, 2008)

Institution type[a]	Distribution of named centers (n = 63)[b]	
	Number	Percent
Research university/very high research activity	23	36.5
Research university/high research activity	14	22.2
Doctoral/research university	3	4.7
Master's/larger programs	12	19.0
Master's/medium programs	4	6.3
Master's/smaller programs	2	3.2
Baccalaureate/arts and sciences	2	3.2
Baccalaureate/diverse	2	3.2
Special focus institutions/ business and management	1	1.6

Notes
a According to the Carnegie Classification of Institutions of Higher Education.
b Named centers in public institutions: 30; named centers in private institutions: 33.

and Rhoades (2004) indicated to be a phenomenon beginning in the late 1970s and early 1980s. Second, namesake funding resulted in the creation of 45 of the aforesaid 63 named centers, while four other centers were named for private sector funding within two years after being created. Thus, a trustworthy conclusion is that private sector funding has had a noticeable effect on the institutionalization of entrepreneurship education, which is a market-oriented phenomenon that has occurred during the academic capitalist knowledge/learning regime.

I do not contend that the preceding namesake trends have captured the entire scope and scale of the privatized dimension of entrepreneurship education. Indeed, my findings are likely to be highly conservative, as private funding does not inherently result in namesake activities. However, my conservative approach is warranted based on the importance of providing a trustworthy discussion.

Discussion and Propositions

The preceding descriptive data contribute valuable insights into the privatized characteristics of entrepreneurship education in the post-secondary academy. The careful consideration of the data included in Katz's (2004) study of endowed faculty positions in or closely related to entrepreneurship reveals entrepreneurship education as being organizationally positioned at the interstices of the academy and the private marketplace. The privatized dimension of entrepreneurship education made evident by the remarkable growth of privately endowed faculty positions demonstrates the strong permeation of private sector forces at the instructional and research core of entrepreneurship education. Also, the normative practice of creating and/or naming entrepreneurship centers in recognition of private sector benefactors that was revealed through my exploration of the GCEC membership provides compelling evidence of the privatized dimension of entrepreneurship education. The namesakes affiliated with endowed faculty positions and centers across the entrepreneurship education field are most often not corporations, but instead are individual benefactors whose personal wealth was created through their own entrepreneurial successes. Regardless of the source, the naming of endowed professorships and centers signals to various audiences (faculty, students, and external interested parties) a clear intersection between the entrepreneurship education field and the private marketplace.

The preceding data illuminate the privatized dimension of entrepreneurship education. However, these data do not lend insights into the effects of such privatization on the learning and socialization of students. Accordingly, I have built on the descriptive contributions of this chapter by developing three tentative propositions specific to the effects of the privatized dimension of entrepreneurship education on students and their learning.

Proposition One

The privatized dimension of entrepreneurship education both influences how students are socialized to view knowledge and contributes to the market-oriented learning conditions of the entrepreneurial classroom.

Entrepreneurship education in part socializes students to view knowledge as more than a source of inquiry and as a lever for creating personal enrichment and contributing to the betterment of society. Instead, students engaged in entrepreneurship education are also trained to assess knowledge for commercial value. In other words, knowledge is introduced to students as intellectual property that may hold monetary value—and not as an inherent public good. Entrepreneurship students are also socialized to view the academy as a place of higher learning and the site where knowledge is produced for the partial purpose of commercialization and economic-value creation. The explicit intersections of entrepreneurship centers and faculty with the private marketplace have likely affirmed and further institutionalized these student beliefs and logics.

Learning conditions are also altered by entrepreneurship students being socialized to understand knowledge and discovery as intellectual property that holds potential commercial value (Mars et al., 2008). Under such conditions, students are more likely to withhold information related to new research, in efforts to protect the innovative underpinnings of their perceived intellectual properties. In other words, within the privatized setting of the entrepreneurial classroom, knowledge and learning are no longer a basis of free exchange and intellectual inquiry. Similarly, the conventional professor–student relationship is sometimes altered when professors and students enter into market-based partnerships based on intellectual properties created in laboratory settings (see Mars et al., 2008 for examples). This relational shift disrupts the traditional learning process that is centered on the professor as a teacher and mentor and the student as a learner and apprentice. Thus, I propose that the privatized dimension of entrepreneurship education likely further encourages students to understand knowledge not as a public good to be shared, but as a commodity to be protected, and to view professors as both mentors and potential entrepreneurial partners.

Proposition Two

The privatized dimension of entrepreneurship education promotes the market agency of college students.

Emergent learning conditions within the capitalist post-secondary academy sometimes enhance the market agency of students, especially those engaged in entrepreneurship education. In particular, certain students who are privileged based on the direct relationship of their disciplinary fields of study to the knowledge-based economy (i.e., hard and applied sciences, engineering, and other technology-based fields) have increased access to institutional capital that is highly valuable to entrepreneurial processes. College and university entrepreneurship centers act as organizational portals to this institutionally held capital. The noticeable contributions of private sector actors to the establishment of such centers show how the privatized dimensions of entrepreneurship education contribute to this expanding market agency of entrepreneurial-minded students.

One potential outcome of the enhanced market agency of student entrepreneurs is that these students will increasingly seek out (if not expect) entrepreneurial opportunities to accompany traditional learning outcomes. Specifically, there exists the potential that entrepreneurial-minded students will engage in higher learning not only to improve their human capital and to further develop their personal character, but also to gain access to capital (intellectual, social, physical, and financial) that is essential to the creation of individual entrepreneurial ventures. In other words, the organizational restructuring of the academic core of the capitalist academy has begun to reshape student expectations of the returns on their investments in higher education. The privatized dimension of entrepreneurship education is reflective of this market-based organizational restructuring of colleges and universities.

Proposition Three

The privatized dimension of entrepreneurship education is an effective strategy for attracting high-market-value students.

The aforesaid market agency afforded to students through entrepreneurship education is particularly relevant to students within disciplinary fields closest to the knowledge-based economy. Specifically, students in science and technology fields are privileged within the capitalist academy based on the anticipated market value of their burgeoning scientific and technological expertise. Also, these students are more likely to develop and commercialize university innovations than are students in less market-oriented fields of study. Proposition three holds that entrepreneurship education centers, which are often hybrid organizational structures based on their location within public institutions (colleges and universities) and concurrent reliance on private market sponsorships, are able to act as connecting points between high market value students and the technology-based markets that are central to the knowledge-based economy. Consequently, the privatized dimension of entrepreneurship education contributes to the privileging of students in fields most closely associated with dominant private market agendas and activities.

Students with developing backgrounds in science and technology are not always passive or uninformed participants in the activities of the academic capitalist knowledge/learning regime. Scholars such as Colyvas and Powell (2007) and Stephan (2009) argue that graduate students in science and technology fields (especially life sciences) are increasingly socialized toward and subsequently engaged in private-industry careers. The market-oriented curricular packages of entrepreneurship centers, which directly reflect the privatized dimension of these centers, are therefore likely to more consistently capture the attention of this high market value student population. Furthermore, the public–private networks that run through entrepreneurship education centers, which are consistent with the organizational premises of academic capitalism as described by Slaughter and Rhoades (2004), are likely to signal market opportunities to entrepreneurial-minded students in the science and technology fields who are looking to leverage their training and expertise in the private marketplace. These centers also provide students with greater access to various forms of institutional capital that are highly strategic to the entrepreneurial process. Thus, I also propose the privatized dimension of entrepreneurship education both targets and attracts students with high market value (perceived and/or real) who themselves are increasingly viewing higher education as an avenue toward self-directed entrepreneurial success.

Discussion

The privatized dimension of entrepreneurship education is an indication of the commoditization and commercialization of the curricular and instructional core of the post-secondary academy. Accordingly, entrepreneurship education provides a conceptual platform on which to more fully explore the implications of academic capitalism on the logics, behaviors, and activities of college student entrepreneurs. These implications have been left largely unexplored by those who study academic capitalism and market permeation in colleges and universities. In order to encourage further scholarly inquiry into this important area, I have offered three propositions on the effects of entrepreneurship education as a privatized academic trend on the emergence of state-sponsored student entrepreneurship. The following brief discussion offers further critique of the effects of the privatized dimension of entrepreneurship education on students.

According to Mars et al. (2008), entrepreneurship education has provided some students with enhanced market agency. Market agency does empower rather than marginalize student entrepreneurs within academic capitalist environments. However, this agency also reshapes the learning experiences of student entrepreneurs in such a way that new knowledge is viewed and understood through a market lens rather than an inquisitive lens. Accordingly, students come to view knowledge not as an inherent public good with the promise of bettering themselves and society, but rather as an avenue toward personal wealth generation and accumulation. One potential outcome of this shift is the further marginalization of non-market-oriented knowledge and the further prioritization of market-oriented knowledge within post-secondary curricula. Consequently, the same shift may also socialize students to minimize the value of engaging in non-market-oriented activities that include social and political activism. Thus, educators concerned about issues of social justice and the welfare of society should be concerned about how market-oriented curricular trends such as entrepreneurship education are reshaping the experiences and viewpoints of college students.

In the broader context of consumption, student entrepreneurs are contributors to the commoditization and commercialization of public knowledge, which are processes that if successful ultimately result in the creation of products or services that become available to consumer markets. In other words, student entrepreneurs are strategic links in the commercial packaging and distributing of innovations developed within colleges and universities. Students, therefore, are assimilated into an entrepreneurial process that has been mostly understood as a phenomenon isolated from the learning dimensions of higher education. The attributes of such academic entrepreneurship, which are both celebrated and highly criticized in various literatures, have traditionally included technology transfer offices, faculty-led start-up ventures, and institution-sponsored commercial parks. Consistent with my earlier critique, the positioning of students in this academic entrepreneurship chain potentially dilutes the purity of higher learning and socializes students to view knowledge less as a public good to be freely shared with society and more as intellectual capital to be protected based on its potential commercial value.

The namesake trend clearly is not exclusive to entrepreneurship education nor is it a trend limited to business schools. For instance, colleges of education are increasingly being named in recognition of large financial contributions of private market actors with examples including the Rossier School of Education at the University of Southern California, the Gevirtz Graduate School of Education at the University of California—Santa Barbara, and the Steinhardt School of Culture, Education, and Human Development at New York University. The extensiveness of the namesake trend stands to perpetuate consumerism within and across the post-secondary academy. Specifically, by making relationships with private sector entities formal and public through namesake activities, higher education is becoming increasingly packaged (seemingly or otherwise) as a commodity available for consumption. Characteristic of such consumerism is the perpetuation of students expecting greater and more market-centric returns on their personal investments in higher education. However, such trends in student expectations and related behaviors and activities have not been fully explored by scholars. The propositions I have put forth in this chapter are intended to serve as threads in a needed line of inquiry specific to the implications of privatization and resulting consumerism at the academic core of colleges and universities.

Conclusion

Throughout this chapter my intention has been to cast brighter light on the commoditization of learning within the contemporary capitalist academy through a careful exploration of the privatized dimension of entrepreneurship education in the U.S. higher-education system. Entrepreneurship education as a (largely) privately subsidized field of study has led to greater market permeation at the curricular and instructional core of the post-secondary academy. As a result, students pursuing an entrepreneurship education are in some cases instructed and socialized to view higher learning and knowledge as commodities to be leveraged for personal market gains. While such trends may undermine student attention to critical issues of social justice and societal welfare, entrepreneurship education should not be viewed as being in complete opposition to the public good dimension of higher education. For instance, some forms of entrepreneurship education can help students develop and enhance the grassroots leadership capacities that contribute to their abilities to act as agents of social change and transformation who are not directly reliant on established state and corporate bureaucracies. However, the remaining challenge facing critical educators who may be interested in using entrepreneurship as a lever for creating social change and transformation is the containing and/or altering of the commercial underpinnings of the traditionally market-oriented field.

Notes

1 I do not refer to the naming of professorships and entrepreneurship centers as "branding." Branding is an intentional and strategic process of establishing distinct images for products and services that are widely recognized by targeted markets (e.g., Aaker, 1996; Keller, 2002, 2003; Keller & Aaker, 1998). My research has not assessed the subtle and likely not so subtle strategies behind assigning namesakes to academic positions and units. This warranted research will require capturing the perspectives and agendas of a variety of actors, which include development officers and other upper and middle college and university administrators, as well as namesake representatives.
2 Katz (2004) indicates in 2003 there were 158 endowed faculty positions in or closely related to entrepreneurship, which marks increase from 34 such positions in 1999 and four such positions in 1991.

References

Aaker, D. A. (1996). *Building strong brands*. New York: Free Press.

Altbach, P. G. (1997). *Student politics in America: A historical analysis*. New Brunswick, NJ: Transaction Publishers.

Bell, J., Callaghan, I., Demick, D., & Scharf, F. (2004). Internationalising entrepreneurship education. *Journal of International Entrepreneurship, 2*(2), 109–124.

Carnegie Foundation for the Advancement of Teaching. (2008). *The Carnegie classification of institutions of higher education* [on-line]. Accessed August 11, 2008. http://www.carnegiefoundation.org/classifications/index.asp.

Colyvas, J., & Powell, W. W. (2007). From vulnerable to venerated: The institutionalization of academic entrepreneurship in the life sciences. *Research in the Sociology of Organizations, 25*, 219–259.

Dana, L. P. (2001). The education and training of entrepreneurs in Asia. *Education + Training, 43*(8), 405–416.

Garavan, T. N., & O'Cinneide, B. (1994). Entrepreneurship education and training programmes: A review and evaluation—part 1. *Journal of European Industrial Training, 18*(8), 3–12.

Global Consortium of Entrepreneurship Centers. (2008). *GCEC members* [on-line]. Accessed July 1, 2008. http://www.nationalconsortium.org/members.cfm.

Harvey, D. (2005). *A brief history of neoliberalism.* New York: Oxford University Press.

Hytti, U., & O'Gorman, C. (2004). What is "enterprise education"? An analysis of the objectives and methods of enterprise programmes in four European countries. *Education + Training, 46*(1), 11–23.

Jack, S. L., & Anderson, A. R. (1999). Entrepreneurship education within the enterprise culture: Producing reflective practitioners. *International Journal of Entrepreneurial Behaviour & Research, 5*(3), 110–125.

Jones, C., & English, J. (2004). A contemporary approach to entrepreneurship education. *Education + Training, 46*(8–9), 416–423.

Katz, J. (2003). The chronology and intellectual trajectory of American entrepreneurship education 1876–1999. *Journal of Business Venturing, 18*(2), 283–300.

Katz, J. (2004). *2004 survey of endowed positions in entrepreneurship and related fields in the United States.* Kansas City, MO: Ewing Marion Kauffman Foundation.

Keller, K. L. (2002). Branding and brand equity. In B. Weitz & R. Wensley (Eds.), *Handbook of marketing* (pp. 151–178). London: Sage Publications.

Keller, K. L. (2003). *Strategic brand management: Building measuring, and managing brand equity* (2nd ed.). Upper Saddle River, NJ: Prentice-Hall.

Keller, K. L., & Aaker, D. A. (1998). Corporate-level marketing: The impact of credibility on a company's brand extensions. *Corporate Reputation Review, 1* (August), 356–378.

King, S., & Slaughter, S. (2004). Sports r' us: All-school contracts, trademarks and logos. In S. Slaughter & G. Rhoades (Eds.), *Academic capitalism and the new economy: Markets, state and higher education* (pp. 256–278). Baltimore, MD: Johns Hopkins University Press.

Klein, N. (2002). *No logo.* New York: Picador USA.

Kuratko, D. F. (2005). The emergence of entrepreneurship education: Development, trends, and challenges. *Entrepreneurship Theory & Practice, 29*(5), 577–598.

Mars, M. M. (2007). The diverse agendas of faculty within an institutionalized model of entrepreneurship education. *Journal of Entrepreneurship Education, 10*, 43–62.

Mars, M. M., Slaughter, S., & Rhoades, G. (2008). The state-sponsored student entrepreneur. *The Journal of Higher Education, 79*(6), 638–670.

Menzie, T. V. (2004). *Entrepreneurship and the Canadian universities.* St. Catharines, Ontario: Brock University.

Peterman, N. E., & Kennedy, J. (2003). Enterprise education: Influencing students' perceptions of entrepreneurship. *Entrepreneurship Theory and Practice, 28*(2), 129–144.

Pfeffer, J., & Salancik, G. R. (2003). *The external control of organizations: A resource dependency perspective.* Palo Alto, CA: Stanford University Press.

Safranski, S. R. (2004). The growth and advancement of entrepreneurship education: An environmental scan/The contribution of entrepreneurship education: An analysis of the Berger Program/ Impact of entrepreneurship education. *Academy of Management Learning & Education, 3*(3), 340–342.

Slaughter, S., & Rhoades, G. (2004). *Academic capitalism and the new economy: Markets, state, and higher education.* Baltimore, MD: Johns Hopkins University Press.

Stephan, P. (2009). Tracking the placement of students as a measure of technology transfer. In G. D. Libecap (Ed.). *Advances in the Study of Entrepreneurship, Innovation and Economic Growth, 19* (pp. 113–142). Bingley, UK: Emerald Group Publishing.

9 Framing Higher Education

Nostalgia, Entrepreneurship, Consumerism, and Redemption

Gustavo E. Fischman and Eric Haas

In this chapter, we argue two main ideas. First, that in the field of higher education in the United States there are three institutional prototypes structuring the general understanding of post-K-12 education. Two of these prototypes, *Educational Entrepreneurism* and *Redemptive Consumerism*, are closely associated with consumerist conceptions of education. Second, we argue that these three institutional prototypes that can be seen in public discourse and the news media are a rich source of data on the dynamics of this on-going policy discussion.

We analyzed the prototypes about higher education in opinion-editorials ("op-eds") of three large circulation and influential metropolitan U.S. newspapers (*New York Times, Los Angeles Times,* and *Washington Post*) over an extended period of time (1980–2005).[1] There is strong empirical evidence supporting the view that the press plays an active part in the determination of what can count as a "public concern," while simultaneously presenting current common "public" ideas about those concerns, in order to be understood (DellaVigna & Kaplan, 2007; Gentzkow, Glaeser, & Goldin, 2004; Gentzkow & Shapiro, 2006; Gerber, Karlan, & Bergan, 2006; Strömberg, 2004). We take an explicitly social constructionist approach, which argues that public policies and the allocation of resources are closely related to the degree that an issue becomes a "public" concern. In that sense, we believe the analytical approach we propose can be applied to other forms of journalistic media, such as television or internet-based reporting.

In the 26-year period analyzed, the *Los Angeles Times, The New York Times,* and *The Washington Post* published 1052 opinion and editorial articles on higher education, representing 27% of the total op-eds on education. There is a clear pattern of increase in total op-eds over time, indicating that education has become a more popular or important topic in the last 26 years for these three newspapers.

In terms of the educational or informational content of these op-eds, the three newspapers we researched published twice as many editorials and opinions about higher education related to issues at the *local and state* levels than at the *national* level. The op-eds discussing *national* level issues represented just below one-third of the total; these usually involved Harvard or other emblematic institutions. Global-level issues received minimal discussion; however, when foreign students were discussed, they were ambiguously portrayed as intelligent and dangerous.

The vast majority of the op-eds (77%) were triggered by an institutional event, such as a court case, pending legislation, or university action. Of the remaining 23%, 13% had no stated trigger, while 10% were triggered by an unexpected or non-institutional event (e.g., student and faculty protests or racial attacks on campus). Approximately 30% of the op-eds also kept exclusively to a managerial frame: they provided a solution to an instance of university mismanagement.

The other 70% discussed policy issues, grounded in six basic purposes of higher education. Listed from most to least prominent, they are: (1) targeted group educational initiatives (such as affirmative action); (2) economic development, both individual, and societal; (3) democratic development, both individual and societal; (4) meritocratic sorting; (5) cultural enlightenment (particularly through classic western liberal arts curriculum); and (6) higher-education institutions as profit-making entities.

In terms of the "objective" characteristic of the authors, we analyzed gender and profession. When it was possible to identify gender, it was clear that the vast majority of the authors were male, with an average male authorship of 84% per year within a range of annual percentages from 76% to 92%. Among authors, journalists were always the most common professional group. They had an annual yearly percentage of 49% within a range from 30% to 60%. The next leading professional group was higher-education personnel, both administrators and faculty, with an average annual percentage of 24%. Business people, think-tank personnel, politicians, and pre-K-12 educators were a third tier of authors, where each was present mostly in the single-digit percentages. All other designees, like K-12 teacher and lawyer, taken together, averaged 12% of the authors annually.

In sum, during the period 1980–2005, the op-eds from these three national newspapers are:

- Paying more attention to educational issues in general;
- Regularly discussing higher-education issues (but less often than K-12);
- Publishing in response to acts by other established institutions;
- Publishing significantly more editorials and opinions about higher education related to local and state level issues, than national or international ones;
- Presenting a variety of "professional" perspectives debating educational issues; however, journalists are by far the most frequent authors.

In other words, the news discourse on higher education in these op-eds can be understood as representing a very narrow range of status-quo-oriented discourses that came in response to institutional events, produced mostly by male journalists, followed by university personnel.

Access, Quality, Private Interest, Public Interest

As a result of close-text qualitative analyses, we determined that the vast majority of the policy op-eds we analyzed were discussed within a narrow ideological range framed by four key tensions: (1) access to higher education; (2) maintaining excellence in higher education; (3) the private benefit to individuals of higher education; and (4) the public benefit to society as a whole from higher education.

One or more of these four issues were present in 88% of the op-eds (220/250). The remaining op-eds (12%, 30/250) concerned sports, foreign institutions of higher education, and personal anecdotes about higher education. The tensions created through the symbolic articulations of these four key issues allowed us to identify: (1) the three most common central prototypes used in understanding the abstract concept of "higher education" in the three newspapers over the 26-year-period—which we have labeled as *Academic Nostalgia, Educational Entrepreneurship,* and *Redemptive Consumerism;* and (2) the use of an ideal prototype versus lesser (possibly anti-ideal prototypes) to demonstrate how these op-ed authors conceive what a university or college is and should be like— what should be taught, how students should be admitted and graduated, how it should be funded, and the purpose of higher education, among others (Lakoff, 1987).

The Prototypes of Higher Education

Academic Nostalgia

This was the *least* common prototype, appearing in 88 of the 250 op-eds; however, in these op-eds, it was mentioned positively in 76 of the 88, negatively in nine, and with a mixed discussion in three more. The *Academic Nostalgia* prototype (AN) depicts higher education as a state-supported, yet autonomous institution where the teaching and learning of great, universal, and timeless truths occurs (e.g., Tyrrell, Jr., 1987). We labeled this prototype Academic Nostalgia because it depicts this structure of higher education as the original form. Here is a fragment of one strong example, a 1987 opinion piece in *The Washington Post,* entitled "The College Student's Journey." The author, a well-known conservative writer and publisher, R. Emmett Tyrrell Jr, describes in an ironic and nostalgic way what higher education should be about:

> The American university has over the past two or three decades moved from being society's preeminent institution for passing on intellectual standards, particularly in the arts and sciences, to becoming an omnium gatherum of reform movements, radical enthusiasms, and childish indulgences that makes yesteryear's Home Economics curriculum appear very cerebral by comparison. Every intellectual distraction imaginable from National Condom Week to lectures by dubious swamis finds hospitality on campus, and always to the enfeeblement of serious education. Take a look at college lecture programs: where once serious minds lectured upon and debated serious issues, you now have patent charlatans and G. Gordon Liddy.
>
> (Tyrrell, 1987, p. A23)

In the AN prototype, students are expected to adapt themselves to the universal truths as presented by this original institutional form. As such, the AN prototype is the antithesis of educational consumerism and stands in strong contrast to the two other prototypes.

Educational Entrepreneurship

This was the *most* common prototype, appearing in 138 of the 250 op-eds. The *Educational Entrepreneurship* prototype (EE) was discussed positively in 103 of the op-eds and negatively in 32. There were mixed discussions in three more. The EE prototype is based on principles of educational consumerism and is, in most aspects, the opposite of the AN. For example, while the AN prototype presents autonomy as a marker of quality in higher education, EE values closer ties to social and business interests. This also appears in the relationship of purpose to structure. The EE emphasizes structural changes to the (once) prevalent AN, based on the assumption that efficient institutions operate according to market principles. There is, therefore, less difference between the purposes of higher education emphasized in the EE prototype, such as individual job skill development, and the structural means for achieving them. In other words, in the EE the market-based structure is a given and the purpose emerges from market forces, while in the AN prototype, the purposes are non-negotiable (such as the teaching of classical western curricula), with flexibility of structure to achieve it.

In a 2005 opinion piece in the *The Washington Post*, president of the public Miami University of Ohio, James C. Garland, states the fundamental belief of the EE mode of thought:

> The historical business model for public higher education is broken and cannot be fixed.
>
> The days are long gone when generous government subsidies allowed public colleges to keep tuition low . . ..
>
> Public higher education is moving down the track toward privatization, and the train is not coming back.
>
> (Garland, 2005, p. A27)

In this mode of thought, higher education is a business, a failed business in most cases, and only privatization—market competition for students-as-consumers—can rescue it. Garland then provides the remedies:

> But states could break the cycle [of decreasing state support and increasing state regulation] by investing their higher education dollars strategically.
>
> First, turn all or part of each public four-year university into a private, nonprofit corporation, with legislation to protect research grants and centers and to honor personnel and pension obligations.
>
> Second, phase out each school's subsidy over, say, six years, to enable campuses to grandfather in current students and adjust to the new environment.
>
> Finally, reallocate the freed-up subsidy dollars to scholarships for new undergraduate and graduate students. The scholarships, valid at any accredited four-year college in the state, would go primarily to middle- and low-income students, with some reserved for engineering majors, math teachers and other groups that meet state needs.
>
> Consider the consequences of this change:

* Middle- and low-income students' degree costs would significantly decrease; others would pay a larger share of their college costs.
* Universities and colleges would scramble to attract scholarship-holding students. Students would choose schools that offered them the highest-quality programs, the most value and a competitive tuition. Colleges that lost market share would either improve their offerings, lower their prices or risk going out of business.
* Lacking an automatic pricing advantage, formerly public colleges would raise tuition to make up their revenue shortfall, but no more than the market would allow.
* Competition would force campuses to become increasingly lean, efficient and strategic.

(Garland, 2005, p. A27)

This last sentence particularly encapsulates the EE mode of thought: competition and consumer power—created here through "scholarships"—are necessary for quality and fiscal responsibility. In the EE prototype, the notion of higher-education institutions being "economically lean" is understood as institutional efficiency.

Garland makes a direct request to turn "all or part of each public four-year university into a private, nonprofit corporation" and maps many business terms onto higher education in support of his idea. Garlands writes about "investing," "market share," and "pricing advantage." In the EE prototype, speaking about teaching and learning using the language of the for-profit business sectors makes perfect sense.

Garland also presents the need for the privatization of higher education as inevitable: "the train is not coming back" (p. A27). This is a common justification by supporters of the EE for a change to market-based management of higher education: it is its natural or existing, but unstated, organizational structure. That is, in the EE, economic markets are assumed to be "natural"—and therefore the most efficient—principles around which to structure an organization. From this unassailable belief, the purpose of higher education is derived: the promotion of economic advantage for individuals and society. For students, this means they are consumers who each seek out the best value for their tuition dollar. In turn, colleges compete for the best students. Higher-education value is measured in increased earning power. For society, higher education should promote a prosperous economy through producing lucrative scientific discoveries and developing students into skilled workers, mostly in engineering and technology.

The belief in the benefits of educational competition, which is central to the EE, has three fundamental assumptions: (1) there is a level playing field for students to compete on; (2) academic merit can be measured fairly and accurately using universal and "objective" data; and therefore (3) the responsibility or accountability for gaining admission to a higher-education institution and then being successful should be placed solely on the individual student. In the EE, the tension between access and value (or quality) is resolved through market competition at all levels. Entrepreneurial students compete for positions in the university that will give them the best economic advantage for the tuition dollar spent. Universities compete for the best students (and faculty and staff) in order to have the best educational product for which they can then charge the highest tuition, secure the most alumni contributions, and win the largest research grants and contracts. The successful thrive; the rest re-invent themselves or solidify their positions in niche areas of education.

Both the EE and the AN models fall short on equal opportunity. The first prototype supports the notion of a level playing field, but in practical terms, life circumstances will leave many behind. The latter ignores it altogether; how a society could provide this type of labor-intensive, individual growth model of education is not addressed. The Redemptive Consumerism prototype (discussed below) has developed as a way to marry expanded access and quality. This is an emerging logic, one that borrows from both the Academic Nostalgia and the Educational Entrepreneurial prototypes.

Redemptive Consumerism

Versions of this prototype appeared in 108 of the 250 news pieces, with 90 positive, 13 against, and 5 mixed. The *Redemptive Consumerism* (RC) prototype is an emergent one, and it is very much the child of neoliberalism mixed with a so-called political pragmatism. Having lost the battle over "progressive" educational perspectives such as affirmative action, many of the advocates for these policies seek to achieve similar ends through other means. In this way of thinking, the RC mode of thought combines many Progressive Era presumptions with market entrepreneurialism. Its central premise derives from scientific rationalism—the idea that social programs can be engineered, now with consumerism, to achieve justice. Its adherents look to complex formulas to find ways to assist marginalized groups in getting greater access and success in higher education indirectly, because it is no longer legal to do so directly through affirmative action (Moses, 2001).

In essence, the RC is the educational version of neoliberalism. It seeks to achieve the progressive goals of more equitable processes for getting a higher-education degree and the benefits that go with it through tinkering with the currently accepted market mechanisms. The tinkering involves developing expanded concepts of merit that will permit marginalized groups to compete through a more level playing field based on the commodification of difference. Its prototype is a university accessible to all students, where there is a mutual responsibility for success by both the individual student and society: students must meet required standards of academic achievement, and society must ensure that students are given every opportunity to develop and demonstrate their abilities.

The central tenet of the RC prototype is universal access to higher education; however, proponents of this prototype contest the definition of "universal." In the RC prototype, proponents contend that there are two primary impediments to universal access to higher education: cost, and academic preparedness. The first, the cost of higher education, is the one most agreed upon by proponents of this prototype. In the RC, the state should ensure that higher education is affordable and, currently, it is simply too expensive for many middle and lower income Americans. An editorial in *The New York Times* from 2002 presents the thinking behind this aspect of the prototype:

The United States set out nearly 30 years ago to ensure that Americans who qualified academically would not be turned away from college for financial reasons. The bedrock of the program was a dual system: state legislatures subsidized public universities to keep tuition low, while the poorest students could get federal Pell Grants that largely covered the remaining costs. Within a few years of setting that goal, the attempt to secure the broadest possible access to college seemed secure. Since then, spiraling tuition and declining support for poor and working-class students have combined to roll back one of the more farsighted policies of the 20th century.

(*The New York Times* Editorial, 2002, Section 4, p. 14)

This editorial does not put any non-financial limitations on access to higher education. However, this conception of universal access as limited only by afford-ability is contested within the RC. Many RC adherents argue for "universal" affordability only for those students who are already academically qualified. A 2004 *The New York Times* editorial makes this academic requirement clear:

The Higher Education Act of 1965, due to be re-authorized by Congress this fall, was meant to ensure that no academically qualified American would be barred from college for financial reasons alone. But the door has been steadily closing, thanks to soaring tuition costs and declining student aid.

(*The New York Times* Editorial, 2004, p. A34)

Among RC proponents, there is agreement that the state must make higher educa-tion affordable for everyone; however, there is less agreement on the second impediment to expanded access to higher education: preparation. No qualified and motivated student should be denied access to a college education, but what support should the state provide to ensure that more students are qualified to enter, motivated to succeed, and therefore likely to graduate? This question leads to others. For example, what is evidence of being qualified and motivated? Is it raw achievement scores or potential as demonstrated through perseverance? And, finally, what is the role of higher-education institutions in the larger state goal of ensuring fully universal access to higher education?

How to overcome the second impediment of academic preparedness is still contested within the RC prototype. One camp, those above, ignores the question. A second camp advocates for more direct state assistance in academic preparation and support for both admission and graduation. They want more pre-college mentoring and academic preparation, active recruiting of under-represented groups, and support within college so that they graduate. A 1985 editorial in the *Los Angeles Times* makes this case:

First, the Cal State trustees approved a new list of courses that students must take in high school before they can enroll as freshmen in 1988 . . . ..

So the new list means that the state Department of Education must work with high schools to ensure that the full complement of courses is available everywhere so that minority students will not suffer simply because their schools are not up to standard.

For the interim, the Cal State trustees authorized "conditional admissions" for students who lack one or more of the required subjects. The trustees still must approve regulations to govern these admissions; certainly chief among them should be a rule governing the percentage of any class that can be admitted conditionally. There should be some ceiling, and there should be a timetable to phase out such admissions . . . .

The trustees have taken a key step, however. Now Cal State, the high schools of California and state officials must do their part to see that the admission standards provide a help and not a hindrance to aspiring university students.

(*Los Angeles Times* Editorial, 1985, Metro, Part 2, p. 4)

The last sentence encapsulates the message: the key here is that measurement against a rigorous standard is necessary, but there must also be sufficient societal support for every student so that the standard is fair and achievable, thereby providing an incentive to do better. We know, however, that these societal supports are not there for many students. This has created a third camp within the RC prototype: those that attempt to use consumer principles to achieve greater access to higher education for marginalized and under-resourced groups.

The RC has emerged out of the social tensions generated from developments associated with "progressive" positions such as affirmative action, expanded scholarship programs, ethnic studies, and so forth. Based on a proclaimed political pragmatism, this third camp of RC proponents seeks structural changes that will achieve its goal of expanded, if not universal, access, believing that direct state aid to currently under-resourced groups is not achievable. According to these RC proponents, sufficient financial support must be institutionalized throughout the system, most notably in the admission process itself. Standardized tests and grades favor the current elites, so the concept of merit and how it is assessed for admission must be expanded.

But there are pitfalls in this logic, a sort of redemptive pathology that allows consumer commodification to undermine its original intent of expanded access by yoking social justice ends to market-based means. Within the RC, differences can be decontextualized, which results in making racial differences equivalent to having musical talent or to home geography. Colby College president William D. Adams supports the commodification of student difference as good for both colleges and students, when he discusses this decontextualized relationship between diversity and a quality college education:

Unlike employment practices, where remediation of the effects of past discrimination has been the primary philosophical and legal hinge of affirmative action, the legitimacy of seeking diversity through the admission process has been linked to educational purposes and effects. That linkage is grounded in the notion that students learn more, and more powerfully, in settings that include individuals from many different backgrounds and perspectives . . . ..

The opponents of affirmative action have tried to reduce the educational pursuit of diversity to the mechanical application of racial preferences. Racial differences are important to any meaningful notion of diversity, but at every liberal arts college I am acquainted with, the commitment to diversity is multifaceted. We have dedicated considerable effort and financial resources, for instance, to recruiting students from different socioeconomic backgrounds, and we have consistently sought diversity of talents—athletes, bassoonists, debaters—in the construction of each class.

More recently, we have increased dramatically the number of international students on our campuses, as well as students from all regions of the U.S. All of these differences have educational value and significance for our students and faculty, and most are considered, though never mechanically, in admission decisions.

(Adams, 2002, M2)

In other words, for these proponents of the RC, it is fair to treat blacks and bassoonists as equivalent based on how an institution wants to package the diversity element of its educational rigor, because in doing so, it will provide more access for more members of currently marginalized and under-resourced groups. This logic, however, is deeply flawed.

Once the equivalence of difference is accepted, the explicit support of already successful groups can be deemed appropriate. But this is only appropriate if discrimination, the impetus for promoting expanded concepts of merit and educational rigor, is over. In a 2002 opinion piece in *The Washington Post*, Columnist Richard Cohen describes a result that can occur if the merit of diversity were to equate all forms of difference—the recruiting by universities and the marketing by students of their group identities, including racial heritage:

Vanderbilt University wants a few good men—preferably Jewish men (or women). The Nashville school, determined to lift its academic standing, thinks that enticing Jews to its campus is a way to do it. It's not the only school doing that. Texas Christian University, for one, offers merit scholarships specifically for Jewish students. You read that right: Texas Christian.

At these colleges and others, Jews are valued for what sounds like a stereotype—that Jews are smarter, for instance . . ..

"Jewish students, by culture and by ability and by the very nature of their liveliness, make a university a much more habitable place in terms of intellectual life," Vanderbilt's chancellor, Gordon Gee, told the Wall Street Journal. "The very nature of their liveliness?" Is this man out of his mind?

Actually, no. Gee is speaking both a specific truth and a larger truth: Not all groups are the same. This, I confess, is why I seized on the Vanderbilt story. For too long in this country, we have been determined not to notice what, literally, is sometimes in our faces: Groups, cultures, call them what you want, have different behavioral characteristics. I don't know if Jews are smarter than other people, but I do know they do better than other groups on the College Boards. That makes them different.

(Cohen, 2002, p. A17)

Vanderbilt's proposal could easily fit into the diversity recruitment of Colby College described earlier, though Mr. Adams did not rank ethnic groups. In contrast, however, Cohen's proposal is based explicitly on his belief that overt racial discrimination has ended and implicitly that there is a level playing field among racial groups.

> Some Jews don't like what Vanderbilt and other schools are doing. I can understand that. If you single out Jews for real characteristics, what stops you from singling them out for fictitious ones? The answer, I both think and hope, is that we are past that.
>   I would say something similar about other groups as well. Jim Crow is dead. Racism exists, but it is waning, a spent force. We must insist on equality before the law. But we must insist also that we are not all the same.
>
> (Cohen, 2002, p. A17)

Cohen's proposal, like that of Adams, appears to commodify race, among a larger commodification of student difference, as a means to legally expand student access and rigor together, though it does not appear to meet the spirit of the affirmative action legislation that it attempts to replace. In this sense, the RC prototype envisions "markets" as an agency with the capacity for disciplining the public sector, and consumerism as the ultimate "disciplinary technology." The general trends towards the commodification of higher education have been widely reported (Fischman, Igo, & Rhoten, in press), and as Olssen and Peters (2005) note,

> marketization has become a new universal theme manifested in the trends towards the commodification of teaching and research and the various ways in which universities meet the new performative criteria, both locally and globally in the emphasis upon measurable outputs.
>
> (p. 317)

There is a rational fallacy here that goes to the heart of the RC logic: attempting to use ahistorical market mechanisms to overcome social problems steeped in centuries of oppression whose vestiges, at a minimum, continue today. The spirit of the RC prototype—expanding access to education of Academic Nostalgia quality—is likely to be colonized by the practices of consumerism of Educational Entrepreneurial thinking.

Conclusions

After identifying, reviewing, and analyzing more than a thousand opinion and editorial pieces, and a large number of articles and books in the relevant literature we have very little doubt about the increased process of mediatization of educational policy as a technology, in the Foucaultian sense, for the commodification of schools and universities. As Norman Fairclough (2000) points out: "Politics has always been about relationships, interactions, languages and discourses, but there are qualitative distinctions that distinguish the present, particularly the 'mediatization' of politics and government" (p. 3).

The concept of mediatization points to the complex ways in which media-related considerations influence policy processes as well the discourses supporting those processes. Mediatization also recognizes that contemporary media conglomerates are simultaneously a very powerful political voice and a key political forum where decisive discursive processes are performed. We are purposely using "voice" and not voices, because in spite of the many actors expressing opinions about higher education in these three national newspapers, that diversity is not reflected in the creation of diverse discourses. Our data demonstrates that there are only three consistent frames about universities in these three newspapers, and two of them—EE and RC—presume that the commodification of higher education will almost magically solve the real social tensions between access to universities offering high-quality education based on the consumer's private interest and the promotion of public benefits.

We understand that in the specific case of educational discourses, the mediatization encompasses a two-way movement. First, media do not merely report or present various events of general interest, but forcefully engage in a kind of performance of the events as they communicate to the public. As Pettigrew and MacLure (1997) argue, "the press plays an active part in the construction of educational issues for its various readerships. Newspapers do not just write about education, they also represent to their readers what education is about" (p. 392). Second, political actors spend considerable energies both preparing their products to have a good media performance and working with media outlets to have good reception.

One of the strongest indicators of this process of mediatization is the increased presence of op-eds about universities over 26 years; however, we cannot say why—has this increase been initiated by the newspapers or it is a response to a demand of their readers? But there is an increase nonetheless, which shows likely greater influence due to at least more presence in the op-ed section of the news. It is important to recall that "education" is one of the most important areas of expenditures for governments as well as for individuals getting educational services in the private sector (Blackmore & Thompson, 2004). That fact alone likely increases media's critical scrutiny about schools and universities.

As we have shown, attention to education in general has increased and these three influential newspapers have treated higher education as a controversial issue in which a diverse number of actors seek to construct their favored prototype about universities as the dominant one in public discourse and thought. The discourses of the newspapers analyzed here followed a pattern that, with variations, was quite clear. Authors often argued for what is presumed to be the ideal structure of higher education, contrasting it to what they also presumed to be the lesser, and possible anti-ideal, typical structure (Lakoff, 2002). That leads, in turn, to providing support to other actors' policies and programs: ones that will embody their ideal model by, in the problem–solution narrative of both politics and the press, moving away from the inferior typical toward the proposed ideal (Fairclough, 1995a, 1995b). We contend that our data demonstrates both aspects of concept construction and contestation regarding the understanding of higher education in the press.

Specifically, we have found that the op-eds of three of the most influential newspapers in the USA have developed a similarly narrow repertoire of narratives about universities in the period 1980–2005. These narratives have two basic models: a "managerial frame" which emphasizes finances and administrative problems and a "policy frame" which emphasizes the goals and possibilities of higher education.

These two frames are consistent over the 26-year period and are structured by a primary discursive tension (quality vs access) and a secondary discursive tension (public vs private benefits). These two frames and discursive tensions are present in almost all the op-eds. They convey distinctive ideas about what a "good university should be," presenting discursive narratives idealized and understood in three prototypes: Academic Nostalgia (present but not dominant); Educational Entrepreneurship (dominant, both positive and negative); and Redemptive Consumerism (emerging). It is important to highlight that these prototypes do not follow a chronological order or represent "pure" ideological perspectives.

These three prototypes suggest that the mediatization of higher-education politics has not changed, but has perhaps accentuated, the discursive frame that sees education as a general and all-powerful "redemptive" institution. It appears that these prototypes cannot escape the older narratives that see formal education as a frontier separating firmly the possibility of achieving society's dreams or failing to uphold those aspirations. Interestingly, in these prototypes universities are transformed into all-powerful institutions, makers and destroyers of hopeful futures (Fischman, 2004), a mythic character in a myth-starved society.

Our study highlights the importance of relating large data to individual articles—addressing issues of validity and credibility—affecting both what we look for and how to express research about media and education. We contend that our analysis is significant because: (1) it was able to identify three key prototypes in media about higher education; (2) it presents a better way of understanding the mediatization of educational policies; and (3) it suggests that the emergence of the RC and EE frames are in part due to the reification of consumerist values, a process characterized by Fairclough (1993) as "marketisation" manifested by the de-legitimization of traditional academic knowledge as impractical and inefficient and the thorough support of commodification, competition, and entrepreneurial values. In doing research about mediatization it is fundamental to describe the prototypes and identify salient examples, because that is how people think. Instead of searching for "perfect categories" we contend that understanding the prototypes of higher education requires us to acknowledge that there are multiple, conflicting, contested ones that change over time. Moreover, identifying the three key prototypes not only helps in understanding the mediatization and marketization of educational policies in general but also adds more analytical density to the phenomenon of the consumerist transformation of higher education over the last 26 years by giving additional conceptual and methodological tools to understand current modifications oriented to increased commodification and what can be done.

Note

1 Over 1,000 op-eds on higher education were gathered from *The New York Times*, *The Washington Post*, and the *Los Angeles Times* at approximately 2-year intervals during the period 1980–2005. The op-eds were gathered predominantly through a keyword search of the Lexis-Nexis database. These newspapers were selected because they have very large

circulations, are usually cited as being influential, and sustain a reputation of being some-what "neutral." Multilevel coding was conducted. First, we conducted coding on "objective-descriptive patterns" (newspaper, date, author, education level, etc.). Second, we conducted a close text analysis of a randomly selected subset of 250 higher-education articles, approx-imately 20% of the total, to describe discourse patterns (Fairclough, 1995a, 1995b) that led to the identification of the three prototype categories. Finally, all articles in the subset were recoded to confirm (or disconfirm) the general presence and strength of these prototype categories. This is an on-going project to provide a situational analysis (Clarke, 2005) of the multiple, often competing, discourses on education.

References

Adams, W. D. (2002, December 29). Race has a place in college admissions; Students learn more, and learn more powerfully, in settings that include individuals from different backgrounds. The *Los Angeles Times*, Opinion, Part M, p. 2.

Blackmore, J., & Thomson, P. (2004). Just "good and bad news"? Disciplinary imaginaries of head teachers in Australian and English print media. *Journal of Education Policy, 19*(3), 201–320.

Clarke, A. E. (2005). *Situational analysis: Grounded theory after the postmodern turn.* Thousand Oaks, CA: Sage.

Cohen, R. (2002, May 28). A study in differences. *The Washington Post*, A17.

DellaVigna, S., & Kaplan, E. (2007). The Fox News effect: Media bias and voting. *The Quarterly Journal of Economics, 122*(3), 1187–1234.

Fairclough, N. (1993). Critical discourse analysis and the marketization of public discourse: the universities. *Discourse & Society, 4*(2), 133–168.

Fairclough, N. (1995a). *Media discourse.* London: Arnold.

Fairclough, N. (1995b). *Critical discourse analysis: The critical study of language.* Harlow, UK: Longman.

Fairclough, N. (2000). *New Labor, new language?* London: Routledge.

Fischman, G. E. (2004). Professor@S, globalização e esperança: Para além do discurso da reden-ção. In Dalila de Andrade, *Educaçao e trabalho* (pp. 149–159). Sao Paulo: Voces Editora.

Fischman, G. E., Igo, S., & Rhoten, D. (in press). Great expectations, past promises, and golden ages: Rethinking the "crisis" of public research universities. In C. Calhoun, (Ed.). *Global transformation in public research universities.* New York: Social Science Research Council.

Garland, J. C. (2005, December 30). How to put college back within reach; Better uses for state education dollars. *The Washington Post*, A27.

Gentzkow, M., Glaeser, E. L., & Goldin, C. (2004). The rise of the fourth estate: How news-papers became informative and why it mattered. NBER Working Paper 10791. Available: http://www.nber.org/papers/w10791P1

Gentzkow, M., & Shapiro, J. M. (2006). Media bias and reputation identifiers. *Journal of Political Economy, 114*, 280–316.

Gerber, A., Karlan, D. S., & Bergan, D. (2006). Does the media matter? A field experiment measuring the effect of newspapers on voting behavior and political opinions. Discussion Paper No. 12, Yale Working Papers on Economic Applications and Policy. New Haven, CT: Yale University.

Lakoff, G. (1987). *Women, fire, and dangerous things: What categories reveal about the mind.* Chicago: University of Chicago Press.

Lakoff, G. (2002). *Moral politics: How liberals and conservatives think* (2nd ed.). Chicago: University of Chicago Press.

Los Angeles Times Editorial. (1985, November 21). New standards on campus. *Los Angeles Times*. Metro, Part 2, p. 4.

Moses, M. S. (2001). Affirmative action and the creation of more favorable contexts of choice. *American Educational Research Journal, 38*(1), 3–36.

Olssen, M., & Peters, M. (2005). Neoliberalism, higher education and the knowledge economy: from the free market to knowledge capitalism. *Journal of Education Policy, 20*(3), 313–345.

Pettigrew, M., & MacLure, M. (1997). The press, public knowledge and the grant maintained schools policy. *British Journal of Educational Studies, 45*(4), 392–405.

Strömberg, D. (2004). Radio's impact on public spending. *The Quarterly Journal of Economics, 119*(1), 189–221.

The New York Times Editorial. (2002, May 5). Public colleges, broken promises. *The New York Times*. Section 4, p. 14. Available: http://query.nytimes.com/gst/fullpage.html?res=9E04EED91E31F936A35756C0A9649C8B63

The New York Times Editorial. (2004, May 6). Congress ducks the college aid crisis. *The New York Times,* Section A, p. 34. Available: http://query.nytimes.com/gst/fullpage.html?res=9802E2DD1F3DF935A35756C0A9629C8B63

Tyrrell, R. E., Jr (1987, August 29). The college student's journey. *The Washington Post*, A23.

10 Politicizing Consumer Education

Conceptual Evolutions

Sue L. T. McGregor

The nature of consumer culture requires consumer education to become political, necessitating that people consciously seek to critically analyze and question the taken-for-grantedness of consumer capitalism (Sandlin, 2005). This entails a critical pedagogy that examines power relationships, especially those related to the ideology of consumerism (McGregor, 2008c), a deep form of structural violence, oppression, and abuse of power (McGregor, 2003a). Consumption is inextricably linked to human, non-human, and environmental oppression (Sandlin, 2005). A more politicized consumer education can help consumers become empowered world citizens concerned with sustainability, solidarity, justice, peace, and the human condition as it is shaped by human consumption. Once it becomes popular, this new politicized consumer education can become the norm, moving in from the margins of an education system that currently favors a neoliberal, free-market, competitive approach.

To illustrate how far consumer education has come during the past half-century, this chapter shares insights into how it has been reconceptualized into its current state—a site ripe for fostering political resistance to the pervasive global consumer culture. In this chapter, I show how consumer education has moved away from teaching consumers how to function efficiently in the free-trade marketplace, towards socializing them to be citizen-consumers striving for citizenship, solidarity, sustainability, and hope for humanity in moral economies.

Consumer Education History Lesson: 1960s–1990s

There have been some 25 initiatives during the past 50 years related to (re)conceptualizing consumer education as a more political site. Space limitations preclude sharing the entire 50-year history of consumer education, starting with President John F. Kennedy's 1962 Consumer Bill of Rights (Green, 1988), followed by inaugural studies of consumer education in the United States (Uhl, 1970) and Canada in the 1970s (Canadian Consumer Council, 1970). Even 50 years ago, consumer educators and scholars saw the complementary potential of connecting consumer education with education for other social roles, including citizens and workers (Uhl & Armstrong, 1971).

In 1978, the American Office of Consumers' Education commissioned a *Consumer Education Development Program* (Green, 1988), which resulted in the *Classification of Concepts in Consumer Education* (Bannister, 1983; Bannister & Monsma, 1982), or *Classi*, which classifies 154 concepts that constitute consumer education. *Classi* defined consumer education as "the process of gaining knowledge and skills needed in managing consumer resources and taking actions to influence the factors which affect consumer decisions" (Bannister, 1983, p. 13), and grouped its constituent concepts into three major categories: decision making, resource management, and citizen participation. Since its conception, it has become the gold standard for consumer education, and has been updated to make it more current in the context of a global consumer culture: Lusby (1992a, 1992b) shifted consumer education from a microscopic, micro-economic, personal perspective of consumer education to a holistic, macroscopic, global, ecologically responsible, humanitarian perspective; McGregor (1994) updated and aligned the concepts of consumer rights and responsibilities; and Steffens (1995) drew attention to a collection of values not usually associated with consumer education: freedom, safety and health, truth, social responsibility, justice, and environmental awareness.

In the 1980s, the International Organization of Consumers Union (IOCU) published two influential innovations to consumer education, a *Charter of Consumer Action* (IOCU, 1980), and *Promoting Consumer Education in Schools* (Hellman-Tuitert, 1985). The former proposed five consumer responsibilities—including social responsibility, ecological responsibility, and solidarity—representing one of the first attempts to match consumer rights with attendant responsibilities. The latter argued consumer education is about understanding how consumer decisions impact the lives of others and how to act conscientiously, taking into account both individual concerns and shared social concerns. Hellman-Tuitert's (1999) update added solidarity with underprivileged members of society and nature, as well as a moral dimension to consumer education. In 1985, the United Nations General Assembly adopted a *Resolution for Guidelines for Consumer Protection*, calling for "education on the environmental, social and economic impacts of consumer choice" and "the promotion of sustainable consumption patterns" (United Nations, 2001, p. 3). This initiative institutionalized consumer education at the global level.

Decade Review of Consumer Education Innovations: 1998–2008

During the early 1990s consumer educators worked to revise earlier innovations. In what follows, I track the period of the late nineties to 2008, profiling 13 innovations of consumer education that helped push it into a more critical, politicized realm. I present them in chronological order, and examine them as a collective at the end of the chapter.

U.K. Framework for the Development of Consumer Skills and Attitudes

Drawing on a consumer education framework developed by Wells (1997) and Wells and Atherton (1998), Atherton, Wells, and Kitson (1999) created a *Framework for the Development of Consumer Skills and Attitudes*. This included three building blocks: consumer values and behavior, consumers in the marketplace, and consumer rights and responsibilities. Operating from the assumption that consumer education "benefits society as a whole by creating more active and better informed [hence empowered] consumers" (p. 4), the learning outcomes—related to both values and behavior, and rights and responsibilities—specified that people educated using this framework would: (a) behave responsibly towards families and wider communities, (b) understand the impact of their behavior locally and globally, and (c) analyze the consequences of their choices on the environment and on social contexts.

Integration of Consumer Education with Citizenship Education

With the intent to motivate consumers to participate in the marketplace as active and informed citizens, McGregor (1999, 2003b) developed a rationale for integrating consumer education and citizenship education, striving to identify synergies that could lead to revised consumer education curricula, which would prepare people to be citizens first and consumers second. Citizenship is defined as the ongoing contribution of citizens to solving community and public problems and creating the world around them (Boyte & Skelton, 1995). McGregor (1999) argued that merging principles, concepts, knowledge, and skills from both consumer education and citizenship curricula could lead to the development of consumer citizens. This conceptualization better ensures the transformation of consumer culture so that people are provoked to reach out of their private worlds to the shared, public, global community.

Participatory Consumerism

McGregor (2002a) continued this dialog about global consumer citizenship in a keynote at the 2002 *International Conference on Developing Consumer Citizenship*, Hamar, Norway. Drawing on earlier work (McGregor, 2001), she tendered a new idea of *participatory consumerism* as a way to pull together the emerging diverse ideas around consumer citizenship for the betterment of the human family and earth, their home. In the spirit of participatory democracy, citizenship, and reflection, this new form of consumerism involves vulnerability, risk-taking, trust, cooperation, public discourse and dialog, openness with healthy suspicion, and being patient with impatience. Perceiving citizens as *participating consumers* is a powerful way to extend consumer education to include: (a) sustainable consumption; (b) the promotion of human dignity and quality of life (human and social development); and (c) interdependence, referring to the interplay between people, economies, and environments.

Consumer Citizenship Network (CCN)

This momentum for a consumer citizenship focus in consumer education continued. Drawing energy from the 2002 Hamar conference, the *Consumer Citizenship Network* (CCN) was born in 2003, under the guidance and conceptual energy of

Victoria Thoresen and Dag Tangen. Comprising educators from the United Kingdom, Europe, Scandinavia, the Baltic, and Canada, CCN brings together expertise and intellectual innovations in the fields of citizenship, environmental, and consumer education, and provides channels for dialog and cooperation in research and development related to consumer citizenship education. Thoresen (2005) explained such education should be guided by seven principles: the art of value-based behavior; critical thinking and critical investigation; optimized opportunities via literacy development; relearning; participatory democracy; global solidarity and connections; and sustainable development. It should be democratic, experimental, holistic, and humanistic, focused on a collection of concepts and themes, including yet going beyond traditional consumer education: life quality, international awareness, gender issues, civic involvement, human rights, sustainability, world citizenship, and fair trade.

These conceptual additions mark true innovations to consumer education. Yearly CCN conferences since 2004 continue to enrich the reconceptualization of consumer education towards consumer citizenship education and political resistance, embracing global solidarity, sustainability, interdisciplinarity, even transdisciplinarity. In 2009, CCN will transform into a new consultant's network called *Partnership for Education and Research for Responsible Living* (PERL) with a mandate to empower individuals to rethink and reorient their consumer choices and the manner in which they live their lives in order to foster sustainable, human development for all (V. Thoresen, personal communication November 25, 2008).

European Module for Consumer Education

In 2001, European Union scholars created a consumer education framework, the *European Module for Consumer Education* (Atschko et al., 2001), informed by Bannister and Monsma (1982) and Wells (1997). Although it contained three traditional concepts (choice, participation, and information), the Module strived to develop a critically aware attitude to consumption, and to change collective citizen behavior as well as the institutional framework of society, including the marketplace and economies. Through an innovative consumer education philosophy, this Module stressed that consumer education includes fostering a "critical conscience" and facilitating the growth of citizens who are "concerned about their duties towards themselves, towards social justice and towards the global environment" (Atschko et al., 2001, p. 11). This requires a "holistic approach . . . a critical analysis of our consumer society [and] an understanding of how society works, of the nature of environmental problems and of their interconnections and contradictions" (p.11).

UNESCO's Teaching and Learning for a Sustainable Future

Agenda 21, signed in 1992, is a blueprint for sustainable development into the twenty-first century (UNDESA, 2004). UNESCO (2002) posited, "Agenda 21 heralded a new approach to consumer education, aligning it with health, citizenship and environmental education as part of a reorientation of education towards sustainability" (p. 1). In this spirit, UNESCO published a multimedia teacher education program called *Teaching and Learning for a Sustainable Future* (UNESCO, 2002). They conceptualized consumer education as a process, which (a) analyzes and appreciates the changing patterns, causes and impacts of consumption; (b) appreciates the ethical dimension of consumption; and, (c) encourages integration of principles for sustainable consumption across the school curriculum.

Norwegian Resource Handbook for Consumer Education

Thoresen (2002) prepared a Norwegian teacher training handbook, the *Resource Handbook for Consumer Education*. A powerful pedagogical tool, it conceptualizes consumer education as: (a) encompassing a connection to the management of the global society's collective life (in addition to individual responsibility); (b) dealing with sustainable development—human, social, economic, and ecological; (c) being an essential aspect of becoming liberally educated (critical thinking, understanding processes, insights into consequences of choice and change); (d) inherently requiring an integrated, holistic interdisciplinary approach; and (e) being concerned with the just distribution of the world's resources, requiring "cooperation for the community's sake, [and] efforts to attain unity to where the global society is headed and how humanity will get there" (p. 8).

Consumerism and Peace

In the same year, McGregor (2002b) expanded consumer education into the realm of peace education, positioning consumerism in a culture of peace. From this approach, consumer education moves beyond teaching how to function efficiently as a consumer agent to teaching for human dignity, a sense of responsibility, world unity, solidarity, and sharing. People are socialized to adhere to social, humanistic values: justice, tolerance, respect, non-violence, security, and equality. Peace-inspired consumer education prepares people to function in a *fair trade* market. Ultimately, people would create and function within *economies of care*, moral economies that replace current free-market economies maintained by consumer capitalism and the consumerism ideology (McGregor 2008c).

Framing Consumer Education as a Political Site

Sandlin (2005) argued that traditional consumer education focuses on teaching technical, how-to knowledge, thereby positioning itself outside the social, political, and cultural realms. For the first time, she conceptualized it as a political site of struggle for knowledge and power, and re-theorized it into a more critical enterprise, using the framework of cultural studies. She offered three different reactions to a consumer culture that can be cultivated by three different kinds of consumer education: embracing consumption, individually questioning consumption, and collectively politicizing and fighting consumption. Sandlin maintained that consumer educators can work towards social justice via a more critical consumer education with a focus on the intersections of power and consumption. The significance and influence of this innovation cannot be overstated.

Typology of Consumer Education (Critical Empowerment Approach)

McGregor (2005) posited a new typology of consumer education, inspired by and building upon the three types of consumer education offered by Sandlin (2005) and Flowers et al. (2001). Type 1, *Consumer Information, Protection and Advocacy*, socializes people to see consumption as good and their role as consumer as natural. Type 2, *Individual Critique for Self Interest*, facilitates learners to downshift in their personal consumption life but not to address consumer society and global capitalism as the real problem. Type 3, *Critical Approach for Self Interest*, educates learners to view consumerism as a social construct that is rife with inequalities and oppression, and to interrupt the taken-for-granted nature of capitalist consumer society. McGregor added a fourth type, the *Empowerment Approach for Mutual Interest*, intended to create empowered, politicized consumers who have found their inner power and voice to advocate for others, the environment, and themselves. With its critical focus, it fosters political freedom by encouraging learners to explore who they are and how they have been shaped by their world. It encourages human, social *and* economic development, sustainability, and a distinction between being a consumer and a global citizen. Within this approach, consumerism is positioned as a form of deep structural violence. People are socialized to question what it means to live in a consumer society, and to know there are alternatives. Consuming for the mutual, common good means living in harmony with all living species—a position that engenders hope, a connection to the future (McGregor, 2007a).

Moral Consciousness Approach to Consumer Education

McGregor (2006) also recommended that consumer educators problematize the morality of consumer choices by augmenting curricula via: (a) adding the affective domain of learning (focused on values); (b) using established moral development models to build a *principled conscience* in consumers; (c) giving more credence to morality within a care and justice framework (instead of the traditional focus on rights); (d) being cognizant of four ethical lenses that can be applied (i.e., normative, descriptive, applied, and meta-ethics); and, (e) remaining open to many interpretations of consuming situations with moral overtones by using the values reasoning process to pose and solve moral consumer multilemmas.

Social Learning Approach to Consumer Education

In another innovation, McGregor (2007b) positioned consumer education at the interface between the precepts of social learning theory (SLT) and the principles of education for sustainable development (ESD). SLT assumes that individuals, their behavior, and their environment, operate in a three-way relationship during learning, mutually influencing each other (Bandura, 1977); people can thus learn consumer behavior by watching others. ESD posits that society, economics, and the environment all affect the possibilities for sustainable learning (UNESCO, 2005). Society refers to the role social institutions play in change and development, with a focus on full, informed participation. Economics touches on people's sensitivity to the limits and potential of economic growth and consumption, and its impact on environment and society. Environment involves people's awareness of its fragility and finiteness, leading to commitment to environmental concerns in social institutions and economic policy. Culture, added by Clugston (2004), reflects the role of values, diversity, knowledge, languages, and worldviews. It provides a lens to help learners gain a sense of the connectedness between themselves and others. At the interface between ESD and SLT, consumer educators create critical, authentic learning situations enabling consumer citizens to appreciate and respect diversity, participation, shared power, interconnectedness, interrelatedness, and value systems and perspectives—to better find their political voice (McGregor, 2009).

Five Orders of Consumer Moral Adulthood

The degree to which people can be morally responsible is contingent on their awareness of their intentions when taking a particular action, the risks involved for themselves and others, and any possible consequences of their actions—for themselves or for others. The more aware they are of these dimensions of morality, the more responsible they can be in the marketplace. In a recent innovation, McGregor (2008b) introduced the idea of five *orders of consumer adulthood*. The orders of consciousness approach represents *principles of mental organization* affecting the way people think, feel, and relate to themselves and others. The first two orders are *egocentric* (focused on *me*), the third order is *ethnocentric* (focused on us), and the fourth and fifth orders are focused on the *world* (all of us). Each level (order) transcends the previous one but still includes the mental functioning abilities of what came before. People grow through these five stages or orders of increasing *competence, care*, and *concern*. Their *mental complexity* increases, as does their capability of making moral decisions. Although the pressures of modern consumer culture require people to operate at the fourth or fifth orders (focus on *all of us*), most operate at the second level (focus on *me*). The third order (focus on *us*) is inadequate for meeting the twenty-first century's complex moral demands of consumer adulthood (see McGregor, 2008a). Sustainable economic, human, and social development hinges on people striving to achieve the fifth order of consumer adulthood; critical consumer educators must work towards creating these transformative changes of consciousness.

A Decade of Conceptual Observations

Over the past 50 years, efforts to conceptualize consumer education have become more refined, progressive, and innovative, especially within the last decade. These innovations have moved us closer to perceiving consumer education as a site of political resistance to the overbearing, oppressive power of a global consumer culture. Over time, scholars have reoriented consumer education, emphasizing its potential to challenge the global consumerist status quo. Whereas the focus in the 1960s and 1970s was on how to be a good consumer and how to function within the local and national market economy (get value for your dollar, live within your income, complain properly, know your rights, and advance your interests relative to the seller), a shift began to occur in the 1980s with the advent of *Classi.*

Bannister and Monsma's (1982) conceptual innovation provided a broader, more proactive view of the role of being a consumer. While respecting the individual consumer interest perspective, they introduced the notions of citizen participation and action for change. Although the former was narrowly defined as involvement in business, government, and community policy decisions, the latter was more progressive: through participation, consumers can *exercise power* to modify policies, institutions, and systems that effect consumers' interests. Granted, the intent of consumers exercising their power was to protect their own—not others'—interests and consumer concerns. Also, although they addressed diminishing natural resources, efficient use of resources, and resource substitutions, they did not articulate a concern for the plight of others who make the goods and services. Instead, when defining the *Conserving* concept, they pondered the social effects of consumption patterns, but as they related to individual happiness of Northern consumers.

On a more progressive note, *Classi* contained both consumer rights and responsibilities. The latter encompassed environmental protection, effective consumption, and ethical behavior, narrowly defined as consumers being honest and not wasteful. In 1980, IOCU tendered a much-needed extension of consumer responsibility, adding social responsibility—a concern for the impact of consumer decisions on others. This innovation extended consumer education beyond immediate, personal concerns to those of others and their communities. In the mid-eighties, IOCU asserted that consumer education should address both *personal* and *social* responsibilities, and is concerned with how consumer, government and industry decisions impact the lives of others, and what it means to behave conscientiously and ethically (see Hellman-Tuitert, 1985, 1999).

The United Nations embraced this theme of ethical, social responsibility when, in its 1985 *Guidelines for Consumer Protection* (updated in 1999), it linked consumerism with sustainability, and became one of the first institutions to use the term *sustainable consumption* (United Nations, 2001). The UN called for consumer education to focus on environmental, social, and economic impacts of consumer choices and to promote sustainable consumption patterns. This innovation extended *Classi's* original conceptualization of *Conserving* beyond resource conservation, to social and economic consequences of unsustainable consumer choices.

In the early 1990s, *Classi* was revised in three different initiatives, addressing sustainable consumption, and holistic, global perspective, and humanistic values. McGregor (2002b) raised the values perspective again when she linked consumer education with peace education, advocating the creation of moral economies informed by a covenant of care. With this peace perspective, she opened the door for the inclusion of a moral imperative. Earlier, buried in the body of *Classi's* text, was a direct reference to the idea that "the moral implications of various attitudes and actions are legitimate areas of discussion and concern in consumer education" (Bannister & Monsma, 1982, p. 22). This idea was not fully embraced again until nearly 20 years later. In 1999, Hellman-Tuitert reiterated the affective, value-focused domain for consumer education, this time adding a moral dimension. McGregor (2005, 2006, 2008a, 2008b, 2008c) reminded consumer educators of the role of morality in consumer education, arguing that a moral dimension helps people learn how to engage in morally conscious consumer behavior.

Starting in 1998–1999, several initiatives reconceptualized consumer education from a consumer citizenship perspective. This innovation offered consumer educators a chance to socialize people to: (a) behave responsibly towards the family and wider community, (b) understand the impact of their behavior locally and globally, and (c) analyze the consequences of their choices on the environment and the social context. Using this conceptualization of consumer education better ensures the transformation of consumer culture so that people are provoked to reach out of their private worlds to the shared, public, global community. McGregor's (2001) conceptualization of participatory consumerism reinforced the peace and consumer citizenship innovations, adding new vocabulary to consumer education: the protection of human dignity, the role of human and social development, peace, justice, democracy, and the betterment of the human family. This approach to consumer education is a far cry from simply helping learners be effective market players.

Especially noteworthy are the conceptual contributions of the CCN in Europe in the early 2000s related to consumer citizenship and sustainability. UNESCO (2002) and Thoresen (2005) continued to entrench likeminded ideas into consumer education: sustainable human, social, economic, and ecological development; a concern for the just distributions of the world's resources; and cooperation for the global community's sake. The latter involved an expanded notion of solidarity than that originally tendered by IOCU (1980), then narrowly defined as ensuring consumer groups were formed to draw adequate attention to the consumer interest. UNESCO's broader interpretation is a timely innovation for consumer educators given the new focus on global citizenship, peace, morality, and humanity.

Politicizing Consumer Education

Recently, Sandlin (2005) identified the need for a critical approach to consumer education so it can become a site of political resistance, meaning we should pay attention to power and how its abuse leads to oppression, exploitation, marginalization, and injustices. The powerful conceptual innovations identified to date provide a potent, vigorous, dynamic approach to consumer education. Noted chronologically (with some slippage), these included: citizen participation; change agents; conserving; consumer responsibilities (including social and ecological responsibility); conscientious consumer behavior; sustainable consumption; a global perspective; a holistic, humanistic approach, including the humanistic values of justice, truth, and freedom; and, a life-long socialization process within the family context. Subsequent innovations included: consumerism and peace; the moral dimension of consumption; the consumer citizenship concept; participatory consumerism; and, sustainable human, social, and ecological development (far beyond conventional economic development). These conceptual advances have been further augmented with very recent innovations dealing with critical consumer empowerment (a fourth type of consumer education), the marriage of principles from ESD with SLT precepts, consumer morality, and the consumer moral adulthood concept.

Taken together, the conceptual enrichments to consumer education that have emerged over the past 50 years have generated a substantial platform from which to politicize consumer education. Socialized from this framework, consumer learners can become critical, empowered, politically nuanced world citizens concerned with sustainability, solidarity, and the human condition as it is shaped by consumption. There is no doubt that consumer education is well situated to become a site for contestation and political resistance to the consumer culture, leading to a sustainable world culture of peace. The field now boasts rich conceptual frameworks, appropriate to the times. With political will, consumer educators can pull these disparate ideas into a coherent whole, using them to shape consumer education programs with political resistance as their *raison d'être*.

References

Atherton, M., Wells, J., & Kitson, M. (1999). *A framework for the development of consumer skills and attitudes—Project report.* London: National Consumer Education Partnership.

Atschko, G., Bailey, S., Gonzalo, C., Kitson, M., Kotisaari, L., Nives, M., Riihiluoma, L., Schuh, M., & Villanueva, M. (2001). *European module for consumer education.* Jyvääskylää, Finland: Jyvääskylää University of Applied Sciences. Retrieved August 24, 2008 from http://web1.jypoly.fi/marata/documents/FINALREPORT.pdf

Bandura, A. (1977). *Social learning theory.* New York: General Learning Press.

Bannister, R. (1983). A classification of concepts in consumer education. *NASSP Bulletin, 67*(467), 10–15.

Bannister, R., & Monsma, C. (1982). *The classification of concepts in consumer education* [Monograph 137]. Cincinnati, OH: South-Western Publishing.

Boyte, H., & Skelton, N. (1995). *Reinventing citizenship.* Retrieved August 27, 2008 from http://www.extension.umn.edu/distribution/citizenship/DH6586.html

Canadian Consumer Council. (1970). *A survey of consumer education in Canada.* Ottawa, ON: Canadian Consumer Council.

Clugston, R. (2004). The UN decade of education for sustainable development. *SGI Quarterly, 38* (October), 2–5.

Flowers, R., Chodkiewicz, A., Yasukawa, K., McEwen, C., Ng, D., Stanton, N., & Johnston, B. (2001). *What is effective consumer education: A literature review.* Sydney, Australia: Australian Securities and Investments Commission. Retrieved August 26, 2008 from http://www.fido.asic.gov.au/asic/pdflib.nsf/LookupByFileName/EffectConEd_report.pdf/$file/EffectConEd_report.pdf

Green, H. (1988). The role of various organizations in consumer education. In S. Maynes and the ACCI Research Committee (Eds.), *The Frontier of Research in the Consumer Interest* (pp. 819–829). Columbia, MI: ACCI.

Hellman-Tuitert, G. (1985). *Promoting consumer education in schools* [Consumercraft 5]. Penang, Malaysia: International Organization of Consumers Unions.

Hellman-Tuitert, G. (1999). *Promoting consumer education in schools* (2nd ed.). Retrieved August 25, 2008 from http://www.konsumentverket.se/Documents/skola_ungdom/promo_cons_edu_schools.pdf

International Organization of Consumers Union [IOCU]. (1980). *Consumer action in developing countries—A consumer action charter [Consumercraft 1]*. Penang, Malaysia: IOCU. Retrieved November 25, 2008 from http://www.scribd.com/doc/133236/Consumer-Action-Handbook

Lusby, L. A. (1992a). *Consumer decision making in a global context.* Wolfville, NS: Acadia University. Retrieved November 25, 2008 from http://eric.ed.gov/ERICDocs/data/ericdocs2sql/content_storage_01/0000019b/80/24/15/4e.pdf

Lusby, L. A. (1992b). Consumer decision making in a global context. *Proceedings of the 38th Annual Conference on American Council on Consumer Interests, 38,* 230.

McGregor, S. L. T. (1994). What next for Classi? *Advancing the Consumer Interest, 6*(1), 21–25.

McGregor, S. L. T. (1999). Towards a rationale for integrating consumer and citizenship education. *Journal of Consumer Studies and Home Economics, 23*(4), 207–211.

McGregor, S. L. T. (2001). Participatory consumerism. *Consumer Interests Annual, 47.* Retrieved January 15, 2009 from http://www.consumerinterests.org/files/public/McGregor–Participatory_Consumerism.pdf

McGregor, S. L. T. (2002a). Consumer citizenship: A pathway to sustainable development? Keynote at the *International Conference on Developing Consumer Citizenship.* Hamar, Norway: Hedmark University College. Retrieved August 27, 2008 from http://www.consultmcgregor.com/PDFs/research/norway%20keynote.pdf

McGregor, S. L. T. (2002b). Consumerism and peace. *Consumer Sciences Today, 3*(3), 8–9. Retrieved August 28, 2008 from http://www.kon.org/publications/cons_peace.htm

McGregor, S. L. T. (2003a). Consumerism as a source of structural violence. *Kappa Omicron Nu Human Sciences Working Paper Series.* Retrieved January 15, 2009 from http://www.kon.org/hswp/archive/consumerism.html

McGregor, S. L. T. (2003b). Globalizing and humanizing consumer education: A new research agenda. *Journal of the Home Economics Institute of Australia, 10*(1), 2–9.

McGregor, S. L. T. (2005). Sustainable consumer empowerment through critical consumer education: A typology of consumer education approaches. *International Journal of Consumer Studies, 29*(5), 437–447.

McGregor, S. L. T. (2006). Understanding consumers' moral consciousness. *International Journal of Consumer Studies, 30*(2), 164–178.

McGregor, S. L. T. (2007a). Consumerism, the common good and the human condition. *Journal of Family and Consumer Sciences, 99*(3), 15–22.

McGregor, S. L. T. (2007b). Sustainability through vicarious learning: Reframing consumer education. In A. E. J. Wals (Ed.), *Social learning: Towards a sustainable world* (pp. 351–367). Wageningen, the Netherlands: Wageningen Academic Publishers.

McGregor, S. L. T. (2008a). Conceptualizing immoral and unethical consumption using neutralization theory. *Family and Consumer Sciences Research Journal, 36*(3), 261–276.

McGregor, S. L. T. (2008b). Five orders of consumer adulthood and their impact on sustainability. In M. O'Donoghue (Ed.), *Global Sustainable Development: A Challenge for Consumer Citizens.* Bonn, Germany: IFHE. Retrieved November 13, 2008 from http://educationforsustainabledevelopment.org/papers/paper_34.doc

McGregor, S. L. T. (2008c). Ideological maps of consumer education. *International Journal of Consumer Studies, 32*(5), 545–552.

McGregor, S. L. T. (2009). Reorienting consumer education using social learning theory: Sustainable development via an authentic consumer pedagogy. *International Journal of Consumer Studies, 33*(2), 258–266.

Sandlin, J. A. (2005). Culture, consumption and adult education: Refashioning consumer education for adults as a political site using a cultural studies framework. *Adult Education Quarterly, 55*(3), 165–181.

Steffens, H. (1995). Classification of values in consumer education. *NICE-Mail*, 4 (November), pp. 17–20. Retrieved August 25, 2008 from http://www.infoconsumo.es/escuela/web/nice/eng/nice_4.pdf

Thoresen, V. W. (2002). *Resource handbook for consumer education.* Oslo, Norway: Consumer Council of Norway. Retrieved August 25, 2008 from http://forbrukerportalen.no/filer/fil_handbook.pdf

Thoresen, V. W. (2005). *Consumer citizenship education guidelines, Vol. 1: Higher Education.* The Consumer Citizenship Network, Hedmark University College, Norway. Available: https://www.hihm.no/content/download/4916/43166/file/4%20 guidelines.pdf

Uhl, J. (1970). The Purdue consumer education study: Some findings and implications. *Journal of Consumer Affairs, 4*(2), 124–134.

Uhl, J., & Armstrong, J. (1971). Adult consumer education programs in the United States. *Journal of Home Economics, 63*(8), 591–595.

UNDESA. (2004). *Agenda 21: Earth summit—The United Nations programme of action from Rio.* Paris, France: United Nations Publications. Retrieved August 24, 2008 from http://www.un.org/esa/sustdev/documents/agenda21/

UNESCO. (2002). *Teaching and learning for a sustainable future.* Paris, France: UNESCO. Retrieved August 24, 2008 from http://www.unesco.org/education/tlsf/TLSF/theme_b/mod09/uncom09.htm

UNESCO. (2005). *United Nations decade of education for sustainable development.* Paris, France: UNESCO. Retrieved August 26, 2008 from fhttp://www.unescobkk.org/fileadmin/user_upload/esd/documents/Final_draft_IIS.pdf

United Nations. (2001). *United Nations guidelines for consumer protection (A/C.2/54/L.24).* Paris, France: UN. Retrieved August 25, 2008 from http://www.unctad.org/en/docs/poditcclpm21.en.pdf

Wells, J. (1997). *Towards 2000—Consumer education in the classroom.* London: Forbes Publications.

Wells, J., & Atherton, M. (1998, Autumn). Consumer education: Learning for life. *Consumer 21 [Consumers International]*, pp. 15–20.

Part III

Consumption, Popular Culture, Everyday Life, and the Education of Desire

11 Consuming the All-American Corporate Burger

McDonald's "Does It All For You"

Joe L. Kincheloe

I was destined to write about McDonald's, as my life has always intersected with the golden arches. As part of my undergraduate comedy routine, I truthfully told my listeners that I had consumed 6,000 McDonald's hamburgers before graduating from high school. In junior high and high school we were allowed to go off campus to eat. My friends and I would tromp through the Tennessee woods daily to the golden arches, obsessed with consuming those burgers. After six years of three-hamburger lunches, including three more for Wednesday dinners with my parents, and several on weekend nights after cruising with friends—the count began to mount. Ray Kroc, the man who made McDonald's a household name, would have been proud.

Somewhere in my small-town-Tennessee adolescent consciousness, I understood McDonald's was the future. I couldn't name it, but the standardized hamburger was a symbol of some vague social phenomenon. Like any immigrant of another place and time, I was ethnic—a hillbilly. And like all children of traditional ethnic parents, I struggled for an American identity. Though it wasn't yet the symbol of America around the world, I knew the McDonald's of the early 1960s was mainstream American. Thus, my participation in the burger–fries ritual was an act of shedding my ethnic identity. Understanding McDonald's regulation of customer behavior, I complied readily, knowing the menu in advance and placing my order quickly and accurately. My parents, on the other hand, raised in the rural South of the early twentieth century, were lost at the ordering counter. They never understood the menu, were always unsure of the expected behavior; the effort to shape their consumer conduct was a disaster.

On a very different level, though, my parents were seduced by McDonald's. Students of cultural studies have come to understand that readings of film, TV, and commercials are idiosyncratic (Steinberg, 2007), differing significantly from individual to individual. So it was in my home. As victims of the Great Depression in southern Appalachia, my parents viewed excessive spending as a moral weakness. Eating out, when it was possible to prepare food at home, was especially depraved. My father entered a McDonald's only if he was convinced of its economic "good sense," and advertisers struck an emotional chord when they pitted McDonald's 15-cent hamburgers and 12-cent fries as an alternative to the extravagant cost of eating out. To my self-identified working-class father, eating at

McDonald's was an act of class resistance. He didn't care much for the food—he would rather eat my mother's country ham and cornbread. But as we McDined, he spoke with great enthusiasm about how McDonald's beat the price of other burgers around town by 50 or 60 cents.

My father consumed a democratic egalitarian ethos. French teenagers accustomed to the bourgeois stuffiness of French restaurants could have identified with my father's class-resistant consumption, as they revel in the freedom of McDonald's "American atmosphere." The inexpensive fare, the informal dress, the loud talk are class signifiers (Leidner, 1993). Such coding is ironic in light of McDonald's right-wing political history, its exploitation of labor, and its cutthroat competition with other fast-food enterprises. That McDonald's continues to maintain an egalitarian image is testimony to the power and expertise of its public relations strategists. In this chapter, I ask: What is the nature of these PR strategies? What do they tell us about McDonald's? And how do they affect American culture—particularly what Shirley Steinberg and I have defined as kinderculture (Steinberg & Kincheloe, 2004)?

Creating a Cultural Consciousness of Burgers

Americans rarely think about efforts by powerful interests in society to regulate populations to bring about desired behaviors. In America and other Western societies, political domination shifted decades ago from police or military force to cultural messages. Such communications are designed to win the consent of citizens for actions taken by power elites (Giroux, 1988). Cultural studies scholars are involved in efforts to expose the specifics of this process of cultural domination, a process taking place in our everyday life experiences. These messages are not sent by a secret group of conspirators or clandestine ministry of propaganda; nor does everyone read them in the same way. But some people understand their manipulative intent and rebel against their authority (Goldman, 1992). McDonald's role in these power dynamics illustrates the larger process—if any corporation has the power to help shape the lives of children, it is McDonald's.

The construction of who we are and what we believe cannot be separated from the workings of power. Americans don't talk much about power. When power is broached in mainstream sociology, discussion revolves around either the macro level, the political relations of governments, or the micro level, the personal relations between two people (Abercrombie, 1994). Power, as I use the term, is neither macro nor micro, nor does it rely on legality or coercion. Power, as it has evolved in the first decade of the twenty-first century, maintains its legitimacy in subtle and effective ways. Consider the power generated by McDonald's use of the media to define itself not simply as an American institution but as America itself—McDonald's attaches itself to American patriotism and the cultural dynamics it involves. Ray Kroc understood early that he was not simply selling hamburgers—he was selling America a vision of itself (Luxenberg, 1985). From the All-American marching band to the All-American sports teams, to the All-American meal served by All-American boys and girls, the All-American of the Year, Ray Kroc, labored to connect the American signifier to McDonald's. The American flag will fly 24 hours a day at McDonald's, he demanded. Using the flag as a backdrop to highlight the hamburger count, Kroc watched the burger numbers supplant the Dow Jones closing average as the symbolic statistical index for America's economic health. In the late 1960s and early 1970s, Kroc saw McDonald's perpetually flying flag as a statement to the war protesters and civil rights "kooks" that McDonald's (America) would not stand for anyone criticizing "our" country (Kroc, 1977).

One of the reasons Americans don't talk much about power is that it works in subtle, hard-to-define ways. Ask Americans how McDonald's has shaped them, and you'll draw blank stares. What does it mean to argue that power involves the ability to ascribe meanings to various features of our lives? Consider the McDonald's All-American ad campaign. Kroc and the McDonald's management sanctioned the costliest, most ambitious ad campaign in American corporate history (Boas & Chain, 1976). Great amounts of money and effort were expended to imbue the McDonald's hamburger with a star-spangled signification—and it worked, in the sense that Americans and individuals around the world began to make the desired connection. Described as the "ultimate icon of Americana," a "cathedral of consumption" where Americans practice their "consumer religion," McDonald's, like Disneyland, transcends status as mere business establishment (Ritzer, 1993). When McDonald's or Disney speaks, they speak for all of us. How could the Big Mac or Pirates of the Caribbean mislead us? They *are* us.

Legitimation signifiers work best when they go unnoticed, as they effectively connect an organization's economic power to acquire property, lobby Congress, hire lawyers, and so on to its power to ascribe meaning and persuade. In the process the legitimated organization gains the power to create and transmit a view of reality consonant with its larger interests—American economic superiority as the direct result of an unbridled free-enterprise system. One McDonald's ad campaign painted a nostalgic, sentimentalized, conflict-free American family pictorial history. The purpose of the ad was to deeply connect McDonald's and America by creating an American historical role for McDonald's where none ever existed. You can almost hear the male voice-over: "Though we didn't yet exist, we were there to do it all for you—McDonald's then, McDonald's now." We're all one big, happy family with the same (European) roots. "We" becomes McDonald's and America— "our" family (Goldman, 1992).

Hegemonically Globalizing Hamburgers

Ironically, as McDonald's became synonymous with America, it outgrew U.S. borders. By the last quarter of the twentieth century McDonald's represented a global enterprise. In this transnational process, the company became the symbol of Western economic development. Often McDonald's was the first foreign corporation to penetrate a particular nation's market. Indian social critic Vandana Shiva (1997) found dark humor in the symbolism of the golden arches. They induce the feeling that you are entering heaven when you walk into McDonald's. Corporate marketers want children around the world to view the "McDonald's experience" as an immersion in celestial jouissance—while they are actually eating junk. In terms reminiscent of the outlook of the Pentagon in the second Iraq war, McDonald's executives refer to their movement into foreign markets as the company's "global realization" (Schlosser, 2001). When statues of Lenin came down in East Germany after reunification, giant statues of Ronald McDonald almost immediately took their place. A couple of months ago, as we disembarked a flight in Amsterdam, and entered into the large and ultramodern Schiphol Airport, Ronald McDonald's ceramic wave greeted us, our first sight of The Netherlands.

Several schoolteachers in Santos, Brazil told me they worried about the impact of McDonald's on their students. One teacher contended: "The danger of McDonald's imperialism is that it teaches children to devalue Brazilian things and to believe that Americans are superior to all of us poor South Americans." The anger these teachers directed at McDonald's and the company's ideological impact on Brazilian children was inscribed on each word they spoke. Western societies, and the United States in particular have created this corporate colonialism via the construction of corporatized governments (Kincheloe, 1999) over the past several decades. To work, such political economic reforms rely on particular types of consciousness—individuals need to dismiss from their consciousness questions of social justice, egalitarianism, and environmentalism. Corporatized, globalized governments and their corporate allies need well-managed, socially regulated, consumption-oriented individuals who understand that economic growth demands "good business climates," antiunion perspectives, and low wages for those lower in the hierarchy.

To gain the ability to introduce these ideas to children across the world, corporations such as McDonald's continue to refine their appeal to the affective dimension. Their ability to produce entertainment for children that adults deem inappropriate is central to this enterprise. After decades of marketing research, the best sellers are items which parents eschew: Toxic High stickers, Garbage Pail Kids, Mass Murderer cards, and McDonald's cuisine. Producers of children's commercial culture understand part of the appeal of children's consumer products lies in vociferous parental disapproval of them (Spigel, 2001)—the more subversive, the better. Schools not only ignore the power of such influences on children but have allowed McDonald's and other marketers into their hallways and classrooms (Kenway & Bullen, 2001; Molnar, 1996).

McDonald's also has practically unlimited ideological access to students by way of such ploys as "job interview seminars." Analysis of such seminars reveals that they are more focused on inculcating particular beliefs about the social benefits of McDonald's and the unregulated free-enterprise system than on helping students practice the interviewing process. I found that students who were savvy enough to recognize the covert ideological dimensions of McDonald's seminars and brave enough to expose them to the school community were often punished for such "misbehavior" by school officials.

A critical pedagogy of consumption cannot ignore these political, economic, social, and ideological dynamics. It is important for children around the world to understand the ways commercially produced children's culture (Kenway & Bullen, 2001) wins their consent to positions that solely serve the interests of multinational corporations and their allies. Children are directly affected by corporate hegemonization and globalization—forces that are central players in the social construction of childhood in hyperreality (Kincheloe, 2002). However, educational researchers must always maintain a delicate balance between structure and agency. The market does not simply snatch children from the innocent garden of child-hood and transform them into crazed consumers. Concurrently the answer is not as easy as providing empowerment for self-sufficient agential children. Corporate producers and marketers must be exerting economic and ideological effects by their efforts, since they keep pouring billions of dollars into advertising directed at children. While children construct their own meanings, the corporate culture of power does exploit them—the corporate effort to ideologically construct children's consciousness is a cold reality.

Educational scholars who do not value the importance of studying the effects of dominant power on the lived world often slam more critical takes on the effects of political economic structures on the lives of children. They often interpret critical charges of ideological exploitation with the assertion that the dominant power of McDonald's, for example, produces standardized and homogenized "corporate children." This is not what McDonald's does. Producers of commercial children's culture reshape everyday places and activities in ways that resonate with corporate economic and ideological interests. In this context, as parents of young children often describe, the relationship of children to, say, eating is reconfigured as children cry out for McDonald's hamburgers.

Consumption and pleasure are intimately connected in the lives of millions of children. Corporate power has entered domains of life once free from market influences. Without their conscious awareness such children may eventually find that this power and the connections it forges exert a significant impact on their life choices. Young boys in China, for example, fantasize about opening chains of McDonald's restaurants in Beijing (Yan, 1997). In a communist country such dreams are ideologically significant and alter the relationship between young boys and Chinese politics. Like the U.S. military in Vietnam and Iraq, corporations work to win the hearts and minds of young consumers; the only difference is that corporate methods are more sophisticated and work much better than the military strategies. Consumer pedagogy is amazingly intrusive, working 24 hours a day to colonize all dimensions of lived experience (Cook, 2004; Kenway & Bullen, 2001).

McDonald's Is for Kids

Using techno power—by which I mean the expansion of corporate influence via the use of recent technological innovation (Harvey, 1989; Kellner, 1989)—corporations like McDonald's have increased their ability to maximize capital accumulation, influence social and cultural life, and even help mold children's consciousness. Since childhood is a cultural construction shaped in the contemporary era by the forces of this media-catalyzed techno power, there is a dire need for parents, teachers, and community members to study it. Let us turn now to McDonald's and the construction of childhood in contemporary globalized society. Even the name, "McDonald's," is kid-friendly, with its evocation of Old MacDonald and his farm. The safety of McDonald's provides asylum, if not utopian refuge, from the kid-unfriendly contemporary world of child abuse, broken homes, and child-napping. Offering something better to escape into, McDonald's

TV depiction of itself to children as a happy place where "what you want is what you get" is very appealing (Garfield, 1992). By the time children reach elementary school, they are often zealous devotees of McDonald's who insist on McDonaldland birthday celebrations and surprise dinners. Obviously McDonald's advertisers are doing something right, as they induce phenomenal numbers of kids to pester their parents for Big Macs and fries. The creation of McDonald's playlands, with brightly colored climbing toys and tunnels—complete with parents' watching tables–has made Mickey D's the favored destination of parents with nowhere to go.

McDonald's and other fast-food advertisers have discovered an enormous, previously overlooked children's market. Children between the ages of 5 and 12 spend almost $5 billion of their own money each year, and influence household spending of an additional $140 billion annually, more than half of which is spent on soft drinks and fast food. Every month 19 out of every 20 kids aged 6 to 11 visit a fast-food restaurant. In a typical McDonald's promotion, where toys with movie tie-ins accompany kids' meals, company officials can expect to sell over 30 million to child customers. By the time they reach two, over four out of five children know McDonald's sells hamburgers. As if this level of child consciousness colonization were not enough, McDonald's, along with numerous other companies, has targeted the public schools as a new venue for child marketing and consumption. In addition to hamburgers-for-A's programs and advertising-based learning packets for various school subjects, McDonald's and other fast-food firms have gained control of school cafeterias, much to the consternation of many child-health advocates (Giroux, 1994; Hume, 1993; Kincheloe, 2002; Ritzer, 1993).

McDonald's and its advertisers want to transform children into consumers; indeed, they see children as consumers in training (Fischer, Schwartz, Richards, Goldstein, & Rojas, 1991). Seiter (1993), however, warns against drawing simplistic conclusions about the relationship between advertisers and children, as have, she says, many well-intentioned liberal children's advocacy groups that fail to capture the subtle aspects of techno power and its colonization of childhood, the complicated interactions of structure and agency. Children are not passive, naive consumers. As advertising professionals have learned, children are active and analytical, and often make their own meanings of both commercials and the products they sell. These social and psychological dynamics between advertisers and children deserve further analysis.

One important dynamic is advertisers' recognition that children feel oppressed by the middle-class view of children as naive and in need of protection. By drawing on children's discomfort with middle-class protectionism and the accompanying attempt to "adjust" children to a positivist "developmentally appropriate" norm, advertisers hit on a marketing bonanza. If we address kids as kids: a dash of anarchism and a pinch of hyperactivity—they will love our commercials; even though parents (especially middle-class parents) will hate them. By the end of the 1960s, commercial children's TV and advertising were grounded on this premise. Such media throw off restraint, discipline, and old views that children should be seen but not heard. Everything, for example, that educational TV embraces—earnestness, child as an incomplete adult, child in need of correction—commercial TV rejects. In effect, commercial TV sets up an oppositional culture for kids.

One doesn't have to look far to find that children's enthusiasm for certain TV shows, toys, and foods often isolates them from their parents. Children turn this isolation into a form of power—they finally know something that Dad doesn't. Battle lines begin to be drawn between children and parents, as kids want to purchase McDonald's hamburgers or action toys. Conflicts in lower-middle-class homes may revolve around family finances; strife in upper-middle-class homes may concern aesthetic or ideological concerns. Questions of taste, cultural capital, or self-improvement permeate child–adult interactions in such families. A child's ability to negotiate the restrictions of adult values is central to the development of an independent self. A common aspect of this developing independence involves the experience of contradiction with the adult world. Children of upwardly mobile, ambitious parents may find it more difficult to negotiate this experience of contradiction because of parents' strict views of the inappropriateness of TV-based children's culture. Thus the potential for parent–child conflict and alienation may be greater in this familial context. Adding to this, with the growing propensity for bourgeois-bohemian parents to go "green" and to avoid many prepared foods—eating at McDonald's can prove to be a political minefield. I recall last year when two of our closest friends, parents to a 16-year-old girl, told us that their worst fights with their daughter Sadie have centered around her insistence to stop training and eat fast food.

The Colonialization of Fun

Play is thus placed in cultural conflict. Over the past several decades psychologists and educators have argued for the importance of play in childhood and child development. With this in mind, our examination of McDonald's opens a window into what can happen when the culture and political economy of play begin to change. New forms of play may accelerate particular forms of intellectual development while concurrently limiting the imagination. With the corporate colonization of play in hyperreality, play begins to lose its imaginative dimensions. Contemporary children's play occurs in the same public spaces as adult labor, as children enter into cyberspace using the same hardware and software their parents use in their professional lives.

Of course, McDonald's is only one producer in an expanding children's commercial culture. Children, in their interactions with McDonald's and other manifestations of this commercial kinderculture, use its symbolic and material dimensions in often unique ways. McDonald's wants children to engage its products and company-produced meanings in an "appropriate" manner. Such engagement would not include "playing" with environmental and health concerns by developing cyber communities of like-minded children calling for corporate responsibility. McDonald's and other corporations do not want power-savvy children, such as the ones who formed the organization Children Against McDonald's, engaging in socially conscious use of their products. Corporate marketers and other protectors of the status quo fear the agential, empowered child. Media corporations and companies like McDonald's work hard to control and structure the way consumers interact with their products. Indeed, child consumers do not experience the freedom and empowerment some advocates of the agential child-hood claim for them. Play as political resistance must be opposed at all costs (Jenkins, 2003).

A covert children's culture has always existed on playgrounds and in schools. The children's culture of the past, however, was produced by children and propagated through personal child-to-child contact. Children's culture of today is increasingly created by adults and dispersed via television for the purpose of inducing children to consume. (The use of the Internet may provide a countervailing trend in this context.) As they carefully subvert middle-class parents' obsession with achievement, play as a serious enterprise, and self-improvement-oriented "quality time" (a subversion that in my opinion probably contributes to the public good), advertisers connect children's culture to their products. McDonald's commercials reflect these themes, although less blatantly than many advertisers.

Attempting to walk a tightrope between tapping the power of children's subversive culture and offending the middle-class guardians of propriety, McDonald's developed a core of so-called "slice-of-life" children's ads. Casting no adults in the commercials, advertisers depict a group of preteens engaged in "authentic" conversations around a McDonald's table covered with burgers, fries, and shakes. Using kid's slang to describe toys in various McDonald's promotions, children discuss the travails of childhood with each other. Twenty-first century McDonald's ads declare: *I'm lovin' it.* Global ads proclaim the slogan in every language, creating the ultimate hyperreal tie-in between desire and consumption. Hip-hop artists and dancers move to the groove of the McHappiness on 30-second spots.

In many commercials children make adults the butt of their jokes or share jokes that adults don't understand (Goldman, 1992; Seiter, 1993). McDonald's subtly attempts to draw some of the power of children's subversive culture onto their products without anyone but the kids knowing. Such slice-of-life ads are opaque to the degree that adults watching them don't see the advertiser's effort to connect McDonald's with this subversive culture. This "oppositional aesthetic" (Jenkins, 1998) has fueled numerous aspects of children's commercial culture (*Malcolm in the Middle, Hannah Montana, Family Guy, The Simpsons,* etc.) that play on children's differences from adults. It is a key weapon in the corporate construction of childhood.

McDonald's Is Home

McDonald's perpetuates what Shelton (1993) referred to as a hegemonic logic—a way of doing business that privileges conformity, callously defends middle-class norms, fights to the death for established virtue, and resists social change. This hegemonic logic holds little regard for concepts such as justice or morality—McDonald's morality is contingent on what sells. This concept is well illustrated in McDonald's emphasis on the primacy of home and family values in its advertising. Kroc and his corporate leaders understood their most important marketing priority was to portray McDonald's as a family kind of place. As they focused on connecting McDonald's to America and the family, they modified the red-and-white ceramic take-out restaurants to look more like the suburban homes that sprang up throughout America in the late 1950s and 1960s. Ad campaigns proclaimed that McDonald's was home, and that anywhere Ronald goes "he is at home." Like many other ads in American hyperreality, McDonald's home and family ads privilege the private sphere, not the public sphere, as the important space where life is lived. As an intrinsically self-contained unit, the family is removed from the public realm of society; such a depiction, however, conceals the ways politics and economics shape everyday family life. The greatest irony of these ads is that even as they isolate the family from any economic connections, they promote the commodification of family life. A form of double-speak is discernible in this situation: The family is an end in itself; the family is an instrumental consumption unit whose ultimate purpose is to benefit corporate profits and growth.

McDonald's ads deploy home and family as paleosymbols that position McDonald's as the defender of "the American way of life." Kroc (1977) never knew what paleosymbols were, but he understood that McDonald's public image should be, in his words, a "combination YMCA, Girl Scouts, and Sunday School." Devised to tap into the right-wing depiction of the traditional family under attack from feminists, homosexuals, and other "screwballs," these so-called legitimation ads don't sell hamburgers—they sell social relations. Amid social upheaval and instability, McDonald's endures as a rock of ages, a refuge in a world gone mad. McDonald's brings us together, provides a safe haven for our children. The needs the legitimation ads tap are real, but the consumption panacea they provide is false (Goldman, 1992). After its phenomenal growth in the 1960s, McDonald's realized that it was no longer the "cute little company" of the 1950s (Love, 1986). The antiwar, civil rights, and other social movements of the late 1960s were repugnant to Kroc's American values. Such views, when combined with the marketing need for McDonald's to legitimate itself now that it was an American "big business," made home and family the obvious battle field in the legitimation campaign. As the public faith in corporations declined, McDonald's used the paleosymbols to create an environment of confidence. Going against the grain of a social context perceived to be hostile to big business, the ads worked. The lyrics of accompanying music read: "You, you're the one. So loving, strong, and patient. Families like yours made all the states a nation. Our families are our past, our future and our pride. Whatever roots we come from, we're growing side by side" (quoted in Goldman, 1992, p. 95).

The world of home and family portrayed by the McDonald's legitimation ads is a terrain without conflict or tension. McDonald's ads are created for demographics; for example, in Atlanta, television ads are almost 100% African American. Urban areas tap into hip-hop for commercials, and middle America has ads that reflect the "heartland." The genius of McDonald's ads creates a seamless union between Rockwellian American life and the hyperreal pulse of house or hip-hop music. Declaring family values and love with every breath, McDonald's has globally become everyone's safe haven. The grand irony of McDonald's family ads reveals that under the flag of traditional family values McDonald's actually undermines the very qualities it claims to promote.

The McDonald's experience depicted in ads does not involve a family sharing a common experience—each market segment experiences it in a different, potentially conflicting way. In terms of everyday life McDonald's does not encourage long, leisurely, interactive family meals. The seats and tables are designed to be uncomfortable to the point that customers will eat quickly and leave. In the larger scheme of things, family values, America, and home are nothing more than cynical marketing tools designed to legitimate McDonald's to different market segments. The cynicism embedded in ads by McDonald's and scores of other companies undermines the social fabric, making the culture our children inhabit a colder and more malicious place. Such cynicism leads corporations to develop new forms of techno power that can be used to subvert democracy and justice in the quest for new markets. Such cynicism holds up Ronald McDonald/Ray Kroc as heroes, while ignoring authentic heroes—men and women who struggle daily to lead good lives, be good parents, and extend social justice. As students of culture, we wait and watch, as McDonald's recreates itself through the decades to replicate its original mandates—set in place by the man himself.

Note

Revised portions of this chapter appeared in Hammer. R., & Kellner, D. (Eds.). (2009). *Media/cultural studies: Critical approaches*. New York: Peter Lang.

References

Abercrombie, N. (1994). Authority and consumer society. In R. Keat, N. Whiteley, & N. Abercrombie (Eds.), *The authority of the consumer* (pp. 43–57). New York: Routledge.

Boas, M., & Chain, S. (1976). *Big Mac: The unauthorized story of McDonald's*. New York: Dutton.

Cook, D. (2004). *The commodification of childhood: The children's clothing industry and the rise of the child-consumer*. Durham, NC: Duke University Press.

Fischer, P. M., Schwartz, M. P., Richards, J. W. Jr, Goldstein, A. O., & Rojas, T. H. (1991). Brand logo recognition by children aged 3 to 6 years. *Journal of the American Medical Association, 266*(22), 3145–3148.

Garfield, B. (1992). Nice ads, but that theme is not what you want. *Advertising Age, 63*(8), 53.

Giroux, H. (1988). *Teachers as intellectuals: Toward a critical pedagogy of learning*. Granby, MA: Bergin & Garvey.

Giroux, H. (1994). *Disturbing pleasures: Learning popular culture*. New York: Routledge.

Goldman, R. (1992). *Reading ads socially*. New York: Routledge.

Harvey, D. (1989). *The condition of postmodernity*. Cambridge, MA: Basil Blackwell.

Hume, S. (1993). Fast food caught in the middle. *Advertising Age, 64*(6), 12–15.

Jenkins, H. (1998). Introduction: Childhood innocence and other modern myths. In H. Jenkins (Ed.), *The children's culture reader* (pp. 1–37). New York: NYU Press.

Jenkins, H. (2003). The poachers and the stormtroopers: Cultural convergence in the digital age. Available: http://web.mit.edu/cms/People/henry3/pub/stormtroopers.htm

Kellner, D. (1989). *Critical theory, Marxism, and modernity*. Baltimore, MD: Johns Hopkins University Press.

Kenway, J., & Bullen, E. (2001). *Consuming children: Entertainment, advertising, and education*. Philadelphia, PA: Open University Press.

Kincheloe, J. (1999). *How do we tell the workers?: The socioeconomic foundations of work and vocational education*. Boulder, CO: Westview.

Kincheloe, J. (2002). *The sign of the burger: McDonald's and the culture of power*. Philadelphia, PA: Temple University Press.

Kroc, R. (1977). *Grinding it out: The making of McDonald's.* New York: St. Martin's Paperbacks.

Leidner, R. (1993). *Fast food, fast talk: Service work and the routinization of everyday life.* Berkeley: University of California Press.

Love, J. (1986). *McDonald's: Behind the arches.* New York: Bantam.

Luxenberg, S. (1985). *Roadside empires: How the chains franchised.* New York: Viking Penguin.

Molnar, A. (1996). *Giving kids the business: The commercialization of America's schools.* Boulder, CO: Westview Press.

Ritzer, G. (1993). *The McDonaldization of society.* Thousand Oaks, CA: Pine Forge.

Schlosser, E. (2001). *Fast food nation: The dark side of the all-American meal.* Boston: Houghton Mifflin.

Seiter, E. (1993). *Sold separately: Parents and children in consumer culture.* New Brunswick, NJ: Rutgers University Press.

Shelton, A. (1993). Writing McDonald's, eating the past: McDonald's as a postmodern space. *Studies in Symbolic Interaction, 15,* 103–118.

Shiva, V. (1997). Vandana Shiva on McDonald's exploitation and the global economy. Available: http://www.mcspotlight.org/people/interviews/vandana_transcript.html

Spigel, L. (2001). *Welcome to the dollhouse: Popular media and postwar suburbs.* Durham, NC: Duke University Press.

Steinberg, S. R. (2007). Reading media critically. In D. Macedo & S. R. Steinberg (Eds.), *Media literacy: A reader* (pp. xii–xvi). New York: Peter Lang.

Steinberg, S. R., & Kincheloe, J. (Eds.). (2004). *Kinderculture: The corporate construction of childhood.* Boulder, CO: Westview Press.

Yan, Y. (1997). McDonald's in Beijing: The localization of Americana. In J. L. Watson (Ed.), *Golden arches east: McDonald's in east Asia* (pp. 39–76). Stanford, CA: Stanford University Press.

12 Barbie

The Bitch Can Buy Anything

Shirley R. Steinberg

Playing Barbies in the fifth grade consisted of lugging plastic cases laden with "outfits" to the playground and constructing scenarios around Barbie and "getting" Ken. I knew at this early age that Barbie (as a female) must have an "outfit" for every occasion and that wearing the same thing within some unspoken frame of time was just not done.

When I was twelve or thirteen I began meticulously recording on a calendar what I wore each day. I made sure that at least a month went by before I wore an outfit again. When I was a high-school teacher, my students called attention to my idiosyncrasy by applauding the first day that I duplicated an outfit in the classroom. Did Barbie construct this behavior, or do I just love clothes? Cultural studies scholars have written in detail on the feminist readings of Barbie, the cultural text of Barbie, and the place of Barbie in childhood. In this chapter, I discuss the cultural and the consumptive aspects of the now-50-year-old Barbie.

Where does the text of Barbie begin? Fifty years ago, Mattel invested in the production of a slim, blonde doll who (that?) wore a variety of coordinated "outfits." While on vacation in Europe, Mattel co-founder Ruth Handler discovered Lily. Lily was a prominent star of comics—a sexy blonde with loose morals who adorned dashboards throughout Germany and Switzerland. Her origin is not well documented, although her lineage has been traced back to a *Lily* comic strip. Handler decided to take the model of Lily back to the States and create a doll that could wear multiple outfits. She named her Barbie, after her daughter, Barbara. The promotional hook that Handler cited was the possibility that the doll could have multiple outfits and girls needed to own only one doll. Ironically, the first Barbie was designed to be the only Barbie for each girl, and the marketing goal was to tap into the supposed innate female desire to own as many clothes as possible. As we all know, the intent changed drastically within 15 years, and the goal became to own as many Barbies as possible; indeed, one cannot buy individual outfits any longer, if you want your doll to change clothes, you buy another doll.

Physiologically, Barbie had perky breasts, a tiny waist and long, slender legs. Much has been written from a feminist perspective about Barbie, discussing the doll's unrealistic body shape, and so on. Barbie was created to be thin so that layers of designer fabric would flow nicely over her body. She was, first and foremost, a model—fabric by Dior, designs by Mackie—nothing was beyond reach for her.

I am not offended by her figure; I do wonder, however, about her poorly constructed private parts—or lack thereof. Barbie is a plastic formation of non-genitalia. Having neither anything "down there," a belly button, nor nipples on her boobs, Barbie has reached a half of a century in age without having sexual organs.

Speaking of private parts, in 1964, Barbie was given a boyfriend, Ken—a boy minus genitals. Ken's crotch was (and is) as flat and smooth as Barbie's. I remember specifically my disappointment in disrobing my first Ken—there was nothing to see. Possibly that physical defect is in line with the personality that Ken has displayed throughout the years (although Earring Ken had a certain flair). Ken and Barbie have gotten as far as their wedding but never past it. The couple never had a wedding night, and Barbie is always seen pushing a stroller of cousins, younger siblings, or friends. Only Ken's friends of color, Derek and Steve, radiate any machismo sexuality, however, they are still crotchless. Finally, after 45 years of never getting it on, Barbie and Ken "announced" they were breaking up—at the time of this writing, they are still "close friends."

Within months of her creation, Barbie was a sensation. Mattel had transformed toys, especially dolls, and Barbie became "us." Young girls were frenzied to own a Barbie, each one coming in her own long, thin box, wearing a black-and-white striped swim suit. Barbie had a blonde ponytail and earrings. She was a teen model. Girls moved from cradling baby dolls to demanding the latest in haute couture à la Mattel. Barbie was sexy, although most of her owners were not even aware of the genre of sexiness—they just loved their Barbies.

Will Shop for Research

I take my work seriously. I am an active researcher. I love the challenge of finding strange and wonderful factoids of trivia in little-known academic nooks and crannies. However, Barbie wreaked financial havoc in my life. About 15 years ago, I became fascinated with Barbie's effect on young girls. I started to pick up Barbies, Barbie furniture, Barbie comics, Barbie books, Barbie jewelry, and Barbie toys wherever I went. I even found Benetton Barbie in the Istanbul airport (under a sign featuring the Marlboro man).

In order to do thorough textual analyses of Barbie and Barbie accoutrements, I needed to purchase my artifacts. I sit now, with great embarrassment, in an office with scores of Barbies, Kens, Skippers, and a plethora of "ethnic" and "special edition" Barbies. I have Barbie watches, a $300 Barbie jacket from F.A.O. Schwartz, a Barbie McDonald's playset, Christmas playset, and bakery set. I bought my husband a Nicole Miller Barbie tie, and silk Barbie boxers (which he immediately re-gifted to me). I have Barbie board games and Barbie computer games—including *Barbie Goes Shopping* and *Babie Design Studio.* I have Barbie books, purses, records, CDs, DVDs, socks, jewelry, and T-shirts. Barbie shopping can get out of control. When children come to visit, they quickly plow through my Barbies and then ask, "Do you have anything else?" Obviously I don't have enough. What kid law was written that expressed the need to have multiples of any and every toy and object? Even the cyber-conscious Webkinz fanatics are not happy with one, or two, or three—they must have every Webkinz made. Barbies are that way: you can never have enough.

My ownership of Barbies and paraphernalia qualifies me as an expert. I am a consumer and a scholar; there is no better combination. Historically, I come by the expertise naturally: I have had Barbies since she was invented. However, as I trace my Barbie autobiography, I am only able to single out my fetish for outfits as a permanent influence à la Barbie. I remain untouched from other taint— unless one looks at my research.

Is There Anything Barbie Doesn't Have?

Discussing what Barbie doesn't have is easier than what she does have. The list is much shorter. Barbie doesn't have a locomotive, a battleship (although she is a sailor), a rocket (although she is an astronaut), or an Uzi submachine gun (although she is a soldier). Thematically, Mattel has not created the Homeless Barbie, the Abortion Barbie, the Alcoholic Barbie, or the S&M Bondage Barbie. As far as special editions, Barbie has not come out as a criminal—she has, however, come out in special editions of fairy tales (never a witch), "true" history, careers, and in different ethnicities—different from white, that is. There is no Northern Barbie, but the Southern Beauty Barbie features "today's Southern belle with charm and style!"

Barbie does not have holes in her clothes (unless placed there by fashion designer Bob Mackie); she never walks because she has a plane, boat, Corvette, bicycle, horse, roller blades, and Ken. Barbie does not have a favorite color other than hot pink; she has one logo and no last name. Actually, I once heard her last name is Roberts; so, where are her people from? Barbie does not have holiday sets for Chanukah or Ramadan, although she does have them for Easter and Christmas. There is no Kmart Barbie, but there are Wal-Mart, Saks Fifth Avenue, Gap, Bloomingdale's, Avon, and Nicole Miller (the fashion designer, whose ties cost $60) Barbies.

It is also easier to look at what Barbie is *not*. Barbie is never sad, never unavailable, and "saves the day" in every story written about her. Barbie is timeless; she existed in the days of the *Mayflower*, she was Dorothy in Oz, and has run for U.S. president several times. She has never been a cook but has been a chef; has never been a construction worker but has been a fashion designer. She has been a soloist, a rock star, and the mythical tooth fairy. Barbie is exclusively thematic; Ken, Christie, and the rest are occasionally given professions.

The Bitch Who Can Buy Everything

And she does. From the pink condo, to the swimming pool, to the RV, to the recording stage, to more friends than anyone. Everyone loves Barbie and Barbie loves everyone. Barbie proves to us that if we try hard enough, we can own anything and everything. Barbie always succeeds. She becomes whatever she sets her mind to. She influences generations of children and adults and exists as a perpetual reminder of all that is good, wholesome, and pink in our lives. Barbie is a true American. She stands for the family values that our country holds dear. She is strictly heterosexual, self-providing, philanthropic, and moral. She is also ready to bring "other" people into her life, no matter what color or ethnicity.

Barbie moves in and out of social circles with ease. Her plate is filled with charity organizations and doing "good." The "Love to Read" Barbie comes with two children (one black and one white) and a book; for every LTR Barbie sold, Mattel donates a dollar to the Reading Is Fundamental organization. As consumers, we can support reading by purchasing this doll—and that makes all the difference.

Barbie and Corporate Lovers

While Barbie may be a virgin in sexual relationships, she is a whore in the corporate world. Barbie has "been in bed" with more Fortune 500 members than anyone. She has worked in and owned her own Pizza Hut and McDonald's, she is a special Wal-Mart edition; she is a star of *Baywatch* and a perennial guest in Happy Meals. Disney's Epcot Center features a Magical World of Barbie show, with dancers, singers, and fireworks. Avon regularly offers a special edition Barbie, and Hallmark issues a new Barbie Christmas ornament each year. eBay is filled with people searching for the rare Holiday Barbie each year. Barbie wanders in and out of corporate headquarters with ease. Companies know that if they tap into her resources, it is a quick ride to higher profits. No one really wants the tiny hamburger in the child's meal; they are, instead, looking for the Barbie—which one is she? The Kenyan? The ballerina? The wedding Barbie? As a professional, Barbie chooses from her cellular phone, her digital camera, and numerous pink briefcases for "just the right thing" for breaking that glass ceiling. Many of the Barbies with store tie-ins come complete with a store credit card and branded shopping bags.

As a professional, Barbie has set records for changing vocations. Early on, she was a nurse, a baby-sitter, and a secretary. Within months of political correctness, she became a doctor, a pilot, and a businesswoman. Naturally, many of her careers still smack of nurturing; how can one avoid it with a perpetual pink motif? One of my favorite fashion sets is the Caring Careers Fashion Gift Set. These "play pieces for Barbie at work" include a firefighter suit with pink trim, a teacher set, and a veterinarian's smock. Dr. Barbie is a pediatrician with a little black child and a little white child, all adorned in pink and blue. Astronaut Barbie came out in the 1980s and reappeared in the late 1990s. As a part of the Career Collection, this Barbie first appeared as a space pioneer. A newer version highlights Space Week and NASA and "encourages children of all ages to discover the past and future of the exploration in space." All of the boxes featuring careers have the slogan "We Girls Can Do Anything!" emblazoned across the front. Police Officer Barbie is a "friend to all in the community! In her glittery evening dress, Police Officer Barbie shines with pride at the Police Awards Ball. Everyone applauds as she receives the Best Police Officer Award for her courageous acts in the community." Police Officer Barbie comes with a badge and a short formal gown for the ball.

No group of careers could be complete without acknowledging our armed forces. As sergeants and majors, these booted girls march to the beat of a proud, patriotic America. Choosing a favorite would be hard, but, well, okay, I guess mine is Desert Storm Barbie. "Wearing authentic desert battle dress uniforms" of camouflage material,

> Sergeant Barbie is a medic, and she's ready for duty! Staff Sergeant Ken is ready too! Their berets bear the distinctive 101st Airborne unit insignia with the motto: Rendezvous with Destiny. Both are proud, patriotic Americans serving their country wherever they are needed.

Rounding up the professions, the Barbie for President Gift Set was introduced in 1992. This text is from a Toys R Us limited edition:

> Barbie hits the campaign trail in spectacular style! Dressed in her winning red and gold suit she's the picture perfect candidate to get out the vote. Then, at her inaugural ball, the festive crowd cheers as Barbie enters in a sensational sparkling gown sprinkled with silver stars!

We girls can do anything. How about the $75 Statue of Liberty Barbie? Holding the torch of freedom, this golden-haired doll stands perched on a plastic island, adorned with a shimmery crown, beckoning all who will listen to join her in liberty and justice for all. Of course, it may be the only way we can see Lady Liberty, as all visits to her shores are now forbidden.

Ethnic Barbies Make for Good Sales

Barbie's other identities lie in ethnic and historical roots. Not satisfied with the existential Barbie, Mattel allowed Barbie to revisit, ergo, rewrite the past through a series of historical dolls. Each doll belongs to a collector's set, usually priced between $5 and $100 more than a regular Barbie. A collector's doll should be kept in her box, appreciating in value as the ages tick by.

To understand how a corporation defines ethnicity, one must take a little boat down Disneyland's or Disneyworld's exhibit *It's a Small World*. As we sail down that channel, listening to hundreds of little dolls sing—incessantly—we see different peoples grouped together on their continents. Northern countries show a preponderance of buildings and clothing, while countries from south of the equator feature dolls wearing scant clothing, selling vegetables, taking a siesta, or climbing trees. There are no buildings evident in Africa, and in South American countries, only huts appear. Taking *It's a Small World* seriously as a metaphor for The World, we can understand the consciousness that constructed Mattel's line of ethnic Barbies—which Mattel calls its "Dolls of the World" collection, and which it first introduced in the early 1980s.

Imagine we are sailing through our own small world, meeting these diverse Barbies, and listening to them describing their heritage. Each Barbie is distinct in native dress and manner. The Jamaican Barbie comes with a red bandana and large hoop earrings. Many exclaim how like Aunt Jemima or a slave she looks. Jamaican Barbie claims that her people speak patois, "a kind of Jamaica talk" filled with African and English words. She also insists Jamaicans are very "happy" people and are "filled with boonoonoonoos, much happiness." Culturally, Jamaican Barbie teaches us that her country is filled with higglers (female vendors or merchants) who sell their food in open markets. Jamaican Barbie is prettily packed in hot pink, along with pictures of Bob Marley, sugar cane, and palm trees. In keeping with the island theme, we next move to the Polynesian Barbie. Her box never mentions which island she is from, just somewhere within the thirteen groups of tropical islands. We are told that people who live on these islands live closely together and are kind to each another. We also learn that Polynesians like luaus and like to eat.

Another Barbie "of color" is the Indian Barbie. Unlike her island cousins, her box shows a picture of a building, the Taj Mahal. The box reminds us that India is a very old country and that most people from India eat only vegetables and rice "with their fingers." We do not learn whether or not Indians are happy or kind. None of these "ethnic" Barbies discuss their skin color or hair texture, and they do not mention physical attributes. Naturally, they are all standing on tiptoe. Puerto Rican Barbie is dressed all in white as she readies herself for—dare I say?—her confirmation. No self-respecting Puerto Rican girlfriend I have has ever done anything but shriek in horror at this plastic sista.

As we visit northern Europe, we do not meet amalgamated Barbies; there are no British Isles Barbies or Scandinavian Barbies. Each Barbie from northern Europe has her own country. The German Barbie looks splendid in her milk-maid's outfit with long blonde braids. We are welcomed to a country known for its "breathtaking beauty and hard-working people." Evidently the south of the equator Barbies do not work, or at least not hard. German Barbie's box mentions modern cities, museums, art galleries, and industries. The Norwegian Barbie tells us of her mythological tradition and describes her people as "tall, sturdy, fair-skinned, blonde and blue eyed." Food is not mentioned nearly as often on northern Barbies as on their southern counterparts. Evidently the farther north one moves, the less people talk or think about food.

There is no specifically "American" Barbie. However, there is a Native American Barbie in the Dolls of the World Collection. Native American Barbie is a part of a "proud Indian heritage, rich in culture and tradition." Long ago her people belonged to a tribe. She is dressed as a Plains Indian, yet she describes homes like those constructed by eastern Indians. She mentions her pride in her people *three times*.

What is going on here? Mattel has defined "ethnicity" as "other than white." Regular blonde Barbie is the standard from which the "others" are derived. As it emulates the dominant culture, the norm is Barbie, without a title. All other Barbies are qualified by their language, foods, and "native" dances. Attempting to be multicultural, parents buy these dolls for their children to teach them about "other" people. No "regular" Barbie ever talks about her regular diet, the personality of "her" people, and her customs. Only the designated "ethnic" dolls have those qualifications. Like the sign in the local Kmart designating where ethnic hair products are located, Barbie has otherized dolls into dominant and marginal cultures. Barbie's whiteness privileges her to not be questioned; she is the standard against which all others are measured.

Corporate Writing of History

In the early 1990s, a few years after the launch of the ethnic Barbie line, Mattel introduced the American Stories Collection, featuring a Civil War Nurse Barbie, a Pilgrim Barbie, a Pioneer Barbie, and an American Indian Barbie (there she is again). Each doll comes with a storybook that places Barbie in the middle of essential historical action. Each book ends with Barbie "saving the day" and changing history for the better.

Predictably, Pilgrim Barbie meets Squanto and he teaches her how to plant corn. We are assured: "He wasn't savage at all." Pilgrim Barbie grows a successful crop of corn and decides to share it with her neighbors; hence, the first Thanksgiving. And Barbie was there! Conveniently neglected are the Pilgrims' grave robbing, stealing of Indian lands, and, yes, the sticky matter of genocide.

Since Betsy Ross already made the flag in 1776, Colonial Barbie decides to make a quilt to celebrate the thirteen colonies. The quilt was embroidered "Happy Birthday America" and Barbie and her female helpers were congratulated for it and treated "with great respect." Western Barbie cleverly brings dried apples on the long journey during westward expansion. When her friends get hungry, Barbie produces the apples and makes a delicious apple pie. American Indian Barbie takes care of a papoose, parentage unknown, and tells stories to the little Indian villagers. I will stop here, to avoid an overload of saccharine.

Each storybook is signed on the back with a personal note from the author. History becomes firm in the eyes of the reader as the author legitimizes it. Here are a couple of examples:

> In writing this story for you, I have learned so much! What I noticed most about the story of the Pilgrims and Thanksgiving is how the Native Americans became their friends and helped these strangers in a new land.
>
> I hope you enjoyed imagining Barbie as a colonial girl. Perhaps you will think of her on the next 4th of July and what it must have been like during the early days when America was first "born."

These authors tell consumers that history is being taught in a friendly way through Mattel. Children now place Barbie within historical contexts in order to under-stand what really happened.

Fairy tales and fiction are not immune from Mattel's rewriting. The Children's Collector Series features heroines from different stories. In this series, "Childhood favorites 'come to life' with Barbie." Young girls are encouraged to, for instance, "Play out the story of Rapunzel" with Barbie. Barbie as Scarlett O'Hara was one of the most successful dolls of the 1990s. Promoted in a 30-minute infomercial by Kathie Lee Gifford (a TV Barbie), the doll was sold as essential for anyone who was affected by the novel or movie version of *Gone with the Wind*: "See Barbie as your favorite character, Scarlett," Kathie Lee chortled. She recalled that when she was a little girl, Barbie was her favorite doll and there is nothing more special than having her best friend become Scarlett. The line between reality and fantasy was blurred. The *real* Barbie was acting as a character?

Buying Barbie Will Teach Us to Read

In its merchandising Mattel recognizes the importance of reading and educa-tion, and has created hundreds of types of reading materials featuring Barbie. Not satisfied with the toy market, Mattel has branched out to magazines, books, newspapers, and film.

The *Adventures with Barbie* book series, from the early 1990s, featured a set of paperback books in which "Barbie stars in her own series of fabulous adventures that tie inspiring messages in with action, suspense and fun with friends—and set an example of independence, responsibility and kindness for young girls every-where." *Barbie Magazine,* a magazine for girls, gives fashion tips, promotes new Barbie themes, teaches fun crafts, and gives beauty advice. On the Internet, girls can explore *Barbie.com,* which "gives" stories, puzzles, style advice, and trend-set-ting tips. Little Golden Books for toddlers include several Barbie titles, including *Very Busy Barbie* (where Barbie is a model who gives up her career), *A Picnic Surprise* (where Barbie finds an old lady's puppy instead of having fun), and *Barbie, the Big Splash* (where Barbie's photo shoot is spoiled, but she is able to take disappointment). We constantly are bombarded by the altruistic blonde (in the books she is usually monocolored) giving up something sensational for the good of all humankind. Girls are taught at an early age that it is more important to give up one's own goal than to disappoint someone else. Disney did it well with *The Little Mermaid* and *Beauty and the Beast.* It is a female's place to sacrifice for the good of others. Remember Pocahontas? Esmeralda? You get the point.

Not to be outdone by three-foot-tall competitors, adults have their own Barbie literature: *Barbie Collector Magazine* and several weekly and monthly newspapers, the most circulated paper being *Miller's Market Report: News, Advice and Collecting Tips for Barbie Doll Investors.* The tabloid features Barbie events; in one issue, 19 "don't miss" gatherings were advertised, including the Great Barbie Show of Southern California, Barbie Comes to Bloomingdale's, Seventh Annual Barbie Grants-A-Wish, and many regional conventions. Barbie clubs adorn the United States from sea to sequined shining sea. There is an annual Barbie world convention, classes on Barbie, as well as various conferences and international summits. To emulate a global con-sciousness, Mattel organizes these summits for women and girls to caucus about their needs and desires from Mattel for the twenty-first century. Always the educator, Barbie proves to us that reading and schooling cannot be left behind. Math becomes essential in order to add up the values of vintage dolls and collectors' items. For many, Barbie is a full-time occupation. Barbie is the only non-human figure in Hollywood's famed wax museum. Naturally, she has her own Barbie Boutique on Fifth Avenue adjoining F.A.O. Schwartz, a store that provides myriads of books, magazines, videos, and objects devoted to Barbie. The market flourishes.

Is She Good or Is She Bad?

Is Barbie good for children? Should we allow our girls to play with them? How many Barbies should a child own? Does Barbie teach us what true beauty is? Can a child have self-esteem and not look like Barbie? Should we bend to peer pressure and allow our children to reside in pink-trimmed junior condos, dreaming of far-away places and exotic men? Does Barbie help construct childhood consciousness? Do Barbie-centered websites increase the obsession with pink consumerism and girlishness?

Of course Barbie helps construct consciousness—just like any other feature of kinderculture. The effect of Barbie's curriculum and pedagogy is idiosyncratic—for some Barbie facilitates conformity; for others, she inspires resistance. Multiple readings aside, Barbie operates within the boundaries of particular cultural logics. She celebrates whiteness—blonde whiteness in particular—as a standard for feminine beauty; she reifies anorexic figures coupled with large breasts as objects of male desire. She supports unbridled consumerism as a reason for living. She unquestioningly embraces American virtue and supports the erasure of the colonial genocide in America's past. Make no mistake: she is a Christian, not a Jew, and *certainly* not a Muslim—she is mainstream and is *not* countercultural. No poor girl is Barbie as she repetitively displays her upper-middle-class credentials. Again, the curriculum may not always take, because no effect is guaranteed, but we must always be aware of the terrain on which Barbie operates.

Barbie enthusiasts feel great anticipation about the next line of Barbies. Having featured professions, movie stars, stories, sports, and fashion, could Barbie ever run out of themes? By maintaining authenticity, Mattel is able to continue rewriting history and life. Re-invention of Barbie is a constant in Mattel world. As Barbie adapts to current lifestyles and girl-fads, cross-marketing with Disney and Hollywood gives her extra earning power.

I'd like to see Barbie a bit more realistic: in keeping with real-life professions, wouldn't we be wise to wait for a factory worker Barbie, a prostitute Barbie, a drug pusher Barbie—can a pimp Ken be far behind? What about more politically active Barbies? Protest Barbie, chained to her dream house, Bisexual Barbie, complete with both Ken and Midge (or Steve and Christie)? Green Barbie? Bo-ho Barbie? Neo-Marxist Barbie?

Barbie is 50 Years Young

As the fiftieth anniversary of Barbie's birth has come and gone (March, 2009 marked Barbie's fiftieth birthday), marketing and publicity for the birthday was unparalleled. Enormous websites were developed to herald in the birth of the modern-day princess of consumerism. Sponsors like Mercedes-Benz, Bloomingdale's, Sephora, and a few plebian corporations were the embedded links that took us directly to corporate sites. Imagine a 10-year-old linking onto the Barbie's-fiftieth website, and being taken directly to the showroom of the new Benz.

The unattainable (at least, for us) ticket to New York Fashion Week 2009 was given to Barbie, as designers Rachel Roy, Michael Kors, Diane Von Furstenberg, and Tommy Hilfiger dressed models as retro-Barbies cum the new millennium. Creating a postmodern collection of original Barbie styles with the new millennial look, the show was premiered on Valentine's Day. Mothers, not daughters, attended the runway show, replete with their own Barbie memories, emulations, and lots of pink—I mean *lots* of it. Karl Lagerfeld created an entire "art" installation celebrating the plastic blonde's half-century. Treating Barbie as a fashion idol, a heroine, she becomes reality as flesh and blood beings retreat into becoming simulacra—is this marketing at its best? Lines blurred between toy and reality have created an industry that marketing has turned into art, culture, memory, and history. One can only wait until the Ken fiftieth, where he finally comes out, does a full three-snap at society and legally marries Steven, and drives off to his honeymoon in a company-supplied Mercedes.

Note

Revised portions of this chapter appeared in Hammer. R., & Kellner, D. (Eds.). (2009). *Media/cultural studies: Critical approaches.* New York: Peter Lang.

13 Consuming Skin

Dermographies of Female Subjection and Abjection[1]

Jane Kenway and Elizabeth Bullen

> The skin figures. It is what we know of others and our selves. We show our selves in and on our skins, and our skins figure out the things we are and mean: our health, youth, beauty, power, enjoyment, fear, fatigue, embarrassments or suffering.
>
> (Steven Connor, 2004, p. 50)

Benthien (2002) talks of "the semantics of the skin" and says it involves "a great many strategies of interpretation and staging" (p. xi). She identifies four main cultural interpretations of skin that have existed over time. We begin by outlining these as they are crucial to an understanding of the many ways skin has been commodified. One view, that has both lost favor and been reinvented, is that the skin is "the mirror of the soul," reflecting psychological, cognitive, and emotional facets of the individual. A second, unpopular, perspective is that skin and the self are irrevocably one and the same—skin is identity and destiny. More common perspectives are, thirdly, that the skin is "the place where identity is formed and assigned" (p. 1); it is a surface for projecting the self and for designating others. Finally, "the skin is the place where boundary negations take place" (p. viii) between self and others. In this view, the skin is a site of contestation over identity.

As this short taxonomy suggests, the skin has considerable semantic depth and anything with such depth lends itself to multiple significations. Of course, multiple significations are the life-blood of the work and world of the commodity:

> In consumer culture we are encouraged to read skin, especially feminine skin, as something that needs to be worked upon in order to be protected from the passage of time or the severity of the external world, or in order to retain its marker of gender difference in the softness of its feel.
>
> (Ahmed & Stacey, 2001, p. 1)

In this chapter, we ask, how does consumer culture "narrate the skin" (Ahmed & Stacey, 2001, p. 11)? How does skin function as a site where female subjection and abjection are produced and reproduced, and what does it teach us about femininity, feminism and consumerism?[2]

Skin Pedagogies

In terms of the commodification of femininity and female sexuality, skin is a powerful signifier of the "material imagination" because it is "both matter and image, stuff and sign" (Connor, 2004, p. 41). According to the aesthetic logic of the commodity, the skin is akin to packaging: the surface of the self women present to the world. For most women, the skin they aspire to and labor to perfect can be compared to the "second skin" of the commodity, which Haug (1986) argues is usually "incomparably more perfect than the first" (p. 50). The second skin, or packaging, mediates the relationship between product and consumer, self and other. In a world in which feminine beauty sells and is sold, the skin is the surface which it is assumed must, through its "amorous glances," do the work of seductive selling. Haug claims that no commodity reflects its "perfect" packaging. For the majority of women and girls in an image-obsessed culture, the converse is true: the skin of real women and girls rarely conforms to the sleek, smooth, blemish-, hair-, and pigment-free perfection of the advertisement. Their "first" skin must therefore be continually worked upon and a "second skin" worked towards. In this context, women consume skin care products and procedures in order to produce and package themselves as feminine, desirable, successful, indeed, "consumable."

A vast array of products, services and perfectly crafted airbrushed, digitally enhanced images, enable/encourage/persuade women and girls to work on their skin or to pay others to do so. There are sprays, bottles, jars, tubes, tubs and pots of creams, butters, oils, perfumes, lotions, gels, glosses, waxes, and exfoliants. There are rubs, scrubs, sponges, scarifiers, razors, wands, pencils, powders, perfumes, concealers, highlighters. Skin treatments include tanning, peeling, lifting, tucking, sucking, inserting, waxing, plucking, and depilation; they can involve laser, botox, and fillers or "insertables." Advertisements, music videos, magazines, television shows, movies, billboards, and websites all convey the message that a female imperative is to nourish and enhance the skin. Giroux (2004) argues that pedagogy can no longer be considered as confined to the site of schooling. It needs to be understood as applying to everyday political sites in "which identities are shaped and desires mobilized" and where "experiences take on form and meaning" (p. 62). Skin pedagogies educate women and girls to work towards the second skin. We read global ideoscapes and mediascapes in terms of Giroux's assumption that culture plays a central role in producing narratives, metaphors, and images that exercise a powerful pedagogical force over how people think of themselves and their relationships to others. The fantasy that all these products, services, and direct and indirect promotions convey is that you can—and need to—perfect your skin. Its natural state can be changed—with the right beauty "remedies" or "therapies."

Connor (2004) argues that "if the skin has become more than ever visible it is as the visible object of many different forms of imaginary and actual assault" (p. 50). With the fetishization of the perfect skin comes the devious "assault" of commerce and the requirement that women and girls enter into a lifetime regime of skin care and beauty consumerism. If regimes of female skin care and adornment are as old as civilization itself, the cultural and historical forces driving the particular forms these regimens take are by no means homogenous. We argue that in the twenty-first century, the dermographies of female subjection and abjection have been shaped by consumer culture and its relationship to femininity and feminism.

Ewen (1976) traces the birth of contemporary consumer culture to the industrial planning and scientific management of the corporate sector in the 1920s; the ascent of the advertising, movie, fashion, and cosmetic industries; and the mass circulation of tabloid newspapers and magazines. The 1920s also marked the peak of the New Woman, the icon of first-wave feminism, who had entered the workforce, pursued higher education, engaged in sport, and remained single longer (Ewen & Ewen, 2008). Zeitz (2006) argues the "new developments in group psychology and behavioral sciences" during this decade informed the "unusual sway" of consumer-media culture "over millions of young women who were eager to assert their autonomy but still looked to cultural authorities for cues about consumption and body image" (p. 8). The New Woman flattened her breasts, bobbed her hair, and wore knee-length skirts. She was often an androgynous figure, but not asexual and certainly not free of the cult of skin. Indeed, Brumberg (1997) argues that the

> massive 'unveiling' of the female body [in the 1920s] meant that certain body parts were bared and displayed in ways that they had never been before. This new freedom to display the body was accompanied, however, by demanding beauty and dietary regimens that involved money as well as self-discipline.
>
> (p. 98)

Second-wave feminism unveiled even more of the female form, as hems rose higher still.

In her analysis of the cult of beauty that arose in the wake of second-wave feminism, Wolf (1991) adds a further psychological dimension to those noted above. Linking increased emphasis on female beauty with increases in emancipation, she argues that

> the ideology of beauty is the last remaining of the old feminine ideologies that still have power to control those women whom second wave feminism made relatively uncontrollable . . ... It is seeking to undo psychologically and covertly all the good things that feminism did materially and overtly.
>
> (p. 10)

Advertising aimed at female consumers works by lowering their self-esteem, by simulating a lack and thus a desire for a product to fill it (Wolf, 1991, p. 276). This state of affairs is arguably even more intensive in a world now regarded as postfeminist than it was when Wolf's (1991) *The Beauty Myth* was first published.

Postfeminism is understood differently in different countries, but whether it is the object of critique or celebration, it is seen to involve an emphasized femininity predicated on consumption. The postfeminist enjoys the fruits of feminism, but rejects feminist solidarity. In a world in which social life is increasingly individualized, if not atomized, she is responsible for her own destiny, and required to plan and monitor her life and lifestyle. Discussing the role of media in the construction of postfeminist identities, McRobbie (2004) contends that girls and women have become "subject to the regulative dimensions of popular culture discourses of personal choice and self-improvement" through consumption. However, choice "within a lifestyle culture," she argues, "is a modality of constraint" (p. 261). These discourses of "self-improvement" intensify the traditional imperatives for women and girls to display and discipline the skin. For, as Bauman (2005) argues, in a society of consumers,

> [The] body is 'autotelic', its own purpose and a value in its own right; in a society of consumers its also happens to be the ultimate value. Its well-being is the foremost objective of all and any life-pursuits, and the final text and criterion of utility, advisability and desirability . . .. The consumer's body therefore tends to be a particularly prolific source of perpetual anxiety, exacerbated by the absence of established and reliable outlets to relieve it, let alone to defuse or disperse it. No wonder marketing experts find the anxiety surrounding the care of the body to be a potentially inexhaustible source of profits.
>
> (p. 91)

In what follows, we examine the dermographics of two regimes of skin care and the mechanisms of consumer-media culture that drive them. The first is hair removal. Even the most cursory examination of advertisements for hair removal products and procedures reveals that they are sold to women and girls through promises of smooth skin. Recently, advertisers have targeted the tween demographic for hair removal products and in the next section we argue that such images are pivotal in the subjection of young girls to discourses of beauty. We then turn to cosmetic and dermatological procedures principally designed for older women, whose skin we suggest is constructed as abject to discourses of beauty. We also take another emerging market as our case study: cosmetic surgery tourism. Via these case studies, we show how the pedagogies of consuming skin rely on processes of subjection and abjection. These processes, we argue, seek to erase the signifiers of girls' and women's life stages and life stories that the skin narrates—even their ethnic ancestry.

Dermographics of Subjection

Smooth. Sleek. Sexy.
Laser hair removal makes you look & feel your best.
American Laser Centers knows what it takes to achieve perfect, hair-free skin—our exclusive laser hair removal protocol.
Kiss your razor goodbye. Toss your tweezers. Lose the wax. Forget about painful nicks and cuts, unsightly stubble and uncomfortable ingrown hair. With laser hair removal from American Laser Centers, every inch of your skin will be as smooth as you want it to be, without pain, hassle or mess.

(American Laser Centers, n.d.)

Early commentators on women's subjection to beauty speculated that women's silence about beauty rituals contributed to the normalization of the cultural ideals of beauty and the silent conformity of the majority of women—in this case, to a potentially lifetime pursuit of hair-free skin. The copy from the American Laser website—and the accompanying advertising promotions in *Bazaar, Brides, Allure, InStyle, People,* and *Self* magazines in September 2008—suggest that hair removal is hardly a "beauty secret" any more. However, the frequency with which hair is mentioned on the American Laser website is not typical of the norm.

More often, hair removal products and procedures are sold through the prom-ise of smooth, sleek, sexy skin, sometimes with no mention of hair at all. Take the advertising for the Gillette Venus range of women's shavers. The Venus Vibrance is "For the goddess seeking more radiant skin" (it exfoliates while you shave), the Venus Divine is "For the goddess who craves divinely smooth skin" (it has "INTENSIVE MOISTURE™" strips) and users of the Venus Embrace will "Embrace a whole new level of smoothness that's fit for a goddess" (Gillete Venus, 2009). What is significant about the advertising for the six types of Gillette Venus razors is that not one of them mentions hair. Although less wary of the mention of fuzz, the trademark slogan for the Schick Quattro line of women's razors is "FREE YOUR SKIN™". Hair removal is a promise not a solution; it is a means to achieving the perfect skin.

As a signifier of femininity, the practice of removing body hair is now so normalized in countries like the United States, United Kingdom, and Australia as to go unremarked. Tiggemann and Kenyon (1998) found that more than 90% of women in Australia remove leg and underarm hair, and in a more recent survey of female university students, that almost 50% remove most or all of their pubic hair (Tiggemann & Hodgson, 2008). However, although the removal of female body hair may have been an ancient practice, it was not one practiced by "respectable" western women of the nineteenth century when clothing cov-ered most of the female body (Toerien & Wilkinson, 2003). The first two waves of feminism, we have suggested, have been accompanied by a reactionary emphasis on femininity, indeed, an emphasized femininity which in the case of postfeminism symbolically renounces the political statement that second-wave feminists made in refusing to shave body hair. Body hair may be feminist, but it is not feminine. While it is natural and normal for women to have body hair, they tend to have less than men. Male hairiness (at least until recently) has been regarded as a signifier of masculine virility. Moreover, unlike breasts, which signify female sexual maturity, underarm and pubic hair—indeed, an increase in body hair post-puberty—are secondary sexual characteristics that are also shared by males. In the logic of binary oppositions, then, smooth hair-free skin is considered the more "feminine," although a state that can only be achieved through regimes of hair removal. The first woman's razor, manufactured by Gillette, came onto the market in 1915.

In insisting on a binary opposition between feminism and femininity, the result is a dis-identification with the politics of feminism (McRobbie, 2004). Instead, the gains of feminism have been appropriated by advertisers as one of a number of lifestyle and identity options and as a means of making sales. This is nowhere more apparent in consumer-media culture's formulation of postfeminist girl-hood, the smart, capable, sassy, pretty "can-do" girl (Harris, 2004) evoked by the advertising campaigns for Nair Pretty. An advertisement for Nair Pretty that ran in *Cosmogirl* and *Seventeen* in 2007 read: "I am a citizen of the world" (Newman, 2007), while the 2009 Nair Pretty Girlfriend of the Year competition run by the Australian teen magazine, *Girlfriend,* exhorts: "Whether your passion is acting, sport, science, art, community service, environmental causes, music or singing, fashion designing, makeup artistry—we want to hear about it!" (Nair Pretty Girlfriend, 2009, ¶ 3). The prizes range from $3,000 towards pre-career training and support to a photo-shoot and a bag full of Nair Pretty products.³ Hair-free skin and accomplishment, this implies, should and must go hand-in-hand.

Nair Pretty is a product specifically designed for first-time hair removers. Like other Nair products, it is designed "For totally touchable skin," but the range seems to be distinguished from the company's other products only by its fruit fragrances ("soft raspberry" and "soft kiwi") and glitter waxes (Nair Pretty, 2008). According to a report in *The New York Times,* Nair first produced products specifically designed to attract girls aged 10 to 15 years in 2007, although many girls of this age were already practicing hair removal (Newman, 2007). It is one of the first skin regimes undertaken in a girl's lifetime. More recently ABC News (Canning, Pflum, & Hagan, 2008) and MSNBC.com (Rao, 2008) have published reports on girls as young as eight being taken by their mothers for bikini waxes.

The emergence of the tween market segment for the hair removal industry has contributed to moral panic about the sexualization of young girls. Such arguments are informed by assumptions about childhood and innocence. There is no doubt that the sexualization of young girls, and the corporate pedophilia that drives it, is of grave concern. However, there is a perverse and unexamined irony implicit in the association between sexualization and pre-teen bikini waxing when pubic hair is, after all, a biological signifier of sexual maturation. In her subjection to advertising that persuades the tween and her peers that smooth, hair-free "bikini area" is a signifier of female sexual maturity, the 10-year-old who has a bikini wax regains her pre-pubescent body. In this respect, she is inducted into a construction of femininity and an embodiment of adult female sexuality that is childlike, passive, immature, and symbolically powerless. The imperative to deny and erase a signifier of their puberty is the beginning of a lifetime of labors compelling them to "restore" their pre-pubescent skin through a multitude of skin technologies. In targeting the tween market, we suggest, the hair removal industry positions girls as subjects of broader discourses about skin.

Author of *Stressed Out Girls,* Roni Cohen-Sandler, is reported as saying "photo-shopped Tinseltown images are only partially to blame [for the sexualization of young girls]. . .. Often the girls are taking cues from their mother" (Canning et al., 2008, ¶ 19). What is lacking here is any critique of the regime of beauty per se; no recognition of the fact that what is offensive in relation to the sexualization of a 10-year-old is also offensive in relation to the sexualization of mature women; and no acknowledgment of the fact that media–consumer culture has a generation's head start on selling the beauty myth to such mothers. They, too, are subjects of the discourses of skin. However, the cult of skin seeks to erase or deny later bodily changes: the signs of aging, of children-bearing, of simply living. As women age, they becomes susceptible to consumer–media cultural discourses that represent the inscriptions of the later stages of women's lives on the skin as abject. Indeed, the female subject in question risks becoming abject herself.

Dermographies of Abjection

Kristeva (1982) theorizes the corporeal, psychological, and social processes associated with the abject. She identified three main forms of abjection associated with food, waste, and sexual difference. The abject has since come to be associated with those bodily fluids, people, objects, and places that are regarded as unclean, impure, and even immoral. The abject disturbs "identity, system, order" (Kristeva, 1982, p. 4) and provokes the desire to expel the unclean, to restore the boundaries upon which the self or subject depend. It involves the erection of social taboos and individual defenses. In so far as the abject challenges notions of identity and social order it "must" be cast out. Abjection is taught and learned: even little girls are taught early to regard aspects of their pubescent bodies as abject.

The abject others of perfect, unblemished, smooth, hairless, youthful skin, include problem skin, tough skin, old skin, spotted, sagging, and spoiled skin. Such skin is "unsightly" and subjected to "a harsher kind of optics" (Connor, 2004, p. 60) by the commercial skin industry. It has constructed an ever-expanding "visual semiotics" (Benthien, 2002, p. 12) that links any skin imperfection with the abject; the multiple signifiers of imperfect skin articulate a semantics of abjection. However, as Grosz (1989) points out, the abject "can never be fully obliterated but hovers at the borders of our existence, threatening the apparently settled unity of the subject with disruption and possible dissolution" (p. 71). Women's skin very soon loses the pre-pubescent perfection that advertising images of skin depict. The subject of beauty discourses soon finds herself to be abject and an outcast. As the signs of age and bodily wear-and-tear reveal themselves on the skin, they disrupt the identity of the female subject of the beauty myth.

The commercial skin industry has created imperfect skin as abject and a social taboo, and casts itself as the agent of remedy. It promotes the skin as a surface with only one texture, free from hair, lines, wrinkles, creases, lumps, bumps, scars, and any sort of flaking, cracking, or roughness. There is no place for flabby, saggy, loose, droopy, dimpled skin; no place for inscriptions of aging or childbirth or hormonal changes upon the tissues of women's biological time. The skin must not reveal the biographical time of the working-class woman's labors of cleaning, scrubbing, washing, let alone the failures of past beauty labor—the age spots and uneven pigmentation created by youthful sunbathing or the burn, scar, broken capillary, ingrown hair, or the results of inept cosmetic interventions. The idea that the "skin remembers," that it bears the marks of our personal biographies, our labors (Ahmed & Stacey, 2001, p. 2), is an anathema to the skin industry which either claims it can defeat time or conceal its consequences. The perfect skin has amnesia—it has no memory, or as Avon promises, it can be born Anew™. The skin industry provides the screen or "second skin" behind which women's life experiences must be concealed. It promises self-determination, not self-subjugation. Skin and self can be transformed. No one need be stuck in their skin, not even those whose skin is considered too white, black, or yellow.

Skin is big business; it has become highly commercialized and standardized. Like capitalism more broadly, it is always on the lookout for expansion possibilities. Welcome cosmetic surgery tourism, a relatively new service in the skin industry, also called "aesthetic surgery vacations," "surgery holidays" or "surgery retreats." Cosmetic surgery tourism follows the path established by medical travel and, indeed, overlaps with it in various respects. Both provide medical treatment, particularly surgical treatment, more cheaply and quickly than in one's own country. In contrast, however, cosmetic tourism involves a combination of cosmetic surgery and a tourist experience, often in luxury medical and hotel environments in countries with appropriately enticing tourist attractions. The advertising rhetoric on the Web bundles medical makeover and holiday as one package: "safari and surgery" and "tango and a tune up." The advertising promises world-class medical facilities and care alongside idyllic holiday resort amenities, lush scenery, and attentive personal care from arrival to departure and sometimes pre- and post-operatively. All of this is evident in the visuals that surround the written promotional texts, including fine-looking skin, perfectly shaped bodies, and exultant, pampered youthful women in top-class settings.

The countries and regions most involved in providing this service include South America, India, Malaysia, Mexico, Philippines, Poland, South Africa, and Thailand—predominantly developing countries where medical services are cheaper. In some cases, cosmetic surgery tourism is part of a larger economic development strategy. The flow of customers, mainly female, is invariably from wealthier to poorer countries. Solid statistics on cosmetic surgery tourism are scarce; however, the *Times of India* reports that on the Subcontinent, "The most sought-after services by foreigners are laser, botox and fillers [and] Americans are the biggest clients, followed by tourists from Eastern Europe, the Far-East and even Japan" (Ramalingam, 2006, ¶ 3 & 4).

Thailand has a thriving industry and has developed the national brand "Cosmetic Surgery Thailand." The image "Total Makeover" on the *Destination Beauty* website features a young woman in a bikini surrounded by arrows pointing to different parts of her anatomy naming the price for 24 procedures involving skin and various body parts and ranging in expense "from" $US2,700 for a Tummy Tuck to $US150 for a facial Botox. A labia reduction costs $US250. Destination Beauty's services also include a "mommy makeover":

> The mommy makeover typically includes a tummy tuck, breast lift and minor liposuction. Childbirth stretches the stomach muscles and results in loose, sagging skin and stretch marks. This cannot be fixed with exercise and diet and thus surgery is the only way to bring the muscles back to normal again. A tummy tuck is ideal for this purpose. . . . Loose skin, stretch marks and sagging breasts are not the only negative effects of pregnancy.
>
> (Hygeia Beauty, n.d., ¶ 2)

The semantics of post-pregnancy skin are the abject symbols that are mobilized here. The advertising is typical in its attempts to naturalize the surgical procedures involved. With abject skin hovering at the borders of women's existence, threatening her "with disruption and possible dissolution" (Grosz, 1989, p. 71), what could be more natural than to turn to the unnatural?

Of course, there are potential clients who may have concerns about the risks of invasive surgery. Always ready to respond to a "need" that it has in fact created, the market steps in with less risky alternatives. Let us visit *Aesthetic Escapes* in Malaysia and consider its product Thermage for "Thighter [sic], Smoother Skin from Head to Toe," an anti-aging regime:

> Thermage is a non-invasive procedure which smoothes, tighten and contour the skin for an overall younger looking appearance—without surgery, injections or downtime.
>
> FACE
> * Tightens sagging jowls and skin under chin
> * Redefines, contours jaw line
> * Improves texture and tone over entire face
>
> EYES
> * Reduces hooding
> * Softens fine lines and crow's feet
> * Smoothes and tightens skin on the eyelids and eye area
>
> ARMS
> * Tightens loose, sagging skin
> * Reduces crepiness
> * Improves texture and tone
>
> ABDOMEN
> * Tightens loose or sagging skin (Perfect for post pregnancy and after liposuction or weight loss)
> * Improves texture and tone
>
> THIGHS
> * Improves texture and tone
> * Tightens and smoothes skin above the knee.
>
> (Aesthetic Escapes, 2007, ¶ 1 & 3)

Here, again, we see the same abject symbols and abject zones needing tightening, redefining, reducing, smoothing, anti-aging treatments—all predominantly expressed through the semantics of skin. With "bad skin" a growing taboo for women, cosmetic intervention becomes an individual defense.

Elliot (2008) attributes the rise of cosmetic surgery and cosmetic surgery tourism to the global force of the cult of celebrity, consumerism, and the new economy. Like McRobbie, he also proposes that constant institutional change in Western societies has heightened individual vulnerabilities and that surgical intervention has become a means of self-reinvention and a means of securing one's prospects. Erynn (2007) sees "cosmetic surgery tourism as a form of globalized consumption, in which women rearranging their bodies becomes a trans-national process of identity construction" (p. 10). This scaling-up will no doubt lead to the mobilization of a commodified global aesthetic of the skin via what we call "scapes of abjection."[4] By this we mean the intensified global flow, even contagion, of the psychic processes of abjection created by the skin industry. Although the "vast majority of customers continue to be Caucasian women," "ethnic surgeries" are also rising (Cognard-Black, 2007, ¶ 16). Dominated by images of Anglo-European beauty, some women seek to erase their "othered" ethnic biography. On a global scale what might such "ethnic surgeries" mean? As the skin and the body and are more widely navigated for profit, we predict that "scapes of abjection" will become even more tightly entangled with the long chains of commodification and representation of the perfect skin. Just as mediascapes of subjection lead adolescent girls to remove the hair that signifies their puberty, and scapes of abjection lead older women to seek to erase their biographical journey from their skin, scapes of abjection are leading women from different racial and ethnic backgrounds to deny their first skin. A global semantics of the skin is being taught by the commercial skin industry on an increasing global scale because, as Connor (2004) says, "The skin figures" (p. 50)—in dollars and cents.

Conclusion

Cosmetic labor is a divisive issue between and amongst feminists and postfeminists. It is seen variously as oppressive, coercive, empowering, resistive, or various combinations of these. For some it is an indication that women and girls are subscribing to a form of aesthetic authoritarianism organized along patriarchal, racial, ethnic, and class lines. For others, the regime of skin is a free lifestyle choice for enlightened women and regarded as an opportunity for creating a new, better, more attractive self who will have more opportunities for success.[5] Ever-younger girls are led to believe that a glamorous and sexually empowered self can be had via consumption, and that the skin is a privileged site where the technologies and disciplinary practices of identity construction can and should be practiced. Skin work is an opportunity to control their bodies and lives. Making a choice within "a modality of constraint" (in McRobbie's terms) may "empower" those individuals who absorb hegemonic ideals of feminine beauty, but this reinforces "the hegemonic ideals that oppress women as a group" (Gagné & McGaughey, 2002, p. 814). Whether it is surgical and dermatological interventions, or beauty products created specifically for girls and tweens, the skin industry is "co-opting, repackaging and reselling the feminist call to empower women into what may be dubbed 'consumer feminism'" (Cognard-Black, 2007, ¶ 6).

Our view is that the processes of consuming skin go beyond the individual and have broader meanings: they may express or challenge social and cultural ideals, feelings, biases, hierarchies, and cultural and sub-cultural membership. The sociocultural normalization of perfect skin is a product of a range of contemporary social and cultural forces overlain by complex pedagogies of power, expertise, and affect. So, with the pressures of subjection and abjection to deal with in the sign-saturated, hyper-individualized, hyper-competitive "skin" of the overdeveloped world, it is no surprise that girls and women want to escape their own skin and thereby erase their biographies and transform their identities. In a society where the commodity promises gratification, and where redesigning, rebadging and rebranding are regular occurrences, it is small wonder girls and women turn to consumerism to fulfill their desires, assuage their anxieties and repackage themselves.

Notes

1 The term "dermography" plays on the notion of advertising images of skin, the female demographic it targets and biographical inscriptions on the skin. It is borrowed from the title of the introduction to Ahmed and Stacey (2001).
2 We are not averse to skin and body care and even enjoy a bit of it ourselves. Our objection is to their extreme commodification and to the inexcusable pressure this places on females of all ages through the processes of subjection and abjection we discuss.
3 At the time of viewing, the *Girlfriend* website also featured a competition promoted by Silkymit (hair removal gloves). According to the promotion, "Using Silkymits to get your legs beach ready is simple AND smart. Because they exfoliate, Silkymits prepare your skin for a more even application of self-tanner. Sweet!"
4 See Kenway, Kraack, and Hickey-Moodey (2006) for an elaboration of this concept.
5 We will not elaborate further on these debates here. For examples on cosmetic surgery see the feminist classic Bordo (1993) and the more recent Blum (2003).

References

Aesthetic Escapes (2007). Thermage—Thighter [sic], smoother skin from head to toe. Aesthetic Escapes. Available: http://www.aestheticescapes.com/Thermage.aspx

Ahmed S., & Stacey, J. (Eds.). (2001). *Thinking through the skin.* New York: Routledge.

American Laser Centers (n.d.). Homepage. Available: http://www.americanlaser.com/

Bauman, Z. (2005). *Liquid life.* Cambridge, UK: Polity Press.

Benthien, C. (2002). *Skin: on the cultural border between self and the world,* translated by T. Dunlap. New York: Columbia University Press.

Blum, V. L. (2003). *Flesh wounds: The culture of cosmetic surgery.* Berkeley, CA: University of California Press.

Bordo, S. (1993). *Unbearable weight: Feminism, western culture, and the body.* Berkeley: University of California Press.

Brumberg, J. J. (1997). *The body project: An intimate history of American girls.* New York: Random House.

Canning, A., Pflum, M., & Hagan, K. (2008). Bikini waxing for tweens! Have spas gone too far? *ABC News,* May 19. Available: http://abcnews.go.com/GMA/BeautySecrets/Story?id=4881675&page=1

Cognard-Black, J. (2007). How the pitch for cosmetic surgery co-opts feminism. *MS Magazine,* Summer. Available: http://www.msmagazine.com/summer2007/extreme makeover.asp

Connor, S. (2004). *The book of skin.* Ithaca, NY: Cornell University Press.

Elliott, A. (2008). *Making the cut: How cosmetic surgery is transforming our lives.* London: Reaktion Books.

Erynn, C. (2007). The whole package: Exploring cosmetic surgery tourism. Paper presented at the annual meeting of the American Sociological Association, New York, New York City, Aug 11, 2007. Available: http://www.allacademic.com/meta/p175877_index.html

Ewen, S. (1976). *Captains of consciousness: Advertising and the social roots of the consumer culture.* New York: McGraw-Hill.

Ewen. S., & Ewen, E. (2008). *Typecasting: On the arts and sciences of human inequality* (revised edition). New York: Seven Stories Press.

Gagné, P., & McGaughey, D. (2002). Cultural hegemony and the exercise of power among women who have undergone elective mammoplasty. *Gender & Society, 16*(6), 814–838.

Gillete Venus. (2009). Gillete Venus: Reveal the goddess in you. Available: http://www.gillettevenus.com/en_US/index.jsp

Giroux, H. (2004). Cultural studies, public pedagogy, and the responsibility of intellectuals. *Communication and Critical Cultural Studies, 1*(1), 59–79.

Grosz, E. (1989). *Sexual subversions: Three French feminists.* Sydney: Allen & Unwin.

Harris, A. (2004). *Future girl: Young women in the twenty-first century.* London: Routledge.

Haug, W. F. (1986). *Critique of commodity aesthetics: Appearance, sexuality and advertising in capitalist society.* Cambridge, UK: Polity Press.

Hygeia Beauty. (n. d.). Mommy makeover. *Destination Beauty.* Available: http://www.hygeiabeauty.com/mommymakeover.html

Kenway, J., Kraack, A., & Hickey-Moodey, A. (2006). *Masculinity beyond the metropolis.* Basingstoke, UK: Palgrave McMillan.

Kristeva, J. (1982). *Powers of horror: An essay on abjection.* New York: Columbia University Press.

McRobbie, A. (2004). Post-feminism and popular culture. *Feminist Media Studies, 4*(3), 255–264.

Nair Pretty. (2008). Feel pretty™ every day! *Nair Pretty.* Available: http://www.nairpretty.com/index.html

Nair Pretty Girlfriend. (2009). Nair Pretty Girlfriend of the Year, *Girlfriend.* Available: http://au.youth.yahoo.com/b/girlfriend/30032/nair-pretty-girlfriend-of-the-year/

Newman, A. A. (2007). Depilatory market moves far beyond the short-shorts wearers. *The New York Times,* September 14. Available: http://www.nytimes.com/2007/09/14/business/media/14adco.html

Ramalingam, A. (2006). Cosmetic tourism gets a face-lift, *The Times of India,* 14 January. Available: http://timesofindia.indiatimes.com/articleshow/1372321.cms

Rao, V. (2008). Too young? Preteen girls get bikini waxes. *MSNBC.com,* August 13. Available: http://www.msnbc.msn.com/id/26182276/

Tiggemann, M., & Hodgson, S. (2008). The hairlessness norm extended: Reasons for and predictors of women's body hair removal at different body sites. *Sex Roles, 59*(11–12), 889–897.

Tiggemann, M., & Kenyon, S. (1998). The hairlessness norm: The removal of body hair in women. *Sex Roles, 39*(11–12), 873–885.

Toerien, M., & Wilkinson, S. (2003). Gender and body hair: Constructing the feminine woman. *Women's Studies International Forum, 26*(4), 333–344.

Wolf, N. (1991). *The beauty myth: How images of beauty are used against women.* London: Vintage.

Zeitz, J. (2006). *Flapper: A madcap story of sex, style, celebrity, and the women who made America modern.* New York: Crown.

14 Happy Cows and Passionate Beefscapes

Nature as Landscape and Lifestyle in Food Advertisements

Anne Marie Todd

The Food Network's slogan, "Taste Life," illustrates contemporary media's approach to promoting all things food. American audiences have become gourmands with the mainstreaming of sun-dried tomatoes, arugula, and truffle oil.[1] As American palates have grown more sophisticated, food marketers have responded with stimulating advertising campaigns. Food has become less of a necessity and more of a commodity as slick food marketing techniques produce global images of highly processed, packaged food products. Advertising is a "profound pedagogical site [that] has helped to elevate consumption to the primary role in defining our social selves" (Hoechsmann, 2007, p. 653). Marketing campaigns associate social values with consumption of food products. Food is above all "a cultural domain that is often elaborated into complex systems of meaning" (Goode, 1992, p. 233). In a global media market, images and narratives of food construct the way consumers *consume* food.

Production and consumption of food has inherent environmental implications: energy and water used by agriculture greatly exceeds that of other production sectors. Factory farms produce massive amounts of soil and water pollution from run-off of animal waste, and "food miles" are gaining prominence as consumers evaluate the carbon footprint of the food they eat. "Our interest in food is associated . . . with our interest in 'nature'" (Goodman & Redclift, 1991, p. xi). The way we consume natural resources helps define our relationship with the environment: the choice to be vegetarian, or eat organic, communicates one's attitude toward sustainability (Pederson, 2000). As increasingly complicated global food markets have expanded the human food chain—Americans buy bananas from Ecuador, shrimp from Thailand, and citrus from Mexico— the food industry uses food as a "rhetorical device against which to rationalize contemporary market practices of consumption" (Shugart, 2008, p. 88). Food advertisements rely on narratives of desire and consumption to construct the environmental persona of food products.

Advertisers are "popular educators" and thus teach the public about the ways of the world (Hoechsmann, 2007, p. 658). Nature is widely used as a symbol in advertisements in general, and in food marketing specifically.[2] Two contemporary advertising campaigns are significant in the way they imbue food products with a natural aesthetic. "Powerful Beefscapes" is a print and radio advertising campaign funded by the National Cattlemen's Beef Association (NCBA) that invites American consumers to "Discover the Power of Protein in the Land of Lean Beef."[3] Two folksy radio ads describe the suburban charm of "the land of lean beef," while six beefscapes, published in glossy magazines, are close-up photographic images of cooked beef artistically arranged to represent landscapes. "Happy Cows" is a television and billboard campaign funded by the California Milk Advisory Board (CMAB).[4] Eighteen 30-second television spots feature cows marveling over the perks for dairy cows of living in California. Each spot ends with the campaign's slogan "great milk comes from happy cows. Happy cows come from California. Make sure it's made with real California milk." Both of these ads campaigns have significant web presence with supplemental information and ephemera.[5]

These two campaigns demonstrate how the meat and dairy lobby cleverly and artistically portray their food products as natural and healthy. These ads commodify their food products in two ways: the use of "foodscapes" to portray the food product as part of the natural landscape, and the use of anthropomorphism to associate food with an eco-personality and a natural lifestyle. These discursive strategies establish an intimate relationship between food and consumers that mystifies the actual production process. Analysis of these campaigns suggests this "natural" discourse has significant implications for public understanding of sustainable food consumption.

Foodscaping Nature: Lands of Plenty

Superficially, these two advertisement campaigns have different purposes: one urges consumers to indulge in the taste of lean beef, while another other hawks the deliciousness of dairy products. A closer look reveals both campaigns foreground a characteristically *natural* landscape. The construction of landscapes in these ads implies a connection between consumers and the environment. These advertisements, as public pedagogy, *seem* to educate consumers about the food production process. Humans understand the environment through landscapes, created by "human acts of conferring meaning to nature and the environment, for giving the environment definition and form from a particular angle of vision and through a special filter of values and beliefs. Every landscape is a symbolic environment" (Greider & Garkovich, 1994, p. 1). Food advertisements subtly associate products with social and cultural values of environmental awareness. "How we view (and treat) landscapes reflects . . . values of the entire social and cultural system in which the sentiment lies" (Corbett, 2006, p. 116). In the beef ads, the cooked beef literally forms the landscape, while the hills of California are the landscape that provides for the happy cows. In these two campaigns, nature is much more than a backdrop—it is a bountiful and imminently consumable landscape.

Passionate Beefscapes: The Land of Lean Beef

In the "Powerful Beefscapes" advertisements, platters of perfectly cooked beef are carefully arranged to visually form landscapes with recognizable natural features. Sirloin, tri-tip, kabobs and other dishes form a beach, canyon, cliff, flat-lands, mountain, and river. A recipe based on the ingredients used in the land-scape accompanies each ad. The radio advertisements expand the visually stunning landscapes: they describe the land of lean beef as a suburban community, with down-home, even agricultural values. The visually appealing foodscapes frame the Land of Lean Beef as lush, pristine landscape, while radio ads evoke a subur-ban community (of meat consumers).

Foodscapes is a technique increasingly used in food advertising of using food to visually represent something other than itself.[6] Turning the pages of *Gourmet*, *Saveur*, or *Bon Appetit*, one sees lamb chops wrapped in a floral bouquet, an egg sunrise over bacon hills, or a cruise ship sailing in a martini glass on a sunset pink Cosmopolitan sea. The "Powerful Beefscapes" are striking advertisements: the beef is larger than life, in explicit representations of lush landscapes with distinc-tive natural features

The beef is the central element of the landscape, In the "Beach" ad (Moroccan-Style Beef Kabobs with Spiced Bulgur), chunks of beef dominate a rocky coastline.[7] The chunks of beef bear an uncanny likeness to rocks. A swath of breadcrumbs smeared on the platter abutting the rocks remarkably evokes a sandy beach with parsley sprigs and leaves blooming behind rocks and dotted in the sand. A distant island of parsley provides texture and the frosted-glass serving platter becomes the glossy sparkle of a calm sea. Cooked perfectly medium rare, the juicy hunks of meat are cut against the grain to reveal enhanced lines, grooves and curves. Importantly, this is the Land of *Lean* Beef, and the beefscape is pristine in its absence of fat. As a dinner dish, this is presented as a healthy plate, supported by the nutrition informa-tion on the recipe. This is the goal of the "Powerful Beefscapes" campaign—to posi-tion lean beef at the center of a healthy diet. The centrality of the meat on the plate explicitly declares meat as the basis of a healthy meal.

As an environmental landscape, the plate is a healthy ecosystem. The beefscapes are lush in the sense of preserved wilderness. In the "Mountain" ad (Hearty Glazed Tri-Tip Roast with Creamy Gorgonzola Sauce), angled tips of meat point up to form tall peaks snow-capped with creamy Gorgonzola sauce. Broccoli surrounds the beef mountains as a healthy vegetable and a healthy forest: stems of broccoli are stand-ins for tree trunks. The Gorgonzola sauce portrays ample snowpack, which, in this ecosystem, provides a source of water for the healthy forest below. Beefscapes are lush, with a wild aesthetic that mimics photographs in *National Geographic.* In the "River" ad (Beef Tenderloin with Savory Saucy Mushrooms and Lentils), pieces of beef represent huge rocks, while mushrooms are boulders and lentils are river rocks, all creating a rocky riverbed. The river itself is a thick swath of rich, brown gravy poured between pieces of beef, which form the high riverbanks. The gravy river flows into the distance where a mound of parsley and lentils suggest a far bank. This is a land of plenty: the lush landscapes have a wild beauty as hunks of meat tower over rushing rivers.

The hunks of beef dominate the plate's landscape, a central part of a natural, healthy ecosystem. The abundance of beef on the plate implies a bounty of resources to support beef consumption. The snow and water are indicative of a healthy ecosystem—providing water, particularly inviting to consumers who grapple with drought. These beef advertisements seek to educate the public about the health benefits of lean protein, which is presented as a natural part of the American diet. The beefscapes position meat as natural food product, one that is sustainable: not only for consumers' personal health, but also to maintain a healthy environment.

California: Land of Happy Cows

In the "Happy Cows" television commercials, the sunny California landscape is the backdrop to the stars of the ads: happy cows. The landscape of California has its own starring role: its great weather is the selling point—the reason for good cheese—and is the subject of the bovine dialog throughout the series. The happy cows exuberantly boast of California's sunshine, clean air, green grass. Elements of the natural world have cultural meaning with which to associate products with "nonmaterial qualities that have disappeared from many people's lives, qualities like solitude, wilderness, lush landscapes, free-flowing water, and clean air" (Corbett, 2006, p. 166). The television spots emphasize the paradise-like qualities of California weather immortalized by the Beach Boys and others.

Omnipresent in the television advertisements, California is larger than life—a legendary place with no rain or snow: In "Dream," cows tease each other about the California weather: "Oops there's a rain cloud . . . Gotcha!" (CMAB, 2008d). Another advertisement, "Weather," opens to a sunny day. The camera pans: not a cloud in the sky. Suddenly, as horror music plays, one cloud appears, causing the cows to scatter, screaming: "Oh my gosh! Cloud! Cloud! . . . Run! . . . Oh mercy!" The scene ends with one cow's lament: "Man I hate the rainy season!" (CMAB, 2008d). The not-so-subtle implication is that it never rains in California. The carefree glee of the cows belies the real problems of drought in California. The fields where the cows roam are lush and vast: resources are plentiful. Images of cows grazing suggest grass-fed beef. This portrayal of California suggests that such environmental abundance creates happy cows.

The campaign positions California as paradise for cows. Several ads show scenes from a far-away, blustery place where other cows live. While never made explicit, the inferred location is the Dairy Belt of the Midwest. In one ad, "Blizzard," a calf asks, "Grandma, how come you never talk about where you come from?" The matriarch becomes agitated: flashing back to an image of cows struggling in a blizzard. A second calf says: "I told you not to ask about that" (CMAB, 2008d). The mere memories of the cold snow are so unpleasant that they are unmentionable. The forbidden quality of these memories means that native Californians have no idea of the world outside of California. In another ad, "Who's She?" a "new girl" approaches a group of cows and comments: "Hey I love it here, no snow! . . . You know, how I hate big snow drifts . . .." Failing to get a response, she walks away as the native cows whisper to each other: "What's snow? . . . I don't know . . .. She's been tipped one time too many!" (CMAB, 2008d). California is a mystic land: cows have never heard of snow, and don't know the trials of feeding or grazing in the cold.

California is paradise due to its remarkable weather, and even the natural disasters are pleasant. One ad, "Earthquake," opens with cows drinking water from a pond. The sky grows dark and the ground starts to shake. The cows "ooh" and "ah," and one cow breathlessly coos: "Ooh foot massage." When the earthquake stops, another cow complains: "Oh, those never last long enough" (CMAB, 2008d). The human experience of an earthquake is quite different: noticeably absent is any mention of earthquake safety or the inherent danger in the shifting of tectonic plates. This advertisement presents the uniqueness of California cheese: one more thing those other cheeses don't have. While the earthquakes may not actually improve the taste of cheese, the mythic qualities of the California climate are associated with good cheese.

The "Happy Cows" campaign presents California as a land of sunshine, where earthquakes are benign, and droughts lead to green grass. In the ad, "To California," a herd watches a lone cow battle a snowstorm attempting to walk to California. This is the most explicit telling of an overall narrative of these ads: cows choose California for the weather; consumers should choose California for the cheese. The advertisements are designed to educate consumers that healthy and happy cows make healthy cheese, which makes happy customers.

Personifying Nature: Food Is Life!

The portrayal of food as part of the environment is also meaningful in the way the ads personify nature. Anthropomorphism, the representation of animals in distinctly human situations, has long been a strategy to sell consumer products—on television, bunnies sell batteries, and a lizard and a duck play insurance agents. Through these narratives, consumers establish a relationship with the animal spokesperson, and therefore the product. Ads develop this character by associating emotional appeals and social values with consumption of the product. In the "Beefscapes" and "Happy Cows" campaigns, natural landscapes are personified in a broader sense to establish a relationship between consumer and the environment. Most of the nine million dairy cows in the United States do not frolic on sunny California hillsides, but live indoors, usually confined to stalls. Recent undercover investigations produced videos of workers at slaughter houses abusing animals too weak or sick to stand (known as "downers") to force them into the slaughter line. Dairy cows are repeatedly impregnated through artificial means to maintain their milk production; they reportedly cry out when separated from their newborn calves, which are destined for two years of confinement before being slaughtered as veal. "As the food we consume has become more processed it has been presented as more 'natural' by the food industry" (Goodman & Redclift, 1991, p. 250). The food's natural persona cultivates a relationship with consumers by embodying the food products with personality, and connecting it to the consumer lifestyle.

The Power of Protein: A Passion for Beef

In the Land of Lean Beef campaign, larger than life cuts of beef create an oversized persona. The consumer passion for beef is attributed to the "Power of Protein." The ads communicate this power: the close-up images of beef are visually stunning, the recipes promise powerful taste. Beef's personality is promoted on the radio with a "voice [that] embodies the personality of beef" (NCBA, 2008a, ¶1). The ad campaign "defines beef as a perfect fit for what drives consumers' protein selection: the eating experience and how it fuels the body" (NCBA, 2008a, ¶1). Beef's personality is based on consumers' "unique passion for beef" and the ads are designed to encourage consumers to "reclaim the dinner they love" (NCBA, 2008a, ¶ 2–3). The ads provide visual stimuli, using succulent meat to construct consumer desire. The ads invite viewers to ogle the meat, providing a view more reminiscent of lascivious looks at a centerfold, than proper attention paid to a plate at the dinner table. The ads urge consumers to indulge their cravings and "reclaim" their passion for beef.

In asking consumers to indulge their guilty pleasures, the beef ads give consumers permission to eat beef. The ads connect desire to healthiness: "Consumers should feel good about loving this protein" that can "satisfy their cravings and deliver good nutrition" (NCBA, 2008a, ¶ 2–3). Consumers are urged to satisfy their desires by first enjoying the pictures, and then enjoying the food. The recipes are an important component of the advertisements because they emphasize the nutritional value of beef. The ads reposition lean beef as a healthy choice for consumers: a passion for beef is healthy. By centrally placing beef at the center of a healthy lifestyle, the ads endeavor to establish consumer loyalty to more than a product, to commit to the *lifestyle* that comes with eating beef.

The lifestyle that emerges when consumers discover the "power of protein," is steeped in community values. The radio ads describe the Land of Lean Beef as a tight-knit community: one with simple pleasures and down-home values. In the "Neighbors" radio spot, music swells and a male announcer begins in a friendly voice:

> You see those hickory smoke signals. That's a sure sign it's grilling season in the land of lean beef. Some strip steak sizzling, tantalizing the entire suburb. That delicious aroma is all the invitation you need to seek out that source . . . . Cause out here, a neighbor's just a friend you haven't fed yet. Discover the power of protein in the land of lean beef. Beef. It's what's for dinner.
>
> (NCBA, 2008c)

The lifestyle of the Land of Lean Beef is suburban. "Out here" is suburbia, a distinctly American place, evoking middle-class values. The community is close-knit, with friendships forged through sharing meat from the grill. The folksy charm of the radio ads suggests one closely connected to agricultural values: as if the farmer that raised that beef is grilling it on the patio next door. This forms a connection between the farmer's field and the consumer's table. In this way, the community is closely rooted in the landscape and the strong bonds of community are linked to a strong bond with nature.

Eating meat transports consumers to that kind of community. The Land of Lean Beef is one of enjoyment and leisure. This is exemplified in the "Gone eatin'" radio spot. As the ad begins, the music swells, and a male announcer begins in a conversational tone:

Gone eatin'. . . .. You'll see this sign often in the land of lean beef. Gone eatin' sirloin . . . gone eatin' t-bone . . . gone eatin' tenderloin. And nobody's sure when they'll be back from those pastures of protein. But when they are, you can bet they'll be satisfied. Discover the power of protein when you go eatin' in the land of lean beef. Beef. It's what's for dinner.

(NCBA, 2008b)

In this ad, listeners discover what sustains the community of the Land of Lean Beef: the happiness that comes from eating beef. Reminiscent of "gone fishin'," the "gone eatin'" signs suggest eating beef is a form of recreation, and one might catch a sirloin as one might catch a fish. Eating is a pastime, part of a relaxation ritual. Eating is a leisure activity that evokes a simpler, pastoral life with a deep connection to nature: consuming the resources of the Land of Lean Beef. "Pastures of protein" refer to the stunning beefscapes, and the enclosed recipes invite consumers to visit by cooking and enjoying this natural bounty. Consumers' passion for beef is portrayed as a passion for nature; the ads encourage consumers to love nature through their appreciation of the beefscapes and enjoyment of the natural lifestyle that comes from eating beef.

California Dreamin'

Just as the beef ads promote eating beef to feel good, the Happy Cows equate dairy products and California with happiness. The happy cows have an exuberant persona: they express their love of California and the happiness that California dairy products bring. "We happy cows are used to making lemonade out of lemons. But our favorite thing is to make great things out of milk. One of our personal summertime favorites is Port Poached Pears and Ricotta" (CMAB, 2008d). The recipes are "cow approved," assuring consumers that California dairy products will make them happy.

Happy Cows provide consumers pleasure through their whimsical commercials, which are designed to add a "little sunshine" to consumers' lives (CMAB, 2008b). "After watching a Real California Cheese TV commercial, we can pretty much guarantee that you'll have an ear-to-ear grin. So, prepare your cheek muscles" (CMAB, 2008d). Ads deploy the emotions of food personalities to project the emotions of consumers: when characters feel emotion, consumers feel emotion. The website promotes Happy Cows merchandise made with 100% "pure happiness" in order to promote the consumer experience: "because sometimes it just feels good to shop" (CMAB, 2008c). The campaign thus urges viewers to invest in the personality of California Cows, in order to capture some of the happiness for themselves.

The Happy Cows have a relaxed lifestyle that embodies the personality of California. An ad, entitled "Alarm Clock," opens with the sound of a rooster crowing, which awakens two cows sleeping in a barn. To one cow's suggestion that they get "an early start on that alfalfa in the back forty," another cow responds: "What's the hurry? Hit the snooze!" The ad flashes to the rooster flying out the barn and into the fence post (CMAB, 2008d). This ad conveys a relaxed California atmosphere with no alarm clocks or deadlines, but the opportunity to roam as they please. Viewers who must wake up to an alarm clock and a daily grind might view this ad wistfully. In "Finish Line," cows race in front of bull spectators, until the opportunity to munch dandelions distracts the contestants (CMAB, 2008d). The campaign claims "fresh air, green grass and beautiful weather definitely make California Cows happy" (CMAB, 2008b). In the vision of these ads, California cows are carefree, without hardships that might befall cows that live elsewhere. Consumers who desire this lifestyle for themselves are told they can achieve it by buying California Cheese.

California weather promotes not just happy cows, but beautiful cows. In one ad, "Workout," one bull tells another "out here the babes are different . . . all the sunshine I guess, clean air, good food, something" (CMAB, 2008d). In another ad, "Wingman," a bull admires a cow walking past: "Ah yeah, here she comes . . . sunshine and clean air have been good to her, boy!" (CMAB, 2008d). California's beautiful landscape supports beautiful healthy cows that thrive on sunshine and clean air. The advertisements suggest that California cows are free-range— roaming on forty acres—and grass-fed—eating alfalfa. The campaign promotes the principle that the "ready availability of California dairy products contributes to the good health and well-being of the state's population" (CMAB, 2008a).[8] In these ads, the "well-being" of the population is understood to mean the physical attractiveness of females. Healthy cows are beautiful cows, and beautiful cows are happy cows. The ad campaign educates the public on the supposed benefits of California dairy products, suggesting that California cows lead a good life; that healthy and beautiful cows make healthful and tasty cheese.

Conclusions

The ways in which food is "produced and consumed" have significant environmental effects (Goodman & Redclift, 1991, p. xii). Dairy and beef production produces massive amounts of animal waste pollution and engenders horrific mistreatment of dairy and beef cattle. This reality is in stark contrast to the happy life of cows seen in the happy cows ads and the luscious images of the beefscapes, which obscure the processes through which cheese and steaks reach the dinner table. Consumers are often unaware of how food arrives at the grocery store, and "restoring the missing associations that connect us to the land is one of the primary aims of environmentalism, and in this sense it is a cultural movement as well as a political ideology" (Killingsworth & Palmer, 1996, p. 237). The advertisements discussed here are a form of public pedagogy that informs consumers of the supposed environmental and health benefits of consumption. The Happy Cows advertisements promote sustainability by portraying dairy cows as nourished by a robust environment. These ads make a connection between the quality of California dairy products and the healthy environment of California. The beefscapes tie the food product to the environment in another way, portraying beef as the foundation of wild landscapes. Both ads belie their messages of sustainability by hiding the environmental impact of the production of beef and dairy food products.[9] These slick marketing techniques offer an anthropocentric perspective of sustainability that provides consumers with a shallow view of the connection between field and table.

California and the Land of Lean Beef are landscapes of abundance. They offer a natural aesthetic that invokes an abundance of natural resources and a sustainability of the environment. The lush beefscapes and the California climate emphasize a strong connection between food and land, but ultimately offer a (dis)connection with place. The association of a beautiful environment and delicious food obscures actual food production processes: agriculture consumes tremendous amounts of energy and water, produces tons of pollution, condones questionable treatment of animals. The ads associate a passion for beef and the pleasures of California with consumers' love of the land, and construct consumers' relationship to food as a healthy relationship to the environment. However, the beefscapes and mystical California are imminently consumable landscapes: the beefscapes are enjoyable scenery precisely because of their imminent destruction at the hands of a diner. California's environmental problems, such as earthquakes and droughts caused by endless sunshine, delight the cows, but create issues for future production. The landscapes constructed in these ads provide short-term happiness, obscuring food production processes that are distinctly unsustainable.

Evernden (1992) emphasizes the importance of understanding how humans construct nature in order to reveal our relationship to it, and thus develop meaningful responses to environmental problems. This analysis demonstrates the importance of consumer awareness of greenwashing—unsubstantiated claims about the environmental benefits of a product—in this case the sustainability of meat production. While Slow Food and other movements are calling for more environmentally sensitive eating habits, food lobbies are producing advertising campaigns that offer messages of sustainability, while actually encouraging consumption. These advertisements are much more than entertainment, they serve as a form of public education campaign that positions dairy and beef products as environmentally sustainable, by obscuring the true environmental impacts of such agricultural products. Through critical evaluation of such advertising claims, consumers can demonstrate true passion for the environment by making informed decisions about the food they eat.

Notes

1 Gourmet food sales increased nearly 25% from 2005 to 2007 (Passy, 2008).
2 See, e.g., Corbett (2006); Cox (2006).
3 Beef Checkoff Program, which funds the campaign, was part of the 1985 Farm Bill, and created funds for a food lobby: the Cattlemen's Beef Promotion and Research Board. The National Cattlemen's Beef Association (NCBA) and its partners are the marketing organization for the largest segment of the food industry (NCBA, 2008a).
4 The California Milk Advisory Board (CMAB) was formed in 1969 by the California Department of Food and Agriculture to promote California dairy products. The Happy Cows television campaign launched in 2000, with additional ads released in 2002, 2005, and 2007. In 2004, the ads expanded to cable television, Spanish-speaking, and Midwest American markets. In 2004 and 2005, the ads aired during the Superbowl. A darling of the advertising industry, the campaign won multiple awards. See Greenwald (2005) for more on the campaign's grand strategy.
5 Included in this analysis are multimedia examples available online: www.realcalifornia cheese.com/ and www.beefitswhatsfordinner.com/

6　Carl Warner creates elaborate artistic *foodscapes:* still-lifes on 8 ft × 4 ft tables. For more on panoramas such as a cheese village, and smoked salmon seas: http://wanhart. wordpress.com/2008/03/17/foodscapes/
7　All descriptions of beefscapes print ads refer to NCBA (2008d).
8　See Ihde (2002): industry analysts termed this cultural category as LOHAS: Lifestyle of Health and Sustainability.
9　PETA sued the California Milk Advisory Board, the lobbying group responsible for the ads, for false advertising (see www.unhappycows.com/). Also see www.humanemyth. org/happycows.htm for how other activist organizations have addressed this.

References

California Milk Advisory Board. (2008a). *About the CMAB.* Retrieved November 14, 2008 from: www.realcaliforniamilk.com/pages/english/aboutCMAB.aspx

California Milk Advisory Board. (2008b). *Happy Cow comments.* Retrieved November 14, 2008 from: www.realcaliforniamilk.com/pages/english/happyCowsComments.aspx

California Milk Advisory Board. (2008c). *Happy Cow merchandise.* Retrieved November 14, 2008 from: www.realcaliforniamilk.com/pages/english/merch/happyCowMerchandise.aspx

California Milk Advisory Board. (2008d). *Happy Cow TV commercials.* Retrieved November 14, 2008 from: www.realcaliforniamilk.com/pages/english/happyCowsTV.aspx

Corbett, J. B. (2006). *Communicating nature: How we create and understand environmental messages.* Washington DC: Island Press.

Cox, R. (2006). *Environmental communication and the public sphere.* Thousand Oaks, CA: Sage Publications.

Goode, J. (1992). Food. In R. Baumann (Ed.), *Folklore, cultural performances, and popular entertainments: A communications-centered handbook* (pp. 233–245). New York: Oxford University Press.

Goodman, D., & Redclift, M. (1991). *Refashioning nature: Food, ecology and culture.* New York: Routledge.

Greenwald, M. (2005). *"Great cheese comes from happy cows"* . . . *and happy farmers: The California Milk Advisory Board's marketing and strategic planning success story.* Available: www.californiadairypressroom.com/CADColumbiaStudy.html

Greider, T., & Garkovich, L. (1994). Landscapes: The social construction of nature and the environment. *Rural Sociology, 59,* 1, 1–24.

Evernden, N. (1992). *The social construction of nature.* Baltimore, MD: Johns Hopkins University Press.

Hoechsmann, M. (2007). Advertising pedagogy: Teaching and learning consumption. In D. Macedo & S. R. Steinberg (Eds.), *Media literacy: A reader* (pp. 653–666). New York: Peter Lang.

Ihde, E. S. (November 25, 2002). Milking the organic market. *Brand Channel.* Available: http://www.brandchannel.com/features_effect.asp?pf_id=133

Killingsworth, M. J., & Palmer, J. S. (1996). Discourse of green consumerism. In J. G. Cantrill & C. L. Oravec (Eds.), *The symbolic earth: Discourse and our creation of the environment* (pp. 219–240). Lexington: University of Kentucky Press.

National Cattlemen's Beef Association. (2008a). *"Beef. It's what's for dinner" advertising campaign invites consumers to discover the power of protein: New campaign boldly depicts passion, protein and strength.* Available: www.beefitswhatsfordinner.com/askexpert/ pressrelease.asp

National Cattlemen's Beef Association. (2008b). *Gone eatin'.* Radio spot. Available: www. beefitswhatsfordinner.com/askexpert/radio.asp

National Cattlemen's Beef Association. (2008c). *Neighbors.* Radio spot. Available: www.beefitswhatsfordinner.com/askexpert/radio.asp

National Cattlemen's Beef Association. (2008d). *Print ads.* Available: www.beefitswhats fordinner.com/askexpert/gallery.asp

Passy, C. (August 14, 2008). Gourmet trends for 2009. *Palm Beach Post.* Available: www.palmbeachpost.com/food/content/food_dining/epaper/2008/08/14/a1fn_fancy_food_web_0814.html

Pederson, L. H. (2000). The dynamics of green consumption: A matter of visibility? *Journal of Environmental Policy & Planning, 2*(3), 193–210.

Shugart, H. A. (2008). Sumptuous texts: Consuming "otherness" in the food film genre. *Critical Studies in Media Communication, 25*(1), 68–90.

15 Creating the Ethical Parent-Consumer Subject

Commerce, Moralities, and Pedagogies in Early Parenthood

Lydia Martens

This chapter is about the constitution of new parents as pedagogical subjects in consumer culture, a process that mirrors an analogous development in the medical-health field. It is identifiable through the diverse instruction services and resources now directed at people going through this transitional phase of life, and which include a growing number of pregnancy and early parenting websites, magazines, advisory services, parenting manuals, and advice books, as well as products with accompanying information. I argue that it is difficult to demarcate medical-health instructions from those deriving from commercial culture, as non-commercial and commercial pedagogic practices are apparently merging in diverse ways. Developing an understanding of the connections between commercial and non-commercial players and practices in this field is therefore salient. This chapter examines how instructional resources targeted at new parents are organized, and asks why we find such proximity in the practices of non-commercial and commercial players in this field.

The discussion is framed by ethnographic research conducted at *The Baby Show*, a U.K. consumer show targeted specifically at this section of the population, and which brings together a variety of commercial and non-commercial exhibitors, and pregnancy and early childhood "experts," with visitors consisting mainly of prospective parents, new parents, parents with young children, grandparents, and friends. The Baby Show illustrates the prominence of medical and health discourses in this field and contains the diverse themes that dominate an early parenthood in which baby care lore is interwoven with specific parenting expectations that feature baby health, safety, and development high on its agenda. While the show operates as an information conduit in its own right, it also serves as a research platform from which to glean the characteristics and *organization* of the informational and instructional resources mentioned above. I move between and across these diverse pedagogic resources in my analysis.

I start with a discussion of theoretical insights on the nature of contemporary parenting and parenting pedagogies, and conclude that, while this literature is clear about the influence of authoritarian medical-health discourses on new parents, there has been little interest in thinking through the fact that commerce has entered this field in the form of an important set of small and large for-profit players. I continue by elaborating how parental instruction is organized and presented, pointing to the blurring between commercial and non-commercial information streams. In an effort to explain this feature, I draw out a set of arguments for what commercial players have to gain by incorporating features of medical-health and scientific practices into their own, the outcome of which is that new parents are confronted with two intertwined and mutually reinforcing moralities: that of *good parenthood* and the *good consumer*.

Parenting Moralities, Pedagogy, and Consumer Culture

New parents are a particular group of adults; they are sketched as essentially "in-the-making" and on a trajectory of "becoming" a parent, with associated conse-quences for the transformation of self-identification (Bailey, 1999; Miller, 2005; Thomson & Kehily, 2008). Parenthood is also a domain of life dominated by strong and specific moralities around good practice. Dominant practice morali-ties exist on maintaining good health during pregnancy, with prospective mothers and fathers being discouraged from smoking, and folic acid prescribed as a stan-dard supplement for women during early pregnancy to prevent the development of brain and spine abnormalities in their babies. New mothers are also told in no uncertain terms that "breast is best" (Blum, 1999; Murphy, 1999) and that over-heating increases the risk of baby cot death syndrome. Prospective parenthood means that those involved are caught up in a power field in which authoritative discourses take a prominent place in the process of formulating parenting moral-ities and specific understandings of good parenthood, motherhood, and father-hood (Miller, 2005). It is therefore not surprising that information and instruction are central devices directed at new parents, and that instruction is at the very heart of early parenthood (Apple, 1995; Arnup, 1994). It is further symptomatic of the historical shift in authority residing in private-domestic pedagogies to public-medical-health pedagogies.

Apple (1995) traces the process she calls "scientific motherhood" to the nine-teenth century, and she argues that the twentieth century saw the medical profes-sions positioning themselves as expert advisers to be trusted over and above advice given by "non-experts." Such discursive struggles are still apparent today. Methods for parenting adopted by family members and others in the social net-work are felt to be quickly outmoded, as ideas about baby care and raising chil-dren change apace over time and models of appropriate parenting pluralize and move in and out of fashion (Miller, 2005). The practice of parenting appears to become an increasingly "sophisticated" enterprise as professionals and experts offer ever more detailed and complex advice to prospective parents. In the United Kingdom this expanding field of experts is dominated by medical and health professionals and their professional organizations and NGO interest groups; these include general practitioners (GPs), pediatricians and obstetricians, midwives and health visitors, and psychologists and social scientists specializing in the fields of children, parenting, and families and their well-being. Underlying the arguments of those commenting on the nature of contemporary parenting is the notion that it has become a more uncertain and intensified experience (e.g., Furedi, 2001; Hays, 1996; Lee, 2008; Nelson, 2008). Parenting pedagogies not only invite pro-spective parents to delve into the specialist knowledge available about new babies and their care, but parenting moralities—becoming and being "good" mothers, fathers, and parents—stimulate a culture of perfection (Apple, 1995; Hardyment, 1995). While this might lead us to think that contemporary parents are more knowledgeable than their parents were before them, Furedi's (2001) main complaint is that, as expert advice has gained in authoritative status, parental certainty and self-confidence has come to be undermined. In previous research on kitchen practices, we have also pointed to this destabilizing quality of domestic pedagogies (Martens & Scott, 2004). It would seem that the prominence of pedagogy in early parenthood is both symptomatic and generative of the reality of this phase of life as "in-the-making" and transformative.

While parenthood scholars are in apparent agreement about the consequences of scientization and medicalization for contemporary parenthood, generally speaking, they pay little attention to the presence and significance of commercial forces as a facet in their explanations. Miller (2005), for instance, concentrates primarily on the prominence of medicalization in relation to pregnancy and childbirth in Western societies, and how this informs the experiences of new mothers. Furedi (2001), on the other hand, illustrates how moralizations about parenting interfere with "objectivity" in scientific explorations of young children, pregnancy, and child birth; and though he includes evidence suggesting that products and commercially sourced advice are part of the story, he does not tease out the significance of this for his overall argument. The most explicit discussion of how marketers have engaged with the scientific approach to parenting know-how is found in Apple (1995), who uses product advertisements to illustrate the trend towards expert reliance discussed above. Apple's work is interesting, as her historical approach points to the fact that the rising prominence of childhood experts is not a new phenomenon, and nor is the meddling of commercial interests with the knowledge that flows from the medical-health field. Yet, as she describes the rise of advice manuals written by professionals like Dr. Spock, we also learn that the American motherhood advice publication with the greatest historical impact in the twentieth century was *Infant Care*, handed to mothers by the U.S. government. Given that the literature on the nature of late modern life has heralded the idea of the market as a primary pedagogue (Bauman, 1987, 1988; Giddens, 1990, 1991; Giroux, 1999), the question arises whether parental pedagogies have become more commercial over time, and directed more by the rules of the market rather than those of the state. However, in this chapter I limit myself to three arguments as to why it is important to scrutinize more closely the interconnections between non-commercial and commercial players in relation to parental pedagogy.

First, medical-health professionals and facets of the knowledge they convey *can* and *do* move between the non-commercial[1] and the commercial, or the public and the private spheres. The growing body of "independent" childhood and parenting experts that form the center of Furedi's account may be seen to operate "on their own," but they frequently collaborate with marketers while becoming elements in commercial products and services such as magazines, websites, product packaging, and advertisements. It is further clear that "experts" frequently make a public name for themselves as parental lore experts by becoming successful authors and media personalities. One way of saying this, borrowing from Hochschild's (2005) discussion of "the wall" that demarcates the commercial from the domestic sphere, is to suggest that commercial players *borrow* across the wall that divides them from their non-commercial counterparts, and that non-commercial knowledge holders at times *move* across the wall. In an attempt to open up the question of what it means to say that early parenthood is increasingly commercialized, my starting point will therefore be to offer an analysis of the ways in which instruction and information from the field of commerce is blending in and merging with that coming from the medical-health field.

Furthermore, parental pedagogies are in a process of continual transformation, being reformulated in a maelstrom of discursive agreements and competitive struggles, deriving from non-commercial *and* commercial sources, through which specific positions of importance are eked out. In the field of consumer research, the rapid transformative quality of commodity culture has been linked to the experience of complexity in everyday life (e.g., Ger & Yenicioglu, 2004). What role the presence of the market plays in the speeding up of change in parenting know-how and associated moralities is thus another question that presents itself. However, here I will be concerned with how the organization of parental pedagogy connects with the quest for authority in commercial environments, or, to say it in a different way, why do we find commerce actively merging with non-commercial themes, actors, and procedures in this field?

This connects with my final set of concerns. Like parenthood, consumer culture has been recognized as a domain in which moralities feature highly (e.g., Miller, 2001; Sayer, 2003; Wilk, 2001). Ongoing debate suggests that consumption-related moralizations connect with a diverse set of concerns that identify specific consumption practices and specific sets of consumers as morally suspect or acceptable (Martens & Casey, 2007). Early parenthood raises the question of how the highly moralistic character of this phase of the life course meets with consumer *and* marketing ethics. One may speculate that commerce colludes with the more general cultural constitution of a "good" parenthood morality, perhaps even exacerbating understandings of what it means to be a "good parent." The informational marketing that comes with specific products hence serve as the discursive elaborations that link parenting normativities with lifestyle challenges and the products in question. However, drawing on Barnett, Cloke, Clarke, and Malpass's (2005) notion of the "governing of consumption" as "strategies used by campaigning organizations, policy-makers, and businesses to facilitate the adoption of ethical consumption practices by consumers" (p. 31), it becomes possible to see that the way in which new parents are addressed through instructional devices entails a coming together of good parenthood and specific understandings of the good parental-consumer subject. The informational and instructional terrain of early parenthood may thus be interpreted as an endeavor which stimulates parental subjects to engage in "ethical self-formation," or "moral selving." Barnett et al. (2005) define this as:

> the mediated work of creating oneself as a more virtuous person through practices that acknowledge responsibilities to others. Moral selving might take the form of explicit performances, or displays, of virtuous conduct. But it also refers to a range of more humble, perhaps even anonymous modes of conduct.
>
> (p. 30)

The examination of the ways in which new parent consumers respond to this invitation to "do" moral selving is the task of a future project. Here, I want to reflect on how the moralistic expectations engendered around early childhood and parenthood rebound onto commercial practitioners and commercial practices.

The Organization of Parental Pedagogy

Parenting has not really been addressed in social and cultural commentaries on consumption and consumer culture. Mothers and mothering have to a degree, with a growing and diverse set of materials focusing on mothers and their caring work in relation to feeding children (DeVault, 1991), to shopping (Miller, 1998), and to children's clothing (Clarke, 2004; Cook, 1995). Related work considers topics as diverse as children's birthday parties (Clarke, 2007), the Yummy Mummy phenomenon (O'Donohoe, 2006), care among low income mothers (Casey, 2007; Pugh, 2004), and empty-nester families (Hogg, Curasi, & Maclaran, 2004). In their introduction to *Consuming Motherhood*, Taylor, Layne, and Wozniak (2004) point to the historical opposition between the values of markets and motherhood, yet there are suggestions in contemporary research that this opposition may be waning with an emergent appreciation, among at least some mothers, of the market as an aid in their practices (e.g., Clarke, 2007). In the contemporary context, new motherhood identity is also understood and formulated increasingly through consumption practices (Thomson & Kehily, 2008) and indications are that the corresponding market for pregnancy and early childhood/parenthood is a growth area (Smith, 2007). Brusdal (in press) offers an explanation of these trends by outlining how the shift to smaller families and changing demographics around parental age and relative wealth at the birth of the first child in Norway stimulates a climate of growing consumerism. In the United Kingdom, this trend is demarcated for instance by The Baby Show, which opened its doors for the first time in 2002 at a London venue, and which in 2008 took place at five different locations throughout the year.

A day at The Baby Show (TBS) offers visitors a number of interrelated opportunities and experiences:

> The Baby Shows are three day events dedicated to pregnancy, birth, babies and toddlers—a great day out with the chance to try and buy all the essentials you need to give your baby the best start in life with expert information and advice.
> (The Baby Show, 2009, ¶ 1)

It is a commercial enterprise in the sense that it is organized by an events organization company, whose profits derive from the entrance fees it charges its visitors and the fees it charges exhibitors. Visiting TBS offers a day out for visitors during which they have the time to concentrate and reflect on their impending parenthood and their status as a (new) family with young children. The show offers the opportunity to shop in all its diverse forms, from seeking advice and information to spending money on a variety of different products, which may be stored for collection at the end. Visitors may also take a rest in one of the many seating areas and cafes, or they may sit down to listen and watch one of the shows on The Baby Show Stage, which is active throughout the day with freebees being handed out alongside fashion shows and "shows" with experts passing on their specialist knowledge.[2]

Two dimensions of parental-consumer pedagogy are evident at TBS. On the one hand, this domain in life offers a diversity of informational products, services and resources, which elaborate on parenting practices and normativities. These include websites, parenting magazines, guidebooks, and experts. As is clear from its online statement (quoted above), TBS functions as an informational resource in its own right, for instance, through the opportunities it offers parents to gain advice on aspects and experiences of pregnancy and early parenthood/childhood from a diversity of experts, ranging from certified midwives to sales staff. It also offers "informational" resources, as was evident at the Manchester 2008 show when various web-based resources and magazines were exhibited. There are interesting parallels between the show, magazines, and websites in the manner in which they bring together these different pedagogic players in the field; one might describe the show as a real-time and real-life formulation of the communication strategies pursued in magazines and on websites.

On the other hand, there is abundant advice on specific products, like prams and other baby carrying and seating equipment; cloth and disposable nappies; food and feeding tools; leisure goods, toys, clothing, and bedding; safety devices; remembrance and celebratory products; and information products associated with pregnancy and early childhood. At the show, product information comes in different formats: as verbal communication between stand representatives and the visiting public; as visual displays on the exhibitors' stands; and as product brochures and company magazines. Visitors typically accrue a wealth of plastic bags containing product samples and leaflets during a day at the show. Explanation of how a product works frequently shades over into practice instruction. The Phillips Avent feeding tool range of products, for instance, offers a diversity of tools for feeding and drinking practices that take a child through from birth to toddlerhood. Explanations of hygiene issues come together with illustrations of how to turn drinking bottles for the baby into drinking cups and food containers for the toddler. A similar scenario was evident in relation to cloth nappies, with sales representatives of various brands illustrating how to use cloth nappies, and how to care for them and for babies' bottoms. Aspects of such products are typically designed to deal with common problems, such as nappy rash and colic in babies, and such features will always be outlined.

I continue now with a discussion on how TBS mixes non-commercial information with commercial pedagogies and entertainment in diverse ways. In their journey through the show, visitors encounter aspects of all of these elements. There was, for instance, a health professionals' stand at every show I visited, which provided open access to visitors to speak with midwives or health visitors. At the Manchester 2008 show, the National Health Service was advertising its new NHS Choice website. Representatives were professional in their dress and in the manner they showed visitors how to navigate the website's content on pregnancy and health related themes pertaining to early childhood and parenthood. The show also had large brands such as Persil, Comfort, or Fairy sponsoring rest areas staffed by midwives and children's nurses. For instance, at the Manchester 2008 show, Fairy sponsored an easy seating area where a professional illustrated baby massage.

These areas at the show are situated among other semi-commercial and commercial stands. One might include the National Childbirth Trust among the show's semi-commercial exhibitors on the basis that it is a registered charity that offers merchandise in the form of information and other products. Other semi-commercial players, such as The Baby Website and Midwives Online, are notable examples of the fact that web-based services targeting this life course phase increasingly exhibit at TBS, demarcating them at the same time as a growth area in parental pedagogy and networking practices and opportunities. Such sites frequently operate as profit-making ventures, though that they do so and exactly how they do so is not obvious. Emma's Diary[3] and Bounty, for instance, are market research companies that gather information on new mothers by providing services (such as websites and pregnancy guides) and goods (freebees). Bounty is a household name in the United Kingdom in the sense that it has a long history and is known through the fact that it has traditionally frequently been one of the first visitors at the hospital bedside of new mothers after they have given birth. In my questioning of a Bounty representative during one of the recent shows that was supported by the company, I discovered how hard it was to get a straight answer from them about Bounty's commercial *raison d'être*. Both companies host popular websites that are not easily distinguishable from others as a means of getting in touch with new parents. The Baby Website and Midwives Online, on the other hand, have their origins in midwives wanting to provide good information to prospective parents, for instance, about breastfeeding. Like some other contemporary informational websites, these sites operate through private sponsorship from advertising. Midwives Online asserted, however, that it only accepts onto its site sponsors it considers ethically sound.

Another excellent example of how parental pedagogies alternate between non-commercial and commercial sources, and entertainment, are the proceedings on The Baby Show Stage. Apart from its fashion shows and Bob-the-Builder sing-along song-and-dance routine, the schedule of activities on the stage is organized around discussions with a variety of commercial and semi-commercial experts, talking about a variety of pregnancy, baby, and toddler concerns. Midwives and child nurses are invited onto the stage to talk about specific baby and childcare issues. Nappy rash was a subject for discussion between the presenter and a child nurse at one of the shows. Their advice blends in with equally confident, assertive, and expert-sounding commercial advisers. For instance, the founder of the Plum Baby organic foods range came on stage with her "food scientist," and together they expounded the ethics and science behind the company's products. These were very likeable people; they had an easy manner, sounded positive and authoritative, and apparently did not have anything to worry about as their product was on the market without any moral "blemishes."[4] Over the years, the stage has featured shows with Jo Frost, Annabel Karmel, Clare Byam-Cook, and Dr. Robert Titzer, and has provided advice on how to deal with "naughty children," how to feed babies and children, and how to teach babies to read.

Elsewhere, midwives may be found on the stands of commercial players. Examples include Pregnacare and Phillips Avent, where stands were populated by registered midwives alongside the company's own representatives. Midwives remain registered if they engage in midwifery practice, and those at the show wore a badge stating they were registered. Their presence here meant that they mixed midwifery practice with commercial work. Over the years, I have spoken to quite a number of midwives, either registered or no longer so, working as National Health Service midwives, working independently from the NHS, having started their own businesses (e.g., in ante-natal classes), or having moved to company work full time. The latter was the case for the representative of the baby-bottle company NUK I spoke with at one of the shows.

Understanding Pedagogic Merging

One explanation for the pedagogic merging found at TBS is that commercial players recognize the ubiquitous presence of medical and scientific discourses in this phase of the life course, and make use of it. One route towards product success is for commercial practices and products to fit in with, and relate to, such discourses, rather than to attempt to reinvent the wheel of pregnancy and early parenthood. Products hence offer themselves as aids around the major and minor concerns and issues facing new parents, which are brought to light through the strategic use of scientific and medical-health discourses and practices.

The power players in this field have their own distinct *raison d'être*, namely: the realization of profit in commercial enterprise and the realization of healthy subjects in the non-commercial medical health enterprise. Even so, the means they adopt to achieve those ends sees them moving closer together in a world that conceives of the new parent in an increasingly uniform manner. While there are different issues at stake in principle—competition between commercial players and the challenges all face regarding successful innovation on the one hand, versus the struggle for and maintenance of authoritative knowledge, trustworthiness, and status in their field by health professionals—they also merge and move across the wall that divides them. For instance, product brand formation may be regarded as an attempt to establish customer trust and loyalty, while brands stake a claim to authority and superiority among the many similar products in the field. Equally, professionals moving towards expertise frequently move from the public to the private sphere, and important facets in establishing expert charisma include the successful identification of knowledge innovation or knowledge needs, frequently packaged in appealing and authoritative ways. The extent to which expertness becomes acknowledged through the professional *performance* of the individuals concerned is an interesting question. Practitioners in both fields share the quest for authority, reputation, and trustworthiness.

Within the commercial environment, this quest means there are distinct benefits to be gained by some players from borrowing across the wall to tap into scientific and medical knowledge in specific ways. This is done in various ways, from adopting a scientific or medical appearance in communication practices, to providing statements of specific scientific outcomes that underscore the rationales for specific products. True, some products in this domain are inherently more "scientific" than others; saving baby stem cells for future ill-health eventualities is a point in case. But scientific content was also apparent in more unlikely products, such as Plum Baby Organics. This relatively new range of baby foods included some unexpected ingredients—such as quinoa and amaranth—that were described as *superfoods*. This baby food was also described as being based on new "scientific" ideas—including that babies have more taste buds than adults and are therefore more discerning when it comes to the taste of foods; and the "fact" that quinoa best resembles breast milk in terms of its protein make-up. I also heard the innovation stories of some products that hold prominent cues to the scientific work or medical knowledge that went into their development. The baby-bottle brand NUK, for instance, was founded by two German orthodontists rethinking the bottle teat[5] to fit in more with the shape of baby mouths. The teat was designed with the hole facing upwards, so that milk would splash against the baby mouth's upper pallet to stimulate salivation and hence digestion. Like other bottle teats exhibited at the show, the NUK product had been designed with a colic valve to reduce baby colic. Adopting a scientific approach in product design is often also necessary. The production of, for instance, food supplements is a point in case, while my discussion with representatives from Fisher-Price indicated the need for careful research around the safety of the products they designed, not only to produce products which were safe to use, but also because there are legal regulations to adhere to.

Along the way, it is hard for the observer to distinguish fact from fiction. While sitting down for a break during one of my show visits, I observed a video that explained about a new mattress for baby beds. It was shaped in a way that allowed the head of the baby to fall slightly backwards, thus opening the baby's breathing organs and making it easier to breath during sleep. There were intonations of baby cot death, with the traditional flat mattress being used to illustrate how it obstructed babies from breathing easily. In its story-telling, the video was scientific and professional, inducing a sense of trustworthiness. But product discourses like these are also, always, efforts in impression and image management. Specific scientific discourses will be selected, or alternatively, discourses are "made up" to sound scientific, in order to highlight the benefits rather than the drawbacks of products. Such commercial stories are thus inevitably partial stories, containing selected and selective information that may be based in "fact" or "fiction."

Underlying all this is an awareness of prospective parents as in need and in search of information and instruction. While the appointment of registered midwives on the stands of, for example, Pregnacare, Fairy, and Comfort may serve as a means to enhance the professional appearance of the brand product, they also serve as reputable knowledge experts on those stands and parents with specific questions may be referred to them. Noteworthy is that parenting and baby care information here comes as a free service. Interviews, and question and answer sessions with experts on The Baby Show Stage, or a visit to the show's *Meet the Midwives* stand, are all part of the package of entering the TBS itself. The same point may be made about the companies that appoint midwives to populate their stands.

The offer of free information and the provision of access points to other prospective and new parents lies at the heart of the growth in Internet sites in this domain. Early parenting magazines, like *Mother and Baby*, *Pregnancy and Birth*, and *Prima Baby and Pregnancy*, now have a prominence online, suggesting they are broadening out their media for communicating with their target group. Various other brands and product groups also host Internet sites, with the "baby club" phenomenon a prominent new theme. Tesco, SMA (baby formula milk), Hipp (organic baby foods), Huggies (disposable nappies), and Nestlé are some of the first brands and firms listed when conducting an Internet search for "baby club." The growth in such sites is interesting, but the speedy rise in their popularity in relation to this life course phase is particularly so. One explanation for this may be the challenges posed by the geographical spread of this population for those wishing to persuade, instruct, and communicate with them (Barnett et al., 2005). By providing online baby and parenting clubs, these companies invite prospective and new parents into a site where they become knowable and where their interests and tastes may be teased out. By hosting chat rooms and blogs, these companies also operate as virtual parenting clubs which may be accessed, from home, at any time of day, with whatever issues or questions the visitor wants to raise. As such, they make available a community of parents "out there" at the click of the computer's mouse.

Creating the Ethical Parent-Consumer Subject

When Barnett et al. (2005) introduce the notion of moral selving, they do so as part of their discussion of the role played by information in communications between businesses and consumers of "ethical" products. Their focus is on product information, and they interpret information, or "mediated strategies" (p. 30), in a broad way. Rather than seeing information as simply about passing on knowledge to consumers, they adopt a Foucauldian interpretation by conceptualizing it as a cultural form of "government" (p. 30) aimed at changing the dispositions of consumers, as generating subjects that engage in ethical self-formation. The applicability of these ideas to the story of educating the prospective parent seems striking. In sociological work on motherhood and baby feeding, the highly instructional and moral character of this phase of the life course has also been interpreted with a Foucauldian toolkit (see, e.g., Murphy, 2003). The difference between these two approaches is that commercial culture stands central in the former, while the prominence of medical-health pedagogies characterizes the latter. In Murphy's Foucauldian iteration, information-instruction around "breast is best" derives from the state-medical-health complex, and serves to generate self-governing good mothers, who breast-feed their babies. The ethical self-formation stimulated through the pedagogies of enterprises discussed by Barnett et al. (2005) essentially works through consumption and choice. They argue that consumption is

> one key site of ethical self-formation in the contemporary period of 'advanced liberalism' (Miller and Rose 1997). It serves as a key arena in which people are made up as selves who can exercise freedom and responsibility by exercising their capacity to choose . . ..
>
> (p. 30)

I want to expand on this by arguing that another understanding of pedagogic merging is to recognize it as a process whereby the goods and services offered through commodity culture offer prospective parents a means through which they may achieve and illustrate good parenthood. Hence, becoming good parents entails becoming and being good consumers. This is a two-pronged process. On the one hand, "moral selving" entails "the mediated work of creating oneself as a more virtuous person" (Barnett et al., 2005, p. 30). Thus, gathering and assimilating information, and reflecting on it, forms part of the process of becoming a "good" parent, and to be seen to be interested in information and to attend information or instructional events, like ante-natal classes or The Baby Show, are ways of appearing to be on the right pathway. In addition, the various products which circulate in this market, and which are subject to continual renewal and innovation, operate as devices for turning the *oughts* of good parenthood into *cans* (Barnett et al., 2005, p. 31): by adopting the appropriate practices with the right products, good parenthood may be both demonstrated and accomplished. Thought about in this way, the pursuit of good parenthood comes to entail the concomitant pursuit of good consumerism, and products, including informational devices, may serve as aids in practices while at the same time serving as icons that mark out the "good" parent. As stated by Douglas and Isherwood (1979), goods are excellent for making stable the categories of culture.

Notes

1 In the United Kingdom, this is represented by the National Health Service (NHS).
2 To get a sense of the vastness of the range of shopping and "entertainment" available at The Baby Show, watch the video featured on The Baby Show website: http://www.thebabyshow.co.uk/video/
3 According to the small print in the website's terms and conditions, Emma's Diary is a division of Lifecycle Marketing (Mother & Baby) Limited. According to another BS exhibitor, Emma's Diary is also financially supported by Lloydspharmacy, which also provides a free gift pack for all members of Emma's Diary.
4 Of course, the product's price tag may be seen as objectionable, but this type of product clearly had an easier PR time than is the case, for instance, for baby-bottle and formula-milk companies.
5 If my understanding is correct, in the United States the word "nipple" is used for the top of the bottle that delivers formula milk into baby mouths.

References

Apple, R. D. (1995). Constructing mothers: Scientific motherhood in the nineteenth and twentieth centuries. *Social History of Medicine, 8*(2), 161–178.
Arnup, K. (1994). *Education for motherhood: Advice for mothers in twentieth-century Canada.* Toronto: Toronto University Press.
Bailey, L. (1999). Refracted selves? A study of changes in self-identity in the transition to motherhood. *Sociology, 33*(2), 335–352.
Barnett, C., Cloke, P., Clarke, N., & Malpass, A. (2005). Consuming ethics: Articulating the subjects and spaces of ethical consumption. *Antipode, 37*(1), 23–45.
Bauman, Z. (1987). *Legislators and interpreters: On modernity, post-modernity, and intellectuals.* Oxford: Polity Press.

Bauman, Z. (1988). *Freedom.* Milton Keynes, UK: Open University Press.

Blum, L. M. (1999). *At the breast: Ideologies of breastfeeding and motherhood in the contemporary United States.* Boston: Beacon Press.

Brusdal, R. (in press). Small emperors in an affluent society. In D. Buckingham & V. Tingstad (Eds.), *Childhood and consumer culture.* London: Routledge.

Casey, E. (2007). Gambling and everyday life: Working class mothers and domestic spaces of consumption. In E. Casey & L. Martens (Eds.), *Gender and consumption: Material culture and the commercialisation of everyday life* (pp. 123–140). Aldershot: Ashgate.

Clarke, A. (2004). Maternity and materiality: Becoming a mother in consumer culture. In J. S. Taylor, L. L. Layne, & D. F. Wozniak (Eds.), *Consuming motherhood* (pp. 55–71). Rutgers, NJ: Rutgers University Press.

Clarke, A. (2007). Making sameness: Motherhood, commerce and the culture of children's birthday parties. In E. Casey & L. Martens (Eds.), *Gender and consumption: Material culture and the commercialisation of everyday life* (pp. 79–98). Aldershot: Ashgate.

Cook, D. T. (1995). The mother as consumer: Insights from the children's wear industry, 1917–1929. *Sociological Quarterly, 36*(3), 505–522.

DeVault, M. (1991). *Feeding the family.* Chicago: Chicago University Press.

Douglas, M., & Isherwood, B. (1979). *The world of goods: Towards an anthropology of consumption.* Harmondsworth, UK: Penguin.

Furedi, F. (2001). *Paranoid parenting.* Chicago: Chicago Review Press.

Ger, G., & Yenicioglu, B. (2004). Clean and dirty: Playing with boundaries of consumer's safe havens. *Advances in Consumer Research, 31,* 462–467.

Giddens, A. (1990). *The consequences of modernity.* Stanford, CA: Stanford University Press.

Giddens, A. (1991). *Modernity and self-identity: Self and society in the late modern age.* Cambridge: Polity Press.

Giroux, H. A. (1999). *The mouse that roared: Disney and the end of innocence.* Lanham, MD: Rowman & Littlefield.

Hardyment, C. (1995). *Perfect parents: Baby-care advice past and present.* Oxford, UK: Oxford University Press.

Hays, S. (1996). *The cultural contradictions of motherhood.* New Haven, CT: Yale University Press.

Hochschild, A. R. (2005). "Rent a mom" and other services: Markets, meanings and emotions. *International Journal of Work, Organisations and Emotion, 1*(1), 74–86.

Hogg, M. K., Curasi, C. F., & Maclaran, P. (2004). The (re-)configuration of production and consumption in empty nest households/families. *Consumption, Markets & Culture, 7*(3), 239–259.

Lee, E. (2008). Living with risk in the age of "intensive motherhood": Maternal identity and infant feeding. *Health, Risk and Society, 10*(5): 467–477.

Martens, L., & Casey, E. (2007). Afterword: Theorising gender, consumer culture and promises of betterment in late modernity. In E. Casey & L. Martens (Eds.), *Gender and consumption: Material culture and the commercialisation of everyday life* (pp. 219–242). Aldershot, UK: Ashgate.

Martens, L., & Scott, S. (2004). *Domestic kitchen practices: Routine, reflexivity and risk: Full Research Report.* ESRC End of Award Report, RES-000-22-0014. Swindon, UK: ESRC.

Miller, D. (1998). *A theory of shopping.* Cambridge, UK: Cambridge University Press.

Miller, D. (2001). The poverty of morality. *Journal of Consumer Culture, 1*(2), 225–243.

Miller, T. (2005). *Making sense of motherhood.* Cambridge, UK: Cambridge University Press.

Murphy, E. (1999). "Breast is best": Infant feeding decisions and maternal deviance. *Sociology of Health and Illness, 21*(2), 187–208.

Murphy, E. (2003). Expertise and forms of knowledge in the government of families. *The Sociological Review, 51*(4), 433–462.

Nelson, M. K. (2008). Watching children: Describing the use of baby monitors on Epinions. com. *Journal of Family Issues, 29*(4), 516–538.

O'Donohoe, S. (2006). Yummy mummies: The clamor of glamour in advertising to mothers. *Advertising & Society Review, 7*(3). Available: http://muse.jhu.edu/login?uri=/journals/asr/v007/7.3odonohoe.html

Pugh, A. J. (2004). Windfall child rearing: Low-income care and consumption. *Journal of Consumer Culture, 4*(2), 229–249.

Sayer, A. (2003). (De)commodification, consumer culture, and moral economy. *Environment and Planning D: Society and Space, 21*(3), 341–357.

Smith, A. (2007). *Baby and toddler essentials: A Which? Essential Guide.* London: Which? Books.

Taylor, J. S., Layne, L. L., & Wozniak, D. F. (Eds.). (2004). *Consuming motherhood.* Rutgers, NJ: Rutgers University Press.

The Baby Show. (2009). *Overview.* Available: http://www.thebabyshow.co.uk/

Thomson, R., & Kehily, M. J. (2008). *The making of modern motherhood: Memories, representations and practice: Full Research Report.* ESRC End of Award Report. RES-148-25-0057. Swindon, UK: ESRC.

Wilk, R. (2001). Consuming morality. *Journal of Consumer Culture, 1*(2), 245–260.

16 Chocolate, Place, and a Pedagogy of Consumer Privilege

David A. Greenwood

How does thinking about geography and place[1]—and the political and economic relationships between people and places globally—impact my own consumption? Everyday consumption and participation in the money economy connects consumers to a wide range of places where other people live, work, and die. Consumption begins with the biophysical and culturally shaped places of production, and the social and environmental conditions surrounding human labor. Extraction, production, consumption, and waste—each of these processes, and the points in between, connects consumers to a great many places and socioecological conditions that are generally and sometimes purposefully obscured from the consumer. An ethic of place requires that I know something about how my consumption is connected to other people and places, and that I endeavor to act, however imperfectly, on this knowledge.

Like many other privileged consumers, I do not want my consumption to support socially and ecologically unjust relationships. But the truth is that despite my desire to guide my consumption by an ethic of place that supports just social and ecological relationships, despite my desire to learn more and to consume less, as an American consumer (that is, I consume a lot), I know very little about where most of my stuff comes from. Worse, caught up in my many acts of consumption, I often choose, unconsciously, not to think about it, choosing instead, again unconsciously, to do what is expedient and economical. Tracking down the full details of each exchange my family of five incurs would amount to something like another full-time job. It would mean we have to unlearn and dramatically change our consumption habits.

Frankly, I am intimidated by the shadow of ignorance that shrouds my consumption, and I don't feel capable of dramatic transformation. In this era of great economic insecurity, I am grateful to have a relatively secure job and manageable debt, just as I am concerned over rising unemployment and horrified that billions of my brothers and sisters live in poverty and other conditions of oppression. Critical of the ravages of global capitalism, I am troubled by my ignorance of how my own economic life is implicated in the lives of other people and places. I am, however, committed to examining my own consumption, and in joining others in the difficult work of incrementally making changes that better reflect my cultural, economic, and environmental values in an ethic of place.

Unpacking the SUV of Consumer Privilege

I know that I am full of contradictions. As Walt Whitman (1855/1977) boldly owned in *Song of Myself*: "Do I contradict myself? / Very well then . . . I contradict myself; / I am large . . . I contain multitudes" (p. 96). I accept this to be more or less true of everyone, and, I also believe what Freire (2005) taught through his consciousness-raising approach to education: conscientization means learning not only to see social and political contradictions, but to *take action* against the oppressive elements of reality. Yet in a world where much of the story of consumption is socially unjust and ecologically irresponsible, where this story is concealed from view in places we do not know, and where the story is hidden deep within selves full of paradox and contradiction, it is not always easy to know what action to take or what parts of ourselves need to change.

A brief teaching story describes this dilemma well, and suggests the presence of many pathways into the issues surrounding place and consumption in the work of education. For several years I have helped lead a Teaching American History (TAH) project with middle and high school teachers in Washington State. TAH may be the largest ever federally funded Department of Education program supporting the humanities. Its purpose, and thus the reason for its long-lived bipartisan support, is to promote teaching the story of "traditional American history." The grant program has a very a-critical "red, white, and blue" reputation, yet the team I work with has been able to shape it into a place-based and social history project that we call *Our Place in History* (Gruenewald, Koppelman, & Kuntz, 2007). As we have traced it together through oral history and place-based historical inquiry, one strand of the American story is that of diverse people struggling for a better life. This story of struggle is not nostalgia, but very much alive, especially in the lives of immigrants, refugees, and exiles who often view and experience the United States, with all of its contradictions, as a land of better opportunity. My own ancestors were dirt-poor farmers from Germany, Ireland, and Slovenia. My grandmother loved America (and the American flag) not only for the ideals of freedom and opportunity that it represents, but for the reality of the opportunities that it actually offered her and her family after they had fled oppression and poverty in Europe.

Any honest approach to American history, however, must eventually confront its legacy of slavery, genocide, ecocide, racism, classism, and other forms of cultural and ecological domination that, paradoxically, continue to make this the land of opportunity for so many people. In other words, understanding history means taking account of the costs of opportunity to other people and places. Tracking the story of consumption is a good window into this history; consumption is the perfect pivot point between the contradictions of opportunity and its costs that characterizes American history and modern American culture.

"The American Dream" is in many ways a dream of consumption. Like others, I want to live a less commodified life, to meet my needs not primarily through the market, but also through relationships. However, I believe that arguing for a less-commodified existence is essentially hypocritical unless one is prepared to reveal the ways in which one's own privilege is encumbered in money and what it provides. If we are to confront the social and ecological costs of capitalism, we need to start unpacking the "invisible knapsack"[2] of consumer privilege that we carry around on our own backs, and the more visible SUVs of consumer privilege that we drive around every day. When we do this, we can acknowledge our own role in a common problem and set the stage for honesty, openness, and transformation in our individual and collective stories of consumption.

For many, myself included, consumption is the backbone of the desire to attain and hold onto a good life and meet one's and one's family's needs for safety, security, and a wide assortment of privileges and luxuries. Most of us are deeply entangled in webs of consumption, and many are trying to untangle ourselves. Like others from the privileged class, I don't believe happiness is purchased with money and possessions, but I still have plenty of stuff I don't really need and, undoubtedly, so do my children. My wife and I try to buy less stuff overall, but such an effort is continually frustrated by the contrary pattern of spending everything we have. Even when I succeed in buying less, more selectively, and more locally, I feel stuck in a cyclone of consuming through my paycheck, my expensive lifestyle (relative to the rest of the world), my wants and needs for myself and my family, my taxes, and through my retirement account. Even if one manages to escape the trance of hyperconsumerism, few really understand or attempt to follow the globalized political ecology that supports each of their privileges. Fewer still use this knowledge to guide all of their consumption practices. Consumer education in America is daily training in economic privilege and ignorance: it means learning the price of everything and the cost of nothing.

Chocolate, Privilege, and Consumer Conscientization

The critique that American "progress," or one's own consumer privilege, is stained by injustice and inequity is often debated by participants in *Our Place in History*. Recently, while comparing historical and contemporary child labor practices in the agricultural industry of Washington Sate, one of our group members made a connection to current reports of child slave labor in the cocoa fields of both Ghana and Ivory Coast. These West African countries are the top two producers of cocoa on earth, and each has been the subject of human rights investigations in connection with human trafficking and child slave labor. Eighty percent of American chocolate comes from cocoa fields where some children may be laboring as slaves. While slave labor may be rare, child labor is not; but regardless of the labor question, very few children actually eat much chocolate in Ghana and Ivory Coast—their families are too poor to buy candy. These countries lack capital for production facilities; grower-owners mainly export the raw cocoa as a cash crop so that other comparatively rich people and their children can eat candy bars elsewhere.

One of our project participants, whose own politics differed from his instructors' "leftist" framing of *Our Place in History*, bristled some at the suggestion that everyday participation in the consumer economy is a privilege somehow connected to systems of oppression and other people's misery. The fact is, he and others contended, that despite the obvious shadow of inequity surrounding chocolate production and consumption, many African people likely *choose* to work the cocoa fields for their livelihood so that they may improve *their* quality of life for themselves and their families.[3] Expressing his frustration to the group, this participant asked with all sincerity, "So I'm not sure what to do, should I buy *less* chocolate or *more* chocolate?"

Many Americans possess a kind of faith in the consumer economy, but most are distressed and outraged by the knowledge that some children labor as slaves while other people's children binge on Hershey bars at Halloween. The wealth and privilege that is taken for granted in the United States has been created through historical practices of violence, slavery, and colonization; the legacy of these forms of exploitation lives in economic globalization and in the huge inequities within and between nations. Everyday consumption connects us to these inequities. Acknowledging the connection in our own lives raises ethical dilemmas and causes discomfort.

The question—Should I buy less chocolate or more?—reflects a paradox: the privileged consumption of chocolate is connected to slave labor and other forms of injustice, but also to the livelihoods of people, some of them children, who choose to work in the fields—not for us, but for themselves. The relationship between laborers in African cocoa fields and chocoholics in the United States is obviously unequal, and it clearly reflects the geopolitical history of colonization, the inequities surrounding globalization, and the costs of privilege. But this critique aside, right now in the present reality, working the cocoa fields offers some Africans the opportunity for a better life than one without the work. Within this paradox is a tension in which privileged consumers are complicit, but for which there is no simple or immediate resolution.

Having a part in raising the issue, and the anxiety, in the first place, I felt responsible for deepening the conversation and providing an outlet for action. Responding to our participant's question with one of my own, I replied, "Do you have the information you need to answer your own question?" We both quickly agreed that neither of us knew enough about chocolate to feel comfortable with our own decisions. The discussion then moved toward identifying consumer options such as boycotting particular brands of chocolate and supporting fair trade initiatives. We wondered together whether boycotting a particular product had more to do with our own guilt, making ourselves feel better, than with actually contributing to more just and equitable economic relationships. The best I could do was to report that the chocolate my wife and I buy for each other—a decadent treat called Divine Chocolate—is labeled fair trade certified, but that I regularly buy less expensive Hershey bars for my kids' smores, and that I have never asked for fair trade chocolate when ordering dessert at a restaurant. I would likely need to go without. I wonder uneasily what it means that so few of my purchases are identifiably fair trade certified or the equivalent.

The point of the story is that most people I know like chocolate, but most don't know much about where cocoa comes from (Ghana and Ivory Coast) or the environmental, economic, and labor practices surrounding the production of everyday consumer wants and needs. I like chocolate and have enjoyed it even more since learning that the kind I like best, the kind with the highest cocoa content, is supposed to be good for you. Chocolate is a great common denominator in American culture. Young and old people of all races and classes buy it often, and collectively, we in the industrialized west eat enormous quantities of it. Most people take it for granted that chocolate is good and indeed it is good. Eating or sharing chocolate is a pleasure, and when I am feeling the pleasures of privilege, I am usually not wanting to be disturbed by the critique that a simple act of consumption implicates me in a tangled web of problematic historical, economic, and geo-political narratives. The same is true for wine and coffee. The privileged class of people likely to read this essay likely also enjoys consuming some or all of these life's pleasures. Food is a good place to start closing the gap of knowledge between one's own consumption and the people and places that produce the things we want or need. I chose to focus on chocolate here, but I could just as easily have picked lettuce or apples, or any of the fruits and vegetables we are all supposed to be eating more of, and that people somewhere labor to produce under social and environmental conditions that we might find objectionable.

The fact is that like all food, chocolate does not come from the grocery store. Like all consumer products, even the best chocolate has a life cycle literally rooted in the land, and also in the lives of people that work the land, probably for very little pay, but nonetheless pay they depend on for livelihood. As with agriculture and manufacturing generally, the people who labor hardest on the land are seldom the ones profiting most from it. Sometimes people work under conditions of oppression, laboring long hours in toxic or sweatshop conditions or worse, so that people of privilege elsewhere can sell at a profit or experience the pleasure and satisfaction of consuming. Although few people know all the details about where their stuff comes from, I believe the basic equation—that people labor for our pleasure elsewhere under questionable environmental and working conditions— is pretty widely known and accepted; it is an obvious fact and a fundamental aspect of the globalized capitalist consumer economy.[4]

The question is: What do we do with this knowledge as consumers? Some would argue that what we might perceive to be unjust and inequitable may be experienced by others as opportunity. But when other people's opportunity collides with my sense of fairness, how should I respond? Conscientization means that I not merely observe or denounce what I believe to be unjust, but that I take some kind of action. I can close the loop between producer and consumer by buying fresh vegetables in season from local farmers, and I can support other local craft businesses with my patronage. Buying locally helps me know something about the labor and environmental practices behind my purchases, but truly local consumption makes up a tiny fraction of my own financial ledger. What about chocolate? Does an ethic of place require deprivation?

I put this question to my friend and colleague Bob Offei Manteaw. A native Ghanaian educated in England and the United States, Bob is a professor of education at Eastern Washington University where he studies local and global sustainability; he also consults with UNICEF around educational reform in Ethiopia. Bob is especially interested in the relationship between discourses of education for sustainability in "developing" countries like Ghana or Ethiopia and "developed" countries like the United States, Canada, and England. When speaking to groups of students and faculty about education and sustainability, Bob often introduces himself as "the Chocolate Man." He tells the story of Ghana as a leading world producer of cocoa (and gold), and explains how few children in his homeland actually get to eat chocolate, except on special holidays like Christmas. As he tells his story, Bob passes out samples of fair trade certified chocolate made from Ghanaian cocoa and produced in one of Ghana's few chocolate factories—he calls it Ghana chocolate.

When I asked Bob to comment on the chocolate dilemma that surfaced in the *Our Place in History* project, he told me he should probably get our group some Ghana chocolate. When I asked him what he thought we should do about our own chocolate consumption, he said he would not tell us to do anything different from what we do now, but that we should be aware that we are fortunate to have such privileged choices—not so in Ghana. From Bob's perspective, chocolate is a moral issue signifying the global inequities and injustices surrounding consumption. He believes we all need to become more conscious of how our privilege is purchased through other people's labor in far away but very real places. Consumer conscientization, in other words, is a learning process.

This is the lesson from the Chocolate Man. It is incredibly simple, and incredibly complex. Bob understands that critique alone changes nothing, and that telling others what to do is seldom the answer, especially when the right decision is often unclear. The ethically charged problems of social and ecological injustice that surround consumption are, from a geopolitical perspective, systemic problems that need to be critiqued, better understood, and hopefully transformed over time. But from the perspective of the privileged consumer, it is also a personal and present problem that one ultimately has to face in oneself. How does one hold the knowledge that something as simple and satisfying as eating chocolate connects us to people we will never know and places we will never see?

I believe there is a growing awareness among privileged consumers such as myself of the social and ecological consequences of consumption. And I also know that those of us who are interested in raising our awareness and making conscious choices are not a monolithic or homogenous group, but a culturally and economically diverse group of learners. Each of us seeking to learn more, and wanting to act with more complete understanding, is on a personal journey. We are all somewhere on a continuum between blind ignorance on the one hand, and intimate knowledge on the other, of what kinds of people and place relationships our consumption supports. Though I try to buy less generally and increasingly attempt to guide my purchases by an ethic of place, as a privileged American consumer, I remain tangled in webs of social and environmental injustice that are hard to escape from. Besides trying to reduce my overall consumption and consuming more selectively, I also try to practice the principle of gratitude. If I slow myself down long enough to judge if I can be truly grateful for something, then I am bringing more consciousness toward the act of consuming. Slowness, gratitude, selectivity, and reduction—these are gestures toward a kind of consumer conscientization, toward a pedagogy of consumer privilege.

I am skeptical of others who would tell us what we should and shouldn't buy. Everyone I know is on a different path around consumption. I know one person who actually does research every product that her dollars touch, trying to ensure each transaction is socially and ecologically just. Another acquaintance buys carbon credits to offset the few times a year he flies home across the country to visit his family. Neither of these individuals claims any moral high ground, and each acknowledges the continuing struggle to come to terms with the social and ecological footprints that spending leaves behind. Incidentally, neither of these acquaintances has children (yet), and I am sometimes stymied by the fact that when it comes to consumption, having children seems to change everything. Probably the most significant decision around consumption that my wife and I have made (besides having children) was joining a local CSA (community supported agriculture). From May through October, we take our kids to pick up a box of fresh organic vegetables from a local organic farm. We know that the people who run the farm love their work because we meet them each week, and we see for ourselves how well they take care of the land. This is a big commitment. At around $500 a season, joining a CSA can strain a family's food budget. But knowing where the money goes, experiencing the beauty of the farm, and enjoying the high-quality produce make the investment worth it. For us, that is value, and we are in a growing process of applying that standard of value to more and more of our family's purchases.

I sometimes feel guilty for being a privileged consumer, and sometimes I feel virtuous for making consumer decisions I believe to be socially and ecologically responsible. But I do not believe guilt and righteousness move us toward greater knowledge and more compassionate acts. Maybe the best we can do is to continue raising each other's awareness of the issues involved in making our choices. Unpacking the knapsack of consumer privilege may be a private and personal journey, but it is also one that really begins to develop once it is shared openly with others, especially others who approach the issues from different experiential, cultural, and geographical contexts. We can give each other some ideas of where to go next without the righteousness that impedes the process of change. Sharing some chocolate together, while learning to appreciate where it comes from, is a good place to start.

Acknowledgment

The author wishes to thank Bob Offei Manteaw for conversation and feedback on this chapter.

Notes

1 On the relationship between place, environment, culture, and education, see Gruenewald (2003a, 2003b); Gruenewald and Smith (2008).
2 The phrase comes from Peggy McIntosh's (1990) classic essay, "White Privilege: Unpacking the Invisible Knapsack."
3 The same is true for Mexican and Mexican Americans laboring in the fields of Washington's fruit and wine industry and for workers around the globe who labor in agriculture for the privileged consumption of others.
4 See *The Story of Stuff* for an introduction to the local and global flow of production and consumption: http://thestoryofstuff.com

References

Gruenewald, D. (2003a). The best of both worlds: A critical pedagogy of place. *Educational Researcher, 32*(4), 3–12.

Gruenewald, D. (2003b). Foundations of place: A multidisciplinary framework for place-conscious education. *American Educational Research Journal, 40*(3), 619–654.

Gruenewald, D, Koppelman, N., & Kuntz, A. (2007). Our place in history: Inspiring place-based social history in schools and communities. *Journal of Museum Education, 32*(3), 231–240.

Gruenewald, D., & Smith, G. (Eds.). (2008). *Place-based education in the global age: Local diversity.* Mahwah, NJ: Lawrence Erlbaum Associates.

Freire, P. (2005). *Pedagogy of the oppressed.* New York: Continuum.

McIntosh, P. (1990). White privilege: Unpacking the invisible knapsack. *Independent School,* Winter, 31–36.

Whitman, W. (1855/1977). *Leaves of grass* (1st ed.). In M. Van Doren (Ed.), *The portable Walt Whitman.* New York: Penguin Books.

Part IV

Unlearning Consumerism Through Critical Pedagogies of Consumption

Sites of Contestation and Resistance

17 Re-Imagining Consumption

Political and Creative Practices of Arts-Based Environmental Adult Education

Darlene E. Clover and Katie Shaw

Contemporary patterns of consumption are symbolic of the power and potential of global capitalism and marketing. Rapid economic growth—assumed to be vital to human existence—is tied inextricably to the production, consumption, and disposal of a variety of products and goods. Quality of life, social status, and even human relations and identities often presuppose a high and constant level of consumption. Critical forces behind contemporary consumption are national, multinational, and transnational corporations and their abilities to encourage a frenzy of buying and selling through highly creative and imaginative marketing and advertising practices (Villeneuve, 1995; Zuk & Dalton, 2003).

For adult educators and community activists across Canada, addressing the complex and multifaceted nature of consumption poses a major challenge. After all, one of the deepest and most pervasive educative processes at work since the Second World War has been teaching and learning to consume (Clover & Hill, 2003; Welton, 1987). Problematically, much of what passes for public environmental education in this country has been woefully inadequate in responding appropriately to consumerism. In one regard, it ignores the politics of over-consumption and waste, choosing instead to focus on the individual and leaving corporations to carry out their activities unencumbered by critique or challenge from a politicized public. Public environmental education has also been unable to match the very creative and imaginative educative practices of advertisers and marketers, choosing instead to focus on awareness-raising and information-sharing rather than critical and creative engagement. Unlike the marketing world, which capitalizes fully on the aesthetic dimension of human kind, public environmental education under-estimates the potential of this human faculty to provide a creative counter-force and means to explore consumerism.

There are, however, examples of environmental adult education activities throughout Canada—in both community and institutions—that help people problematize diverse aspects of consumption in creative ways. Our aim in this chapter is to highlight four of these, exploring how arts-based practices are used to broaden and re-politicize the discourse of consumerism. Their aim is to provoke creative ways of explaining, understanding, and acting in and on the world, or develop new partnerships and alternative symbolic representations. We suggest these environmental adult education initiatives are a critical force for change because they tap into the aesthetic dimension—the imaginative and symbolic realm. As Greene (2000) so aptly notes, "consciousness always has an imaginative phase, and the imagination, more than any other capacity, breaks through the 'inertia of habit'" (p. 21).

Consumption in the Canadian Context

Like most other western countries, Canada began in the 1950s to experience the unprecedented growth of a "consumer society." This term came to signify not just affluence and the expansion of production and markets, but also the increased penetration into the culture of everyday life of the meaning and images associated with consumption. The free and abundant choice of goods increasingly available came to symbolize for Canadians, freedom, affluence, and the good life (Nava, 1992). According to consumer ideology, the more people consumed, the higher their standard of living, and by association, their quality of life. In fact "forced consumerism was extolled by the markets as a must: things had to be consumed, burned, used, replaced and discarded at a constantly accelerating pace" (Lahaye, 1995, p. 60) if economic prosperity was to be maintained. Lister (2000) identified the suburbs around Canada's largest cities in particular as "exclusive enclaves of private splendour" and therefore, the critical and ultimate reflection of "our consumer-driven narcissistic obsession with the private realm" (p. 1).

Today, the Canadian economy, like many others, is dominated by large trans- or multinational corporations with the ability to control costs, prices, labor, and materials through long-term, global planning. They are also able to generate internal capital and thereby "ignore government efforts to fine-tune the economy through traditional monetary and fiscal policies" (Clarke 1997, p. 16). However, governments are not innocent bystanders of corporatization and globalization forces. Rather, they create policies that provide vast amounts of freedom to corporations. Moreover, successive right-wing governments in Canada have cut spending for environmental protection and monitoring to such an extent that problems such as water contamination are increasing. From an economic point of view, water contamination (like war) is actually a "good" thing as people are compelled to purchase bottled water from multinational corporations.

Corporations are enabled in two other ways. First, much of the right-wing mainstream media, especially the print media, is owned by one conglomerate—CanWest Global Communications Corporation—with vested interests in the status quo. This special interest group has the ability to portray corporations in specific lights, enacting a great deal of public control by hiding or depoliticizing corporate socio-environmental impacts. Consumption, we are told through this media lens, is merely a personal choice and corporations generously—perhaps we should even say altruistically—give people what they want. Within this corporate-controlled ideology, it is demand, after all, that fuels supply.

Or is it? The second corporate enabler is advertising and marketing. As Duval, an adverting executive in Montreal, states so adamantly, "our work more often than not boils down to boosting sales of a product in a particular market and thus to encourage consumption . . . to claim otherwise would be a lie" (in Villeneuve,

1995, p. 57). Academics have long been concerned about the possible negative effects of a constant diet of commercials and propaganda and the ways in which people are "being corrupted or duped by entreaties to buy" (Nava, 1992, p. 172). Equally problematic is the amount of creative artistry that goes into the marketing and advertising of goods. The arts are powerful tools that transform how we see the world by creating worlds before our very eyes (Clover & Stalker, 2007). This power and potential—the arts and what they symbolize—have therefore become essential elements of advertising (Zuk & Dalton, 2003). Posters, billboards, and commercials are alive in design, color, and symbols that stimulate strong emotion, frequently with spectacular results in terms of spurring on consumption (Florida, 2002). For example, the arts construe meanings that go beyond the product itself. We begin to identify with these products as symbols of say, our identity—the "good life." They become both a need and want to make us feel complete (Klein, 2002). In addition, commercials are extremely entertaining—often making us laugh and feel good about the world the product symbolically represents and where we should somehow be. Propaganda becomes both an art and a craft. The subset of what we can call the imaginative is unrestrained; the act of consumption becomes a source of power.

Public Environmental Education

Situated within both the political and creative advertising contexts are two major problems with what passes for much public environmental education in Canada today. To begin, there is an overwhelming emphasis on individual behavior modification that is at best simplistic and at worst naïve, disempower-ing, and often, useless. Emphasis is placed on the individual learning to recycle all those water bottles, to shut off the lights or the taps, or to comply voluntarily with "Buy Nothing Day." Let us make it clear that we are not suggesting indi-vidual actions do not make a difference and that small measures are not impor-tant. Certainly, we believe in the consumer power of individuals. Rather, we are suggesting that in terms of education, we need to think more about how to encourage critical thinking and deeper reflection and empower people to engage more fully as citizens.

Behavioral changes in populations can often be undermined by political/cor-porate interests as we will illustrate in the next section of this chapter. But to illustrate our point here on critical thinking and deeper reflection, we return to Lister's (2000) comments above on the problematic of the suburbs vis-à-vis con-sumption and environmental degradation. Several factors behind this so-called "consumer-driven obsession" need to be unpacked if those living in suburban enclaves are to feel empowered rather than victimized. To begin, we acknowledge that some people move to the suburbs by choice. They want more land, a larger home and/or to remove their children from what they perceive to be the dire consequences of urban living (i.e., drugs, gangs, pollution). However, there are many others who are forced to move from—or never had the opportunity to choose—the more desirable and accessible inner city locations of Canada (all of which are vibrant) for financial reasons: they simply could not afford to purchase a home. For instance, much of the suburban population comprises new Canadians and people of color who, primarily due to racism, work in menial jobs with low salaries that negate living downtown (Mojab, 2001). Moreover, public transport to these areas is most often limited, forcing use of a car. U.S.-style shopping centers or mega-malls move in to provide the consumer goods these people "need." While many of these shops were at one time locally or even Canadian-owned, they certainly are not now. Globalization and corporatization brought American fast food and big-box stores, all of which sell products made outside Canada and plenty of them at cheap prices. The quality of these products is equally cheap and they are soon disposed of into landfills. Through the lens of public environmental education with its individualistic focus and process, the individual has made a poor "choice" and has to change his or her (and predominantly "her" since women make most household purchases) behavior in order to "fix" the problem. This neatly eliminates having to explore the complexity of urban sprawl or the tougher work of encouraging collective action around public transport, local ownership, and other more political responses (since governments are still, at least in theory, responsible to the public). Educator-activist Clarke (1997) noted quite aptly that a quarter-century ago there was a much higher degree of political literacy in Canada about corporations and their power than exists today. In the 1970s and 1980s there were lively debates but today there is almost no emphasis in public environmental education practice on the political, social, and environmental influences of modern corporations, or on what needs to be done to change things around and return the blame to where it belongs.

The second problematic of public environmental education is the lack of creativity in educational practice. The emphasis rests almost exclusively on awareness-raising through information sharing from "experts." This approach reinforces the idea that we can attribute different levels of status to knowledge, based on the rationale that professionals would know but so-called ordinary people would not. The practice of teaching becomes expository and didactic rather than engaging and critical. Not only is people's knowledge ignored as a basis to explore a problem, but symbolism, metaphor, and humor which the media understands to be so powerful, too are excluded. What counts as going beyond the obvious—what may actually require the *imagination*—is neglected in public environmental education. The advertising world fully recognizes the need to stimulate the human resources of imagination and creativity. It is therefore imperative that public educators understand the power and emancipatory potential of the aesthetic dimension to develop new ways of seeing, exploring, and challenging the world being created for us (Clover & Stalker, 2007; Greene, 2000). It is to examples of this potential we now turn.

Critical and Creative Environmental Adult Education Responses

In Canada there is a shift taking place in terms of environmental thinking and citizen action, placing more emphasis on the arts. Below we outline four examples of critical and creative pedagogical practices that go well beyond the stifling, limited, and pedantic aspects of so much public environmental education. Practices of arts-based adult education are in fact emerging in communities across Canada as a way to challenge the didactic, behaviorism model and encourage aesthetic ways of knowing for radical, social learning. Arts-based adult education is an imaginative, participatory approach based on working and learning collectively through artistic processes to develop new paradigms for comprehending contemporary problems, promoting consciousness and knowledge, stimulating imaginative critique, and enhancing people's abilities to challenge processes and practices that marginalize and disempower (Clover & Stalker, 2007). Using arts and other symbolic, performative, metaphoric, and visual forms, adult environmental educators can address environmental degradation and injustices. Engaging the aesthetic dimension enhances, or has the potential to enhance, the transformative, democratic, and emancipatory objectives of environmental adult education.

Adbusters Media Foundation

Zuk and Dalton (2003) suggest

> If we are to attempt to understand the power of advertising art, we need to learn more about how and why it works . . . .. Viewers are better able to respond intelligently when they learn . . . the ways advertising artists select and compose images to alter or extend . . . values through connecting them with goods and services.

> (p. 287)

Adbusters Media Foundation, based in Vancouver, British Columbia, is one space that aims to help citizens think differently about taken-for-granted advertisements, reconnecting them to social issues. Although not without critique for its sometimes lack of cultural understanding (i.e., Sandlin & Milam, 2008) this group of very creative public educators aims to change the way information flows and meanings are produced. *Adbusters* magazine carries philosophical articles and activist commentary around corporations and the power they wield. But what is most compelling and creative is the use of counter-imagery based on pervasive mainstream advertisements that deconstruct or turn those mainstream adverts on their head. As Zuk and Dalton (2003) note, "these advertisements have all the savvy and glitz of advertising campaigns launched by major corporations" (p. 286) but they are subversive, entertaining, and poignant. In one Adbusters "subvertisement" (as these counter-ads are called by Adbusters founder Kalle Lasn) the outline of an Absolut Vodka bottle comprises chairs in a circle reminiscent of an Alcoholics Anonymous meeting. In another, there is an image of a young woman originally associated with the GAP brand retail store. But the caption draws attention to eating disorders and their health impact on young women. Another subvertisement sells a pair of old boots to "kick corporate ass." As Adbusters itself notes on its website "we want folks to get mad [sic] about corporate disinformation, injustices in the global economy, and any industry that pollutes our physical or mental commons" (www.adbusters.org). "To create symbols is to generate power" and the arts have always had a great power over and in society (Griffiths, 1997, p. 31). The growing influence of visual media in advertising in Canada makes it "all the more necessary that we understand the power of images, how they are constructed, what they mean, and how they affect us" (Zuk & Dalton, 2003, p. 293). Creative advertising has an impact even if many do not fully realize just what that impact is. Adbusters currently has over 79,000 individuals and organizations as part of its network. Beyond the *Adbusters* magazine, they are actively engaged in challenging the active censorship in Canada of citizen-produced advertisements. It is their contention that "Canadians should be able to . . . buy 30 seconds of airtime under the same rules and conditions as corporations do" (Adbusters, 2008, ¶ 4).

Tales from the Sari-Sari

In the mid 1990s, Footprints International at the University of Calgary initiated a creative, Canada–Philippine arts-based learning project titled *Tales from the Sari-Sari: In Search of Bigfoot*. The primary objective of this program was to improve students' skills in using popular theater as a critical and creative educational tool vis-à-vis the issue of over-exploitation of natural resources. Over approximately 10 weeks, students worked together in both countries to create a performance that addressed issues of over-consumption, such as over-fishing and corporate greed, in comical yet poignant ways (Keough, Carmona & Grandinetti, 1995). Over 3,000 people in communities in Canada and the Philippines attended the 17 interactive performances in community centers, church basements, and school auditoriums. While there were many cultural and environmental differences between the two countries, the life-and-death struggles of fishers in Matabas, Philippines, and those on the east coast of Canada due to foreign over-fishing, destructive technologies, and unresponsive politicians had striking parallels. Although these creative experiences "were at times inspired, at times hair-pulling and frustrating; and frantic, exhilarating, sweaty and . . . seat of the pants" (p. 7), the work resulted in a greater understanding of cultural imperialism, corporate power, unsustainable consumption, and the power of the arts and collective processes. In particular, there was a "renewed understanding of the depth, breadth and wisdom of people's knowledge" (p. 9). In other words, what came creatively to light was a powerful source of knowledge held by ordinary people in terms of the root causes of over-consumption and community/environmental degradation. Throughout Canada and the Philippines, people in remote mountain communities or small coastal villages shared what they knew and strategies for change. What became clear was the value of recognizing that this is an interdependent global world and that not taking collective action is done at our peril.

The Garbage Collection

The Garbage Collection was an environmental adult education project aimed at building links between sanitation workers (members of the Canadian Union of Public Employees, CUPE), environmental activists (Toronto Environmental Alliance) and artists in Toronto. Twelve members of these groups came together one weekend in a workshop to share knowledge about the issues of production, consumption, and waste. Working collectively, the group developed shared stories and a series of colorful and poignant images of various signs of danger due to over-consumption—such as farmland under threat—and painted these images as murals on the sides of municipal 'mobile canvases' or garbage trucks (Barndt, 2008; Clover, 2000). Through storytelling "the artists revealed their complicity in creating trash from the toxic materials they use, the [sanitation] workers exposed the dangers they face as they pick up the garbage, and the environmentalists unearthed the impact current garbage disposal systems have on the planet" (Barndt, 2008, p. 358). The City of Toronto approved the drawings, the murals were all painted onto the trucks, and they, along with the workshop participants and even city Counselors, assembled in a downtown sanitation yard to celebrate the art. In order to bring visibility to the project, television media were invited to this unveiling. While events began calmly enough, one image creatively depicting a current initiative to have millions of tons of trash shipped by train from Toronto to a small town site in northern Ontario caught the eye of the media, turning the ceremony into a volatile circus that had major political implications. In front of a bank of savvy media, a Counselor pointed directly to the image, arguing vociferously that it depicted two Counselors (with train carriages and money bags swirling around their heads—trash is, after all, a lucrative business) as pigs; he ordered the trucks off the lot to be "whitewashed." CUPE officials, the artists, sanitation workers, and many others protested immediately and organized a major press conference. This, they argued, was an issue of democracy and freedom of voice. The decision to whitewash the design was undemocratic, an act of censorship.

This act of censorship should not, however, come as a surprise. As Griffiths (1997) notes, attention by authorities in public situations is often directed at stamping out creative elements "because they are the most vigorously effective" (p. 31). And effective they were. Four important actions resulted from this arts-based project. First, the trucks belong to the City but copyright belongs to the artists, so the murals were simply repainted in very public places, which proved more effective in terms of public education than trucks that simply ghost through a neighborhood in the early morning hours. Second, the City canceled plans to ship the garbage. One media source suggested it was due to the contractors but this was not the full story. Third, and related, the Counselor who ordered the truck whitewashed was voted out of office shortly thereafter. The media suggested this loss was due to a recent merger but the Counselor himself appeared on CBC radio and publicly blamed the Toronto Environmental Alliance for his downfall. Finally, it was revealed through the project that recyclables were being dumped into landfill, rather than being taken to recycling stations. The sanitation workers—seldom asked for their knowledge—revealed that in many instances, they were simply shipping the blue boxes of recycling materials to landfill since it was a cheaper alternative for the City. Millions of Torontonians who had been washing bottles, peeling off labels and dutifully carrying blue boxes to the curb each week were incensed. It became clear that behavioral modification, so encouraged by public environmental education activities, had been in vain. With an angry and knowledgeable public at their doorstep, the City was forced to change its practice!

The Means of Production Project

Linking consumption patterns to the production of art is another step in understanding the collective responsibilities and opportunities for creative adult environmental education. The Means of Production Project from North China Creek Park in the Mount Pleasant Neighborhood of Vancouver, British Columbia was conceived to meet three main objectives: to challenge artists' understandings and practices of consumption in the production of their art, create viable urban green space where artist materials could be locally produced and fostered, and develop a new critical tipping point for local artists to link with youth. Connecting to youth through this project allows a different type of capacity building; building a sense of place-based, local resilience among emerging youth artists to look to local opportunities for material production versus relying on external, transnational resources. Initiated in 2002 by artist Oliver Kellhammer and three community stakeholders,[1] the physical building of the green space/ecoforest was first viewed as simply a community garden, but the arts-infused objective allowed for a creative and sustainable practice of art supply and engagement within the community. The garden continues to flourish today as it produces an expansive scope of raw materials for the art and youth community (such as regular harvesting of materials such as basketry, garden fencing, drawing charcoal, hand-made paper, tea pot handles, rustic furniture, etc.). Kellhammer has crafted a botanical intervention by creating an inclusive community-owned process of building community-scale, urban ecoforestry in a low-income, inner-city neighborhood.

Originally, artist Oliver Kellhammer envisioned the design and function for The Means of Production through an artistic and environmental sustainability lens. However, the art of the original concept was meant to continue adapting and shifting, to represent the true and organic growth of communities themselves. The original "artistic" structures and even selection of plans for the urban ecoforest have since evolved and responded to community suggestions and local needs of both artists and manufacturers. Kellhammer himself acknowledged during the conception of the project that the role of the artists in this case was to set a landscape for more artistic, ecological, and functional interpretations to emerge—for the forest to eventually represent social, economic, and environmental needs within the roots of the community itself. The catalyst for this art manifested into sustainable productions; the purpose focused on community engagement and education, not individual impact or perception.

This project also sought to shift the conception of the role art could play *in* and the impact art could have *on* re-imagining environmental adult education. The Means of Production Project raises questions about the artistic integrity of an ever-evolving and complex ecosystem and beckons the need to magnify the collective contribution of art as a means for political engagement. Deconstructing consumer patterns and developing a more collective understanding of the intersecting uses for local materials, modes of production, and means of supply requires collaborations across sectors and disciplines be re-invigorative and supported. This project demonstrates that a collaborative effort between two large stakeholders—Community Arts Council of Vancouver and the Vancouver Parks Board—and a local youth-led community organization could create tangible, long-term change. This is particularly impressive during a time where land continues to soar in economic value and redirecting development towards a green, urban, multifunctional ecoforest is not only creative, but almost unheard of. Systems change is necessary for comprehensive community impact on consumption patterns, and the pivotal role of art and collaboration cannot be underestimated.

The means of production, in this case, were creatively infused to meet local artists' needs while manifesting an action-based project within a community, which critically engaged local citizens across generations around issues of common area, common space, and consumption patterns for future generations. The respectful inclusion of youth into the production of the ecoforest and the fact that it remains a community space, free for use and visit by anyone, exemplifies a creative educational practice.

Conclusions

To paraphrase Arundhati Roy who spoke in 2003 at the World Social Forum in Porto Alegre, the aim of the kinds of pedagogical activities outlined above is to not only confront the empires of corporatization and marketing but to mock them, with art, stubbornness, joy, brilliance, and the sheer relentlessness of creatively telling different stories from the ones we are brainwashed to believe. We concur with Zuk and Dalton (2003) who argue that many citizens today feel a "growing discomfort with the power and influence exercised by multi-national and corporate giants" (p. 285). However, individuals seldom have anywhere to turn to critically or creatively explore or discuss these feelings. More often than not, they are bombarded with messages of "blame" and told by experts what to think, while their own substantial knowledge is disregarded.

These four examples demonstrate the power and potential of arts-based environmental adult education to re-politicize creatively and vibrantly the issue of consumption and its local and/or global implications. The arts are far more than mere self-expression; they are tools of emancipatory and critical learning that can inflame politicians, force people to see the taken-for-granted differently, and engage the imagination in explorations of consumerism (Clover & Stalker, 2007; Greene, 2000). As marketing executives and corporations have discovered, the symbol-maker has immense power and control in society (Griffiths, 1997). These educational initiatives offer ways to both take back and generate power and citizen control. These examples also create spaces for communities of practice, such as artists, to engage more critically and politically around their consumption practices. Arts-based adult education lights the creative spark for environmental change, using the imagination to challenge current systems and structures of mass production.

Part of this re-imagining of arts-based environmental adult education involves educators having the courage to take risks through multisectoral collaborations.

Environmental practices are impacted by a variety of systems, sectors, and disciplines. As these examples show, the arts can be used as catalysts to bring a variety of community and global stakeholders around tables and spark more holistic partnerships to address complex issues. The examples also illustrate that challenging sectors to work more holistically will not happen immediately. Changing global, colonial, imperialistic value systems that uphold individualistic "blaming" around environmental change will not be easy, but critically examining and identifying entry points (such as arts-based environmental adult education) for this change is crucial.

Arts-based environmental adult education is about re-engaging the imagination and the aesthetic dimension and trusting in and building upon ordinary people's knowledge. The arts are powerful tools to publicly illuminate the 'other' stories and activities so often hidden behind a veil of political double-speak, corporate lobbying, and media omissions. These are examples of "art used for common causes; not only to raise emotions but to direct that passion into actions" (Griffiths, 1997, p. 30). To us, this is the promise of an arts-based environmental adult education—a promise fulfilled through an efficacy in helping people to collectively, creatively, and aesthetically reflect upon and transform the planet's current consumerist trajectory.

Note

1 The Means of Production Project was funded by the *Art and Environmental Initiative* of the Community Arts Council of Vancouver, the Vancouver Parks Board and with the support and guidance from the Environmental Youth Alliance in Vancouver.

References

Adbusters. (2008). *A legal action for media democracy.* Available: http://www.adbusters.org/campaigns/updates/legal_action_media_democracy.html

Barndt, D. (2008). Touching minds and hearts: Community arts as collaborative research. In J. G. Knowles & A. L. Cole (Eds.), *Handbook of the arts in qualitative research* (pp. 351–362). Thousand Oaks, CA: Sage Publications.

Clarke, T. (1997). *Silent coup: Confronting the big business takeover in Canada, Ottawa and Toronto.* Ottawa: Canadian Centre for Policy Alternatives and James Lorimer & Company Limited.

Clover, D. E. (2000). Community arts as environmental adult education and activism. *Convergence, 33*(3), 19–30.

Clover, D. E., & Hill, L. (Eds.). (2003). *Environmental adult education: Ecological learning, theory, and practice for socio-environmental change.* New Directions in Adult and Continuing Education Series, 99, San Francisco: Jossey-Bass.

Clover, D. E., & Stalker, J. (Eds.). (2007). *The arts and social justice: Re-crafting adult education and community cultural leadership.* Leicester: NIACE.

Greene, M. (2000). *Releasing the imagination.* San Francisco: Jossey-Bass.

Florida, R. (2002). *The rise of the creative class.* New York: Basic Books.

Griffiths, J. (1997). Art as a weapon of protest. *Resurgence, 180,* 35–37.

Keough, N., Carmona, E., & Grandinetti, L. (1995). Tales from the Sari-Sari: In search of bigfoot. *Convergence, 28*(4), 5–11.

Klein, N. (2002). *No logo.* New York: Picador.

Lahaye, M. (1995). The consumer and "green" products. *EcoDecision, 16,* 60–62.

Lister, N. (2000). Beyond sprawl. *Alternatives, 26*(2), 1.

Mojab, S. (2001). The power of economic globalization: Deskilling immigrant women through training. In R. M. Cervero & A. L. Wilson (Eds.), *Power in practice: Adult education and the struggle for knowledge and power in society* (pp. 23–41). San Francisco: Jossey-Bass.

Nava, M. (1992). *Changing cultures: Feminism, youth and consumerism.* London: Sage.

Sandlin, J. A., & Milam, J. L. (2008). "Mixing pop (culture) and politics": Cultural resistance, culture jamming, and anti-consumption activism as critical public pedagogy. *Curriculum Inquiry, 38*(3), 323–350.

Villeneuve, C. (1995). Advertising, consumption and environment: An interview with Jacques Duval, Advertising Executive. *EcoDecision, 16,* 57–59.

Welton, M. (1987). *Knowledge for the people.* Toronto: OISE Press.

Zuk, B., & Dalton, R. (2003). Satirical counter-ads as critical pedagogy. In R. Roth (Ed.), *Connections* (pp. 285–293). Victoria: University of Victoria.

18 Using Cultural Production to Undermine Consumption
Paul Robeson as Radical Cultural Worker

Stephen D. Brookfield

Working in the belly of the beast to challenge and dismantle the beast is an enter-prise fraught with contradiction. Yet artists and cultural workers through the ages have used popular cultural forms that are bought, traded, and consumed in the capitalist marketplace to undermine the logic of that same marketplace. Within adult education there has been interest among educators and scholars in how popular culture can be used to animate social change. European Marxist scholar-ship and critical theory, particularly the work of Gramsci, Benjamin, and Adorno, laid a rich foundation for contemporary cultural studies. In the United Kingdom much of the work of the Welsh cultural critic, Raymond Williams, the British–Caribbean intellectual Stuart Hall, and the first (and only) chairman of the National Advisory Council for Adult and Continuing Education, Richard Hoggart, was conducted within university extra-mural adult education. Williams (1995) consistently declared that the foundations of contemporary cultural studies were laid in English adult education.

The form of cultural consumption Williams and Hoggart were most interested in was the consumption of popular culture, particularly the role of popular cul-tural consumption in the development of class identity. Growing up in Liverpool, England, in the 1950s and 1960s I was well aware of how cultural consumption was stratified by social class, and by its associated variable, education. As a teen-ager it was clear to me that the culture one consumed, and how one consumed it, were political matters. For example, it was a revelation to me to understand, through the work of C. L. R. James, the Caribbean Marxist, that the consumption of cricket in the West Indies was crucial to the anti-colonial movement. From being a vestige of British upper-class social control, cricket became a way to humiliate British imperialism (James, 1993). The Indian Bollywood film *Lagaan: Once Upon a Time in India* (Gowariker, 2002) portrays the same dynamic in colonial India.

Sport and popular music were clearly two forms of cultural consumption that framed the identity development of millions of British teenagers like myself. But we had no public figure who crossed these areas of cultural production and who used their influence to undermine the logic of the system that had produced them. In America, however, I knew of two lauded sporting or musical figures who had used fame as a spur to greater political activism. First, there was Cassius Clay, the Boxing Heavyweight Champion of the World, who changed his name to

Muhammad Ali and joined the Nation of Islam, and registered as a conscientious objector to the Vietnam War. That was an impressive statement against Black Exceptionalism—the notion that because an African American attains fame and status that racism has thereby been overcome. Even more impressive than Ali, however, was Paul Robeson's decades of work for nuclear disarmament, his 30-year connection to the Trade Union movement, his championing of anti-colonial struggles across the globe, his support of the Soviet Union as the super-power aiding those struggles, and his commitment to socialism. Here was a man who was a superstar in both sport *and* popular music—an All American football player, a massively popular singer, and a film star who, the more famous he became, the more he moved leftward into radical activism. Robeson was an iconic American sporting, music, and film figure in the 1930s and 1940s—certainly the most well-known African American in the world. Yet he intentionally used this fame to fight against the American demonization of the Soviet Union and to promote Socialist ideals. Robeson spent a lifetime living the contradiction of producing art that requires significant capital investment while simultaneously and intentionally using that art to explore how power could be exercised by individuals, groups, and movements independent of capital's formations.

Paul Robeson

Paul Robeson was one of the towering American public intellectuals of the twentieth century. His biographer claims that at one point in his life he was the most well-known and most admired Black man alive (Duberman, 1988). Foner (1978) notes that Robeson's emphasis on racial pride, racial unity, the connection between civil rights organizing in the USA and anti-colonial struggles across the globe, and the importance of mass action and collective unity amongst African Americans, means he must be considered the intellectual catalyst for, and forerunner of, Malcolm X, Stokely Carmichael, Huey Newton, and Eldridge Cleaver. Indeed, Malcolm X's well-known distinction between House Negroes (Blacks willing to cooperate with the White power structure to curry temporary favor and an easier life) and Field Negroes (those whose rebelliousness meant they rejected servility to Whites) was one repeatedly drawn by Robeson. Foreshadowing the later radical stance of the Black Panthers, Robeson castigated the leadership of the NAACP as his own radicalism exploded after World War II. He wrote in 1949:

> How Sojourner Truth, Harriet Tubman, Fred Douglass must be turning in their graves at this spectacle of a craven, fawning, despicable leadership able to be naught but errand boys, and—at the lowest level—stooges and cowardly renegades, a disgrace to the Negro people and to the real and true America of which they so glibly talk.
>
> (Robeson, 1978a, p. 203)

For many people in the USA, Robeson is known mostly for his pop culture fame as the singer of "Old Man River" from the musical *Showboat,* and as the theatrical star of *Othello* and films such as *The Proud Valley.* American football fans also remember "Robeson of Rutgers," the first African American, All American football player. Less well known, perhaps, are his tireless efforts at organizing, building mass movements, working within a radical Presidential campaign, singing to and supporting labor unions, cultural work within the Hollywood studio system, support of colonial struggles across the globe, and his long-standing involvement in the anti-nuclear movement. Most people who have heard of him are probably dimly aware that he was caught up in the McCarthyite witch hunt of communists in the 1950s and that he famously refused to name names when called in front of the House on Un-American Activities Committee (HUAC). To the end of his life he refused to buckle under pressure to denounce the Soviet Union, which, for him, represented the best hope of providing support for anti-imperialism.

At the height of his mainstream popularity Robeson was one of the best-known American entertainers in the world, pulling down an enormous salary in the 1940s. As he became a target of the HUAC that rapidly dwindled to $6,000 per year. In addition, the State Department's confiscation of his passport denied Robeson the chance to earn a living overseas where he remained hugely popular. Although the White establishment tried to separate Robeson from the Black community by portraying him as a wealthy dilettante, he was deeply involved in union organizing, and particularly active in trying to persuade African Americans to join mainstream labor unions, which he saw as the best hope for advancing Black interests. He also played a major role in the Progressive Party's campaign to elect Henry Wallace as President in 1948. Like Gramsci, he felt the interests of the working class needed to be represented by a revolutionary Party.

Robeson maintained a strong interest in popular culture throughout his adult life and was suspicious of the ways it disseminated dominant ideologies of capitalism and White supremacy. For Robeson, popular culture was a site for struggle and he strove to use the Hollywood studio system against itself by promoting films he felt could help undermine White supremacy. Robeson became an expert on musicology, studied a number of African and Asian dialects, and explored African cultural values, philosophy, art, music, and spirituality. This eclecticism was evident in his internationalism. He traveled the world constantly, initially as a singer, and then as a political activist concerned to connect the disenfranchised and dispossessed of different countries and racial groups. As a Socialist, Robeson was used to thinking politically and internationally and argued workers and racial minorities had more connecting them than dividing them. This was true linguistically, musically, and politically. Robeson was consistent in his efforts to point out the international dimensions of, for example, the struggle for racial equality.

Robeson was one of those rare examples of a successful, admired and feted leader who sees through the sham of ideological manipulation and risks everything to move to the left. His growing wealth, fame, and international acclaim did not soften his growing criticism of American imperialism and its hostility to the Soviet Union (which Robeson thought was grounded in the Soviet Union's championing of anti-colonial struggles across the globe). The more his fame propelled him into international tours and travel, the more he learned of the growing anti-colonial movements across the world and the link these had to fighting White supremacy in the USA (and vice versa). Robeson's influence on U.S. affairs was tempered by his growing public and private commitment to socialism (which grew concurrent with the advent of the cold war) and his refusal to disavow the Soviet Union, even after Khrushchev's 1956 address publicizing Stalin's repression. When the State department confiscated his passport as he faced the HUAC he was, in effect, an exile in his own country.

Critical Reflection and Transformative Adult Learning

As a movement leader Robeson was a practitioner of critical reflection on experience, so frequently lionized as the quintessential form of adult learning. As he developed his own conception of race leadership—in a direction other Black leaders wished him to abandon—he continually examined both his motives and assumptions, changing quite significantly his ideas on tactics and strategy regarding how best to challenge White supremacy. He drew insights from his analysis of his experiences, which grew ever wider as he struggled with the Hollywood studio system, with the need to internationalize the U.S. Black liberation struggle to become part of the world anti-colonial movement, and with his attempts to forge alliances between Blacks and Whites in the Trade Union movement. From a career that began with fame on the football field, on the stage, on the screen, and in the concert hall, Robeson moved through experiences with anti-colonial movements across the globe and with picket lines and rallies in countless union halls to become, with DuBois, an outspoken critic of White racism and White capitalism. To move from a life of privilege to a lifelong advocacy of socialism that effectively killed his earning potential shows a willingness to reappraise assumptions borne of equal parts intellectual honesty and critical conviction.

Robeson was also increasingly committed to developing collective leadership in the African American community, particularly through Negroes assuming prominent positions within Trade Unions. He is thus squarely in the tradition of adult educators such as Ella Baker and Septima Clark, both of whom were skeptical of the prevalence of charismatic leadership, in particular that of Reverend Martin Luther King, Jr. For Robeson a strategy for African American advancement based on individual leadership exercised by prominent spokespersons shot itself in the foot. Leadership had to be *collective* for any true change to occur, because in collectivity lay the strength of solidarity, and also because radical leadership could only hope to survive all the enmity and punishment that was visited on it by the White supremacist power structure if those involved had a sense that they were representatives of, and supported by, a much wider force. He also sought to learn how to practice democracy, consistently framing himself as both Democrat and Socialist. In his view there was no inherent contradiction between the two. Indeed, for Robeson socialism *was* democracy—the fullest possible realization of political and economic equality. Like radical educator Myles Horton, Robeson viewed representative democracy as a sham. True democracy could only exist if the massive economic disparity between rich and poor, Black and White, was redressed.

Robeson was consistently open to new ideas, not only in political theory and strategy. If we look for examples of transformative learning—the development by adults of meaning schemes and perspectives that are ever more comprehensive and discriminating—Robeson's life represents transformative learning par excellence. He explored widely and seriously his passion for musicology, languages, and the heritage of African culture, being particularly intrigued by the similarities in musical structures he found between African American spirituals and work songs and Eastern modalities. His growing internationalism led him to learn about other cultures and about the different facets of anti-colonial struggles across the globe. Indeed, his internationalism prompted and nurtured his radicalism, particularly his socialism. Had he not traveled to the Soviet Union and been astounded by the lack of racism he experienced there, and had he not been open to listen to striking Welsh miners he bumped into outside the Savoy hotel in London, it is hard to imagine him developing the views he did and the fortitude he subsequently needed to hold them. Robeson also turned his critical gaze on the evolution of what he felt was an imperialist American foreign policy, on the unwarranted demonization of the Soviet Union by the White Right, and on the use by the White ruling class of what critical race theorists have subsequently labeled Black Exceptionalism: the idea that because Robeson had a successful career as athlete, singer, and actor, that structural barriers to all African Americans had significantly weakened, if not disappeared.

Robeson displayed a heroic, steadfast, and hopeful independence of thought, despite the considerable cost to himself and the mounting evidence of hostility heaped upon him. His commercial career as a singer was destroyed by his commitment to socialism and his refusal to abandon his support of the Soviet Union, even as his artistry flourished. In contrast to the ideological trajectory of many artists and intellectuals who begin as radicals and then temper their convictions as they enjoy success, Robeson moved in the opposite direction. The more success he gained, the more he realized how the White power structure was trying to use that success to demonstrate that true equality of opportunity existed for African Americans in the USA. The more he achieved personal wealth and fame, the more he allied himself with the labor movement, anti-colonial struggles, and the Soviet Union's efforts to create a Socialist, non-racist state.

Robeson's support of the Soviet Union caused the White press either to delete his presence entirely from the cultural–intellectual landscape of the USA or to portray him as an unpatriotic, un-American, communist subversive. As Duberman (1988) notes, by 1960 "his image (was) converted by a now hostile establishment from public hero to public enemy . . . an outcast, very nearly a nonperson" (p. xiii). Popular culture has also framed the early biography of this freedom fighter as a minstrelian entertainer, a singer of sanitized show tunes. Robeson fought against this stereotyping. One small example of this is his changing the lyrics in concert of "Old Man River" from "Tote that barge, lift that bail, you get a little drunk and you land in jail" (which portrayed Negro laborers as human oxen and seeking solace in drink) to "Tote that barge, lift that bail, you show a little grit and you land in jail" (which emphasized the laborer's refusal to buckle under capitalism and the White supremacist power structure).

Popular Culture

Robeson's work with popular culture is probably the best-known area of his life. Beginning as a singer Robeson expanded his activities to include film and theater, starring as "Othello" at Stratford on Avon in the United Kingdom once the State Department had returned his passport. For him art was always politically charged and he famously declared in 1937 at a rally in support of the anti-fascist forces in the Spanish Civil War: "the artist must take sides. He must elect to fight for freedom or slavery. I have made my choice. I had no alternative" (Robeson, 1978b, p. 119). He tried to work in the commercial studio system to develop race pride by providing historically accurate representations of Africans in films such as *Sanders of the River*. After disavowing the film in 1938 as "a piece of flag-waving, in which I wasn't interested" (Robeson 1978c, p. 121) he declared "the big producers insist on presenting a caricature image of the Black, a ridiculous image, that amuses the white bourgeoisie, and I am not interested in playing their game" (1978d, p. 126). He kept faith in film as a medium of social change, however, arguing in Gramscian mode in 1939 that film "is the medium through which to express the creative abilities of the masses" (Robeson, 1978e, p. 130).

In 1937 he complained that "things were twisted and changed and distorted" (Robeson, 1978f, p. 120) whenever he worked with film and said again in 1942:

> I thought I could change the picture [*Tales of Manhattan*] as we went along . . . but in the end it turned out to be the same old thing—the Negro solving his problem by singing his way to glory. This is very offensive to my people. It makes the Negro child-like and innocent and is in the old plantation tradition.
>
> (1978g, p. 142)

Because of his disillusionment with Hollywood's White bankrollers he gradually moved away from commercial films and ceased to target his appeal to a broad audience. Increasingly, he aimed his acting at members of labor unions, believing art could help demonstrate the common economic interests of poor working-class Whites and Blacks and thus play a part in creating a viable working-class movement. He elevated the singing of Negro spirituals to the status of serious, socially committed art—and hence made it a political act—believing it was one way to educate African Americans and Whites of the rich heritage of African culture. Robeson thus viewed popular culture as a powerful medium through which millions outside formal education could be reached.

When it was clear that the Hollywood studio systems as currently comprised could not be subverted from within, Robeson reappraised his commitment to film. In 1937 he concluded, "one man can't face the film companies. They represent about the biggest aggregate of finance capital in the world . . . So no more films for me" (1978f, p. 120). Declaring in 1937 that "what I won't do is work for the big companies, which are headed by individuals who would make me a slave, like my father, if they could" (1978d, p. 126) he came up with two strategies. First, he proposed an alternative model of financing, producing, and distributing films that bypassed the major studios. Such films would be financed by unions, cultural associations, or wealthy independent backers, and would allow him to make films on such topics as the life of a Black commander of the Lincoln Brigade in the Spanish Civil War (a project he was never to realize). Second, he suggested that African Americans, Union members, and progressive Whites boycott studio-produced films, hoping such a stand would inspire similar boycotts in international markets. In 1951 he argued that "the mounting of the right kind of campaign could shake Hollywood to its foundations" (1978h, p. 302).

Using Popular Culture to Develop Race Pride

Robeson devoted his life to using use mass culture to develop race pride amongst African Americans. This project had two dimensions: educating adults about the richness of the African cultural heritage, and about the values and practices that lay at the heart of authentic African culture. Like DuBois, Robeson believed that a commitment to Pan-Africanism and a commitment to socialism were compatible. While in London he conducted a series of substantial adult learning projects, studying at the School of Oriental Languages and learning a number of African languages such as Swahili, Yoruba, Efik, Benin, Ashanti and Tivi. Indeed, he often said that it was in England that he became an African, partly as a result of his language studies, and partly through his conversations with African seamen in London, Liverpool, and Cardiff. Increasingly he became a passionate advocate of African Americans learning about the rich heritage of African culture, believing that a lack of knowledge of their culture meant they were denied a potent source of race pride. As early as 1934 he declared that "in my music, my plays, my films I want to carry always this central idea: to be African" (1978i, p. 91). The next year he declared: "for the rest of my life I am going to think and feel as an African—not as a white man . . .. To me it seems the most momentous thing in my life" (1978j, p. 91). In common with the contemporary Africentric turn away from Eurocentrism he maintained "it is not as imitation Europeans, but as Africans, that we have a value" (1978j, p. 92).

The heritage Robeson sought to educate people about was that of Africa's "great philosophy and epics of poetry" (1978k, p. 352), which, in 1953, he maintained, were comparable to the achievements of Greek and Chinese poetry. He celebrated what he felt was the "great precision and subtlety of intonational structure" found in African languages, the "rich oral folklore . . . distinctive decorative art" of African culture and the "highly developed and original musical art distinguished by an extraordinary wealth of rhythm" (1978k, p. 352) he found in his studies of Africa. Yet, he lamented, in 1949, none of these was evident in the "savage and cannibalistic" images of half-naked Black people presented as examples of Africans "as the newspapers, radio, book and lecture propagandists would make them" (1978l, p. 228). In the pursuit of an authentic Africentrism he urged an educational campaign to make African Americans aware of their African roots. In 1934, he stated,

> the dances, the songs, and the worship perpetuated by the Negro in America are identical with those of his cousins hundreds of years removed in the depths of Africa, whom he has never seen, of whose very existence he is only dimly aware. His peculiar sense of rhythm alone would stamp him indelibly as African.
>
> (1978i, p. 90)

As Robeson conducted this educational project he became more aware of the political underpinnings of the opposition he faced. As he put it in 1953,

> there was a logic to this cultural struggle, and the powers-that-be realized it before I did. The British Intelligence came one day to caution me about the political meanings of my activities. For the question loomed of itself: If African culture was what I insisted it was, what happens to the claim that it would take 1,000 years for Africans to be capable of self-rule? Yes, culture and politics were actually inseparable here as always.
>
> (1978k, p. 352)

After reflecting critically on his earlier assumptions regarding the significance of education about African culture, Robeson switched his emphasis to advocating cultural adult education as a central political component in the Black liberation struggle. Particularly frustrating for Robeson was the fact that African Americans shared the White supremacist stereotypes of Africa that viewed Africans as uncultured savages. Hence the major purpose of his studies of African language and folk music, he stated in 1934, was "to dispel this regrettable and abysmal ignorance of the value of its own heritage in the negro race itself" (1978m, p. 87). His decision to sing only Negro spirituals in concert, to charge low admission prices, and to make independent films financed outside of the studio system, were all manifestations of this project. These were political statements, not simply cultural choices. As his career evolved, he continued learning the importance of integrating the cultural and political dimensions of educating people about African culture. This became reframed as an important element in the anti-colonial struggle rather than an act of purely aesthetic or anthropological education.

Early in his career, in fact, Robeson spoke of Black culture as emotional and instinctual, a sort of primal connection to a Jungian race memory or cultural DNA. In 1931, for example, he referred to Negro culture as manifesting "a deep simplicity, a sense of mystery, a capacity for religious feeling, a spontaneous and entirely individual cheerfulness" (1978n, p. 84). Again, in 1934, he wrote that "the Negro feels rather than thinks, experiences emotions directly rather than interprets them by roundabout and devious abstractions, and apprehends the outside world by means of intuitive perception instead of through a carefully built up system of logical analysis" (1978m, p. 86). Contrast this with his much more politicized comments on Black culture some 20 years later, in 1951, that emphasized the way White capitalists had robbed Blacks of their economic and cultural due: "billions of dollars, have been earned and are being earned from their creation, and the Negro people have received almost nothing" (1978h, p. 299). In 1949, he framed Negro culture as the response of "this enslaved people, oppressed by the double yoke of cruel exploitation and racial discrimination" that produced "splendid, life-affirming songs" (1978o, p. 212). He also castigated the way capitalism distorted and perverted Negro music, arguing that commercial jazz has: "debased many talented Negro musicians in order to satisfy the desires of capitalist society" (1978o, p. 217).

The change in emphasis outlined above illustrates how Robeson's critical reflection on his experiences with movements for social change caused him to alter dramatically his understanding of, and role within, movements against White supremacy. One of his earliest lessons in this struggle was his quick realization of how the White Supremacist power structure used his cultural success as evidence of the lack of racism in the USA. Robeson professed himself always to be aware of the wider struggle his life represented. In 1946, speaking of his college football days, he said "from the time I played on the football field I felt I was struggling for the Negro people, my people, and I was conscious of that struggle" (1978p, p. 180). Gradually, his understanding of how his success was being manipulated by Whites caused him to speak out against it more forcefully. In 1951 he stated: "I got tired of serving as an excuse for these cruelties to my people" (1978q, p. 266).

As already mentioned, in 1937 he made one of his earliest, and most renowned, declarations of how he had come to place his art—his cultural work—in the service of struggle, stating: "The artist must take sides." (1978b, p. 119). Ten years later, this solidified into an abandoning of his lucrative singing and film career for direct political action: "In 1947, on an NAACP picket line in St. Louis, I decided to retire from the concert stage and enter the day-to-day struggle of the people from whom I spring" (1978r, p. 319). Having learned of how his success was being used to justify White supremacy Robeson turned the ideological tables and decided to use it to fight that same supremacy. In contemporary terms, this would be as if Michael Jordan or Michael Jackson—at the height of their fame and their ability to secure millions of dollars in recording contracts and lucrative sponsorships—had announced they were devoting their talents and energies to forging a mass movement between Blacks and Labor Unions to fight White capitalism, or to reviving the Black Panther Party. Robeson's artistic and political trajectory was the opposite of the typical tale of early radicalism transmogrifying into mainstream co-optation and commodification, and constitutes a vivid example of political principle maintained within, and sometimes transcending, the confines of the mainstream market.

References

Duberman, M. B. (1988). *Paul Robeson.* New York: Knopf.

Foner, P. S. (Ed.). (1978). *Paul Robeson speaks: Writings, speeches, interviews 1918–1974.* New York: Brunner/Mazel.

Gowariker, A. (2002). *Lagaan: Once upon a time in India.* Sony Home Pictures Entertainment.

James, C. L. R. (1993). *Beyond a boundary.* Raleigh, NC: Duke University Press (Originally published 1953).

Robeson, P. (1978a). For freedom and peace. In P. S. Foner (Ed.), *Paul Robeson speaks* (pp. 201–210). New York: Brunner/Mazel.

Robeson, P. (1978b). The artist must take sides. In P. S. Foner (Ed.), *Paul Robeson speaks* (pp. 118–119). New York: Brunner/Mazel.

Robeson, P. (1978c). Paul Robeson tells us why. In P. S. Foner (Ed.), *Paul Robeson speaks* (pp. 121–122). New York: Brunner/Mazel.

Robeson, P. (1978d). Paul Robeson in Spain. In P. S. Foner (Ed.), *Paul Robeson speaks* (pp. 123–126). New York: Brunner/Mazel.

Robeson, P. (1978e). A great Negro artist puts his genius to work for his people. In P. S. Foner (Ed.), *Paul Robeson speaks* (pp. 127–130). New York: Brunner/Mazel.

Robeson, P. (1978f). Why I joined labor theatre. In P. S. Foner (Ed.), *Paul Robeson speaks* (pp. 119–120). New York: Brunner/Mazel.

Robeson, P. (1978g). Hollywood's "old plantation tradition" is "offensive to my people". In P. S. Foner (Ed.), *Paul Robeson speaks* (p. 142). New York: Brunner/Mazel.

Robeson, P. (1978h). The Negro artist looks ahead. In P. S. Foner (Ed.), *Paul Robeson speaks* (pp. 298–304). New York: Brunner/Mazel.

Robeson, P. (1978i). I want to be African. In P. S. Foner (Ed.), *Paul Robeson speaks* (pp. 88–91). New York: Brunner/Mazel.

Robeson, P. (1978j). Negroes–Don't ape the Whites. In P. S. Foner (Ed.), *Paul Robeson speaks* (pp. 91–93). New York: Brunner/Mazel.

Robeson, P. (1978k). How I discovered Africa. In P. S. Foner (Ed.), *Paul Robeson speaks* (pp. 351–352). New York: Brunner/Mazel.

Robeson, P. (1978l). My answer. In P. S. Foner (Ed.), *Paul Robeson speaks* (pp. 224–229). New York: Brunner/Mazel.

Robeson, P. (1978m). The culture of the Negro. In P. S. Foner (Ed.), *Paul Robeson speaks* (pp. 86–87). New York: Brunner/Mazel.

Robeson, P. (1978n). Thoughts on the colour bar. In P. S. Foner (Ed.), *Paul Robeson speaks* (pp. 82–84). New York: Brunner/Mazel.

Robeson, P. (1978o). Songs of my people. In P. S. Foner (Ed.), *Paul Robeson speaks* (pp. 211–217). New York: Brunner/Mazel.

Robeson, P. (1978p). Excerpts from testimony before the Tenney Committee. In P. S. Foner (Ed.), *Paul Robeson speaks* (pp. 178–180). New York: Brunner/Mazel.

Robeson, P. (1978q). Negro history—History of the whole Negro people. In P. S. Foner (Ed.), *Paul Robeson speaks* (pp. 265–267). New York: Brunner/Mazel.

Robeson, P. (1978r). Voting for peace. In P. S. Foner (Ed.), *Paul Robeson speaks* (pp. 319–322). New York: Brunner/Mazel.

Williams, R. (1995). *The sociology of culture*. Chicago: University of Chicago Press.

19 Beyond the Culture Jam

Valerie Scatamburlo-D'Annibale

A recent documentary suggests that $300 billion (U.S.) is spent annually by the North American advertising industry and that the average North American is exposed to more than 6,000 marketing messages a day.[1] This is hardly surprising if one surveys our contemporary cultural landscape. Advertising is plastered all over our environment; it provides a constant visual and verbal backdrop to our experiences; shapes our fantasies and desires and molds our very identities and subjectivities. It embodies and conveys frameworks of meaning—notions of what is good and bad, normal and perverse. Advertising is one of the central "storytelling" mechanisms in our society and it increasingly defines our collective forms of social consciousness. Moreover, the endless epistles emanating from the "captains of consciousness" (Ewen, 1976) sell not only commodities but an entire way of life—one of endless and excessive consumerism.

Kilbourne once stated that advertising is a system of education that is powerful precisely because it is not considered education.[2] Jhally (2006) takes this even further by claiming that "advertising is the most powerful and sustained system of propaganda in human history"—one whose cumulative effects, if unchecked, could potentially be responsible for "destroying the world as we know it" (p. 99). Advertising is the main voice of "the capitalist threat" insofar as it "pushes us down the road to increased economic production" and leads to the kind of over-consumption that is leading to environmental ruin (Jhally, 2006, p. 111).

Advertising also performs an ideological function within capitalist societies—it addresses us as individual private consumers rather than as citizens and therefore marginalizes discussions of the public good and the commons. As such, advertising narratives proclaim, much like Margaret Thatcher once did, that there is no such thing as society—no identifiable collective interests that we may share. Its focus on immediate satisfaction—the "here and now" also circumscribes our ability to think long-term and to imagine alternative forms of economic and social organization. In this regard, advertising also reinscribes another Thatcherian mantra—"there is no alternative"—by which she meant, of course, that there is no alternative to capitalist globalization.

Given that the ubiquity of advertising and the commercial colonization of our culture have become so pervasive, "culture jammers" have sought to confront the hegemonic discourses of consumer society. However, as I argue below, culture jamming fails to provide an adequate challenge to the fundamental injustices of capitalism and often perpetuates the very ideological discourses it claims to resist.

Jamming the Culture

The phrase *culture jamming* was introduced into the popular lexicon by the band Negativland in 1985. One of their recordings on JamCon84 referred to "billboard activists," those known to alter billboards with subversive meanings, as the embodiments of culture jamming—noting that a "skillfully reworked billboard" could potentially serve the purpose of directing public attention to "a consideration of the original corporate strategy" (Negativland, 1985/1994).

Echoing these sentiments, Klein (2000) contends that culture jamming is a form of dissent that produces "counter-messages that hack into a corporation's own method of communication to send a message at odds with the one that was intended" (p. 281). This is often achieved by satirizing advertisements in order to disrupt or alter the advertiser's original encoding of the message, thus undermining the ability of corporate discourses to make meaning in predictable ways; creating anti-advertisements or "subvertisements"; engaging in billboard "liberation"; and revealing the ideological veneer of particular corporations in order to expose the harsh realities (i.e., environmental destruction) that are obfuscated by the glossy images of contemporary branding practices.

In a more grandiose fashion, Kalle Lasn (1999), founder of the Adbusters Media Foundation and author of *Culture Jam*, states that "culture jammers" constitute a "loose global network of media activists" who are "the advance shock troops" of "the most significant social movement" and whose aim is "to topple existing power structures and forge major adjustments to the way" people conduct their everyday lives (p. xi). Among academics, culture jamming has been heralded as a critical intervention that opposes corporate brand culture and the omnipresent advertising ethos (Harold, 2004; Rumbo, 2000; Zuk & Dalton, 2003). Others, arguing in a similar vein, have suggested that culture jamming is a form of critical public pedagogy that is animated by a "shared vision of a more just society" (Sandlin & Milam, 2008, p. 324). However, Haiven (2007) argues, rightly in my view, that culture jamming has largely escaped serious academic criticism because of the "ambivalence it inspires" in two major tendencies within cultural studies— the "neo-Gramscian and the audience-oriented" (p. 87).

Within a neo-Gramscian cultural studies framework, popular culture is conceived of as an active process, where cultural commodities and texts are not simply passively consumed, but rather are the materials people use to create popular culture. For example, Fiske (1989) refers to *excorporation* as the process by which groups (often marginalized populations) make their own culture out of the "resources and commodities provided by the dominant system"—it is how people *use* those resources, within various contexts of power relations, which is of import in this framework (p. 15). From this perspective, therefore, popular culture is viewed as a contested arena—one in which the struggle for hegemony is waged and sometimes resisted (Storey, 1998). However, given the populist bent of neo-Gramscian formulations, the ability to "resist" dominant narratives including those of advertising and consumer culture is lauded—often times uncritically—as an end in and of itself. Haiven (2007), therefore, contends that while some academics (particularly those on the "left") have been reluctant to critically interrogate the politics of culture jamming, it is necessary to sound some caution at the "premature valourization" of culture jamming as a "form of cultural politics and public pedagogy" (p. 88).

The Quest for Authenticity and Privatized Resistance[3]

Culture jammers place themselves on a "revolutionary continuum" and claim inspiration from the "Situationists," a group of "European intellectuals and conceptual artists" led by Guy Debord who believed that the "spectacle had kidnapped" the real lives of individuals and co-opted whatever "authenticity" people once had (Lasn, 1999, p. 102). According to Debord (1967/1983), in the society of the spectacle, capital is accumulated to such an extent that it becomes an image that represents a distorted, if not falsified, version of reality. Just as the economy had subjugated workers, so too had the spectacle to the extent that workers themselves became complicit in their own subjugation and incapable of envisioning forms of economic and social organization beyond capitalism (Debord, 1967/1983, p. 5). The Situationists argued that the spectacle was a "novel mode of social domination in which the industrial age's coercive manual labor was replaced by capitalism's deceitful promise of fulfillment through entertainment and consumption" (Harold, 2004, p. 192). To combat this state of affairs, one of the main strategies of the Situationists was *détournement*. Literally, a "turning around," *détournement* involves "rerouting spectacular images, environments, ambiences, and events to reverse or subvert their meaning, thus reclaiming them" (Lasn, 1999, p. 103).

According to Lasn (1999), *détournement* may provide people with new, more *authentic* choices about how to live their lives:

> many times a day, each of us comes to a little fork in the path. We can then do one of two things: act the way we normally, reflexively act, or do something a little risky and wild, but genuine. We can choose to live our life as "a moral, poetic, erotic, and almost spiritual refusal" to cooperate with the demands of consumer culture.
>
> (p. 101)

Here, Lasn implies that culture jammers reject the spectacle in favor of "authenticity." However, there is a conceptual murkiness in the way that he and others employ the term—while the presumably "inauthentic" spectacle is contrasted with some vaguely defined authentic gesture, exactly what constitutes the "authentic" remains largely unarticulated. In fact, all that Lasn (1999) provides are nebulous references to "real living," "living in the moment," and "living close to the edge" as somehow constitutive of authenticity (p. 106).[4] Presumably, one could surmise that the "authentic" is something which is free from the taint of commercialism, something that exists outside market-structured consciousness. Yet, this rather simplistic formulation tends to ignore that discourses of authenticity have been co-opted. One of the hallmarks of what some have dubbed "postmodern consumer culture" is that individuals have willingly embraced "consumption as an activity through which identity could be constructed . . . authentically" (Carducci, 2006, p. 121). Brands such as Nike that were perceived to be "more 'authentic'" began to capture more of the consumer market when the company positioned its brand as one that promised "authentic athletic performance" (p. 121). In short, the notion of the "authentic" itself has been hijacked and has become part of marketing strategies for brands that are increasingly "said to represent a kind of authenticity" (p. 127).

More troubling, however, is that some forms of culture jamming tend to privilege *individual* acts of resistance. Whereas the Situationists were concerned with challenging the totalizing logic of the spectacle within capitalist social formations and reclaiming the "commons" through *collective* political action, contemporary culture jammers object to the spectacle not "insofar as it dissuades the oppressed from rising up or colonizes all of life, but more that it eschews the 'authenticity' of the individual" (Haiven, 2007, p. 94). In this regard, culture jamming may perpetuate the ideological individualism that animates the very commercial messages it purports to subvert. Furthermore, while the Situationists treated inauthenticity as "part and parcel of workers' alienation from the means of production, the fruits of their labor, and a society evacuated of democratic relationships," for Lasn and many academic champions of culture jamming, inauthenticity is merely a "mark of deviation from a romantic notion of unmediated transcendent human freedom for its own sake" (Haiven, 2007, p. 94). Yet one could certainly ask proponents of culture jamming why the quest for authenticity and what Carducci (2006, p. 134) refers to as "transcendent strategies of individual emancipation" should, in and of themselves, be held up as beacons of radical political praxis given that they tend to undermine, or at least marginalize, collective political action.

Hyperculturalism and Its Discontents

Culture jamming, for the most part, privileges the cultural terrain as a site of political action and has tended to favor the representational realm in that its main targets have been the *texts* of consumer culture. However, it is important to note that producing counter-discourses, subvertisements, and the like may reinforce the kind of "discourse radicalism" that has been a key feature of an ineffectual postmodern politics. As Harvey (1998) has argued, such discourse radicalism has tended to circumvent a serious analysis of capitalism—a point to which I will return. In making the text the marionette theater of the political, contesting only the *symbols* of corporate brand culture, and elevating the "cultural," jammers have tended to valorize a form of textual resistance while contributing to what Bannerji (2000) has called the "culturalization" of politics.

This culturalization of politics is evident among neo-Gramscians who view culture jamming as the quintessential embodiment of counter-hegemonic resistance. In invoking Gramsci to accentuate the political relevance of the cultural domain, many have denuded Gramsci's thought of its fundamental concern with class struggle and the economic constitution of capitalist social formations largely because they adopt a post-Marxist—not to mention, partial—rendering of Gramsci's thought. In such narratives, the "cultural" is often treated as a separate and autonomous sphere severed from its embeddedness within sociopolitical and economic arrangements—a theoretical sleight-of-hand which represents a perversion of Gramsci's thought. While Gramsci clearly assailed a specific version of Marxism that tended to reduce everything to the economic level, thereby simplifying the structure of social formations and their complexities by flattening the *mediations* between different levels, he never suggested that analyses of economic and class relations were epiphenomenal or subordinate to cultural considerations (Scatamburlo-D'Annibale & McLaren, 2008).

Far too many neo-Gramscians have committed the errors of overemphasizing the significance of culture and ideology while abstracting class struggle out of existence. Gramsci was insistent that the building of

> mass counter-hegemonic movement does not take place on a strictly cultural plane or as some rarified intellectual process of ideological dissent. Counter-hegemonies, he argues, are created through political struggle, movements in which *economic resistance* [italics added] and ideological combat go hand in hand.
>
> (McNally, 1997, p. 38)

The current deployment of Gramscian theory without acknowledging its emphasis on economic resistance and class analyses is, at best, a liberal dilution of his radical formulations. As Verdicchio (1995) argues, if Gramscian thought may be regarded as "post-Marxist" and therefore emptied of its commitment to class politics, "it is due only to its decontextualization" (p. 172).

Similarly, culture jammers have obfuscated the *Marxist* roots of Situationism and "de-class-ified" its politics. For example, Lasn's selective reading of the Situationists' legacy conveniently ignores that they were committed to a Marxist understanding of capitalism, consumer culture, and the potential for *working-class* resistance. The Situationists' "vision of politics was informed by a notion of, and dedication to, the historical struggle between classes and was motivated by a desire to quicken the revolutionary potential of humanity" (Haiven, 2007, p. 94). Unfortunately, many scholars who have written approvingly of culture jamming as a "radical," "counter-hegemonic" strategy of "resistance" have done little to remedy Lasn's historical amnesia—something which may, in part, be due to their own aversion to Marxist theory.

What is even more perplexing is that many self-proclaimed progressives have enthusiastically and uncritically embraced Lasn's formulations despite his contempt for "leftist" politics and his privileging of free-market philosophies. Lasn (1999) has explicitly stated that culture jammers are not "lefties" because the left has presumably become "tired, self-satisfied and dogmatic" and because the "collapse of the Soviet empire undermined the Left's whole philosophical base" (p. 118). Lasn adds that while "free market philosophies" are flawed, they are "far better" than "social democracy" (p. 118). In calling on cultural jammers to work *around* leftists rather than *with* them and in referring to the collapse of the left's philosophical base (read: Marxism), Lasn evinces a form of doctrinaire anti-Marxism that has become all too commonplace. And, in suggesting that free-market philosophies (read: capitalism) can be given a more human face, Lasn echoes those who claim "there is no alternative."

> It is important to recall that according to the Situationists, the working class's oppression and docility was confirmed and compounded by the development of a 'Society of the Spectacle' in which social life was increasingly routinized and organized into banal, contrived, and stayed rituals and spectacles of work, play, and political participation . . .. Situationism's objective was to use techniques many would identify as 'art' as weapons of class war to provoke thought and action which would lead to a society where . . . the capitalist mode of production (and the society built to sustain it) would be replaced by a radical form of socialism suffused with a deep collective intentionality.
>
> (Haiven, 2007, p. 93)

In short, the Situationists were profoundly committed to class struggle and socialism but this is a part of their revolutionary legacy that has largely been disregarded by culture jammers and their academic admirers.

Undoubtedly, culture jamming has encouraged some individuals to rethink their consumption practices and it has been successful in promoting forms of textual resistance aimed at subverting the dominant codes of advertising. However, contrary to what Lasn claimed a decade ago, culture jammers have not constituted themselves as a "significant social movement," nor have they realized the aim of toppling "existing power structures." In fact, Bennett and Lagos (2007) argue that due to a desire for anonymity, there is often a lack of communication between culture jamming groups. They further suggest that these groups have often presented conflicting ideals rather than a cohesive political identity. Additionally, like so many other forms of culturalist politics, "resistance" has remained mostly at the level of a politics of representation. And, in this politically amorphous arena, the cultural turn towards "sign value" and "meme warfare" has been the hallmark of a "radicalism" that detaches the social relations of production from the cultural sphere and deftly side-steps the enduring conundrums of class.

In concealing, or at least downplaying, the socialist underpinnings of Situationism, culture jamming has led to a fashionable apostasy that has severed the critical links between Marxist theory, class politics, and social transformation. In many ways, culture jammers are reminiscent of the "Young Hegelians" whom Marx chastised. Of the Young Hegelians, Marx (1978) stated that they were "in spite of their allegedly world-shattering statements, the staunchest conservatives" (p. 149); Marx argued that they were simply fighting "phrases" and had forgotten that to those phrases they themselves were merely opposing other phrases and in no way "combating the real existing world" (p. 149).

Taking a cue from Marx, I contend that much of culture jamming tends towards the superficial. Too often, it represents little more than a form of textual resistance or discourse radicalism that leads us willy-nilly down a path where collective politics takes a back seat to individual gestures of transcendence and where serious engagement with the material conditions of capitalist production is precluded. In many ways, it is a kind of pseudo-radicalism, a "verbal radicalism of the word without deed, or rather, of the word *as* deed." In response to actual "structures and practices of oppression and exploitation," culture jamming offers the "rhetorical gesture, the ironic turn of phrase." Such politics are, in practice, if not intent, obstacles to "the rebuilding of mass movements of protest and resistance" (McNally, 1997, p. 27).

Rather than disavowing the Marxist left, culture jammers would do well to revisit the Situationists' commitment to working-class struggle and socialism. Sadly, many like Lasn and his academic bedfellows have embraced the inevitability of capital and, in lending their voices to the symphony of TINA (there is no alternative), have served as ideological ventriloquists of the capitalist class and revealed the utter superciliousness of their radical posturing. Their countercultural criticism often masks an aristocratic radicalism underwritten by a liberal affective politics that rarely challenges the capitalist system as a whole or at its core. It is not enough to turn texts on their heads, not enough to rewrite the American dream so that "empowered citizens" can decide "for themselves what's 'cool'" (Lasn, 1999, p. 168). It is not enough to try to "uncool" consumption. Rather, a politics that truly honors the legacy of the Situationists would necessarily entail a reconsideration of class.

Beyond the Culture Jam: Reclaiming Class Politics

> There's class warfare all right, but it's my class, the rich class, that's making war, and we're winning.
>
> (Buffet, cited in Stein, 2006)

> Progressive social change will ultimately involve the working class or it will not happen.
>
> (Gindin, 2003, p. 19)

Culture jamming, like advertising, addresses us as consumers. It often seeks to influence our behavior as consumers and, in the case of campaigns such as those for Adbusters' Black Spot sneakers—allegedly, a brand of "subversive" running shoes—it prods us to consume more "ethically." Yet, as Heath and Potter (2004) have argued, such forms of "cultural rebellion" hardly constitute a "threat to the system" (p. 1). In fact, far from representing "a revolutionary doctrine," they are actually more reflective of a "warmed-over version" of "countercultural thinking" that has been one of the "primary forces driving consumer capitalism" for several decades (Heath & Potter, 2004, p. 2). Moreover, in focusing almost exclusively on the realm of consumption, culture jamming has, in effect, precluded any discussion of a class politics that would speak to the level of capitalist production.

When Marx and Engels penned the *Communist Manifesto*, capitalism as we know it was still confined to a few countries. Today, the reign of capital is more absolute than ever and central passages of the *Manifesto* ring truer today as "key features of nineteenth-century capitalism are clearly recognizable, and even more strongly developed, in the early twenty-first century" (Saad-Filho, 2003, p. 1). Moreover, as capitalism has become "increasingly global the number of people in a proletarian position is greater than ever before" (Brosio, 2008, p. 13). While capitalism has undergone considerable shifts since Marx's day, Marx nonetheless provided us with *fundamental* insights into class society that have held true to this day and a return to the tough, simple truths that lie at the core of Marx's analyses is essential for effective political praxis. Of course, the sentinels of intellectual fashion and those whom Kelsh and Hill (2006) refer to as revisionist leftists constantly tell us that class analyses and indeed class struggle is obsolete. Yet, such a struggle does, in fact, exist in the form of the "struggle by capital for profit," the struggle by capital to exploit labor, the struggle of capital to impose "its form of social relations" on all of us (Holloway, 2003, p. 233).

Within educational theory, an iron wall whose purpose is to further ghettoize Marxist conceptions of class from less combative Weberian and neo-Weberian conceptualizations confronts us. Even within discourses of critical pedagogy, we are surrounded by a motivated amnesia with respect to the strategic potential of a Marxist analysis of class. Or when class *is* discussed by educationalists, they follow Weber in referring to class as "social divisions, social strata, that are effects of market forces that are understood to be (relatively) autonomous" from "the relations of exploitation between labor and capital" (Kelsh & Hill, 2006, p. 3). Individuals are perceived as belonging to *strata* on the basis of occupational status, income, consumption patterns, etc., and these various strata are then taken as *proxy* social classes. Yet, such conceptualizations do not reveal much about class relations for these base categories are *not* social class ones at all but categories of social stratification founded on the combination and aggregation of various measures of social inequality and relative social status. Such formulations (1) ignore the existence of the capitalist class that owns the means of production as well as the means of distribution and exchange and which therefore dominates society economically and politically; (2) "gloss over and hide, the fundamental *antagonistic* relationship between the two main classes in society"—the capitalist class and the working class which consists not only of manual workers but millions of white-collar laborers whose work conditions are similar to those of manual workers; (3) work ideologically to segment the working class and to hide "the existence of *a* working class." They "serve the purpose of 'dividing and ruling' the working class" by "segmenting different groups of workers" and thus inhibiting the "development of a common (class) consciousness against the exploiting capitalist class" (Hill & Cole, 2001, pp. 152–153).

In order to get a real grip on class we must veer from the safe path of the mainstream to the lost highway of Marxist theory for as Brosio (2008) reminds us, Marx "sought to develop a form of common language for politics so that the scattered and disunited working-class people could understand their plight and make common cause in solidarity to overcome their oppression" (p. 5). While it is certainly the case that class is, in many ways, a lived culture and lived experience, this should not prevent an understanding of class as an objective entity. Marxists well understand that class has an objective existence as an empirical category and a subjective existence in terms of the way in which it is lived and interpreted.

However, in jettisoning Marxism and/or positing class as an effect of culture, many have fallen prey to an ahistorical "culturalism" that separates class from the relations of production. In such theoretical trickery, class is effectively cut off from the political economy of capitalism and severed from an exploitative power structure in which those who control and benefit from collectively produced resources only do so because of the value generated by those who do not. In this sense, class is not simply *another* ideology that serves to legitimate oppression; rather class denotes "exploitative relations between people mediated by their relations to the means of production" (Gimenez, 2001, p. 24). Furthermore, classes "do not come into being by subjective fiat"; rather, "they are organized by the capitalist class to appropriate value" (Petras, 1999, p. 63).

In his attempt to make sense of capitalism as a *social* relation, Marx identified the historical specificity of value-producing labor. He argued that the value of any given commodity is determined by the socially necessary labor time that is used in production. As he puts it, "the labour-time socially necessary is that required to produce an article under the normal conditions of production, and with the average degree of skill and intensity prevalent at the time" (Marx, 1887/1967, p. 41). In the context of his labor theory of value, commodities are exchanged in the market at costs that correspond to the necessary labor time embodied in them. However, surplus value is realized when a commodity is sold or exchanged for more than its labor value.

Capital relies for its very existence on the generation of surplus value—that is, value over-and-above necessary labor. Surplus value—profit—is the value determined, ultimately by capitalist class practices in their totality, to be above and beyond ("surplus") the value that owner must pay in wages to the laborer to ensure she is able to reproduce her labor-power. Marx argues that to "extract the greatest possible amount of surplus-value, and consequently to exploit labor-power to the greatest possible extent" is the "directing motive, the end and aim of capitalist production" (1867/1967, p. 331, cited in Kelsh & Hill, 2006, p. 4). Exploitation, through the extraction of surplus value, "is a systemic feature of capitalism" and capitalists "*must* exploit their workers if they are to remain in business" since exploitation is the fuel that moves capitalist production and exchange." Without "surplus value there would be no wage employment, no capitalist production, and the system would grind to a halt" (Saad-Fihlo, 2003, pp. 35–36).

Within capitalism, the fundamental opposition is between labor and capital—a relation that is constituted at the *level of production*. Hence, the primary social contradiction within capitalism is the specific antagonism that exists between classes under the totalizing logic of capital and commodification. Capitalism "is a system based on the imposition of universal commodification, including, centrally, the buying and selling of human life-time. Its tendency is to subordinate all activity to the law of value—the socially imposed law of exchange." Such a "system operates by process of massive reduction" that "perceives and processes the world solely as an array of economic factors. Under this classificatory grid . . . human subjects figure only as so much labor power . . . and their natural surroundings as so much raw material" (Dyer-Witheford, 1999, p. 9).

To counteract the politically debilitating narratives that undermine a critical understanding of capitalism, the relationship between capital and labor must be properly understood. But, it is also imperative to note that the labor–capital relation is not a symmetrical one—while "capital's dependency on labor is *absolute*— in that capital is absolutely nothing without labor, which it must permanently exploit—labor's dependency on capital is *relative, historically created and historically surmountable*" (Meszaros, 2001, pp. 76–77). In other words, "capital, a relation of general commodification predicated on the wage relation, needs labor. But labor does not need capital. Labor can dispense with the wage, and with capitalism, and find different ways to organize its own creative energies" (Dyer-Witheford, 1999, p. 68). Hence, revolutionary critical pedagogues believe, much like the Situationists, that the best way to transcend the limits to human liberation set by capital are through practical mass movements centered around class struggle.

While the clarion cry of class struggle is spurned by culturalists, there is a class struggle—indeed class warfare—being carried out as billionaire Warren Buffet has suggested. It is a class struggle being waged by those few who continue to reap outrageous profits on the backs of the laboring masses. If Buffet can readily admit that class warfare is being waged, we must ask ourselves why there is such reluctance on the part of "critical" educators and neo-Gramscians to vigorously engage the concept of class.

The emphasis on working-class struggle and resistance is precisely what the Situationists' political project was about, for they understood the "strategic position of the working class in terms of their needs, which repeatedly come up against the logic of capitalism," and as a result of their unique power and position in the economy—a position that could enable them to "disrupt and potentially act to affect change" (Gindin, 2003, p. 19). In this context, it is imperative to transcend the traditional conceptualization of the working class as a white male phenomenon and to take the notion of working class beyond the factory floor and unions. Today, the global working class is very diverse in terms of its racial and gender composition which makes it a much more inclusive social agent (Panitch, 2000). And, if we think of workers concretely rather than as abstractions, it is clear that "workers are people of colour, men and women, immigrants, people with disabilities, individuals who differ in terms of sexual preferences, . . . those that are both organized and unorganized" (Gindin, 2003, p. 19).

Culture jamming, forms of meme warfare, and textual resistance cannot topple existing power structures; nor can they lead us to imagine alternative forms of social and economic organization beyond capital. This is not to say that culture jamming simply be dismissed as inconsequential. Rather, culture jammers need to remind themselves that the Situationists from whom they claim inspiration were interested in replacing the capitalist *mode of production* with socialism and using art as a weapon of class war to promote action to that end. Any "counterhegemonic" strategy must therefore address not only the realm of consumption but *by necessity* the realm of production and the economic exploitation of labor by capital. It must also encourage us to think beyond the horizons of *what is* to what *might be*. The challenge before us lies, partially, in the recognition that alternatives to capitalism do exist—they are not merely idealistic dreams in the face of the capitalist behemoth. Amin (1998) states the challenge explicitly: humanity may let itself be led by capitalism's logic to a fate of collective suicide or it may pave the way for an alternative humanist project of global socialism. To this end, Marx still matters:

> Experiences have taught us that understanding things holistically is difficult and organizing around Marxist ideas and calls for solidarity have never been easy. There are so many 'identities' thought to be more important and easier to recognize and rally around than class. However, this has resulted in spotty ameliorative progress at best . . . There have been unjust systems before capitalism; however, this system, in all its complexities, is the most powerful secular system in the world today; furthermore, those who suffer, directly and indirectly, must understand how it works in order to oppose it. Marx and Marxists have been our most informative teachers on this subject; therefore, it is within and around the best of this intellectual-activist tradition that promises the best results.
>
> (Brosio, 2008, pp. 15–16)

Armed with Marxist understandings of capitalism and guided by the imperative of class struggle, the Situationists sought to transcend capitalism and create a world where labor would no longer be alienated, exploited, instrumentalized, and commodified—a world where the full development of human capacity was encouraged. A new generation of activists should reinvigorate that agenda, move beyond contemporary forms of culture jamming, reclaim class politics, and resurrect the spirit of socialism.

Notes

1 See *The Selling Game* at www.cbc.ca/doczone/sellinggame/
2 Quoted in the documentary, *The Ad and the Ego* (Boihem, 1997).
3 I am appropriating the phrase "privatized resistance" from Haiven (2007).
4 Unfortunately, many academic explorations of culture jamming merely adopt Lasn's ill-defined use of the term without striving for greater clarification.

References

Amin, S. (1998). *Spectres of capitalism: A critique of current intellectual fashions.* New York: Monthly Review Press.

Bannerji, H. (2000). *The dark side of the nation: Essays on multiculturalism, nationalism, and gender.* Toronto: Canadian Scholars' Press.

Bennett, W. L., & Lagos, T. (2007). Logo logic: The ups and downs of branded political communication. *Annals of the American Academy of Political and Social Science, 611*(1), 193–206.

Boihem, H. [Director/Editor/Producer]. (1997). *The ad and the ego* [Motion picture]. (Available from Parralax Pictures, Inc., 715 Fitzwater Street, Philadelphia, PA, 19147.)

Brosio, R. (2008). Marxist thought: Still primus inter pares for understanding and opposing the capitalist system. *Journal for Critical Education Policy Studies, 6*(1). Available: http://www.jceps.com/?pageID=article&articleID=113

Carducci, V. (2006). Culture jamming: A sociological perspective. *Journal of Consumer Culture, 6*(1), 116–138.

Debord, G. (1967/1983). *Society of the spectacle.* Detroit, MI: Black & Red.

Dyer-Witheford, N. (1999). *Cyber-Marx: Cycles and circuits of struggle in high-technology capitalism.* Urbana and Chicago: University of Illinois Press.

Ewen, S. (1976). *Captains of consciousness: Advertising and the social roots of the consumer culture.* New York: McGraw-Hill.

Fiske, J. (1989). *Understanding popular culture.* Boston: Unwin Hyman.

Gimenez, M. (2001). Marxism and class, gender and race: Rethinking the trilogy. *Race, Gender & Class, 8*(2), 23–33.

Gindin, S. (2003). Social justice and political capacities. *Marxism, 1,* 15–19. Available: http://www.web.net/sworker/Journal/m2003/04-SocialJusticeAndPolitic.html

Haiven, M. (2007). Privatized resistance: Adbusters and the culture of neoliberalism. *Review of Education, Pedagogy, and Cultural Studies, 29*(1), 85–110.

Harold, C. (2004). Pranking rhetoric: Culture jamming as media activism. *Critical Studies in Media Communication, 21*(3), 189–211.

Harvey, D. (1998). The practical contradictions of Marxism. *Critical Sociology, 24*(1/2), 1–36.

Heath, J., & Potter, A. (2004). *The rebel sell: Why the culture can't be jammed.* Toronto: Harper Perennial.

Hill, D., & Cole, M. (2001). Social class. In D. Hill & M. Cole (Eds.), *Schooling and equality: Fact, concept and policy* (pp. 137–159). London: Kogan Page.

Holloway, J. (2003). Where is class struggle? In A. Saad-Fihlo (Ed.), *Anti-Capitalism: A Marxist introduction* (pp. 224–234). London: Pluto Press.

Jhally, S. (2006). *The spectacle of accumulation: Essays in culture, media, and politics.* New York: Peter Lang.

Kelsh, D., & Hill, D. (2006). The culturalization of class and the occluding of class consciousness: The knowledge industry in/of education. *Journal for Critical Education Policy Studies, 4*(1). Available: http://www.jceps.com/print.php?articleID=59

Klein, N. (2000). *No logo: Taking aim at the brand bullies.* Toronto: Vintage Canada.

Lasn, K. (1999). *Culture jam: How to reverse America's suicidal consumer binge—and why we must.* New York: HarperCollins.

Marx, K. (1978). *The Marx-Engels reader* (2nd ed.). New York: Norton.

Marx, K. (1887/1967). *Capital, Vol. 1.* New York: International Publishers.

McNally, D. (1997). Language, history, and class struggle. In E. M. Wood & J. B. Foster (Eds.), *In defense of history: Marxism and the postmodern agenda* (pp. 26–42). New York: Monthly Review Press.

Meszaros, I. (2001). *Socialism or barbarism.* New York: Monthly Review Press.

Negativland. (1985/1994). *Over the edge, Vol. 1: JamCon'84'.* CAS (SST 223)/CD (re-issue Seeland 004).

Panitch, L. (2000). Reflections on strategy for labour. In L. Panitch & C. Leys (Eds.), *Working classes, global realities* (pp. 367–392). New York: Monthly Review Press.

Petras, J. (1999). *The left strikes back: Class conflict in Latin America in the age of neoliberalism.* Boulder, CO: Westview Press.

Rumbo, J. D. (2000). The case of *Adbusters:* 'Culture jamming' as an act of resistance against the acritical discourse of mass advertising. *University of Notre Dame Department of Sociology Working Paper and Technical Report Series #6.* Available: http://www.nd.edu/~soc2/workpap/2000/rumbo2.pdf

Saad-Filho, A. (Ed.). (2003). Introduction. In *Anti-Capitalism: A Marxist introduction* (pp. 1–11). London: Pluto Press.

Sandlin, J. A., & Milam, J. L. (2008). "Mixing pop (culture) and politics": Cultural resistance, culture jamming, and anti-consumption activism as critical public pedagogy. *Curriculum Inquiry, 38*(3), 323–350.

Scatamburlo-D'Annibale, V., & McLaren, P. (2008). Contesting the new 'Young Hegelians': Interrogating capitalism in a world of 'difference.' In P. Trifonas (Ed.), *Worlds of difference: Rethinking the ethics of global education for the 21st Century* (pp. 137–178). Boulder, CO: Paradigm Publishers.

Stein, B. (2006, November 26). In class warfare, guess which class is winning? *New York Times,* Available: http://www.nytimes.com/2006/11/26/business/yourmoney/26every.html

Storey, J. (1998). *An introduction to cultural theory and popular culture* (3rd ed.). Athens, GA: The University of Georgia Press.

Verdicchio, P. (1995). Reclaiming Gramsci: A brief survey of current and potential uses of the work of Antonio Gramsci. *Symposium, 49*(2), 169–177.

Zuk, B., & Dalton, R. (2003). Satirical counter-ads as critical pedagogy. In W. M. Roth (Ed.), *Connections '03 Conference Proceedings.* Available: http://www.educ.uvic.ca/Research/conferences/connections2003/17Zukuk103.pdf

20 Global Capitalism and Strategic Visual Pedagogy

David Darts and Kevin Tavin

Yes (Men) We Can: Artful Critiques of Global Capitalism

It started with an email. On November 29, 2004, the website DowEthics.com received an electronic request from BBC World Television for an interview concerning Dow Chemical's position on the 1984 Union Carbide Bhopal chemical plant disaster. The news agency planned to run a story about the twentieth anniversary of the industrial accident, estimated to have killed 20,000 residents of Bhopal, India and to have made many thousands more ill, and wanted to discuss Dow's corporate responsibilities and reparation efforts since acquiring Union Carbide in 2001 (Goodman, 2004).

Four days later, a spokesperson for Dow Chemical appeared in a BBC Paris studio and announced on live television that Dow now took full responsibility for the disaster. The company intended to immediately begin cleaning up the Bhopal site and would, finally, adequately compensate the victims:

> I'm very, very happy to announce that for the first time, Dow is accepting full responsibility for the Bhopal catastrophe. We have a $12 billion plan to finally, at long last, fully compensate the victims—including the 120,000 who may need medical care for their entire lives—and to fully and swiftly remediate the Bhopal plant site. When we acquired Union Carbide three years ago we knew what we were getting. Union Carbide is worth $12 billion. We have resolved to liquidate Union Carbide, this nightmare for the world and this headache for Dow, and use the $12 billion to provide more than the $500 per victim which is all that they've seen, a maximum of just about $500 per victim. That is *not* "plenty good for an Indian," as one of our spokespersons unfortunately said a couple of years ago. In fact, it pays for just one year of medical care. We will *adequately* compensate the victims.
>
> (The Yes Men, 2006, p. 176, italics in the original)

The entire interview lasted five and half minutes and aired twice during the BBC World morning news program. As word of Dow's surprising new plans for Bhopal spread across the news wire and the story rose to be the top item on Google News, shares of Dow Chemical began to precipitously drop. In fact, over the course of a 23-minute period, Dow's share price fell an astounding 4.24% on the Frankfurt exchange, wiping two billion dollars off its market value (Goodman, 2004). This clearly caught the attention of Dow executives who contacted the BBC and angrily informed them that the story was a fake (O'Neill, 2004). Two full hours after the first interview had run, the BBC began broadcasting retractions of the story explaining they had fallen victim to an elaborate prank. Other media outlets picked up on the BBC's blunder and as news of the hoax spread, Dow's share price promptly rebounded.

As the day wore on, it became clear that the Yes Men, a group of artists and social activists who use satire, political theater, and spoofs to expose government hypocrisy and corporate social injustices, had struck again. This was confirmed later in the afternoon when Yes Men member Jacques Servin (AKA Andy Bichlbaum) appeared again on BBC Television to corroborate the Yes Men's involvement in the hoax (The Yes Men, 2006). By creating a bogus Dow Chemical website and then posing as a spokesperson for the company, Servin and his accomplices were able to enact a trope the Yes Men describe as "identity correction," a culture jamming tactic in which members impersonate corporate and governmental officials in an effort to reveal the true ideology of a given organization (Darts, 2008). By artfully presenting Dow's fictional plans for compensating the victims and cleaning up the Bhopal site, the Yes Men successfully drew attention to the company's failures to meaningfully address these issues. In the process, they also challenged the credibility of global media news organizations, particularly the reliability of their fact-checking procedures.

More poignantly, however, the Yes Men's performance clearly exposed the tenuous relationship between corporate social responsibility and free-market capitalism. By appearing to be doing the right thing for the victims and people living in Bhopal, the Yes Men demonstrated that Dow would clearly be doing the wrong thing for its bottom line. The hoax thus illustrated the severe limitations of corporate social responsibility within an unregulated free-market system. As Deborah Doane (2005), Director of the Corporate Responsibility (CORE) Coalition points out, "companies can't do well while also doing good" (p. 23). She explains that, counter to the rhetoric of corporate social responsibility campaigns, short-term corporate profits and long-term benefits to society are generally not compatible under the dominant free-market economic system.

Watching What We Learn: Lessons of Global Capitalism

Placed within the context of global capitalism, the Yes Men's artful critique of Dow Chemical exists in stark contrast to the ideological lessons about free-market economics and democratic citizenship embedded within our visual culture. With the increasing confluence of culture and politics over the last century, the cultural realm has emerged as a key site of political propaganda and education (Jameson, 1984; Stauber & Rampton, 1995). This phenomenon has intensified in recent years with the global expansion of digital technologies and networks, a burgeoning visual culture, and the consolidation of ownership and control of the media by megacorporations (McChesney, 2000). The result is that key political ideas and values are regularly implanted within the commercial products and entertainment vehicles of our visual culture. As Kincheloe (2003) explains, "[a]reas that were once considered trivial venues of entertainment by political analysts are now used for profound political 'education'" (p. 78).

Giroux (2004) labels the lessons embedded within dominant culture as a "transnational public pedagogy" (p. 52). He explains that this public pedagogy has emerged from the market-driven discourse of neoliberalism and describes it as a pedagogy in which "the production, dissemination, and circulation of ideas emerge from the educational force of the larger culture" (Giroux, 2005, ¶ 10). One of the key ideological lessons taught by global capitalism is that unregulated free markets are inseparable from democratic principles. As Carey (1997) points out, the decades-long business-driven propaganda campaign to marry capitalism to democracy has been fundamental to the project of protecting corporate power *against* democracy. This linking of free-market ideology to democratic ideals has served as the chief moral rationale for United States military interventionism (Mitchell, 2005) and has been integral to expanding the unregulated flow of capital and commodities across national borders. Sold directly to our desires and insecurities through spectacular images and designer products, capitalism's public pedagogy has helped maintain the neoliberal fantasy that infinite economic growth is possible within a finite system of natural resources. Conversely, it has helped obscure the stark reality that the health of our consumer culture is intimately connected to the sickness of our planet (Darts, 2008).

Such forms of public pedagogy vigorously promote a politics of privatization, thereby relegating citizenship and the public domain to the commercial confines of the free market. Giroux (2004) explains that the values, ideologies, and social relations taught by public pedagogy define global citizenship as "a private affair, a solitary act of consumption" (p. 52). Within this capitalist paradigm, citizenship is reduced to a predetermined selection of consumer choices. Acts of civic engagement are limited to buying organic, driving a hybrid, or wearing sweat-free clothing, just as acts of patriotism are reduced to shopping sprees and family vacations. As President Bush infamously urged just two weeks after the September 11, 2001 terrorist attacks, "Get *down* to Disney World in Florida . . .. Take your families and enjoy life, the way we want it to be enjoyed" (Bacevich, 2008, ¶ 2, italics in the original). And while these ideological lessons are pervasive, much of their educational force lies in their apparent imperceptibility. Duncum (2002) explains that by working through everyday commercial artifacts and channels, "ideology establishes the parameters for thinking and experiencing outside of which it is difficult to think or experience, let alone to act" (p. 5). He argues that while "culture is always a site of struggle to define how life is to be lived and experienced, the struggle is often rendered invisible" (p. 6).

Part of the value then of the Yes Men's artistic interventions is their creative ability to expose the ideological lessons of the dominant culture. By producing tactical media events like the Dow Chemical hoax, the Yes Men temporarily subvert the power of capitalism's public pedagogy by offering a glimpse into an alternate reality where capitalist interests do not supersede basic human rights or environmental obligations. This enacting of a better world, even if only temporary, is an important tool for inspiring critical reflection and awakening social consciousness. As Duncombe (2007) explains, "counterideologies work best when they are not just imagined but performed" (p. 173). Borrowing from the Situationist International (SI), the Yes Men's identity corrections utilize the concept of *détournement* which, roughly translated, is a "turning around," essentially the act of pulling an image or situation out of its original context to create a new and socially improved meaning (Darts, 2004). Building on Marx's (1867) theory of commodity fetishism, the SI declared in the 1960s that our real lives had been co-opted by the spectacular media events and commodity consumption of the modern world. As a response to this society of the spectacle, they advocated fighting commercial culture with its own weapons. This approach is akin to Alinsky's (1989) metaphor of "mass political jujitsu," which he describes as "utilizing the power of one part of the power structure against another part . . . the superior strength of the Haves becomes their own undoing" (p. 152).

Both the SI and Alinsky have contributed to a theoretical framework that informs contemporary culture jamming, a movement that has its roots in a number of artistic, intellectual, and social movements from over the last 80 years (Lasn, 2000). While the term "culture jamming" was first used in 1984 by the San Francisco audio-collage band Negativland, the concept itself dates back to the suffrage and avant-garde movements of the early twentieth century. The Dadaist, Surrealist, Situationist International, Civil Rights, Anti-War, Environmental, Human Rights, Culture Jamming, and Anti-Globalization movements have all successfully employed and contributed to culture jamming ideas and techniques. As a form of artistic and sociopolitical intervention, culture jamming involves the creative appropriation and subversion of symbols, media channels, and technologies to reveal and subvert dominant structures and socio-political inequities of the status quo. Through artistic interventions, hoaxes, tactical media pranks, or what the SI called "situations," culture jammers direct public attention to the caesura between the fundamental values of a society (e.g., justice, democracy, civil rights, freedom) and its normative social, political, and environmental practices, with the intention of inspiring renewed debate and meaningful social transformations. Culture jammers regularly work to reveal corporate power and to subvert the ideologies of consumer-driven culture. At its best, culture jamming creates counterideologies, or what Duncombe (2007) labels "ethical spectacle" (p. 124), that subvert capitalism's public pedagogy and redirect it towards more socially just aims.

Strategic Visual Pedagogy: Art Education Towards Critical Citizenship

The creative tactics used by culture jammers to expose, critique, and subvert the ideologies of overconsumption promoted by global capitalism are, in many ways, analogous to the pedagogical approaches promoted by progressive art educators who have called for an art education that includes conscious and critical forms of student sociopolitical engagement (Darts, 2004; Duncum, 2007; Freedman, 2003; Tavin, 2003). Art educators have long argued for the importance of an education that supports critical self-expression and political agency and that encourages careful interrogations of our consumer-driven culture. Yokley (1999), for instance, has encouraged art educators to "combine the power of artistic means with political action as they question ideological formations, and indeed all facets of life, through projects of possibility" (p. 24). jagodzinski (2007) meanwhile, has proposed what he terms a "strategic visual pedagogy" (p. 341). Inspired in part by Hardt and Negri's (2000) call for the creative forces of the multitude to reorganize and redirect the global flows and exchanges of Empire to build a "counter-Empire" (p. xv), a strategic visual pedagogy involves teaching students to identify and repurpose the multimodal techniques used to sell the wares and values of global capitalism. jagodzinski (2007) cites the "graphic rhetoric" used by Al Gore in *An Inconvenient Truth* to powerfully visualize and "theatrisize" the statistical evidence of global warming as one such example (p. 355). Other instances of strategic visual pedagogy include the Yes Men's identity corrections and the faux sermons and exorcisms performed at the Disney store and other corporate retail outlets by Reverend Billy (a character created and performed by performance artist and activist Bill Talen) of the Church of Stop Shopping.

A defining feature of strategic visual pedagogy is its embrace of critical citizenship, including a commitment to revealing hidden forms of power and challenging corporate ideologies of consumption. Critical citizenship begins "with the principle that individuals and communities should have a direct role in the determination of the conditions of their own lives" (Sholle & Denski, 1994, p. 26). Critical citizens are individuals who are self-reflexive—setting themselves and their world in question— and have a deep concern for the lives of others. Teaching about global capitalism and consumer culture through art education offers opportunities to work toward critical citizenship, where students see themselves as agents of change. By connecting creative expression, theoretical knowledge, everyday experiences, and social critique though art education, students may have a stronger basis for investigating the implications of global capitalism (Tavin, 2003).

The goals laid out above—to develop a critical citizenship in response to corporate public pedagogy— are the underlying objectives for a graduate art education course that focuses on cultural sites and the public sphere. While the curriculum includes many forms of visual cultural critique, a special emphasis is placed on interrogating the pedagogical and ideological dimensions of consumer culture. Pre-service art education students investigate how particular forms of visual culture are understood within and across different circuits of culture that, in turn, characterize the wider society in relation to consumer culture and everyday life. As Giroux (2000) contends, central to any project that investigates global capitalism and corporate public pedagogy "is the need to begin at those intersections where people actually live their lives and where meaning is produced, assumed, and contested in the unequal relations of power that construct the mundane acts of everyday relations" (p. 355). Corporate-produced visual qualities, as perceived, exert their force on personal and social experiences in everyday life. Formal qualities and symbolic meanings exert influence on what and how we think. In this sense, students explore how individuals and groups are affected by particular forms of visual culture that constrain and/or enable various forms of agency in the context of global capitalism.

At one point in the semester, individual students present their critical response to readings on critical pedagogy and cultural studies (for example, Giroux, 1992; Kellner, 1995; Steinberg & Kincheloe, 1997) and engage the class in a dialogic seminar that encourages discussion, debate, and exchange. Through this seminar, students link theoretical issues about cultural studies and consumption with wider practical and pedagogical concerns. Students are encouraged to position themselves as reader, author, critic, and participant by situating the selected texts within a field of other texts, and knowledge in the context of other knowledge. Put differently, students respond to the articles through their own experiences and concerns, discovering and sharing "the connections between the text and the context of the text [and] the context of the reader" (Freire as cited in Shor & Freire, 1987, pp. 10–11).

During another point in the semester, individual students engage the class in a visual culture presentation where they make connections to the production of art or other forms of visual culture, and the teaching of visual culture through projected images, DVDs, guest speakers, or other collaborative projects. At the end of the semester, each participant in the class analyzes and interprets a cultural site, text, image, and/or set of images through critical theories that investigate what, when, and how discourses are produced, consumed, and regulated. Emphasis is placed upon visual phenomena and their influence on our thoughts and actions. The final project culminates with an outside field trip, culture jam, or other critical activity led by an individual student. In the past, students focused their attention on specific corporate and commodity sites in and around the city of Chicago. Many students engaged these sites by enacting a critical pedagogy of consumption inspired by culture jamming.

One example of this critical pedagogy of consumption is from a student-led "fieldtrip" to the Hard Rock Café in Chicago, one of approximately 110 chain restaurants in over 40 countries. Participants were guided through the restaurant and asked to explore the visual narratives and artifacts deployed on the walls in the context of global capitalism. One student pointed out a large proclamation, "All is One," spread across the wall in gold letters and surrounded by rock-and-roll icons, video screens, and other memorabilia. The students handed out a flyer to customers that discussed what the proclamation might signify as a form of neoliberal discourse contextualized within corporate public pedagogy. One of the conclusions made by students was that problems of race, class, gender, and sexual identity in the music industry are erased, and complex relations of global power get lost amidst the celebration of individualism and consumption in the Hard Rock Café.

With these ideas in mind, the class took note of who was represented, how the stories about those individuals were signified, and what stories were missing in the many narratives of popular culture on display. Students also discussed the corporate ownership of the restaurant chain, including the various locations around the globe and the how the corporate structure functions in particular contexts and communities (Kincheloe & Steinberg, 1997). After discussing these issues together as a group, individual students in the class began to talk with some of the workers and guests. In one sense, all the conversations dealt with how global capitalism constructs and helps maintain particular cultural memories—where ideology, belonging, pleasure, and passion are taught through corporate public pedagogy, and anchored in hyperreality.[1] These conversations, while not necessarily a blatant activist intervention, reflect the spirit and philosophy of culture jamming while enacting a critical pedagogy of consumption. By exposing various registers of power produced through the Hard Rock Café, "their specific manifestations in different places [and] the manner in which struggles of meaning and identity articulate with struggles over resources" (Kenway, 2001, p. 61).

Another student from the course led the class to Niketown, a corporate mega-complex replete with swirling shoes, video rooms, museum cases, and thousands of retail products. The student divided the class into five sections, asking each group—drawing upon readings for the class—to focus on one element from Du Gay, Hall, Janes, Mackay, and Negus' (1997) concept of "the circuit of culture," which includes identity, representation, production, consumption, and regulation. Participants were asked to analyze and interpret representations of athletes (their gender, ethnicity, sexual identity, nationality, age, etc.), promotional material, architecture, consumers, and the placement, type, and cost of Nike products. Students inspected product labels to determine the country of origin and then contextualized the materials within the discursive space of Nike's capitalist self-promotion as innovative, youthful, irreverent, authentic, fun, and all-American (Tavin, 2003).

Like Caffrey and Hunter (2002), the students understood that "Nike promotes athletic participation and discourages discrimination here at home, while the workers in the factories halfway around the world can barely afford to live" (p. 3). The students then discussed how visual representations throughout Niketown cultivate a particular notion of political efficacy through consumption and fantasy (Cole, 2000). In the end, members of the five student groups compared and contrasted notes from their critical readings of Niketown's pedagogy of consumption and together wove a discursive tale of the all-encompassing corporate pedagogy of Nike, while critiquing Nike's self-promotion and marketing of authenticity as a form inauthentic authenticity. As a way to help mobilize oppositional practices that demand corporate and social responsibility locally and globally all the students brought into focus the contrast between constructed reality and the lived contradictions for Nike factory workers.

Another critical reading of consumption's pedagogy involved "peeking into the past" at American Girl Place in Chicago, where corporate culture celebrates "girlhood through enchanting and fun play" (American Girl Place, 2008). Established first as the Pleasant Company and later acquired by Mattel Inc., American Girl Place has stores in Chicago, New York, Los Angeles, Atlanta, Dallas, Boston, and Minneapolis. The company developed and now makes huge profits from "historical" characters sold as dolls and marketed in books, magazines, and everywhere else on their cultural horizon. The company sells "Just Like You Dolls," Bitty Babies, and has "American Girl Place Boutiques and Bistros." According to their website, 23 million people visit and shop in their stores and 14 million dolls have been sold since their first store opened in Chicago to celebrate the life of dreams of girls.

The participants in the class wanted to know what girls were being celebrated and at what cost (financially and ideologically). In order to position the theoretical work they were learning about global capitalism against corporate power, the class was once again divided into teams to cover all four floors of the superstore. One group of students investigated the lower level of the complex where large dioramas of each doll's life are on display; students considered what and whose history was being exhibited. The group concluded that all the dolls, regardless of the temporal context (1774, 1854, 1864, 1904, or 1994), were represented in a safe, one-dimensional ontological zone—living a simple, wholesome, innocent, and privileged life, free from the struggles, conflict, and atrocities of the past. The only possible exception was Addy Walker, an African-American doll whose life takes place during the civil-war era. However, the students recognized and discussed how Addy's story was a site for both corporate pedagogy and commodified exotification—a form of objectification in which "the other" becomes alien, dehumanized and, ultimately, consumable—by failing to contextualize issues of race as part of the wider discourse of power and knowledge.

Other participants in the class re-searched different areas of the mega-store, including the bistro, theater, clothing, and other retail sections. Students explored American Girl books, toys, computer games, accessories, make-up, beach towels, blankets, and raised questions around the consumption of those products. Each group in the class problematized the American Girl products and the company's philosophy using a particular set of questions from Brady's (1997) article, *Multiculturalism and the American Dream*. These questions included: "Do these texts provide the opportunity to name the experience of oppression and then identify structures of dominance that function to cause the oppression?" "Do [these products] erase America's shameful character?" and, How does American Girl Place "legitimate diversity as a marketing strategy" (pp. 219–226)? While the students did not engage in direct "action" with the consumers or repurpose particular products in the store, their insight and questions around how American Girl Place deploys public pedagogy can be understood as an enactment of a critical pedagogy of consumption inspired by culture jamming. Here their questions about the norms, values, and roles taught through American Girl Place directly problematize how corporate power and global capitalism operates, by connecting visual representations with their material effects.

A final example comes from another student who escorted the class to Chicago's Rock and Roll McDonald's, a massive site of glass, overcrowded dining rooms, and cased collections of memorabilia, American icons, and images from the 1950s and 1960s. As Duncum (2001) states, McDonald's is "arguably the single most important icon of global culture" (p. 6). The student provided the class with a 15-page self-produced zine, complete with appropriated articles and essays and questions to consider. The readings included critiques of McDonald's global practices by Kincheloe (1997, 2002) and Ritzer (1996), and other articles from the McSpotlight website (www.mcspotlight.org), a site developed by British protesters who were sued by McDonald's. In addition, the zine contained promotional material from McDonald's and other pro-McDonald's essays from business journals and magazines. After reading the material, a student leader asked the class to consider the following questions: How does the production and consumption of McDonald's commodities affect the global and local environment? How does McDonald's two-billion-dollar advertising budget influence the construction of your identity and other global, collective, and regional identities? How has your life and the life of others been affected by multinational corporations, such as McDonald's, encroaching on all areas of the globe? What are the working conditions and labor practices of McDonald's in the United States and abroad?

The projects outlined above interpreted global capitalism to analyze, critique, and challenge real-life issues regarding real-life struggles. During these projects, students operated on and through contemporary theories learned in class (for example, Du Gay et al., 1997; Giroux, 1992; Kellner, 1995; Steinberg & Kincheloe, 1997) in order to set their world and themselves in question. Students challenged each other to become politically engaged by confronting specific and substantive historical, social, and/or economic issues, "drawing upon provided cultural signs [and] resignifying them to address the local politics of home" (Morgan, 1998, p. 126).

In art education practice, the analysis and interpretation of public and corporate spaces should engage students in confronting specific and substantive issues. Adopting a strategic visual pedagogy can help equip students with the intellectual and artistic tools necessary to evaluate and challenge global capitalism's public pedagogy. Such an approach includes teaching students to critically identify and artfully repurpose the multimodal techniques used to sell the products and ideas of commercial culture. While this may include utilizing the tactics and strategies used by culture jammers to reveal corporate power and expose ideologies of over-consumption, such direct actions are not necessarily required. As the student projects outlined above underscore, enacting critical pedagogies of consumption *inspired* by culture jamming can also provide powerful modes of response to the historical, social, and ideological dimensions of living in a consumer-driven culture. This does not mean, however, that there must be predefined political entailments or culture jams that offer emancipatory guarantees (Tavin, 2001). It merely suggests that art educators engage in a political project that addresses global capitalism while recognizing a whole host of complex issues and problems confronting students when negotiating identities within the terrain of visual culture. Telling students what to think and what to do about global capitalism in visual culture, for example, is inadequate and irresponsible. It plays into the logic of traditional teacher authority where educators speak uncontested truths that erase the complicated relationship students have to everyday life. Instead, educators should address issues of how to question the effects of global capitalism through multiple perspectives, performative interpretation, and meaningful production. As Buckingham (1998) states:

> If we want to enable students to explore theoretical issues in a genuinely open-ended way—rather than simply using practical work to demonstrate our own agenda—we have to acknowledge the possibility that they will not arrive at the correct positions that we might like them to occupy.
>
> (p. 85)

Building on Buckingham's gentle warning, the student culture-jam-inspired critiques focused on global capitalism could be seen as a "contextual practice which is willing to take the risk of making connections, drawing lines, mapping articulations, between different domains, discourses and practices, to see what will work, both theoretically and politically" (Grossberg, 1994, p. 18).

Note

1 Hyperreality is a term that usually describes a postmodern phenomena where it is difficult, if not impossible, to tell the difference between "real" experiences and reproductions of reality (Baudrillard, 1988).

References

Alinsky, S. (1989). *Rules for radicals: A practical primer for realistic radicals.* New York: Vintage.

American Girl Place (2008). Celebrating girls and all that they can be. Retrieved November 2, 2008, from http://www.americangirl.com/corp/corporate.php?section=about&id=1

Bacevich, A. J. (2008, October 5). He told us to go shopping. And now the bill is due. *The Washington Post.* Retrieved February 27, 2009, from http://www.washingtonpost.com/wp-dyn/content/article/2008/10/03/AR2008100301977.html

Baudrillard, J. (1988). *Jean Baudrillard: Selected writing.* London: Polity Press.

Brady, J. (1997). Multiculturalism and the American dream. In S. Steinberg & J. Kincheloe (Eds.), *Kinderculture: The corporate construction of childhood* (pp. 219–226). Boulder, CO: Westview.

Buckingham, D. (1998). Pedagogy, parody, and political correctness. In D. Buckingham (Ed.), *Teaching popular culture: Beyond radical pedagogy* (pp. 63–87). London: UCL Press.

Caffrey, E., & Hunter, M. (2002). *The female athlete in advertising.* Retrieved July 10, 2008, from http://it.stlawu.edu/~advertiz/womenath/conclusi.html

Carey, A. (1997). *Taking the risk out of democracy: Corporate propaganda versus freedom and liberty* (edited by A. Lowrey). Champaign, IL: University of Illinois Press.

Cole, C. (2000). The year that girls ruled. *Journal of Sport & Social Issues, 24*(1), 3–7.

Darts, D. (2004). Visual culture jam: Art, pedagogy and creative resistance. *Studies in Art Education, 45*(4), 313–327.

Darts, D. (2008). Art and pedagogy in the age of neo-liberal globalization. *Journal of Cultural Research and Art Education, 26*(1), 80–85.

Doane, D. (2005). The myth of CSR: The problem with assuming that companies can do well while also doing good is that markets don't really work that way. *Stanford Social Innovation Review,* Fall. Available: http://www.ssireview.org/articles/entry/the_myth_of_csr/

Du Gay, P, Hall, S., Janes, L., Mackay, H., & Negus, K. (1997). *Doing cultural studies: The story of the Sony Walkman.* London: Sage.

Duncombe, S. (2007). *Dream: Re-imagining progressive politics in an age of fantasy.* New York: The New Press.

Duncum, P. (2001). Theoretical foundations for an art education of global culture and principles for classroom practice [Electronic version]. *International Journal of Education and the Arts, 2*(3), 1–15.

Duncum, P. (2002). Theorising everyday aesthetic experience with contemporary visual culture. *Visual Arts Research, 28*(2), 4–15.

Duncum, P. (2007). Aesthetics, popular visual culture, and designer capitalism. *International Journal of Art & Design Education, 26*(3), 285–295.

Freedman, K. (2003). *Teaching visual culture: Curriculum, aesthetics and the social life of art.* New York: Teachers College Press.

Giroux, H. A. (1992). *Border crossings: Cultural workers and the politics of education.* New York: Routledge.

Giroux, H. A. (2000). Public pedagogy as cultural politics: Stuart Hall and the 'crisis' of culture. *Cultural Studies, 14*(2), 341–360.

Giroux, H. A. (2004). Cultural studies and the politics of public pedagogy: Making the political more pedagogical. *Parallax, 10*(2), 73–89.

Giroux, H. A. (2005). Cultural studies in dark times: Public pedagogy and the challenge of neoliberalism. *Fast Capitalism, 1*(2). Retrieved December 3, 2008, from http://www.uta.edu/huma/agger/fastcapitalism/1_2/giroux.html

Goodman, A. (2004, December 6). Yes Men hoax on BBC reminds world of Dow Chemical's refusal to take responsibility for Bhopal disaster. *Democracy Now!* Retrieved November 7, 2008, from http://i1.democracynow.org/2004/12/6/yes_men_hoax_on_bbc_reminds

Grossberg, L. (1994). Introduction: Bringin' it all back home—Pedagogy and cultural studies. In H. A. Giroux & P. McLaren (Eds.), *Between borders: Pedagogy and the politics of cultural studies* (pp. 1–25). New York: Routledge.

Hardt, M., & Negri, A. (2000). *Empire.* Cambridge, MA and London: Harvard University Press.

jagodzinski, j. (2007). The e(thi)co-political aesthetics of designer water: The need for a strategic visual pedagogy. *Studies in Art Education, 48*(4), 341–359.

Jameson, F. (1984). Postmodernism: Or, the cultural logic of late capitalism. *New Left Review, 146,* 59–92.

Kellner, D. (1995). *Media culture: Cultural studies, identity and politics between the modern and postmodern.* New York: Routledge.

Kenway, J. L. (2001). Remembering and regenerating Gramsci. In K. Weiler (Ed.), *Feminist engagements: Reading, resisting, and revisioning male authority in education and cultural studies* (pp. 47–65). New York: Routledge.

Kincheloe, J. L. (1997). McDonald's, power, and children: Ronald McDonald (aka Ray Kroc) does it all for you. In S. R. Steinberg, & J. L. Kincheloe (Eds.), *Kinderculture: The corporate construction of childhood* (pp. 249–266). Boulder, CO: Westview Press.

Kincheloe, J. L. (2002). *The sign of the burger: McDonald's and the culture of power.* Philadelphia, PA: Temple University Press.

Kincheloe, J. L. (2003). Says who? Who decides what is art? In K. Rose & J. L. Kincheloe, *Art, culture, & education: Artful teaching in a fractured landscape* (pp. 49–104). New York: Peter Lang.

Kincheloe, J. L., & Steinberg, S. R. (1997). *Changing multiculturalism.* Buckingham, UK: Open University Press.

Lasn, K. (2000). *Culture jam: How to reverse America's suicidal consumer binge—and why we must.* New York: Quill.

Marx, K. (1867). *Capital: The process of production of capital* (F. Engels, Ed.) (S. Moore & E. Aveling, Trans.). Moscow: Progress Publishers.

McChesney, R. (2000). *Rich media, poor democracy: Communication politics in dubious times.* New York: New Press.

Mitchell, W. J. T. (2005). *What do pictures want?: The lives and loves of images.* Chicago: University of Chicago Press.

Morgan, R. (1998). Provocations for a media education in small letters. In D. Buckingham (Ed.), *Teaching popular culture: Beyond radical pedagogy* (pp. 107–131). London: UCL Press.

O'Neill, S. (2004, December 4). Cruel $12 billion hoax on Bhopal victims and BBC. *Times Online.* Retrieved November 7, 2008, from http://www.timesonline.co.uk/tol/news/uk/article398896.ece

Ritzer, G. (1996). *The McDonaldization of society.* Thousand Oaks, CA: Pine Forge Press.

Sholle, D., & Denski, S. (1994). *Media education and the (re)production of culture.* Westport, CT: Bergin & Garvey.

Shor, I., & Freire, P. (1987). *A pedagogy for liberation.* Granby, MA: Bergin and Garvey.

Stauber, J., & Rampton, S. (1995). *Toxic sludge is good for you: Lies, damn lies and the public relations industry.* Monroe, ME: Common Courage Press.

Steinberg, S. R., & Kincheloe, J. L. (Eds.). (1997). *Kinder culture: The corporate construction of childhood.* Boulder, CO: Westview.

Tavin, K. (2001). Swimming up-stream in the jean pool: Developing a pedagogy towards critical citizenship in visual culture. *The Journal of Social Theory in Art Education, 21,* 129–158.

Tavin, K. (2003). Wrestling with angels, searching for ghosts: Toward a critical pedagogy of visual culture. *Studies in Art Education, 44*(3), 197–213.

The Yes Men (2006). Dow Chemical just says "yes" to Bhopal. In T. Corby (Ed.), *Network art: Practices and positions* (pp. 173–183). New York: Routledge.

Yokley, S. H. (1999). Embracing a critical pedagogy in art education. *Art Education, 52*(5), 18–24.

21 Turning America Into a Toy Store

Henry A. Giroux

The specific appeal of Disneyland, Disney films and products—family entertainment—comes from the contagious appeal of innocence.

(Michael Eisner)

The Southern Baptist Convention in June 1997 generated a lot of media attention when it called for a boycott of the Disney Company for promoting "immoral ideologies such as homosexuality." The Southern Baptists were angry because Disney sponsors "Gay Days" at its theme parks, provides health benefits to the domestic partners of gay employees, and publishes books about growing up gay. According to Herb Hilliger, a convention spokesman, the last straw came in April with the lead character of the sitcom Ellen had the audacity to come out as a lesbian on the Disney-owned ABC.[1]

The Baptists got it right in assuming that something was amiss in Disney's image as an icon of clean childhood fun and healthy family entertainment, but they got the reason wrong. Disney should not be condemned because it refuses to endorse homophobic practices in its labor operations and television programming but because its pretense to innocence camouflages a powerful cultural force and corporate monolith—in Eric Smoodin's words "a kind of Tennessee Valley Authority of leisure and entertainment"[2]—that commodifies culture, sanitizes historical memory, and constructs children's identities exclusively within the ideology of consumerism.

Far from being a model of moral leadership and social responsibility, Disney monopolizes media power, limits the free flow of information, and undermines substantive public debate. Disney poses a serious threat to democracy by corporatizing public space and by limiting the avenues of public expression and choice.[3] Disney does not, of course, have the power to launch armies, dismantle the welfare state, or eliminate basic social programs for children; Disney's influence is more subtle and pervasive. It shapes public consciousness through its enormous economic holdings and cultural power. Michael Ovitz, a former Disney executive, says that Disney is not a company but a nation-state, exercising vast influence over

This chapter first appeared as chapter five of Giroux, H. A. (1999). *The mouse that roared: Disney and the end of innocence.* Lanham, MD: Rowman and Littlefield. Reprinted with permission.

global constituencies.[4] Influencing large facets of cultural life, Disney ranks fifty-first in the Fortune 500 and controls ABC, numerous TV and cable stations, five motion picture studios, 728 Disney Stores, multimedia companies, and two major publishing houses. In 1997, Disney pulled in a record $22.7 billion on revenues from all of its divisions.[5] Not content to peddle conservative ideologies, it now provides prototypes for developing American culture and civility, including a model town, a prototype school system, and the Disney Institute, where it offers the intellectually curious vacations organized around learning skills in gardening, radio and television production, cinema, fitness regimens, and cooking.

Disney has always understood the connection between learning and power and their relationship to culture and politics. As one of the most powerful media conglomerates in the world, Disney promotes cultural homogeneity and political conformity, waging a battle against individuals and groups who believe that central to democratic public life is the necessity of democratizing cultural institutions, including the mass media. Extravagant, feature-length animated films, theme parks, and the Disnification of West Forty-second Street in New York City certainly may have entertainment and educational value, but they cannot be used as a defense for Disney's stranglehold on the message and image business, its stifling of unpopular opinions, or its relentless corporatizing of civic discourse—all of which undermine democratic cultural and political life.

What the Southern Baptists missed was that Disney's alleged transgression of family values and morality has nothing to do with its labor policies or representations of gays and lesbians. On the contrary, Disney's threat to civic life comes from its role as a transnational communications industry capable of ideological influence over vast segments of the American cultural landscape and, increasingly, the rest of the world. In the "magic kingdom," choice is about consumption, justice is rarely the outcome of social struggles, and history is framed nostalgically in the benevolent, patriarchal image of Walt Disney himself. In the animated world of Disney's films, monarchy replaces democracy as the preferred form of government, people of color are cast as either barbarous or stupid, and young Kate Moss-like waifs such as Pocahontas, Megara in *Hercules*, and Mulan support the worst kind of gender divisions and stereotypes. Combining economic control with pedagogical influence, Disney has become a major cultural player in American life, and the first casualties of its dominance in popular culture are, of course, the most defenseless—children.

Most insidiously, Disney uses its much-touted commitment to wholesome entertainment to market toys, clothes, and gadgets to children. Beneath Disney's self-proclaimed role as an icon to American culture lies a powerful educational apparatus that provides ideologically loaded fantasies. Walt Disney imagineers have little to do with "dreaming" a better world or even commenting on the world that today's kids actually inhabit. On the contrary, fantasy for Disney has no basis in reality, no sense of real conflicts, struggles, joys, and social relations. Fantasy is a marketing device, a form of hype rooted in the logic of self-interest and consumption.

Disney's view of children as consumers has little to do with innocence and a great deal to do with corporate greed and the realization that behind the vocabulary of family fun and wholesome entertainment is the opportunity for teaching children that critical thinking and civic action in society are far less important to them than the role of passive consumers. Eager to reach children under twelve, "who shell out $17 billion a year in gift and allowance income and influence $172 billion more spent by their parents," Disney relies on consultants such as the marketing researcher James McNeal to tap into such a market.[6] McNeal can barely contain his enthusiasm about targeting children as a fertile market and argues that the "world is poised on the threshold of a new era in marketing and that . . . fairly standardized multinational marketing strategies to children around the globe are viable."[7] For McNeal and his client, the Walt Disney Company, kids are reduced to customers, and serving the public good is an afterthought.

In its search for new markets and greater profits, Disney presents its films, theme parks, and entertainment as objects of consumption rather than as spheres of participation. Art in the Magic Kingdom becomes a spectacle designed to create new markets, commodify children and provide vehicles for merchandizing its commodities. Films such as *The Lion King, Pocahontas, The Hunchback of Notre Dame, Hercules,* and *Mulan* are used to convert J. C. Penney, Toys 'R Us, McDonald's, and numerous other retailers into Disney merchandizing outlets. But the real commercial blitz is centered in Disney's own marketing and distribution network, which includes the Disney Store, the Disney Channel, Disney magazine, Disneyland, and Walt Disney World.[8]

Given the recent media attention on the exploitation of children and young adults over the use of heroin chic in the fashion industry, the sexualization of young girls in the world of high-powered models, and the eroticization of six-year-olds in children's beauty pageants, it is surprising that there is little public outcry over the baleful influence Disney exercises on children. The Southern Baptists and the general public appear indifferent to Disney's role in attaching children's desires and needs to commodities, convincing these children that the only viable public space left in which to experience themselves as agents is in the toy sections of Wal-Mart or the local Disney Store.

Growing up corporate has become a way of life for American youth. Corporate mergers, such as Disney's buyouts of ABC, consolidate corporate control of assets and markets. An accelerated commercialism has become apparent in all aspects of life, including the "commercialization of public schools, the renaming of public streets for commercial sponsors, Janis Joplin's Mercedes pitch, restroom advertising, and [even the marketing] of an official commercial bottled water of a papal visit."[9] Accountable only to the bottom line of profitability, companies such as Disney carpet bomb their audiences with aired commercials and magazine ads.[10] Michael Jacobson and Laurie Ann Mazur estimate that each day, "260 million Americans are exposed to at least 18 billion display ads in magazines and daily newspapers [as well as] 2.6 million radio commercials, 300,000 television commercials, and 500,000 billboards."[11]

Although it is largely recognized that market culture exercises a powerful role educationally in mobilizing desires and shaping identities, it is still a shock that an increasing number of pollsters report that young people, when asked to provide a definition for democracy, refer to "the freedom to buy and consume whatever they wish, without government restriction."[12] Growing up corporate suggests that, as commercial culture replaces public culture, the language of the market becomes a substitute for the language of democracy; at the same time, the primacy of commercial culture has an eroding effect on civil society as the function of schooling shifts from creating a "democracy of citizens [to] a democracy of consumers."[13] One consequence is that consumerism appears to be the only kind of citizenship being offered. Confusing democracy with the market does more than hollow out those public spheres whose roots are moral rather than commercial; it also fails to heed an important insight expressed by Federico Mayor, the director general of UNESCO, who argues that "you cannot expect anything from uneducated citizens except unstable democracy."[14]

Disney's role as the arbiter of children's culture may seem abstract when expressed in these terms, but in the aftermath of the promotional blitz for Disney's animated film *Hercules*, the mix of educational strategy and greed was brought home to me with great force. My three boys were watching television news clips of the Disney parade in New York City and were in awe of Disney's extravaganza, which held up traffic in thirty city blocks and pulled out every stop in the creation of glitz, pomp, and spectacle. Of course, they couldn't wait to see the film, buy the spin-off toys, and be the first on their block to wear a *Hercules* pin. "Pin? What pin?" I asked. I hadn't watched the promotional ad carefully enough. It seems that Disney was providing a special showing of the film Hercules on June 21, 1997, a few weeks before its general release. But to get a ticket for the special showing, I (and thousands of other parents) had to go to an authorized Disney Store to buy a box, for seven dollars, that contained a ticket, a pin of one of the characters in the film, a brochure, and a tape of a song in the show, sung by Michael Bolton. Disney was in full force in this instance making sure that every kid, including my own, knew that along with the film came stuffed animals, figurines, backpacks, lunch boxes, tapes, videos, and a host of other gadgets soon to be distributed by Mattel, Timex, Golden Books, and other manufacturers of children's culture. Once again, children become the reserve army of consumers for the industrial state. (Not to mention that Disney's products are sold by companies like Mattel, Hasbro, and others that routinely exploit workers in China, Mexico, Indonesia, and elsewhere.)

Disney is shameless in turning the film hero Hercules into an advertisement for spin-off merchandise. Once Hercules proved himself through his brave deeds, Disney turned him into a public relations hero with a marketable trade name for products such as Air Hercules sneakers, toy figurines, and action-hero dolls, all of which can be bought in an emporium modeled shamelessly in the film after a Disney Store. Michael Eisner claims that the film is about building character, about "sophisticated style, and [about] a hip sense of humor."[15] Clearly, "character" has less to do with developing a sense of integrity and civic courage than with getting a laugh and building name recognition in order to sell consumer goods. *Hercules* suggests that the Disney dream factory is less a guardian of childhood innocence than a predatory corporation that views children's imaginations as simply another resource for amassing earnings.[16]

As market culture permeates the social order, it threatens to cancel out the tension between market values and those values representative of civil society that cannot be measured in commercial terms but that are critical to democracy, values such as justice, freedom, equality, health, respect, and the rights of citizens as equal and free human beings. Without such values, students are relegated to the role of economic machines, and the growing disregard for public life is left unchecked.

History is clear about the dangers of unbridled corporate power in the United States. Four hundred years of slavery (ongoing through unofficial segregation), the exploitation of child labor, the sanctioning of cruel working conditions in coal mines and sweatshops, and the destruction of the environment have all been fueled by the law of maximizing profits and minimizing costs, especially when there has been no countervailing power from civil society to hold such powers in check. This is not to suggest that corporations are the enemy of democracy but to highlight the importance of a strong democratic civil society that sets limits to the reach and effects of corporate culture. John Dewey was right: democracy requires work.[17]

Alex Molnar is also right in warning educators, parents, and others that the market does not provide "guidance on matters of justice and fairness that are at the heart of a democratic civil society."[18] The power of corporate culture, when left to its own devices, respects few boundaries and even fewer basic social needs, such as a safe food supply, universal health care, and safe forms of transportation. Moreover, as multinational corporations become more powerful by amassing assets and increasing their control over the circulation of information in the media, there remains little countervailing discourse about the role they play in undermining the principles of justice and freedom and in limiting the range of views at the center of our civic institutions.[19] This is particularly true for public schools, whose function, in part, is to teach about the importance of critical dialogue, debate, and decision making in a participatory democracy.[20]

What strategies are open to educators, parents, and others who want to challenge the corporate Disney barons who are shaping children's culture in the United States? First, it must become clear that Disney is not merely about peddling entertainment; it is also about politics, economics, and education. Corporations such as Disney do not give a high priority to social values, except to manipulate and exploit them. With every product that Disney produces, whether for adults or children, there is the accompanying commercial blitzkrieg aimed at excessive consumerism, selfishness, and individualism. This commercial onslaught undermines and displaces the values necessary to define ourselves as active and critical citizens rather than as consumers.

Moreover, driven by the imperatives of profit, Disney and other megacorporations reward ideas, messages, and values that are supportive of the status quo while marginalizing dissident views. A vibrant democratic culture is not served well by shrinking the range of critical public spheres, discourses, and relations necessary for the full, active participation of its citizens in shaping political culture. Disney, Time-Warner, and other corporate giants constitute a media system or national entertainment state that has "negative implications for the exercise of political democracy: it encourages a weak political culture that makes depoliticization, apathy and selfishness rational choices for the citizenry, and it permits the business and commercial interests that actually rule U.S. society to have inordinate influence over media content."[21]

Second, battles must be waged on numerous fronts to make clear the political, economic, and cultural influence that media industries such as Disney exercise in a democratic society. This suggests at the least the hard pedagogical and political work of getting the word out that "fewer than ten transnational media conglomerates dominate much of our media; fewer than two dozen account for the overwhelming majority of our newspapers, magazines, films, television, radio and books."[22] Public debate must be waged in numerous venues by academics, teachers, parents, and others over the implications of such media concentration for commercializing public discourse, limiting the range of dissent, limiting access to channels of communication, and shaping national views, desires, and beliefs.

While the traditional liberal response to such media concentration has been the traditional liberal call for regulation, progressives must interrogate the limits of such regulation and press for more radical structural changes. Educators, parents, community groups, and others much call into question existing structures of corporate power in order to make the democratization of media culture central to any reform movement. In part, this suggests taking ownership away from the media giants and spreading these resources among many sites in order to make media culture diffuse and accountable. Such monopolies are a political and cultural toxin, and their hold can be broken through broad-based movements using a variety of strategies, including public announcements, sit-ins, teach-ins, and boycotts, to raise public consciousness, promote regulation, and encourage antitrust legislation aimed at breaking up media monopolies and promoting the noncommercial, nonprofit public sphere.[23]

Progressives also need to press for a combination of state-supported, nonprofit, noncommercial television, radio, journalism, and other cultural formations impervious to the pernicious influence of advertisers and corporate interests. At the same time, progressives must be vigilant in not tying public broadcasting to state control.[24] In 1990, the federal government spent an estimated "$171 million on the National Endowment for the Arts, less than it allocated to the Pentagon for military bands."[25] Clearly, any commitment on the part of the government to cultural democracy must be tied to subsidies that allow independent media to flourish outside of the commercial sphere.

Defending media democracy is not tantamount to demanding that schools teach media literacy, nor is it simply about providing students with more choices in what they watch, hear, buy, or consume. These issues are important but become meaningless if abstracted from issues of institutional and economic power and how it is used, organized, controlled, and distributed. For example, as important as it is to teach students to learn how to read ads critically in order to understand the values and worldviews the ads are selling, it is not enough. Such literacy should not be limited to matters of textual interpretation or to the recognition that media culture is about business rather than entertainment. Parents, educators, and others need to actively question the manufactured myths, lifestyles, and values created by media giants like Disney to sell identities and increase profits.

Media literacy as a political commodity and pedagogical strategy means teaching strategies of interpretation and strategies of social transformation. As a form of political education, media literacy teaches students how to interpret critically the knowledge, values, and power that are produced and circulated through diverse technologies and public spaces while linking such understanding to broader public discourses that invoke the interrelated nature of theory, understanding, and social change. Makani Themba claims that "media literacy must be more than helping children and families take a discerning look at media. We need to work together to forge new partnerships—new covenants—that address corporate irresponsibility and government neglect. We must not only talk with kids and admonish them to stay on track, we must also hold those businesses accountable who prey on our young people."[26]

Children are growing up in a world shaped by a visual culture under the control of a handful of megacorporations that influence much of what young people learn. We need a new language to address these forms of power and their interlocking systems that dominate the production of knowledge. Against the power of a global culture industry driven by commercialism and commodification, it is crucial that we reclaim the language of critical citizenry, democracy, and social values. Financial and institutional support is necessary to develop those public cultures and spaces in which open deliberation, critical debate, and public education are not undermined by the imperatives of big business and advertising but are shaped by those social and critical values necessary for building democratic communities, identities, and social relations. This suggests curbing the power of big media and weakening the influence of advertising in shaping cultural life. Media giants such as Disney must be challenged. Disney has created a national entertainment state capable of exercising unchecked corporate power within "the injustices of an unregulated global economy."[27]

The time has come to challenge Disney's self-proclaimed role as a purveyor of "pure entertainment" and take seriously Disney's educational role in producing ideologically loaded fantasies aimed at teaching children selective roles, values, and cultural ideals.[28] Progressive educators and other cultural workers need to pay attention to how the pedagogical practices produced and circulated by Disney and other mass-media conglomerates organize and control a circuit of power that extends from producing cultural texts to shaping the context in which they will be taken up by children and others.

In addition, as a principal producer of popular culture, Disney's films, television programs, newscasts, and other forms of entertainment should become objects of critical analysis, understanding, and intervention both inside and outside of schools. It is almost a commonplace that most of what students learn today is not in the classrooms of public schools or, for that matter, in the classrooms of higher education but in electronically generated media spheres. Consequently, students need to acquire the knowledge and skills to become literate in multiple symbolic forms so as to be able to read critically the various cultural texts to which they are exposed. This is not to suggest that we should junk the canon for Disney studies but to suggest that we refashion what it is that students learn in relation to how their identities are shaped outside of academic life.

Students need to become multiply literate and focus on diverse spheres of learning. The issue of what is valuable knowledge is not reducible to the tired either/or culture war arguments that pervade the academy. Maybe the more interesting questions point in different directions: What is it that students need to learn to live in a substantive democracy; to read critically in various spheres of culture; to engage those traditions of the past that continue to shape how we think about the present and the future; and to critically analyze multiple texts for the wisdom they provide and the maps they draw that guide us toward a world that is more multicultural, diverse, and democratic?

Students need to learn how to produce their own newspapers, records, television programs, music videos, and whatever other technology is necessary to link knowledge and power with pleasure and the demands of public life. But for such skills to become useful, they must be connected to the larger project of radical democracy and technological justice, that is, to the struggle for local communities to have universal access to the internet, public broadcasting, and the institutional spaces for theater, newspaper, and magazine productions. Put simply, young people need access to subsidized, noncommodified public spheres that allow their artistic, intellectual, and critical talents to flourish.

Corporate power is pervasive and will not give up its resources willingly. Resistance to dominant corporate culture means developing pedagogical and political strategies that both educate and transform, that build alliances while recognizing different perspectives, and that foreground the struggle over democracy as the central issue. Any attempt to challenge media giants such as Disney demands linking cultural politics with policy battles. Changing consciousness must become part of practical politics designed to change legislation, to reorganize and distribute resources, and to redefine the relationship between pedagogy and social justice, between knowledge and power. Building alliances is especially important, and progressives need a new language for bringing together cultural workers that ordinarily have not worked well together. This suggests finding ways to organize educators at all levels of schooling in order to gain control over those pedagogical forces that shape our culture. And this means addressing the pedagogical force of those cultural industries that have supplanted the school as society's most important educational force.

There is also the imperative to reinvigorate unionized labor, whose funds and power can help us fight for social justice, particularly through gaining access to the media as a site for public pedagogy, especially as that pedagogy shapes the lives of young people.[29] Unions must be convinced that the struggle over wages, better working conditions, and health benefits becomes more meaningful and just when linked to the broader discourse of democracy and its impact upon those populations who are often marginalized.

Finally, we need to organize those who inhabit cultural spheres that produce, circulate, and distribute knowledge but who seem removed from matters of education, pedagogy, and cultural politics. Artists, lawyers, social workers, and others need to acknowledge their role as public intellectuals engaged in a pedagogy that offers them an opportunity to join with other cultural workers to expand the noncommodified public space.

These are highly general suggestions, but they offer a starting point for making the pedagogical more political and for making hope the basis for practical resistance. Disney got its eye blackened when its attempt in 1995 to create a theme park on a historical Virginia landmark was successfully resisted by active citizens. This victory, while modest, suggests that dominant power is never total, resistance is possible, and pedagogical work is fundamental to the struggle for social justice. While we cannot underestimate the political power and cultural force of corporations such as Disney in undermining democratic public life and in turning every aspect of daily life into either a commercial or an appendage of the market, we must continually make visible the threat such corporations pose to democracy everywhere.

Challenging the ideological underpinnings of Disney's construction of common sense is the first step in understanding the ways in which corporate culture has refashioned the relationship between education and entertainment, on the one hand, and institutional power and cultural politics, on the other. It is also a way of rewriting and transforming such a relationship by putting democracy before profits and entertainment and by defining such a project within the parameters of a broad political and pedagogical struggle. The aims of this struggle are (1) creating public spheres that educate for critical consciousness, (2) closing the gap in wealth and property between the rich and poor, and (3) providing the resources for creating a democratic media linked to multiple public spheres.

Notes

1 Lori Sharn, "Southern Baptists Denounce Disney, Urge Boycott," *USA Today*, June 19, 1997, p. 1A.

2 Eric Smoodin, "How to Read Walt Disney," in Smoodin, ed., *Disney Discourse: Producing the Magic Kingdom* (New York: Routledge, 1994), p. 3.

3 For an analysis of the emerging "national entertainment state," along with a chart that tracks the acquisitions of four major media conglomerates, including Disney, see Mark Crispin Miller and Janine Jaquet Biden, "The National Entertainment State," *Nation*, June 3, 1996, pp. 23–26. See also Mark Crispin Miller, "Free the Media," *Nation*, June 3, 1996, pp. 9–15.

4 Peter Bart, "Disney's Ovitz Problem Raises Issues for Show-biz Giants," *Daily Variety*, December 16, 1996, p. 1.

5 Figures from *The Walt Disney Company 1997 Annual Report* (Burbank, Calif.: Walt Disney Company, 1997).

6 Andrea Adelson, "Children's Radio Pioneer is Challenged by Disney," *New York Times*, July 21, 1997, p. D10).

7 James U. McNeal, *Kids as Consumers: A Handbook of Marketing for Children* (New York: Lexington Books, 1992).

8 With properties in a variety of markets, Disney can generate enormous profits from these outlets even if an animated film does not do well at the box office. For instance, Robert McChesney points out that "the animated films *Pocahontas* and *Hunchback of Notre Dame* were only marginal successes at the box office, with roughly $100 million in gross US revenues, but both films will generate close to $500 million in profit for Disney, once it has exploited all other venues: TV shows on its ABC network and cable channels, amusement park rides, comic books, CD-ROMs, CDs, and merchandising (through 600 Disney retail stores)." "Making Media Democratic," *Boston Review* 23: 3–4 (1998), p. 4.

9 George R. Wright, *Selling Words: Free Speech in a Commercial Culture* (New York: New York University Press, 1997), p. 181.

10 McChesney uses the term "commercial carpet bombing" and argues that "advertising should be strictly regulated or removed from all children's programming." "Making Media Democratic," pp. 6–7.

11 Don Hazen and Julie Winokur, eds., *We the Media* (New York: New Press, 1997), p. 40.

12 Wright, *Selling Words*, p. 182.

13 Gerald Grace, "Politics, Markets, and Democratic Schools: On the Transformation of School Leadership," in A. H. Halsey, Hugh Lauder, Philip Brown, and Amy Stuart Wells, eds., *Education: Culture, Economy, Society* (New York: Oxford University Press, 1997, p. 315).

14 Burton Bollag, "Unesco Has Lofty Aims for Higher-Education Conference, but Critics Doubt Its Value," *Chronicle of Higher Education*, September 4, 1998, p. A76.

15 Michael Eisner, with Tony Schwartz, *Work in Progress* (New York, Random House, 1998), p. 414.

16 For an excellent critical analysis of how toys limit the imaginations of children, see Stephen Kline, *Out of the Garden: Toys and Children's Culture in the Age of TV Marketing* (London: Verso, 1993). For an analysis of how marketing is spreading to different populations of youth in a variety of sites, see Larry Armstrong, "Is Madison Avenue Taking 'Get 'Em While They're Young' Too Far?" *Business Week*, June 30, 1997, pp. 62–67. For a critique of the commercialization of public schools, see Alex Molnar, *Giving Kids the Business* (Boulder, Colo.: Westview, 1996).

17 John Dewey, Democracy and Education (New York: Free Press, 1916).

18 Molnar, *Giving Kids the Business*, p. 17.

19 Andre Schiffrin, the director of the New Press, brilliantly illustrates how the takeover of the book publishing industry by conglomerates is eliminating books that cannot be made into films or television series or achieve instant blockbuster status. The result has been that important literary works, scholarly books, books that are critical of corporate power, and others that do not fit into the for-profit formula driving the big publishing houses simply do not get published. This is no small matter, considering that independent and university publishers constitute only about 1 percent of the total sales in book publishing. See "Public-Interest Publishing in a World of Conglomerates," *Chronicle of Higher Education*, September 4, 1998, pp. B4–B5.

20 Benjamin Barber, "The Making of McWorld," *New Perspectives Quarterly* 12:4 (1995), pp. 13–17.

21 Robert W. McChesney, *Corporate Media and the Threat to Democracy* (New York: Seven Stories Press, 1997), p. 7.

22 McChesney, "Making Media Democratic."

23 See Mark Crispin Miller, "Free the Media," *Nation*, June 3, 1996, pp. 9–15; see also John Keane, *The Media and Democracy* (London: Polity, 1991); Noam Chomsky, *Manufacturing Consent* (New York: Pantheon, 1988); George Gerbner, Hamid Mowlana, and Herbert I. Schiller, *What Conglomerate Control of Media Means for America and the World* (Boulder, Colo.: Westview, 1996).

24 Robert W. McChesney argues that this is not a call to abolish the commercial media but to make sure that it is not the dominant sector of the culture industry. Moreover, if the dominant sector is to be nonprofit, noncommercial, and accountable to the public, the commercial media should have a 1 percent tax levied on them to subsidize the noncommercial sector. He also calls for the leasing of spectrum space. These combined taxes, he estimates, would bring in over $3 billion in revenue—no small matter, considering that in 1997 the total federal subsidy to public broadcasting was $250 million. See McChesney, *Corporate Media and the Threat to Democracy*, p. 67.

25 Sut Jhally, "Moving beyond the American Dream," in Hazen and Winokur, *We the Media*, p. 41.

26 Makani Themba, "Holding the CEO's Accountable," in Hazen and Winokur, *We the Media*, p. 88.

27 Eyal Press, "Barbie's Betrayal: The Toy Industry's Broken Workers," *Nation*, December 30, 1996, p. 12.

28 This argument is used by many media conglomerates. For a devastating critique of this position, see McChesney, *Corporate Media and the Threat to Democracy*; Hazen and Winokur, *We the Media*. Also see Charles Deber, *Corporation Nation* (New York: St. Martin's Press, 1998).

29 Robert McChesney argues that labor could subsidize non-profit and noncommercial media without micromanaging them. For such media to flourish, they must remain independent. "We need a system of real public broadcasting, with no advertising, that accepts no grants from corporations or private bodies, and that serves the entire population, not merely those who are disaffected from the dominant commercial system and have to contribute during pledge drives." "Making Media Democratic," pp. 4–5.

22 United We Consume?

Artists Trash Consumer Culture and Corporate Green-Washing

Nicolas Lampert

Collage is a form of recycling, a medium whereby images and their meanings are recycled and re-contextualized. The image "United We Consume" (the image on the cover of this book) is an example of this; it takes two found images and rearranges them to make a political statement. The end result is a critique on consumerism—a theme that runs central in much of my artwork and the courses I teach to college art students.

"United We Consume" juxtaposes a found photograph of two women sewing American flags and positions them in the foreground of a found photograph of a garbage pile that was used as a barrier wall in Alaska. The image itself (including the original photographs) can conjure up multiple readings, but the title serves as an indicator of what I wished to communicate with the image. I created "United We Consume" shortly after September 11th and the subsequent attacks on Afghanistan and Iraq by the Bush Administration. The title is a play upon the slogan "United We Stand" that dominated speeches by the Bush Administration as it pitched the need for war to the American people. The drumbeat for war and the carefully construed slogan found itself everywhere—on bumper stickers, T-shirts, song titles and the graphics of corporate newscasts. Despite the fact that the country was more divided then ever, very few voices asked who was the "we" we are standing behind and if a "we" even exists in a country as diverse as the United States. Nonetheless, the message of "United We Stand" coming from the president and the corporate media implied that the country was united behind the U.S. government's decision to retaliate with force.

For my image, I wanted to critique the "United We Stand" slogan, the Bush administration, and the war climate that followed. I wanted to critique the political and cultural climate that had become pre-occupied by terrorism, and specifically I wanted to draw attention to the issues that were not being discussed, issues such as environmental collapse and poverty—both on global and domestic levels. Instead of focusing on these issues (which I would argue are some of the primary root causes of war and acts of terror), Americans were asked to be blind consumers. The message coming out of Washington and the mass media was to wave the flag, be uncritical, shop, consume, and stand behind the government's actions to wage war.

Counter Images/Counter Approaches

Dissident words, images, and actions can offer a counter perspective. In visual culture, the medium of collage is well suited for this critique because it uses a common visual language of photographic images and mass media images that derive from popular culture. Additionally, collage has a long history of being a subversive medium. Examples range from John Heartfield's photomontages against Hitler, Peter Kennard's anti-nuclear images, the cut-and-paste aesthetic of punk rock flyers, the collages by Winston Smith, John Yates, Gee Vaucher, and many other examples too numerous to list. Collage is also a medium that often employs humor—an important tactic that invites the viewer into the conversation no matter how troubling the subject matter may be. And lastly, the medium is easily disseminated; images can be showcased in exhibitions, reprinted in books and periodicals, and spread far and wide through websites.

The dissemination of the work is as crucial as the image itself. In the 1930s, John Heartfield reached a vast audience with his collage art through the weekly illustrated news magazine *AIZ*, or *Arbeiter-Illustrierte-Zeitung* (in English this translates to "Workers Illustrated Newspaper") and by wheatpasting thousands of posters in the streets of Berlin. Today, the largest audience an artist can reach is often through the Internet, although one can make the argument that images posted in the street (depending on the city and the location) can reach a potentially larger audience. That said the longevity of street art is often limited due to weather conditions, and by the work being removed if it was put up illegally.

In the case of my own work, I choose to disseminate images through a variety of tactics. I show images in galleries, museums, in the street, in publications, and on the Internet. I also license the work through Creative Commons, which circumvents rigid copyright restrictions and allows the images to be reproduced and shared as long as people credit my name and do not profit from any of the images.

Gone Tomorrow

Creating art with political and social content has led me to teach college courses on the topic. One course I have taught on a number of occasions is a hybrid studio/theory/contemporary art history course that examines how visual artists have tackled the immense subject of consumerism, and how artists, designers, and architects have provided critique and solutions for a more sustainable and equitable world.

In this course, students read *Gone tomorrow: The hidden life of garbage* by Heather Rogers (2006) and learn about the work of contemporary artists including Mierle Laderman Ukeles (the artist in residency at the New York Department of Sanitation for the past two decades), Reverend Billy and the Church of Stop Shopping (who perform exorcisms on the cash registers of Starbucks, among other things), Tyree Guyton (who created the Heidelberg Project in Detroit where he attaches discarded consumer goods to the houses and empty lots of Heidelberg Street), and the "Trashball" performance (where an art collective called "Men and Women" rolled a giant ball of trash down Chicago's "Magnificent Mile" on a Saturday afternoon during the peak time of shopping madness.) Another facet of the course is a critique of images found in popular culture and public space, including corporate advertisements and the insidious practice of corporate green-washing.

Additionally, the studio component of the class asks students to create their own visual projects and to place them in public. Projects have run the full gamut, including posters, performances, video, sculptures, and street art. In many cases, the preferred subject matter explored by students often revolves around an investigation of their own consumer habits, the politics of recycling, the amount of trash on the streets, or a critique of car culture. Some of the more memorable projects included a student who created a tag that read "Your Bicycle Misses You" that was attached to the handles of numerous cars throughout Milwaukee. Another project involved two students who altered a 50-gallon metal drum barrel into a rain catchment system with a filter and spigot that caught rain water. The students redistributed the water for free in a public park to encourage people not to buy water sold in plastic bottles. And one student created series of "mud stencils"—street stencils that use mud as a medium instead of spray paint. His classic image in this series was an outline of a plastic bottle with text that simply read "oil."

Think Green

The student projects that derive from this course never fail to amaze me and I find that teaching the class influences my own visual artwork. For example, one specific classroom discussion that focused on the "Think Green" advertising campaign by Waste Management (WM) inspired me to create a visual project in response.

To provide background context, the WM ad campaign has been ongoing for the past two years and has appeared in magazines, on the WM website, and on the sides of their garbage collection trucks (conveniently painted green). Through this campaign WM attempts to pass itself off as the most environmentally sound corporation that has ever graced the face of the earth. The primary slogan revolves around the words "Think Green." In the ads, various designs and text state that WM's landfills are now thriving homes for birds and other wildlife; the ads also include images depicting a near perfect green scene. The class found this ad campaign to be particularly egregious for numerous reasons.

To begin with, WM does nothing to challenge over-consumption, nor does it critique the excessive packaging and waste produced by manufacturers that lead to massive landfills. Of course, WM profits from industry creating more products and from consumers throwing away more trash so the few "green" practices the company practices do little to counteract the systemic issues of hyperconsumerism and resource extraction. Additionally, WM's "green" practices need to be questioned, because a large percentage of the recycled materials the company collects ends up in landfills; additionally, the entire process of recycling and a fleet of garbage trucks use an exorbitant amount of fossil fuels. Thus, the emphasis is never on creating less waste, reducing unnecessary packaging, re-using materials, or keeping biodegradable materials such as food—materials a household or business could easily compost—out of landfills. Nonetheless, "Think Green" has been an effective advertising campaign from the perspective of WM because it dupes the public into thinking otherwise and presents WM as a model corporate citizen.

Think Green®

WASTE MANAGEMENT

The more you throw away, the more we profit

Figure 22.1 Sticker Mimicking WM Campaign.

Figure 22.2 Sticker Placed on a WM Dumpster.

To visually critique the green-washing by WM, I decided to create a counter advertising campaign. I (along with Max Estes, a graduate student) designed a sticker, mimicking the WM campaign, but adding the slogan "Think Green: The More You Throw Away, The More We Profit" to the WM logo (see Figure 22.1). The sticker was then placed on WM dumpsters in a number of Midwestern cities during a three-month period (see Figure 22.2).

In retrospect, one could argue that this was a small gesture considering the hundreds of thousands of WM dumpsters that exist in the world, but it was a symbolic act nonetheless. And one that at least made me, and perhaps others who came across the intervention, feel better. Additionally, it was a lesson in scale and a reminder that corporations such as Waste Management have budgets in the millions to advertise and employ visual images and slogans to influence the public discourse, while the majority of artists (myself included) co-exist with limited resources, time, and budgets.

That said, artists and educators should not be discouraged from engaging in this critical work, for these types of creative actions are all part of the larger struggle over who owns public space during an era of massive privatization and corporate control. And from a broader perspective, these types of visual projects are all part of the larger struggle to challenge consumerism, corporate green-washing, and green capitalism. In the end, they are creative actions where art becomes a tool for social action and artists situate themselves in the most important place of all: within movements.

Reference

Rogers, H. (2006). *Gone tomorrow: The hidden life of garbage.* New York: New Press.

List of Contributors

Faith Boninger is a Research Analyst at the Commercialism in Education Research Unit at Arizona State University. Her recent publications include a yearly review of commercialism activities in schools, and a national survey of school officials that assessed schoolhouse commercialism activities by corporations that sell foods of minimal nutritional value. She brings to this work a special interest in persuasion processes, social influence, and social cognition.

Stephen D. Brookfield, since his days as a lecturer/organizer in community development in the 1970s, has worked in Britain, Canada, and the United States exploring how adults learn to think and act critically in the face of ideological manipulation. He has written, edited, and co-authored 12 books on adult learning, dialogic teaching, critical thinking, and critical theory and is currently Distinguished University Professor at the University of St. Thomas in Minneapolis-St. Paul, Minnesota.

Elizabeth Bullen is a Senior Lecturer in Literary Studies at Deakin University, Australia, where she teaches in the children's literature Masters Program. Her research interests include class, consumer, child, and youth cultures, with a focus on narrative. She is currently investigating representations of social class in contemporary children's texts. Her forthcoming article in the journal *Media, Culture, Society*, "Inside story: product placement and adolescent consumer identity in young adult fiction," links consumption with new class formations.

Darlene E. Clover is a photographer and Associate Professor in Leadership Studies, Faculty of Education, University of Victoria, British Columbia. Her research and teaching focus on feminist pedagogy, environmental adult education, and community cultural leadership through the arts. Darlene's latest publication (with Joyce Stalker) is titled *The Arts and Social Justice: Recrafting Adult Education and Community Cultural Leadership*.

David Darts is Assistant Professor of Art and Art Education and Associate Director of the NYU Steinhardt MA in Studio Art Program in Venice, Italy. His research and writings about contemporary art, public pedagogy, digital media and creative citizenship have been published in top scholarly journals and books. Darts is Curatorial Director of *Conflux*, the annual art and technology festival for the creative exploration of urban public space. He teaches courses on media literacy, art education, and theory and research in contemporary art.

Ramin Farahmandpur is an Associate Professor in the Department of Educational Leadership and Policy in the Graduate School of Education at Portland State University. His most recent book is entitled *Class, Ideology and Hegemony: Rethinking Marxist Educational Theory* (2008). His previous book (coauthored with Peter McLaren) is entitled *Teaching Against Global Capitalism and the New Imperialism* (2005). Dr. Farahmandpur's work has been translated and published in Spanish, Portuguese, Arabic, Turkish, Chinese, and Russian language journals.

Gustavo E. Fischman is an Associate Professor at the Mary Lou Fulton Institution and Graduate School of Education, Arizona State University. His areas of specialization are comparative education, educational policy studies, and critical pedagogy. Dr. Fischman is currently coordinating two research projects. The first is titled "Strengthening the academic and scientific scholarly publishing capacity in Latin America." The second project analyzes the political-pedagogical discourses of influential newspapers. He actively teaches and collaborates on research projects in Argentina, Brazil, Mexico, and the USA. He is one of the editors of *Education Review* and *Educational Policy Analysis Archives*, and the author of two books and numerous articles and chapters on critical pedagogy, teacher education, higher education, and gender issues in education.

Joseph Fogarty is Principal of Corballa National School in Sligo, Ireland. He is chairperson of the Campaign for Commercial-Free Education and brings a knowledge of commercial trends in Irish schools.

Henry A. Giroux currently holds the Global TV Network Chair Professorship at McMaster University in the English and Cultural Studies Department. His most recent books include *The University in Chains: Confronting the Military-Industrial-Academic Complex* (2007), *Against the Terror of Neoliberalism* (2008), and *Youth in a Suspect Society: Democracy or Disposability?* (2009). His primary research areas are: cultural studies, youth studies, critical pedagogy, popular culture, media studies, social theory, and the politics of higher and public education.

David A. Greenwood (formerly Gruenewald) is an Associate Professor at Washington State University. His research, teaching, and activism revolve around place-based, environmental, and sustainability education. Widely published in these areas, David recently co-edited the book *Place-Based Education in the Global Age: Local Diversity* (Lawrence Erlbaum, 2008). David earnestly believes that institutions of education need to be radically transformed to meet the challenges of local and global sustainability. He can be reached at greenwood@wsu.edu.

Eric Haas is a Senior Research Associate at WestEd, a national U.S. educational research organization. His work has been published in academic journals and books as well as in the popular press. In 2004, Dr. Haas was awarded a visiting fellowship at the Institute of Advanced Studies at the University of Lancaster (England) for his work on framing and discourse analysis. Dr. Haas began his professional career as a Peace Corps Volunteer in Liberia. Since then, he has worked as a lawyer, a teacher in international schools, a middle school principal, and an Assistant Professor of Education at the University of Connecticut.

Michael Hoechsmann is an Associate Professor in Education at McGill University. His research interests are in the areas of media, new technologies, literacy, new literacies, youth, cultural studies, and education. He is the author, with Bronwen E. Low, of *Reading Youth Writing: "New" Literacies, Cultural Studies and Education* (Peter Lang, 2008). For four years, he was the Director of Education of Young People's Press, a non-profit news service for youth 14–24.

Richard Kahn is an Assistant Professor of Educational Foundations and Research at the University of North Dakota. The Chief Editor of *Green Theory & Praxis: The Journal of Ecopedagogy*, he is the author of two forthcoming books, *Critical Pedagogy, Ecoliteracy, and Planetary Crisis: The Ecopedagogy Movement* (Peter Lang) and *Ecopedagogy: Educating for Sustainability in Schools and Society* (Routledge). Additional information about him can be obtained at his website: http://richardkahn.org.

Jane Kenway is a Professor of Education, Monash University, Australia. Her expertise is in the politics of educational change in the context of wider social, cultural and political change. Her more recent jointly written books are *Masculinity Beyond the Metropolis* (Palgrave, 2006), *Haunting the Knowledge Economy* (Routledge, 2006), and *Consuming Children* (Open University Press, 2001). Her most recent jointly edited book is *Globalising the Research Imagination* (Routledge, 2008).

Joe L. Kincheloe was the Canada Research Chair of Critical Pedagogy at the McGill University Faculty of Education, Montreal. He was the founder of the Paulo and Nita Freire International Project for Critical Pedagogy. He was the author of numerous books and articles about pedagogy, education and social justice, racism, class bias, sexism, issues of cognition and cultural context, and educational reform. His books included: *Knowledge and Critical Pedagogy* and *The Sign of the Burger: McDonald's and the Culture of Power*. His co-edited works with Shirley Steinberg include *Christotainment: Selling Jesus Through Popular Culture*, and *White Reign: Deploying Whiteness in America*.

Nicolas Lampert is a Chicago-based artist and writer. Collectively, he works with Justseeds (www.justseeds.org) and Mess Hall, an experimental cultural center in Chicago (www.messhall.org). He was a co-editor for *Peace Signs: the Anti-War Movement Illustrated* (2004). Past essays include "Recent Struggles at Haymarket: An Embattled History of Static Monuments and Public Interventions" (*Realizing the Impossible: Art Against Authority*, edited by Josh MacPhee and Erik Reuland, AK Press, 2007). His visual art website is: www.machineanimalcollages.com.

Sue L. T. McGregor is a Canadian home economist and Professor in the Faculty of Education at Mount Saint Vincent University, Nova Scotia, Canada. She is the Director of Graduate Education and has been a home economics and consumer studies educator for 35 years. Her current work focuses on pushing the boundaries of consumer education and research and home economics thinking toward transdisciplinary inquiry, transformative approaches (leadership and education), a moral imperative, and the new sciences approach.

Peter McLaren is a Professor in the Division of Urban Schooling, the Graduate School of Education and Information Studies, University of California, Los Angeles. He is the author or editor of 45 books. Professor McLaren's writings have been translated into 20 languages. Four of his books have won the Critic's Choice Award of the American Educational Studies Association. A Marxist humanist, he lectures widely in Latin America, North America, Asia, and Europe. His most recent book (co-authored with Nathalia Jaramillo) is *Pedagogy and Praxis in the Age of Empire* (Rotterdam and Taiwan, Sense Publications). With Steve Best and Anthony Nocella, he has co-edited a forthcoming book, *Academic Repression: Reflections from the Academic Industrial Complex* (AK Press). Professor McLaren's work has been the subject of two recent books: *Teaching Peter McLaren: Paths of Dissent*, edited by Marc Pruyn and Luis M. Huerta-Charles (New York: Peter Lang Publications), and *Peter McLaren, Education, and the Struggle for Liberation*, edited by Mustafa Eryaman (New Jersey: Hampton Press).

Matthew M. Mars is an Assistant Professor in the Division of Applied and Advanced Studies in Education at California State University, Los Angeles. Mars's research focuses on the entrepreneurial dimensions of contemporary higher education environments with particular emphasis on student entrepreneurship. His research has been published in education and management journals that include the *Journal of Higher Education* and the *Journal of Management Inquiry*.

Lydia Martens is a Senior Lecturer in Sociology at Keele University. She is working on an ongoing research agenda on children, families, and consumer culture. As part of this, she has conducted fieldwork at The Baby Show since 2005, and is working on a related book project entitled "Consuming the Precious Child." Her publications include *Eating Out: Social Differentiation, Consumption and Pleasure* (2000, with Alan Warde), and *Gender and Consumption: Domestic Cultures and the Commercialisation of Everyday Life* (2007, with Emma Casey). She is co-author of "Bringing Children (and Parents) into the Sociology of Consumption" (*Journal of Consumer Culture*, 2004). Lydia is currently on the UK DCSF panel, which assesses the impact of the commercial world on children's wellbeing.

Alex Molnar is a Professor of Education Policy and Director of the Education Policy Research Unit and Commercialism in Education Research Unit at Arizona State University. He has published numerous articles on social and educational policy and practice. For the past several years, he has studied and written about commercial activities in the schools and market-based school reforms such as private school vouchers, charter schools, and for-profit schools.

Jennifer A. Sandlin is an Assistant Professor in the Division of Advanced Studies in Education Policy, Leadership, and Curriculum at Arizona State University. Her research focuses on consumer education; the intersections of education, learning, and consumption; and various sites of ideological education for children, youth, and adults. Her recent work investigates sites of public pedagogy and popular culture-based, informal, and social movement activism centered on "unlearning" consumerism. Her work has been published in *Adult Education Quarterly*, *Journal of Curriculum and Pedagogy*, *Curriculum Inquiry*, and *Teachers College Record*. She is currently co-editing, with Brian Schultz and Jake Burdick, the *Handbook of Public Pedagogy: Education and Learning Beyond Schooling* (forthcoming, Routledge). She can be reached at Jennifer.Sandlin@asu.edu.

Katie Shaw is a graduate student in the Faculty of Education at the University of Victoria, in Leadership Studies. For the past nine years Katie has worked in a variety of community based NGOs with a special focus on youth engagement, capacity building initiatives, and collaborative community development. She is currently the Regional Facilitator for BC Healthy Communities, Vancouver Island and also a Program Manager with the LifeCycles Project Society.

Valerie Scatamburlo-D'Annibale is an Associate Professor and Chair of the Graduate Program in Communication and Social Justice at the University of Windsor, Ontario, Canada. An award-winning author and educator, she has authored numerous book chapters and journal articles, the latter of which have appeared in such publications as the *International Journal of Progressive Education*, *Educational Philosophy and Theory*, *Cultural Studies/Critical Methodologies*, *Public Resistance*, and *Journal for Critical Education Policy Studies*.

Joel Spring has published over twenty books on American and global educational policy. His great-great-grandfather was the first Principal Chief of the Choctaw Nation in Indian Territory and his grandfather, Joel S. Spring, was a district chief at the time Indian Territory became Oklahoma. Joel is an enrolled member of the tribe. He lived for many summers on an island off the coast of Sitka, Alaska. His novel, *Alaskan Visions,* includes many of these Alaskan experiences.

Shirley R. Steinberg is the Director of the Paulo and Nita Freire International Project for Critical Pedagogy at McGill University. She is the author and editor of numerous books and articles and co-edits several book series. The founding editor of *Taboo: The Journal of Culture and Education,* Steinberg's most recent books are: *Christotainment: Selling Jesus Through Popular Culture* (with Joe Kincheloe), *Media Literacy: A Reader* (with Donaldo Macedo) and *The Encyclopedia of Boyhood Culture.* Steinberg has also edited *Teen Life in Europe*; and with Priya Parmar and Birgit Richard, *The Encyclopedia of Contemporary Youth Culture* (Library Reference Award Winner). Her areas of expertise and research are in critical media literacy, cultural studies, urban education, social drama, and youth studies.

Kevin Tavin is an Associate Professor in the Department of Art Education at The Ohio State University. He holds a BFA, M.Ed., and a Ph.D. in art education and has taught K-12 and post-secondary courses since 1990. Tavin's research focuses on visual culture, critical pedagogy, cultural studies, Lacanian psychoanalytic theory, and art education. His work is published in numerous journals and presented at various international, national, and regional conferences and symposia.

Anne Marie Todd is an Associate Professor of Public Communication in the Department of Communication Studies at San José State University. She received her Ph.D. from the Annenberg School for Communication at the University of Southern California in 2002. She publishes in the areas of environmental communication and media studies, including articles on green consumerism, environmental rhetoric in popular culture, and social movement activists' use of new media.

Robin Usher is a Professor of Research Education and Director of Research Training at RMIT University, Melbourne, Australia. He is the author (with Richard Edwards) of *Postmodernism and Education: Different Voices, Different Worlds* (Routledge, 1994) and *Globalisation and Pedagogy: Space, Place and Identity* (Routledge, 2008); and (with David Scott) *Researching Education: Data, Methods and Theory in Educational Inquiry* (Cassell, 1999).

Gary Wilkinson is a Lecturer in Education Policy in the Institute for Learning at the University of Hull. Gary's research interests center on analysis of education and social policy and, in particular, on professionalism, power and control within education systems, and mechanisms of commercialization in the public sector.

Index